MEMORY AND MORTALITY
IN RENAISSANCE ENGLAND

Drawing together leading scholars of early modern memory studies and death studies, *Memory and Mortality in Renaissance England* explores and illuminates the interrelationships of these categories of Renaissance knowing and doing, theory and praxis. The collection features an extended Introduction that establishes the rich vein connecting these two fields of study and investigation. Thereafter, the collection is arranged into three subsections, 'The Arts of Remembering Death', 'Grounding the Remembrance of the Dead', and 'The Ends of Commemoration', where contributors analyse how memory and mortality intersected in writings, devotional practice, and visual culture. The book will appeal to scholars of early modern literature and culture, book history, art history, and the history of mnemonics and thanatology, and will prove an indispensable guide for researchers, instructors, and students alike.

WILLIAM E. ENGEL is the Nick B. Williams Professor of English at the University of the South, in Sewanee, Tennessee, USA, and author of six books on literary history including *Mapping Mortality* (University of Massachusetts Press, 1995), *Death and Drama in Renaissance England* (Oxford University Press, 2002), and *The Printer as Author in Early Modern English Book History: John Day and the Fabrication of a Protestant Memory Art* (Routledge, 2022); and, with Rory Loughnane and Grant Williams, *The Memory Arts in Renaissance England* (Cambridge University Press, 2016) and *The Death Arts in Renaissance England* (Cambridge University Press, 2022).

RORY LOUGHNANE is Reader in Early Modern Studies at the University of Kent, UK. He is the author and editor of many books and play editions, including, for Cambridge University Press, *Late Shakespeare, 1608–1613* (2012), *The Memory Arts in Renaissance England* (2016), *Early Shakespeare, 1588–1594* (2020), and *The Death Arts in Renaissance England* (2022). He is a series editor of Cambridge's Elements in Shakespeare and Text and a general editor of The Revels Plays.

GRANT WILLIAMS is Associate Professor of English Literature at Carleton University, Ottawa, Canada, and has coedited five books:

Forgetting in Early Modern English Literature and Culture (Routledge, 2004), *Ars reminiscendi* (Centre for Renaissance and Reformation Studies, 2009), *Taking Exception to the Law* (University of Toronto Press, 2015), *The Memory Arts in Renaissance England* (Cambridge University Press, 2016), and *The Death Arts in Renaissance England* (Cambridge University Press, 2022). With Donald Beecher, he has coedited Henry Chettle's *Kind-Heart's Dream and Piers Plainness: Two Pamphlets from the Elizabethan Book Trade* (Centre for Renaissance and Reformation Studies, 2022).

MEMORY AND MORTALITY IN RENAISSANCE ENGLAND

EDITED BY

WILLIAM E. ENGEL
University of the South, Sewanee

RORY LOUGHNANE
University of Kent

GRANT WILLIAMS
Carleton University, Ottawa

CAMBRIDGE
UNIVERSITY PRESS

CAMBRIDGE
UNIVERSITY PRESS

University Printing House, Cambridge CB2 8BS, United Kingdom

One Liberty Plaza, 20th Floor, New York, NY 10006, USA

477 Williamstown Road, Port Melbourne, VIC 3207, Australia

314–321, 3rd Floor, Plot 3, Splendor Forum, Jasola District Centre,
New Delhi – 110025, India

103 Penang Road, #05–06/07, Visioncrest Commercial, Singapore 238467

Cambridge University Press is part of the University of Cambridge.

It furthers the University's mission by disseminating knowledge in the pursuit of
education, learning, and research at the highest international levels of excellence.

www.cambridge.org
Information on this title: www.cambridge.org/9781108843393
DOI: 10.1017/9781108918565

© Cambridge University Press 2023

First published 2023

A catalogue record for this publication is available from the British Library.

Library of Congress Cataloging-in-Publication Data
NAMES: Engel, William E., 1957– editor. | Loughnane, Rory, editor. |
Williams, Grant, 1965– editor.
TITLE: Memory and mortality in Renaissance England / edited by William E.
Engel, Rory Loughnane, Grant Williams.
DESCRIPTION: Cambridge ; New York, NY : Cambridge University
Press, 2023. | Includes bibliographical references and index.
IDENTIFIERS: LCCN 2022022794 | ISBN 9781108843393 (hardback) |
ISBN 9781108918565 (ebook)
SUBJECTS: LCSH: English literature – Early modern, 1500-1700 – History and
criticism. | Memory in literature. | Mortality in literature. | Death in
literature.
CLASSIFICATION: LCC PR428.M44 M46 2023 | DDC 820.9/3548–dc23/eng/20220728
LC record available at https://lccn.loc.gov/2022022794

ISBN 978-1-108-84339-3 Hardback

Why recount they not oft, with Philip the King of the Macedons, that they are born as other, and are men, and no more? For he, after many luckily achieved enterprises in his wars against the Athenians, his enemies vanquished and put to flight … commanded one his servant[s], every morning at his uprising, to cry to him 'Remember, thou art a man'. Would our nobles in like manner charge herewith some one of their servants … [to] sing this song in their deaf ears and revive to their dulled memory their frail mortality.

Laurence Humphrey, *The nobles or of nobilitye*
(London: 1563; STC 13964), R5ʳ.

The day wherein we first behold the light,
Begins our *Death,* for life doth daily fade,
Our day of *Death* begins our happie life
We are in danger, till our debt is paid.
Life is but lent, we owe it to the Lord.
When 'tis demanded, it must be restor'd.

Rachel Speght. *Mortalities memorandum*
(London: 1621; STC 23057), F2ʳ.

How necessary a thing it is for all degrees of men, as well the high as the low, noble and ignoble, rich and poor, and how behooveful to their soul's welfare both now and hereafter, to represent to their remembrance the memory of death and mortality by some good means whatsoever, in any sort howsoever … in regard as well of the misery of this present life, which is transitory, as of the happiness of the life in expectancy, which is everlastingly enduring.

Paul Wentworth, *The miscellanie, or, A registrie, and methodicall directorie of orizons* (London: 1615; STC 25244), Z4ʳ⁻ᵛ.

Twice hath sad Philomele left off to sing
Her mortifying sonnets to the spring.
Twice at the sylvan choristers' desire
She hath lent her music to complete their choir,
Since all devouring Death on her took seizure,
And Tellus's womb involved so rich a treasure.
Yet still my heart is overwhelmed with grief,
And time, nor tears, will give my woes relief.
Twelve times hath Phoebe, hornéd, seemed to fight,
As often filled them with her brother's light,
Since she did close her sparkling diamond eyes;
Yet my sad heart, for her still pining, dies.

Hester Pulter, 'Upon the Death of my Dear and Lovely Daughter, Jane Pulter', *Poems breathed forth by the nobel Hadassas* (c. 1661; University of Leeds Library, Brotherton Collection, MS Lt q 32).

Contents

Figures

Notes on Contributors

JONATHAN BALDO is Professor of English in the Eastman School of Music, the University of Rochester. He is the author of *Memory in Shakespeare's Histories: Stages of Forgetting in Early Modern England* (Routledge, 2012) and co-editor, with Isabel Karremann, of *Forms of Faith: Literary Form and Religious Conflict in Shakespeare's England* (Manchester University Press, 2017).

BRIAN CHALK is Associate Professor of English at Manhattan College. He is the author of *Monuments and Literary Posterity in Early Modern Drama* (Cambridge University Press, 2015) and has published essays on early modern literature and culture in journals such as *Studies in Philology* and *Studies in English Literature, 1500–1900*. His current project is a book on the relationship among dreaming, sleeping, and theatrical experience in Shakespeare's plays and poems.

WILLIAM E. ENGEL is the Nick B. Williams Professor of English at the University of the South, in Sewanee, Tennessee. He has published eight books on literary history and applied emblematics including, with Rory Loughnane and Grant Williams, *The Memory Arts in Renaissance England* (Cambridge University Press, 2016) and *The Death Arts in Renaissance England* (Cambridge University Press, 2022).

JOHN S. GARRISON is Professor of English at Grinnell College. He is co-editor of three essay collections and author of five books, as well as co-editor of the book series Spotlight on Shakespeare. He is the recipient of numerous fellowships and prizes and was named a Guggenheim Fellow in 2021.

REBECA HELFER is an Associate Professor of early modern English literature at the University of California-Irvine and the author of *Spenser's Ruins and The Art of Recollection* (University of Toronto Press, 2012),

'The State of the Art of Memory and Shakespeare Studies', in *The Routledge Handbook of Shakespeare and Memory* (2017), and essays on cultural memory in *Renaissance Quarterly, Spenser Studies,* and *English Literary Renaissance.*

ANDREW HISCOCK is Dean and Professor of Early Modern Literature at Bangor University, Wales, fellow of the English Association and research fellow at the Institut de Recherche sur la Renaissance, l'Âge Classique et les Lumières, Université Paul-Valéry, Montpellier 3. He is series co-editor for the *Arden Early Modern Drama Guides,* English Literature co-editor for *Modern Languages Review* and series editor for the *Yearbook of English Studies.* His most recent monographs are *Reading Memory in Early Modern Literature* (2011) and *Shakespeare, Violence and Early Modern Europe* (2022), both published with Cambridge University Press.

RORY LOUGHNANE is Reader in Early Modern Studies at the University of Kent. He is the author and editor of many books and play editions, including, for Cambridge University Press, *Late Shakespeare, 1608–1613* (2012), *The Memory Arts in Renaissance England* (2016), *Early Shakespeare, 1588–1594* (2020), and *The Death Arts in Renaissance England* (2022). He is a series editor of Cambridge Elements in Shakespeare and Text and a general editor of The Revels Plays.

MICHAEL NEILL is Emeritus Professor of English at the University of Auckland. He is the author of *Issues of Death* (Oxford University Press, 1997) and *Putting History to the Question* (Columbia University Press, 2000). His numerous editions of Renaissance plays include *Anthony and Cleopatra* (1994) and *Othello* (2006) for the Oxford Shakespeare. More recently, he co-edited *The Oxford Handbook of Shakespearean Tragedy* (2016).

SCOTT NEWSTOK is Professor of English and founding director of the Pearce Shakespeare Endowment at Rhodes College. A parent and an award-winning teacher, he is the author of several books including, most recently, *How to Think like Shakespeare* (Princeton University Press, 2020) and the editor of Montaigne's writings on education in a new translation by Tess Lewis (forthcoming from Princeton University Press).

PATRICIA PHILLIPPY is Professor of Material and Cultural Memories and Director of the Centre for Arts, Memory and Communities at

Coventry University. Her publications include *Shaping Remembrance from Shakespeare to Milton* (Cambridge University Press, 2018), *Women, Death and Literature in Post-Reformation England* (Cambridge University Press, 2002) and *A History of Early Modern Women's Writing* (Cambridge University Press, 2018). Her current research examines memory, climate change and mortality in seventeenth-century England and America.

CLAIRE PRESTON is Emerita Professor of Renaissance Literature, Queen Mary, University of London. Her book *The Poetics of Scientific Investigation in Seventeenth-Century Literature* (Oxford University Press, 2015) won the British Society of Literature and Science's annual prize. She is the general editor of *The Complete Works of Sir Thomas Browne* (forthcoming, Oxford University Press), and the recipient of the Rose Mary Crawshay Prize from the British Academy, a Guggenheim Fellowship, a British Academy Research Development Award, and an Arts and Humanities Research Counsel five-year research grant.

PHILIP SCHWYZER is Professor of Renaissance Literature at the University of Exeter. He is the author of studies including *Shakespeare and the Remains of Richard III* (Oxford University Press, 2013), *Archaeologies of English Renaissance Literature* (Oxford University Press, 2007), and *Literature, Nationalism and Memory in Early Modern England and Wales* (Cambridge University Press, 2004). His current projects include a new edition of Michael Drayton's *Poly-Olbion*.

PETER SHERLOCK is Vice-Chancellor of the University of Divinity, Melbourne, Australia. His research examines cultures of death, remembering and forgetting in early modern Europe, especially monumental commemoration. He is author of *Monuments and Memory in Early Modern England* (Ashgate, 2008).

ANITA GILMAN SHERMAN is Professor of Literature at American University, Washington, DC. She is the author of *Skepticism in Early Modern English Literature: The Problems and Pleasures of Doubt* (Cambridge University Press, 2021) and *Skepticism and Memory in Shakespeare and Donne* (Palgrave, 2007). She has published essays in journals and edited collections on various authors, including Garcilaso de la Vega, Thomas Heywood, Montaigne, and W. G. Sebald.

GRANT WILLIAMS is Associate Professor of English Literature at Carleton University, Ottawa, Canada, and has coedited five books: *Forgetting in Early Modern English Literature and Culture* (Routledge, 2004), *Ars reminiscendi* (Centre for Renaissance and Reformation Studies, 2009), *Taking Exception to the Law* (University of Toronto Press, 2015), *The Memory Arts in Renaissance England* (Cambridge University Press, 2016), and *The Death Arts in Renaissance England* (Cambridge University Press, 2022). With Donald Beecher, he has coedited *Henry Chettle's Kind-Heart's Dream and Piers Plainness: Two Pamphlets from the Elizabethan Book Trade* (Centre for Renaissance and Reformation Studies, 2022).

Acknowledgements

It is a special grace that the primary research for this book was conducted by the contributors to this volume prior to the closing of the libraries in 2020–21 during the global pandemic. We are grateful to Emily Hockley at Cambridge University Press for seeing right away the value of a collection of essays by a dozen internationally renowned scholars of early modern literary history working on topics pertaining to the cultural cross-pollination of the death arts and the memory arts.

Portions of the work, including especially the editors' Introduction, have been discussed and presented at the following venues and conferences: Carleton University English Department (2017); Centre for Medieval and Early Modern Studies at the University of Kent (2019); Eton College (2019); Renaissance Society of America (Toronto, 2019; New Orleans, 2018; Chicago, 2017; Boston, 2016); Shakespeare Association of America (Denver/virtual, 2020); and Sixteenth Century Studies Conference (Milwaukee, 2017; Albuquerque, 2018; St. Louis, 2019). We are especially grateful to Bill Sherman and the staff at the Warburg Institute for allowing us to host 'Memory and Mortality: An Interdisciplinary Symposium', on 17 May 2019, and to all the contributors, attendees and correspondents who made it such a memorable and useful event.

For support with securing images, we are especially grateful to Adam Hawkins, Associate Director of Informational Literacy and Instructional Technology at Sewanee, The University of the South; and Cressida Williams, Head of Archives at Canterbury Cathedral Archives and Library.

William Engel would like to thank the Office of the Dean at Sewanee, the University of the South, for granting a research leave (2020–21); Sewanee's Alderson-Tillinghast Fund for supplementing travel to archives abroad (2018–20); and the English Department Reading Group: Stephanie L. Batkie, Matthew Irving, Maha Jafri, James Ross Macdonald,

Benjamin Mangrum and Jennifer Michael. Rory Loughnane was very grateful to receive a Francis Bacon Foundation Fellowship at the Huntington Library for research related to this project. He would like to thank Dympna Callaghan, William Engel, Catherine Richardson, Goran Stanivukovic and Grant Williams for their advice upon, and support with, his application. Grant Williams would like to thank Carleton University and Social Sciences and Humanities Research Council for a Development Grant (2018), which facilitated related research at the British Library.

Introduction
Between Memory and Death

William E. Engel, Rory Loughnane, and Grant Williams

In the early summer of 1533, Desiderius Erasmus received the following written request: 'I implore you again and again to take care to finish a little book on the preparation for death, as soon as you can'.[1] Erasmus, by then sixty-three years of age, took to this task immediately, and his *De praeparatione ad mortem* was published in early 1534, dedicated to the author of the letter, Thomas Boleyn.[2] The study was to be a transcontinental publishing phenomenon with some twenty editions published in Latin and translations made into French, German, Spanish, and English. The first Latin copies found a readership among London's elite, including, somewhat ironically, the woman whom Boleyn's daughter had recently supplanted. According to Eustace Chapuys, the Imperial Ambassador to England, Catherine of Aragon found much solace and comfort in Erasmus's words as she lay on her deathbed at Kimbolton Castle, Cambridgeshire, in January 1536.[3] When news of Catherine's death reached the royal court, the reaction was mixed. For some, the true Queen had died; for others, including Henry and Anne, the death enabled the living to move on from the past.

By the time the first English translation of his work appeared, in an anonymous translation in 1538, both Erasmus and Anne were also deceased.[4] A wider English readership was now reminded, in an *ars moriendi* that combines tropes from both *contemptus mundi* and *memento mori* traditions, that the best way to live is in ever-readiness for death; after all, 'This holle lyfe is nothinge elles but a rennynge to deathe, and that very shorte, but death is the gate of euerlastynge lyfe' (A4ʳ). Thus, Erasmus cautions, remember to prepare your estate, give charity widely, forgive your enemies and pray that they forgive you (L6ʳ–L7ʳ). Repeatedly, Erasmus invokes this state of vigilance and preparedness, for, he suggests, it is a foolish person who neglects, or, more precisely, forgets their mortal condition. What is significant, however, about Erasmus's work is not its instructional wisdom, which *ars moriendi* treatises had been recycling for decades. What is significant about it is that Erasmus, the prince of humanists, had used his scholarly publishing platform to broadcast the teachings of *memento mori*.

Early modern English writing tirelessly underscores the complicity between memory and mortality thanks to the widely disseminated *ars moriendi*. For example, Christopher Sutton's *Disce mori. Learn to Die*, bears the telling subtitle *A Religious discourse, moouing euery Christian man to enter into a serious remembrance of his ende.*⁵ To remember one's end was a familiar injunction that served to guide the experience of the living. As was frequently asserted in the scores of how-to-die-well manuals and sermons published in the sixteenth and seventeenth centuries, a virtuous life is the best preparation for death. Befitting the high stakes involved, such preparation was a serious business that required daily practice: as Jeremy Taylor advises in his popular *The Rule and Exercises of Holy Dying*, 'every night we must make our bed the memoriall of our grave, so let our Evening thoughts be an image of the day of judgement'.⁶ Mortality, an entropic step towards oblivion and thus a natural enemy to memory, must be kept uppermost in one's mental storehouse.

The struggle between memory and mortality went well beyond theological treatises, inspiring the plots and conceits of various literary genres. From the morality plays of the late fifteenth and early sixteenth centuries, where an eponymous figure such as Everyman or Mankind must learn to live virtuously to prepare himself for death, to Shakespeare's extraordinary sonnets about the relentless march of time (think of Sonnet 60: 'Like as the waves make towards the pebbled shore / So do our minutes hasten to their end'⁷) where the grave threatens to efface the image of the living, scenes of *memento mori* captivated the poetic imagination. Stephen Batman's *The Travelled Pilgrim* (1569), a loose translation of Olivier de La Marche's *Le Chevalier Délibéré*, features an allegorized everyman who follows Dame Memory, his personal guide and governor, as she leads him through life, corrects his judgements with continual reminders, and 'comforteth him to provide and arm himself against Thanatos': 'the ugly corpse, that bony figure he, / Is Thanatos which ends the life of every degree'.⁸ Both personifications loom over the pilgrim's existential condition and look forward to Spenser's sophisticated allegory of the House of Alma in *The Faerie Queene*, where the librarian Eumnestes works to preserve faerie and human genealogies in his turret archive, while outside Maleger, the skeletal captain, lays siege to the fortified building.⁹

Chroniclers from the period also reminded their readers repeatedly that they must look to the lessons of the past to better live their lives in humble anticipation of the grave. Among the period's popular historical books,

The Mirror for Magistrates, which underwent multiple editions, memorialized accounts of famous heroes and princes, many of whom take the form of ghosts to reflect upon their earthly deeds and their precipitous falls from fortune,[10] while John Foxe's *Acts and Monuments* (or *Book of Martyrs*, the 1563 edition, the first of several in English), with its compilation of instances of proto-Protestant and Protestant martyrology from the Lollards to the Marian persecutions, contributed to a wave of anti-Catholic feeling through its vivid *exempla* of past deaths.[11] Such creative and historiographical engagements indicate the extent to which memory and mortality were at once in opposition and agreement.

This volume's chapters examine the interplay between memory and death in the lives, literature, and visual imagination of Renaissance England. Although each of the guiding concepts has been developed over the decades by its own separate scholarly field, we want to highlight their intense friction and collaboration within the period. While acknowledging the lasting importance of both memory studies and death studies, this Introduction argues for the benefit of mapping out their areas of intersection, where the chapters broadly situate themselves. One cannot regard memory and mortality in isolation from one another, since the period's cultural activities and products bear the deep impression left by their never-ceasing encounters.

Memory Studies

Whether personified, figured as a constituent aspect of the soul, or put to work as a method in all manner of activities and crafts both sacred and secular, memory long has been subject to the metaphorical process associated with the classical rhetorical tradition which has enabled – and taught – us to think through images. The names with which to conjure in this field of endeavour justifiably are well known: Volkmann, Rossi, Yates, Carruthers, Bolzoni.[12] And this area of intellectual enquiry has blossomed considerably as a result. Among the studies that offer descriptive surveys of recent activities in the emerging subfields associated with memory studies are those by Neil Rhodes and Jonathan Sawday, on 'knowledge and technology in the first age of print' involving Renaissance systems of memory that locate objects of knowledge in terms of schematized places; Rebeca Helfer, on the application of applied mnemonics in English literary history; and Raphael Lyne, on the diachronic movement from the claim that artificial memory was 'vital to intellectual life in the period' to taking this as a scholarly 'starting point in a literary-critical enquiry'.[13] Historians and literary scholars, variously using the headings of mnemology, mnemotechny, and memory studies, have juxtaposed and aligned a wide range of topics and approaches pertaining to early modern efforts to counteract the effects of sinfulness, ignorance, forgetfulness, idleness, and oblivion.[14] And this encompasses sacred meditative practices and visualization techniques both private and public,[15] as well as secular pedagogical uses of mnemonic schemes, and extends also to take into account Neoplatonic and pseudo-scientific treatises on recovering and interpreting, generating and deploying symbols, ciphers, and emblems so as to make things happen in the world. But the net has been cast further still, as exemplified in the essays in this volume, to apply analytical frameworks that are at once hermeneutic and heuristic, specific to particular cases and also instructive more generally for what they reveal about the ways memory both conditioned and intersected with every facet of cultural life and lived experience in the Renaissance. As Frances Yates presciently argued in *The Art of Memory*, renewed attention to the memory arts is a prerequisite for advances in Renaissance scholarship. She was convinced that the history of the organization of memory touches at vital points on the history of religion and ethics, of philosophy and psychology, of art and literature, of scientific method, and of political and social life broadly conceived – all of which has been borne out, among other places, in the recent six-volume set *A Cultural History of Memory*.[16] It is in the interest of Renaissance scholarship to continue recovering and applying some of the key assumptions underlying an ongoing tradition involving mnemonic thought and a wide range of both fairly standard and also sometimes quite idiosyncratic memory practices. Among the benefits of such a line of enquiry is that it provides fresh insights into the period by focusing on the writings as well as other modes and media of cultural production that incorporate and augment, whether by design or unintentionally, the memory arts – and memory's art.

Death Studies

Death studies has grown up separately from memory studies, having made a significant contribution to Renaissance history, literature, and art. The pioneering work of Philippe Ariès invigorated the field with the social constructionist assumption that death is not a natural given but something historically variable and culturally specific; however, his methodology, stemming from the *l'histoire des mentalités*, which developed out of the Annales school of historiography, has had a negligible influence on shaping the approaches pursued in the English context.[17] The field of death studies in Renaissance England began in earnest during the 1990s with a spate of important monographs, which are committed less to affirming epochal narratives about changing mental dispositions than to recovering a diversity of practices, experiences, and testimonies as they unfold within institutional settings. Inductively accumulating a comprehensive range of archival evidence and detail, David Cressy and Ralph Houlbrooke respectively gave contours to the incipient field and demonstrated its potential for continued investigation.[18] Around this time further ground-breaking scholarship by Nigel Llewellyn, William E. Engel, and Michael Neill sounded the theoretical implications of analysing death's images and artefacts, acknowledging the influential Germanic tradition of the *totentanz* and the French *danse macabre*.[19] The early research performed in this field collectively indicated the great degree to which death, far from being a solitary terminal event, constitutes an ongoing dimension of daily living and social activity.

Since the 1990s, death studies has increasingly expanded its domain. One way of spatializing the field today is to envision an individual's biological expiration as only one point in a continuum stretching from birth through the ante-mortem period to the posthumous. We may group death studies according to five broad areas that correspond to temporal zones along this continuum.[20] The first area covers the lifelong devotional preparations leading up to the deathbed, epitomized by the *ars moriendi*, prayer, and meditation, which include depictions of the Dance of Death and other pictorial renderings of the Grim Reaper, *vanitas*, and *contemptus mundi*.[21] The second deals with the public side of dying, drawing within its ambit plague deaths and state-sanctioned execution,[22] such as regicide, the hanging of criminals, and the martyrdom of saints. The third focuses on the funeral with its processions, customs, and rituals in and around burial.[23] The fourth encompasses grief, mourning, and bereavement – the affective response to the loss of a loved one.[24] And the fifth examines the beliefs in and manifestations of a person's afterlife, whether otherworldly, as with ceremonies and doctrine revolving around heaven and hell,[25] or earthly, as with epitaphs,[26] monuments,[27] and exhumed ruins.[28] These five areas of study – the art of dying, public death, funerals, mourning, and memorializing the dead – suggest that individuals and their communities in Renaissance England were continually paying tribute to mortality.[29] Since death was not just an abstract topic of learning in philosophy and theology, but a part of ordinary thinking, activity, and craft, it has left behind tangible signs of its fundamental importance to the social imaginary. In its methodological approach, current death studies thus has leaned more towards material culture than towards a straight-up history of ideas.

Areas of Intersection

Even though memory and death studies lend themselves towards being demarcated as distinct fields of Renaissance research, the division of the two areas tacitly minimizes if not ignores their inseparability in premodern societies, where they complement, supplement, and even depend upon one another. Their separation may be a by-product of modernity's secular-izing impulse, which brackets off religion's fundamental role in cultural production – albeit the religious turn in contemporary early modern schol-arship has questioned the previous generation's prevalent Enlightenment assumptions. One of the major binding agents between memory and mor-tality in the period is clearly faith, confession, creed.

This volume merges the two thematic fields to acknowledge the his-torical importance traditionally ascribed to their intersection. The com-bination, we want to argue, is a methodological prerequisite for studying today the relevant aspects of Renaissance England. To understand one field requires us to engage with and understand the other. With their com-bination, too, in-between spaces emerge. The double focus not only sig-nals a heuristic for further thinking but also stakes a claim for fertile yet overlooked territories in which intriguing research can take place. A few problems arise, however, when we map out the territories. One needs to disentangle the accidental from the necessary, since polyvalent terms and competing definitions may lead us away from the historical particularity of Renaissance memory and death. The memory studies conducted in the Anglo-American context should be distinguished from the German social-science field of cultural memory studies, which conceptualizes culture in terms of a 'collective memory'.[30] It should also be distinguished from a French tradition that separates memory and history, such that 'far from being synonymous appear now to be in fundamental opposition'.[31] In the Anglo-American context, within which our project is conceived, mem-ory is not privileged over historiography. Moreover, the interrelationship between the two thematic fields of memory studies and death studies is not strictly reciprocal and will require careful parsing.

As the contributions to this volume bear out, memory holds greater prominence within death studies than does death within memory studies. The zones of the previously mentioned continuum corroborates this obser-vation, revealing the two dominant kinds of culturally specific remem-bering that tenaciously cling to mortality.[32] During the ante-mortem phase, deathward preparations fall back on what can be generally called *memento mori* – the remembrance that you too will die – while during the posthumous phase, the areas of the funereal, bereavement, and the afterlife draw upon commemorative remembering. These two types of memory can easily be conflated and confused because they regularly occur in the same context where they often bolster each other's ends; for example, brasses, tombstones, and Protestant funeral sermons may at once memorialize the deceased and invite the viewers or listeners to reflect upon their own mortality, pressuring them to remember because it will be only a matter of time before they suffer the same fate. *Memento mori* remembering is a self-reflexive activity, which, looking towards one's future deathbed, shakes one out of the here and now. It considers death to usher in the climactic event when God's final sentence will be passed on the soul's spiritual condition, and thus for the period, the four last things did not treat death in isolation but deemed it a transition from the earthly to a supernatural reckoning yielding either infernal punishment or heavenly reward.[33] Recalling the thinker from ephemeral, fleshly concerns, that is, the day-to-day distractions of the senses and their concomitant desires, the existential jolt of gazing upon a skull or a *danse macabre* prompts her or him to enter a higher mental state, intent on bringing the soul into conformity with biblical teachings. This type of remembering does not consist in the retrieval of a single idea. It involves a reminder to alter one's entire mindset and focus on caring for one's spiritual life to properly prepare for the final judgement. *Memento mori* cognition thus relies upon visual and verbal cues to initiate the intensely individualized introspection associated with Protestant and Catholic Reformation teachings.

Commemorative remembering, in contrast, is oriented to others, essentially conferring upon a dead person an afterlife through ritual, artefact, or writing. Such an afterlife can be sorted according to secular and sacred modes. In the latter case, the Reformation disrupted commemorative practices that honoured the dead. Christianity, a memory religion ('do this in memory of me'), foregrounds through its repeated services and traditions various forms of engagement with the past. The most controversial church teaching to emerge from this, and one which helped precipitate the Reformation, was the existence of Purgatory and the idea that the living could intercede on behalf of the dead. The living, fearful for their post-mortem state, thought they would be reliant on those they left behind to remember and pray for them. Being forgotten, in this context, would only lead to longer suffering. The flourishing of memorializing practices (month's minds, obits, trentals) in the late medieval and early modern period attest to the influence of the idea of the communion of the living and the dead. The English Reformation, which jettisoned

Purgatory from state church instruction, severed this memorial connection between those living and those departed. So, too, it brought with it, through its dissolution or destruction of church properties, objects, and images, an enforced collective forgetting of the past.[34] Still, traditions hold strong within communities, and long-assumed ideas about death, how it should be remembered and memorialized, remained pervasive in the newly Protestant state.[35]

Protestantism shifted remembering's attention from the afflicted Purgatorial soul to the individual's former life. Because scholars no longer take the Reformation to be a single event of rupture but a protracted religious revolution to reinvent the nation's confessional, liturgical, and devotional forms,[36] the Protestant proscription of masses and prayers for easing the suffering of the departed not only created new means of commemoration but also left lingering resistance to these reforms as the Laudian Church of England and the Restoration attest. The secular mode of commemoration allowed more scope to fame and honour than did the Reformers, basing its remembrance upon the dead's exemplary active virtue in contradistinction to heraldic memory's emphasis upon rank and pedigree. Both secular and religious commemoration, though admitting different blends, involves discharging a debt or duty to the dead by revivifying them in memory. Such a mapping out of the dominant intersections clarifies why memory is so integral to death studies. Memory is the Renaissance social remedy *par excellence* – ultimately a balm, anodyne, and palliative – for the terminal affliction of mortality: *memento mori* reflection tends towards the pre-emptive and the prophylactic, whereas commemorative remembering strives to be therapeutic and restorative.[37]

Death thus does not hold the equivalent sway in memory studies. When we consider the individual with respect to cognitive and personal – which is to say existential – memory, then death as an object of thought is only one of many things that life offers us to reflect upon. Memory, always implicated in some way with the full range of mental activity, potentially mediates most of what we think and do. Death bears no comparable relation as implied by the imperative of *memento mori*: it all too easily slips out of one's mind, given the pressure of immediate experiences, the world's countless diversions. However, when we change our perspective from the individual to the social, memory, especially evinced by early modern institutions, can be seen to significantly grapple with mortal issues. The law, heraldry, and antiquarianism channelled its resources towards preserving the continuity of the family name, whether it be royalty, nobility, or gentry.[38] For a society that valorized primogeniture, the genealogical line's termination with the dissolution of an estate or the lack of an heir signalled a death worse than death itself.[39]

Although church ceremony need not be mentioned again, religious education provides another crucial nodal point where memory studies touches upon mortality. Death played a formative role in the primary Christian narrative and throughout the narrative's supporting doctrines. By introducing sin into a perfectly created world, Adam's fall necessitated the punishment of humankind with the mortal condition. However, the sacrifice of the second Adam, Christ, lifted the curse of death that the first Adam introduced. This narrative, in effect, bestowed upon humanity more than one kind of death: along with the natural (external or bodily), there was a spiritual (internal or 'ghostly') and an eternal (of both body and soul).[40] More dangerous than the first death was the second, since if one died spiritually, then the third – the most terrifying – death was assured. In conformity with the teachings of Paul and Augustine, believers thus fought off spiritual moribundity by contemplating and studying God's word.[41] And how did the believer contemplate God's word? By storing it up in his heart as the Psalmist says.[42] Memory held a privileged cognitive position with respect to studying Scripture because it was through permitting the divine word to grow in one's heart that one could overcome the barrier between God and one's moribund humanity.[43] This death-bound theology was thus mnemocentric. The period's steady stream of print products – catechisms, commentaries, prayer books and psalters, doctrinal treatises, meditation and devotional guides – stored up scriptural knowledge and facilitated its ready recollection.[44] The student's memory whilst serving the highest power of the soul, which Aristotelian psychology designated as the intellect in contrast to perception and nutrition, sought to embrace the eternal truths of the Bible, since, aside from the elect, only God's word would last forever where earthly matters were concerned.[45]

In reviving the study of classical languages and literature with their values, mores, and ideas, humanist education cultivated the student's faculty of memory too and that faculty could address questions of mortality. Humanism did not promote learning for learning's sake but argued for the ethical dimension of memory in the service of civic virtue. A syncretic moral philosophy based on the ancients could be accessed by recycling sayings and *exempla*, which the educated civil servant would remember at the appropriate time to help guide him in his decision-making and advance his social status.[46] Philip Sidney's view of poetry as a speaking picture that impresses upon the reader's mind a noble ideal for emulation is a literary elaboration of what Erasmus, Elyot, and others recognized as occurring when one read classical texts for memorable and edifying commonplaces.[47] Hence, humanist students implemented a cult of the dead that enshrined noble action, while humanist writers recalled, to a lesser degree, the ethical significance of the deaths of Greek and Roman ancients, such as the sui-cides of Socrates, Cato, and Seneca, suggesting alternative models to saints and Protestant martyrs, inspiring numerous Elizabethan and Jacobean tragedies, and fuelling a different kind of *memento mori* and *contemptus mundi* thinking.[48] It would be wrong, however, to regard humanism as diametrically opposed to religious education with reference to death; for example, both Elyot and, as we have seen, Erasmus contributed treatises to the *ars moriendi* tradition. Both types of education shared mnemonic resources as well. Ramist schemes were applied to the Bible as well as clas-sical texts,[49] and, though strongly associated with the occult tradition and the development of science, the loci and place method, derived from clas-sical rhetoric, was used by some divines to structure sermons and religious treatises and by some auditors to memorize sermons.[50]

Memory studies does not reserve an essential place for death in the same way that death studies does for memory. And yet if we consider how death was for early modern culture much more than the mere cessation of vital functions, then the intersected area between the two fields comes into greater focus and achieves a greater relevance. The worst fate that could befall an early modern individual was not physiological termination in and of itself. Because the afterlife, the worldly and the otherworldly, deeply mattered to a culture consumed by questions of honour, virtue, and salvation, the irre-versible state of being forgotten posed the greatest existential threat to the individual. The relationship between the two fields is accurately described by the period's term 'oblivion', the common foe against which both the memory arts and death arts applied their energies. In early modern culture, there were at least three major kinds of oblivion: damnation,[51] that is *being forgotten by God*; erasure or erosion from the record, that is, *being forgot-ten by humanity and society*; and, as opposed to knowing thyself, forgetting thyself, that is, *being forgotten by yourself*. Forgetting thyself was a classically inflected form of spiritual death, which explained moral deterioration in the here and now.[52] To be clear, oblivion was not physical death, but a more permanent form of annihilation, which occurred in the afterlife. The threat of oblivion best explains the interrelationship between death studies and memory studies. Life was a matter of preparing one's memory for the afterlife and this started with cultivating one's own mnemonic faculty. No one can avert his or her mortal fate, but to a certain degree everyone can do something in the here or now to be remembered when he or she is gone.

Memory Arts and Death Arts

The ubiquitous early modern motto *memento mori*, like the death's head, reminds viewers that someday they too must die and so should make proper provisions towards this end. Confronting and contemplating such expressions of mortal temporality also can bring something else into view, which might be considered the metacognitive dimension; namely, the ways in which and the extent to which a wide range of related early modern cultural activities fuse the memory arts with the death arts. While the death arts depend on monitory and commemorative cues, not every memory art involves the death arts, but of course many do – going back to the origin story of the classical memory arts involving the performative poet, Simonides, identifying the dead bodies in the collapsed banqueting house of Scopus based on his recollection of where each was seated.[53] And so too this volume, full of essays that engage creatively with and tease out the strands relating to the death arts and those of the memory arts, links our two critical anthologies. Put differently, this present volume of essays bridges the epistemological brook between the territories covered in our two previous studies, *The Memory Arts in Renaissance England* (2016) and *The Death Arts in Renaissance England* (2022).

Even as we began laying the foundation for the first volume nearly a decade ago, we were aware that we were embarking upon a much larger project. The critical essays of this present collection are in effect practical applications of the kinds of materials we wanted to make available to a wide range of readers. *The Memory Arts* anthology, we were aware from the outset, needed to contain a representative sampling of entries involving mourning, loss, and mortality; even as we recognized that *The Death Arts* anthology would need to explore also early modern cultural expressions of remembrance, commemoration, and active recollection. Our two anthologies in effect have recuperated over 130 printed works and associated images with the goal of curating, organizing, and annotating, so as to offer a way to comment critically on these mutually involved cultural activities and forms of expression engaged with memory and mortality. This present volume realizes and makes explicit the kinds of connections that remain implicit throughout our two previous anthologies between these two modalities of creative expression during the English Renaissance: the memory arts and the death arts.

To be sure, some entries in *The Memory Arts* book just as easily might have been included in *The Death Arts*, and vice versa. Moreover, some of the same authors appear in both volumes (though using different passages), so representative and exemplary did we consider their writings, but

Figure 0.1a   Memento Mori Anamorphosis, portrait (view from left), 1580. Called Mary, Queen of Scots. Scottish National Portrait Gallery. Accession number: PG 1989. Photo Credit: Antonia Reeve.

of course examined with an eye towards the memory arts in the first volume and the death arts in the second.[54] Although we want to highlight the most productive points of contact between the two fields, we must recognize that the terrain shifts depending on where one stands to evaluate and assess the traces of these expressive forms. Another way to think of it, in terms familiar to the people in Renaissance England, would be to consider what Robert Burton, in his *Anatomy of Melancholy*, refers to as 'turning pictures': 'stand before which you see ... on the one side an ape, on the other an owl ... wise on the one side ... fools on the other'.[55] Among the extant 'turning portraits' from the period, painted on angled wooden slats, is the likeness of a lady of consequence (possibly Mary, Queen of Scots, *c.* 1580) looked at from left to right to reveal the human head changing into a death's head (Figures 0.1a and 0.1b).[56]

This three-dimensional work of art evokes the same eerie sense of recognition of one's mortality as that experienced with Holbein's famous

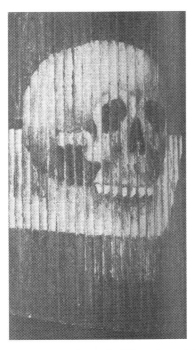

Figure o.1b   Memento Mori Anamorphosis, skull (view from right), 1580. Called Mary,
Queen of Scots. Scottish National Portrait Gallery. Accession number: PG 1989.
Photo Credit: Antonia Reeve.

distorted anamorphic shape at the bottom right of his justifiably celebrated
vanitas double portrait, *The Ambassadors*, that resolves into a death's head
when viewed at an extreme sidelong perspective. Another version of this
dialectical relationship of memory and mortality is foregrounded, among
other places, in one of the border illustrations in the series of allegorical
virtues depicted trampling – which is to say triumphing over – their oppo-
sites in *A Book of Christian Prayers* (see Figure 0.2).[57]

Memory is personified in classical habiliments, shown as a recorder with
her stylus and book: 'Memory is a treasure house' whereas 'Oblivion is as
a grave'. She stands over, seemingly unconcerned by the presence of, a
shrouded corpse positioned beside a spade (the visual metonymy associated
with work involved in Christian burial) crossed by a scythe (the traditional
symbol of reaping, associated originally with Saturn or Chronos and later
with the skeletal figure of Death). And even health manuals and books
about medicine and surgery, insofar as they provide memorial records of

Figure 0.2   Memory and Oblivion. *A Book of Christian Prayers*, 1608, S4ʳ.

what has been attempted and been proven successful for the preservation
and extension of life, at the same time express an anxiety over the need to
keep death at bay.[58] In this regard both *The Memory Arts* and *The Death
Arts* participate in representing the larger cultural activities and daily practices that the present volume of essays explores in further – and in more
particularized – detail.

***

Memory and Mortality in Renaissance England is organized around three
perspectives on the conjunction between memory and mortality. Part I,
'The Arts of Remembering Death', covers chapters that explore the ways
in which writers prepare for death by marshalling variations on the *ars
moriendi* and the *ars reminiscendi*. While weaving together rich traditions, learning how to die – consistent with other premodern arts – could
be surprisingly pliable, plastic, and inventive. Part II, 'Grounding the
Remembrance of the Dead', raises the issue of establishing the place of
commemoration. Before the dead could be remembered, they needed to

have a stable monument. Far from stable, however, such a ground often betrayed anxieties over posterity's ability to make good on its duty to remember. And Part III, 'The Ends of Commemoration' presents four different treatments of how remembering the dead in the period served disparate and often oblique agendas. The cultural work of mourning royals and nobles could advance different objects of remembrance altogether.

The volume's contributors offer a range of approaches through their case studies, drawing on literary criticism, intellectual history, art history, historiography, performance studies, theology, church history, and religious studies. But, as their chapters highlight, we remember the past as we anticipate the future. The present enterprise thus offers a roadmap for studies at the intersection of memory and mortality and, at the same time, realizes that there are many further territories to explore. The fraught problems raised by these two conceptual domains are inextricably intertwined in some of the most engaging and most frequently taught works of Renaissance English literature, including Shakespeare's *Hamlet*, his sonnets, the poetry of John Donne and of George Herbert, Browne's *Urne-Buriall*, and Milton's *Paradise Lost*. But, as the contributors make clear in their case studies, literature is only one area in which such creative interplay exists between the domains. Our goal with this volume is to illuminate and explore the interrelationships of these fundamental categories of Renaissance knowing and doing, theory and praxis, establishing the rich vein connecting these two fields of investigation, and gesturing towards new directions and future work.

Notes

1 The letter is translated in *Correspondence of Erasmus: Letters 2803 to 2939*, trans. by Clarence H. Miller, in *Collected Works of Erasmus*, vol. 20, ed. by James M. Estes (Toronto: University of Toronto Press, 2020). See letter 2824 'From Thomas Boleyn, Greenwich, 29 June 1533'. Boleyn's letter is dated 19 June 1533 as England's calendar was ten days out of sync with the continent in this period. The original letter can be found at MS Rehd 254 152 (University Library at Wrocław). For a modern translation of Erasmus's work, see *Preparing for Death* in *Spiritualia and Pastoralia*, trans. by John N. Grant, vol. 70, *Collected Works of Erasmus*, ed. by John W. O'Malley (Toronto: University of Toronto Press, 1998).

2 Erasmus, *De praeparatione ad mortem* (Basel: Froben and Episcopius, 1534).

3 Chapuys's letter to Erasmus can be read in Percy Stafford Allen, *Opus epistolarum Des. Erasmi Roterdami*, vol. 11 (Oxford: Clarendon Press, 1906), letter 3090, pp. 29–53. The original letter can be found at MS Rehd 254 49 (University Library at Wrocław).

4 Erasmus, *Preparation to deathe*, trans. by Anon. (London, 1538; STC 10505). Cf. entry III.1 in William E. Engel, Rory Loughnane, and Grant Williams, eds., *The Death Arts in Renaissance England* (Cambridge: Cambridge University Press, 2022).

5 Christopher Sutton, *Disce mori. Learne to die* (London, 1600; STC 23474). See also Chapter 4 regarding Sutton, 'Learn How to Die' by Scott Newstok.

6 Jeremy Taylor, *Holy Dying* (London, 1651; Wing T361A), D5ᵛ. See entry I.14 in *The Death Arts*, ed. by Engel, Loughnane, and Williams.

7 *Shakespeare's Sonnets*, ed. by Francis X. Connor, in *The New Oxford Shakespeare: Modern Critical Edition*, gen. ed. by Gary Taylor, John Jowett, Terri Bourus, and Gabriel Egan (Oxford: Oxford University Press, 2016), pp. 2819–82 (p. 2843).

8 Olivier de La Marche, *The Travelled Pilgrim*, trans. by Stephen Batman (London, 1569; STC 1585), M4ᵛ, M3ʳ.

9 Edmund Spenser, *The Faerie Queene*, ed. by A. C. Hamilton et al., 2nd ed. (Harlow, UK: Pearson Education, 2007), 2.9.55–58, 2.11.20–23.

10 See entry VI.4 in *The Memory Arts in Renaissance England*, ed. by William E. Engel, Rory Loughnane, and Grant Williams (Cambridge: Cambridge University Press, 2016); and entry III.4 in *The Death Arts*, ed. by Engel, Loughnane, and Williams.

11 See entry V.2 in *The Memory Arts*, ed. by Engel, Loughnane, and Williams; and entry II.4 in *The Death Arts*, ed. by Engel, Loughnane, and Williams.

12 It would be redundant to list here all of the works by these authors, the bulk of which are referenced in the following chapters; but we would be remiss not to give their touchstone texts, basically the first wave of memory studies in the pan-European intellectual tradition: Ludwig Volkmann, *Ars memorativa* (Vienna: Schroll, 1929); Paolo Rossi, *Clavis universalis* (Milan: Ricciardi, 1960); Frances A. Yates, *The Art of Memory* (London: Routledge & Kegan Paul, 1966); Mary Carruthers, *The Book of Memory* (Cambridge: Cambridge University Press, 1990); and Lina Bolzoni, *La stanza della memoria* (Turin: Einaudi, 1995). Translations of the German and Italian works are listed as well in the Bibliography. For a more fulsome bibliography of the second wave of memory studies published at the opening of the current millennium, see William E. Engel, 'What's New in Mnemology?', *Connotations* 11.2–3 (2001–2002), 241–61; and *The Memory Arts*, ed. by Engel, Loughnane, and Williams, pp. 1–38.

13 Neil Rhodes and Jonathan Sawday, eds., *The Renaissance Computer* (London: Routledge, 2000), p. 13, Rebeca Helfer, 'The State of the Art of Memory and Shakespeare Studies', in *The Routledge Handbook of Shakespeare and Memory*, ed. by Andrew Hiscock and Lina Perkins Wilder (London: Routledge, 2018), pp. 315–28; and Raphael Lyne, *Memory and Intertextuality in Renaissance Literature* (Cambridge: Cambridge University Press, 2016), pp. 4–7.

14 Most notably, Alexandra Walsham, Bronwyn Wallace, Ceri Law, and Brian Cummings, eds., *Memory and the English Reformation* (Cambridge: Cambridge University Press, 2020); Peter Sherlock, *Monuments and Memory in Early Modern England* (London: Routledge, 2016); Rebeca Helfer,

Spenser's Ruins and the Art of Recollection (Toronto: University of Toronto Press, 2012); Andrew Hiscock, *Reading Memory in Early Modern Literature* (Cambridge: Cambridge University Press, 2011); Donald Beecher and Grant Williams, eds., *Ars Reminiscendi: Mind and Memory in Renaissance Culture* (Toronto: Centre for Reformation and Renaissance Studies, 2009); Philip Schwyzer, *Literature, Nationalism, and Memory in Early Modern England and Wales* (Cambridge: University Press Cambridge, 2005); Christopher Ivic and Grant Williams, eds., *Forgetting in Early Modern English Literature and Culture: Lethe's Legacies* (London: Routledge, 2004). There is a wealth of major studies on memory in Renaissance drama and Shakespeare, exemplarily Garrett A. Sullivan, Jr., *Memory and Forgetting in English Renaissance Drama: Shakespeare, Marlowe, Webster* (Cambridge: Cambridge University Press, 2005); Anita Gilman Sherman, *Skepticism and Memory in Shakespeare and Donne* (New York: Palgrave Macmillan, 2007); Jonathan Baldo, *Memory in Shakespeare's Histories* (New York: Routledge, 2012); Lina Perkins Wilder, *Shakespeare's Memory Theatre* (Cambridge: Cambridge University Press, 2010); Isabel Karremann, *The Drama of Memory in Shakespeare's History Plays* (Cambridge: Cambridge University Press, 2015); Patricia Phillippy, *Shaping Remembrance from Shakespeare to Milton* (Cambridge: Cambridge University Press, 2018); and Peter Holland, *Shakespeare and Forgetting* (London: Bloomsbury, 2021).

15 With special reference to memory in early modern religious practices, analysed in terms of models derived from theories of 'Extended Mind' and 'Distributed Cognition', see Evelyn B. Tribble and Nicholas Keane, eds., *Cognitive Ecologies and the History of Remembering Early Modern England* (London: Palgrave, 2011).

16 See Marek Tamm and Alessandro Arcangeli, eds., *The Early Modern Age*, vol. 3, *A Cultural History of Memory*, gen. ed. by Stefan Berge and Jeffrey K. Olick (London: Bloomsbury, 2020).

17 At the time, Ariès entered into a debate with Michel Vovelle, a Marxist historian, whose *La Mort et l'Occident de 1300 à nos jours* (Paris: Gallimard, 1983) is another major contribution to death studies. Vovelle criticized him for 'spiritualizing the history of mentalities, recasting it in such a way that it acquired an autonomy divorced from social and economic realities' (Patrick H. Hutton, *Philippe Ariès and the Politics of French Cultural History* (Amherst: University of Massachusetts Press, 2004), p. 123). See Philippe Ariès, *The Hour of Our Death: The Classic History of Western Attitudes toward Death over the Last One Thousand Years*, trans. by Helen Weaver, 2nd ed. (New York: Vintage Books, 2008).

18 David Cressy, *Birth, Marriage, and Death: Ritual, Religion, and the Life-Cycle in Tudor and Stuart England* (Oxford: Oxford University Press, 1997); and Ralph Houlbrooke, *Death, Religion, and the Family in England, 1480–1750* (Oxford: Clarendon Press, 1998).

19 Nigel Llewellyn, *Art of Death: Visual Culture in the English Death Ritual, c. 1500–c. 1800* (London: Reaktion, 1991); William E. Engel, *Mapping Mortality: The Persistence of Memory and Melancholy in Early Modern England* (Amherst:

University of Massachusetts Press, 1995); and Michael Neill, *Issues of Death: Mortality and Identity in English Renaissance Tragedy* (Oxford: Clarendon Press, 1997).

20 The selected examples that will follow in this paragraph come mostly from literary studies, as do most of those discussed by our collection's contributors.

21 On the emblems of death, see William E. Engel, *Death and Drama in Renaissance England: Shades of Memory* (Oxford: Oxford University Press, 2002).

22 Mary J. Dobson, *Contours of Death and Disease in Early Modern England* (Cambridge: Cambridge University Press, 2002); and Andrea McKenzie, *Tyburn's Martyrs: Execution in England, 1675–1775* (London: Bloomsbury, 2007).

23 Patricia Phillippy, *Women, Death and Literature in Post-Reformation England* (Cambridge: Cambridge University Press, 2002).

24 Margo Swiss and David A. Kent, *Speaking Grief in English Literary Culture: Shakespeare to Milton* (Pittsburgh, PA: Duquesne University Press, 2002). This is no place to map out the recently flourishing field of cognition, emotion, and affect studies, which we acknowledge as being of signal importance in early modern cultural studies.

25 See Ramie Targoff, *Posthumous Love: Eros and the Afterlife in Renaissance England* (Chicago: University of Chicago, 2014), and John S. Garrison, *Shakespeare and the Afterlife* (Oxford: Oxford University Press, 2018).

26 Scott L. Newstok, *Quoting Death in Early Modern England: The Poetics of Epitaphs Beyond the Tomb* (Basingstoke: Palgrave Macmillan, 2009).

27 Brian Chalk, *Monuments and Literary Posterity in Early Modern Drama* (Cambridge: Cambridge University Press, 2015).

28 Philip Schwyzer, *Archaeologies of English Renaissance Literature* (Oxford: University of Oxford Press, 2007) and *Shakespeare and the Remains of Richard III* (Oxford: University of Oxford Press, 2013). Claire Preston, 'The Laureate of the Grave: *Urne-Buriall* and the Failure of Memory', in Claire Preston, *Thomas Browne and the Writing of Early Modern Science* (Cambridge: Cambridge University Press, 2005), pp. 123–54.

29 On the flourishing critical interest in early modern ruins and ruined structures, see Andrew Hui, *The Poetics of Ruins in Renaissance Literature* (New York: Fordham University Press, 2017); Susan Stewart, *The Ruins Lesson: Meaning and Material in Western Culture* (Chicago and London: University of Chicago Press, 2020); and Stewart Mottram, *Ruin and Reformation in Spenser, Shakespeare, and Marvell* (Oxford: Oxford University Press, 2019). Apropos of the latter reference especially, see Chapter 1, 'Death and the Art of Memory in Donne' by Rebeca Helfer, which builds productively on her research in *Spenser's Ruins*; and see also in this regard Chapter 6, 'Scattered Bones, Martyrs, Materiality, and Memory in Drayton and Milton' by Philip Schwyzer; and Chapter 12, '"Superfluous Men" and the Graveyard Politics of *The Duchess of Malfi*' by Michael Neill.

30 On the crucial distinction between Anglo-American and German memory studies, see Mary Carruthers, 'Moving Back in Memory Studies', *History Workshop Journal*, 77 (2014), 275–82 – a review of Jan Assmann, *Cultural Memory and Early Civilization: Writing, Remembrance, and Political Imagination* (Cambridge: Cambridge University Press, 2011). The concept of 'cultural memory' was first developed at length by Maurice Halbwachs, *On Collective Memory*, ed. and trans. by A. Coser (Chicago: University of Chicago Press, 1992).

31 Pierre Nora, 'Between Memory and History: Les Lieux de Mémoire', *Representations*, 26 (1989), 7–24 (p. 8).

32 Of course, there are other less prominent, yet productive types of memory suggested by death studies. Mourning and bereavement raise the issue of affective memory, and public dying and execution broach the issue of disciplinary memory, whereby the state manages society through fear.

33 That is, death, judgement, heaven, hell; for more on this cultural context, see the introduction in *The Death Arts*, ed. by Engel, Loughnane, and Williams.

34 Eamon Duffy, *The Stripping of the Altars: Traditional Religion in England, 1400–1580* (New Haven, CT: Yale University Press, 1992); Bruce Gordon and Peter Marshall, eds., *The Place of the Dead: Death and Remembrance in Late Medieval and Early Modern Europe* (Cambridge: Cambridge University Press, 2000); and Peter Marshall, *Beliefs and the Dead in Reformation England* (Oxford: Oxford University Press, 2004).

35 For a suggestive history of Purgatory in England, with special reference to its survivals and echoes in works by Shakespeare, see Stephen Greenblatt, *Hamlet in Purgatory* (Princeton, NJ: Princeton University Press, 2001).

36 See Walsham et al., *Memory and the English Reformation*, pp. 3–4, 11–15.

37 The utility of memory is not always championed in the period; for example, see the entry on Pierre Charron in *The Memory Arts*, ed. by Engel, Loughnane, and Williams, p. 303.

38 See entry IV.10 on William Dugdale in *The Memory Arts*, ed. by Engel, Loughnane, and Williams.

39 See Chapter 5, 'Memory, Climate, and Mortality: The Dudley Women among the Fields' by Patricia Phillippy.

40 See Thomas Tuke, *A Discourse of Death, Bodily, Ghostly, and Eternal* (London, 1613; STC 24307), B3r, and George Strode, *The Anatomy of Mortality* (London, 1618; STC 23364), B1v. Samuel Otes, *An Explanation of the General Epistle of Saint Jude* (London, 1633; STC 18896), CC2v, credits Augustine with making the division. John Bradford postulates just such a quadratic scheme; see Engel, Loughnane, and Williams, eds., *The Death Arts in Renaissance England*, entry I.6.

41 Ephesians 2:1–3. All references to the Bible are taken from the KJV, *The Holy Bible* (London, 1611; STC 2216).

42 'Thy word have I hid in mine heart, that I might not sin against you' (Psalms 119:11).

43 The Parable of the Sower of Seed (Matthew 13:1–9, 18–23).

44 For complaints about the press's overproduction of books on divinity, see Robert Burton, *The Anatomy of Melancholy*, ed. by T. C. Faulkner, N. K. Kiessling, and R. L. Blair, 6 vols. (Oxford: Clarendon Press, 1989–2000), vol. 1, pp. 21–2.

45 1 Peter 1:24–25.

46 See Mary Thomas Crane, *Framing Authority: Sayings, Self, and Society in Sixteenth-Century England* (Princeton, NJ: Princeton University Press, 2016).

47 Philip Sidney, *Sidney's 'The Defence of Poesy' and Selected Renaissance Literary Criticism* (London: Penguin, 2004), pp. 16–18. See Erasmus, *The Education of a Prince*, trans. by Neil M. Cheshire and Michael J. Heath, in Desiderius Erasmus, *Panegyricus: Moria; Julius Exclusus; Institutio Principis Christiani; Querela Pacis; Ciceronianus; Notes; Indexes*, ed. by Anthony Levi (Toronto: University of Toronto Press, 1986), p. 210. Thomas Elyot, *The boke named the Gouernour* (London, 1537; STC 7636), structures his book around many examples of noble persons performing virtuous deeds. See, for instance, p. 229.

48 See Lorraine Helms, '"The High Roman Fashion": Sacrifice, Suicide, and the Shakespearean Stage', *PMLA*, 107.3 (1992), 554–65.

49 On Ramism, see the classic study by Walter J. Ong, *Ramus, Method, and the Decay of Dialogue: From the Art of Discourse to the Art of Reason* (Cambridge, MA, and London: Harvard University Press, 1958).

50 See, for example, the Ramus-structured interpretations of the Song of Songs written by Dudley Fenner, *The Song of Songs That Is, the Most Excellent Song Which Was Solomon's* (Middelburg, 1587; STC 2769). For a sermon that employs an elaborate art of memory, see entry V.6 on Daniel Featley in *The Memory Arts*, ed. by Engel, Loughnane, and Williams. The art of memory was taught to auditors who wanted to improve their ability to remember sermons: see entry I.8 on Henry Herdson in *The Memory Arts*, ed. by Engel, Loughnane, and Williams.

51 This kind of oblivion is dramatized in Shakespeare's *Hamlet*, with the Ghost's rousing appeal to Prince Hamlet to 'remember me'; and in Marlowe's *Doctor Faustus*, the final scene in which Faustus wishfully reasons that oblivion is preferable to eternity in Hell – a scene examined with verve and acuity by Rebeca Helfer in Chapter 1 of this volume, 'Death and the Art of Memory in Donne'.

52 Sullivan, *Memory and Forgetting*, pp. 12–15.

53 Frances A. Yates, *The Art of Memory* (London: Penguin, 1978), pp. 17–18. Supplementarily, Helfer, in *Spenser's Ruins*, carefully explores the perennial significance of Simonides.

54 Most notably Francis Bacon, Margaret Cavendish, John Foxe, Abraham Holland, Alexander Ross, Mary Wroth, and authors of the *Mirror for Magistrates*. See entries IV.3, VI.9, V.2, VI.5, II.10, VI.15, and VI.4 in *The Memory Arts*, ed. by Engel, Loughnane, and Williams, and entries III.10, III.15, II.4, III.9, III.13, IV.14, and III.4 in *The Death Arts*, ed. by Engel, Loughnane, and Williams.

55 Burton, *The Anatomy of Melancholy*, vol. 1, p. 105.

56 www.nationalgalleries.org/art-and-artists/3239/anamorphosis-called-mary-
   queen-scots-1542-1587-reigned-1542-1567
57 See *The Memory Arts*, ed. by Engel, Loughnane, and Williams, pp. 246–54.
58 Cf. Levinus Lemnius, *The Touchstone of Complexions* (1576), entry III.3 in *The
   Memory Arts*, ed. by Engel, Loughnane, and Williams; and Helkiah Crooke,
   Mikrokosmographia: A description of the body (1631), entry III.11 in *The Death
   Arts*, ed. by Engel, Loughnane, and Williams.

The Arts of Remembering Death

Preface to Part I

The chapters in this opening part identify intersection points between the arts of memory and death, as broadly conceived. The former is associated with the architectural mnemotechnics of the classical *ars memorativa*. Such mnemonic practice, formalized in the rhetorical tradition, as outlined by Cicero, Quintilian, and the anonymous author of *Rhetorica ad Herennium*, was adapted in Christian traditions stretching from Augustine through the scholastics and beyond, and then re-secularized in sixteenth and seventeenth-century humanist and self-help writing.[1] Less formally, the memory arts, a much more capacious category, became integrated with early modern habits of thought and practice that helped individuals in their daily preparations and activities. This extended to preparations for and activities surrounding death – described in *ars moriendi* manuals but also informing broader cultural work – creating much overlap between the arts of memory and mortality.[2] In the four chapters of this first part, by drawing in forms of intellectual, social, and spiritual practice, contributors observe the manifold ways in which formalized approaches to memory and death speak to one another in the period.

The arts of remembering death refer to a host of cultural activities in the period that informed the living to remember both the dead and their own mortality. To think upon one's end was a habit of thought, reinforced by sets of visual, aural, and verbal reminders about death's proximity, ranging from tomb-making to bell-ringing to habits of speech (see Chapter 2 by Jonathan Baldo for the colloquial phrase of 'owing' God a death).[3] An illustrative material example was the wearing of mourning rings: often designed with a *memento mori* insignia, such as a death's head, the wearer wore such jewellery to remember a specific person who has died while also reminding them daily of their own inevitable end. Lest we think such reinforcement was always miserable for the individual, we should recall that death was also understood, in the Christian tradition, as a welcome return to God after the trials and tribulations of life, a bridging point rather than a terminus. Quite where the individual went next and how much that path was pre-determined were, of course, some of the major bones of contention of the European Reformation. But what was generally agreed was that whatever death brought it was best to remember to prepare diligently for it.

The wearing of mourning rings offers an example of such memorative practice at the conservative end of the scale. At the more radical end, consider the following advice from Richard Braithwaite's *A Spiritual Spicery* (1638), where he outlines a five-day 'exercise' to remember death:

> There are [those] who all the year long present the figure and feature of Death before them by some certain exercise, and prepare themselves no otherwise for death than if they were even then to die, and that for the space of five days continually. The first day, they meditated of the griefs and infirmities which go before death, and [the] horror of death, unto all which they resign themselves. The next day, they think of their sins, confessing them with so great diligence and intention as if they were to die presently after their confession. Therefore, they spend this day in sighs and tears. The third day, they come unto the blessed Eucharist with all the fervour they may, receiving it as their viaticum in their passage from this their exile. The fourth day, they make continual supplications unto God for the unction of the Holy Spirit, whereby they might be illuminated and the hardness of their hearts mollified. And this they do, as it were, for extreme unction. The fifth day, they become most fervent supplicants unto God for a spiritual death: whereby they may perfectly die to the world and to themselves, and live with God. And to every of these days may be applied proper psalms and prayers, as also divine invocations, and giving of thanks, for all benefits conferred by God upon them all their life long. (L12^v–M1^v)[4]

Frances A. Yates famously described a lost social practice of the arts of memory – imagining a student of memory walking around a deserted space memorizing sites for their locational memory technique – and here Braithwaite outlines a further set of lost practices for the arts of death. Like Braithwaite's student of death, the idea that death is something to be remembered daily, to be anticipated and prepared for, and to be understood and engaged with, informs each of the subsequent chapters in this part.

Rebeca Helfer's opening chapter, Chapter 1, draws the most explicit connection between the memory and death arts. Identifying textual inter-play and indebtedness between Augustine's *Confessions*, Marlowe's *Doctor Faustus*, and Donne's *Holy Sonnets*, Helfer describes how the speaker or character's uncertainty about their own salvation connects the *ars memorativa* and *ars moriendi* through the evocation of confessional practice. Donne famously writes that 'the art of salvation is but the art of memory',

yet Helfer argues that Donne ironizes this in his *Holy Sonnets* by revealing how his speaker longs for forgetfulness, or divine oblivion, which,
like Marlowe's play, dramatizes the problem of salvation in Reformation
England. The desire to forget rather than remember problematizes Donne's
depiction of the art of death, and it serves as an ironic reminder of the
relationship between the art of salvation and the art of memory, through
which Donne fashions the *Holy Sonnets* as a memory theatre built upon
the ruins of the past.

Jonathan Baldo identifies a series of debt/death puns in Shakespeare's
plays and outlines how debt and death are conceptually linked through the
influence of pre-Reformation teaching about Purgatory. Baldo describes
Purgatory as a sort of debtor's prison, with the dead paying off their sins,
or spiritual debts, through their own endured punishment and the inter-
cessionary prayers and payments by those left behind. With the abolition
of Purgatory in the Protestant Reformation, the link between spiritual
debt and death had to be reconfigured, and Chapter 2, like Helfer's,
explores the cultural preoccupation with uncertain salvation. The chapter also marks a rich connection between the emergence of double-entry
bookkeeping, with its emphases upon symmetry, proportion, and balance,
and the idea of God's divine design for the world. Baldo identifies such
an ordered way of thinking about the world, where the individual is either
in debt or credit, whether financially or spiritually, in Shakespeare's plays,
and specifically in the blurring of the language of debt and death, homo-
phones that would be indistinct in performance.

Staying with Shakespeare, in Chapter 3 John S. Garrison teases out the
connections between forgetting and remembering, absence and presence,
in the Sonnets. Similar to Baldo's analysis of the symmetry of debt and
credit, Garrison observes the presence of absence in Shakespeare's poems
and describes how the process of forgetting also requires remembering.
As the sonnets work to immortalize both the speaker and the beloved
addressee, and, in effect, immortalize Shakespeare as author, they defy
death and the threat of oblivion. Garrison focuses upon the poems' work
to bring pleasure into the present moment, as the sonnets both reflect
upon the past and anticipate the future. Such memory work, at once elegiac for the past and endlessly deferring future mortality, shows how literary creation can act as a bulwark against death.

Concluding this part, Scott Newstok, in Chapter 4, shifts our attention
to the craft, rather than art, of dying. Describing the culture of mortality
that Shakespeare and others were educated and apprenticed in, Newstok
marks a connection between the habits and practices of death – scripted

death scenes that were rehearsed and then performed – and dramatic performance. Such labour and discipline surrounding death, which finds parallels in the spiritual work in the world described by Helfer and Baldo, understood mortality as an end, an output, or limit. Newstok observes the phenomenon of 'craft of dying' manuals across the sixteenth and seventeenth centuries, which advised, in often overtly performative descriptions, how the dying should act in their final moments, again raising the spectre of uncertain salvation and oblivion analysed in the preceding chapters.

Notes

1 See the Introduction to *The Memory Arts in Renaissance England*, ed. by William E. Engel, Rory Loughnane, and Grant Williams (Cambridge: Cambridge University Press, 2016) for the art of memory's circuitous path to English intellectual and popular culture (pp. 1–32).
2 Nancy Lee Beaty's *The Craft of Dying: A Study in the Literary Tradition of the Ars Moriendi in England* (New Haven, CT: Yale University Press, 1970) remains a foundational study in this area. See also the set of entries in Part I ('Preparatory and Dying Arts') in *The Death Arts in Renaissance England*, ed. by William E. Engel, Rory Loughnane, and Grant Williams (Cambridge: Cambridge University Press, 2022).
3 Some particularly influential studies of how memory and death figured and intersected in early modern English culture include: David Cressy, *Bonfires and Bells: National Memory and the Protestant Calendar in Elizabethan and Stuart England* (Berkeley and Los Angeles: University of California Press, 1989); Nigel Llewellyn, *The Art of Death: Visual Culture in the English Death Ritual, c. 1500–c. 1800* (London: Reaktion, 1991); and Peter Marshall, *Beliefs and the Dead in Reformation England* (Oxford: Oxford University Press, 2002). For the cultural commonplace of thinking upon one's end, see Rory Loughnane, 'Studied Speech and *The Duchess of Malfi*: The Lost Arts of Rhetoric, Memory, and Death', *Sillages Critique* 26 (2019), http://journals.openedition.org/sillagescritiques/6847.
4 Richard Braithwaite, *A Spiritual Spicerie containing sundrie sweet tractates of devotion and piety* (London, 1638; STC 3586). The excerpted section is described as 'The Dying Man's Diary, or A Christian's *Memento Mori*; Divided into a five days' exercise'. We have modernized the excerpt.

CHAPTER I

Death and the Art of Memory in Donne

Rebeca Helfer

In the *Holy Sonnets*, Donne ruminates incessantly on death and the problem of salvation that death's seeming imminence produces for his persona – a figure clearly distinct from the poet he so closely resembles. At the start, Donne's speaker issues an eleventh-hour plea for salvation, as though he were in the face of death and damnation:

> Thou has made me, and shall Thy work decay?
> Repair me now, for now mine end doth haste;
> I run to death, and Death meets me as fast,
> And all my pleasures are like yesterday.
> Despair behind, and Death before doth cast
> Such terror, and my feeble flesh doth waste
> By sin it in, which it towards hell doth weigh.[1]

Here, as throughout the *Holy Sonnets*, Donne would seem to enact the drama of salvation as an 'art of death': originally, broadly speaking, this meant Catholic practices for achieving a 'good death' that might save a sinful soul at the hour of death, in which confession and contrition, remembering and repenting, play a central part; and writ small, the medieval manuscripts that describe this method of dying well, which often include a series of final temptations by the devil for those at death's door, as it were, who must resist these temptations in order to save their souls.[2] The apparent nearness of death – 'I run to death, and Death meets me as fast' – motivates Donne's urgent demand for divine intervention, presented as though it were a near-deathbed confession of sin and plea for salvation. But though death clearly presents itself as a terrifying prospect, and despite his time running out, Donne nevertheless remains torn between two loves, a dividedness between the divine and the diabolical that he despairs of resolving as though he were a Petrarchan lover. 'When towards Thee / By Thy leave I can look, I rise again; / But our old subtle foe so tempteth me, / That not one hour myself I can sustain', he confesses, though 'Thy grace may wing me to prevent his art / And thou like adamant draw mine

iron heart' (1.9–14). Donne appeals to God for grace, which would answer
Satan's temptations and which would give him the strength 'to prevent
his art': his craft, his cunning, his courtship, all of which reflect ironically
upon Donne's own representation of art within, and as, the *Holy Sonnets*.
Yet therein lies the problem at the heart of the *Holy Sonnets* – the question of where to find or fathom such saving 'grace', particularly given its
different role in Catholic and Protestant soteriology. What complicates
the 'art of death', an art reformed in part by Protestant writers, for Donne
turns on the problem of grace and its relationship to good works: whereas
for Roman Catholics, penitence has a sacramental role to play in enacting
a 'good death' that might earn forgiveness for the sinful soul, for English
Protestants such contrition might be seen as an enactment or evidence of
the unearnable gift of grace, but it also might be seen as acting – an empty,
even deceptive performance.[3] The speaker's Manichean division between
good and evil, grace and damnation, relates to the question of theatricality in a still more specific sense, as I will show. Donne constructs the *Holy
Sonnets* as a memory theatre: a memorial space in which to remember his
persona's sin and soul, his divided loves, and in which to enact the drama
of salvation by re-enacting the role of Faustus from Marlowe's *Doctor
Faustus* to Augustine's *Confessions*. By playing the part of Faustus, I argue,
Donne dramatizes a version (and perversion) of his well-known sermonic
assertion that 'the art of salvation is but the art of memory': the method
of architectural mnemonics that Augustine in the *Confessions* converts for
Christianity, and through which he remembers divine love and reforms his
soul.[4] In so doing, Donne suggests the ways in which his poetic persona
represents his own anguished conversion process, as though confessing to
his own dividedness between Catholic and Protestant paths to salvation.
In the context of sonnets rather than sermon, Donne explores 'the art of
salvation [as] the art of memory' as a problem rather than a solution, and
dramatizes their relationship ironically by spotlighting his persona's persistent desire to forget. 'The so-called art of memory becomes, in [Donne's]
hands, an art of doubt', Anita Gilman Sherman astutely argues, identifying a scepticism – a dialectical and dialogic aesthetic that allows Donne to
wrestle with questions of faith in unorthodox terms – that is central to the
Holy Sonnets.[5]

To see the *Holy Sonnets* as a memory theatre is to rethink what the 'art
of memory' means.[6] As I have previously argued, building upon William
E. Engel's extensive work on the 'mnemonically oriented principle of early
modern aesthetics', the art of memory is more than an *ars* or artificial
method of rhetoric, used to construct imaginative spaces – metaphorically,

a building or book of memory, which often double for one another to create a book-as-building and vice versa – filled with vivid images designed both to store memory and to spur and maintain an orator's recollection.[7] Rather, I understand the art of memory first and foremost as a literary 'art' form, a mnemonic poetics used to create memorable tales of ruin and recollection both on the page and in performance. This mnemonic method is clearly one that poetry's image-rich, metaphor-laden stanzas, or 'rooms', naturally lend themselves to and even emblematize. Yet Donne's treatment of the art of memory is more complex than the use of an ancient method for novel poetic purposes. With the *Holy Sonnets*, Donne does not obviously 'build in sonnets pretty rooms', as he writes in 'The Canonization' in mock-salvific terms, in which the poem becomes a 'well-wrought urn' for the memory of the once sinful lovers-turned-saints.[8] Yet by focusing on forgetting, he paradoxically fashions the *Holy Sonnets* as a memory theatre in another sense: as a meta-poetic space in which to remember earlier art about the relationship between memory and salvation, from the sonnet to the stage, from Catholic Italy to Protestant England, from Dante to Donne himself.[9]

Memory Theatre: Death and *Doctor Faustus*

In the midst of the *Holy Sonnets*, Donne borrows a theatrical metaphor that frames his sonnet sequence as a memory theatre on multiple levels:

> This is my play's last scene …
> … my minute's latest point;
> And gluttonous Death will instantly unjoint
> My body and soul, and I shall sleep a space;
> But my ever-waking part shall see that face
> Whose fear already shakes my every joint.   (6.1–8)

Donne then imagines the separation of his body and soul – 'as my soul to heaven her first seat takes flight, / And earth-born body in the earth shall dwell' – and with this separation, a release from his sins: 'so fall my sins … / To where they're bred and would press me to hell' (6.9– 14). In this fantasy of liberation and salvation, this dress rehearsal for death, Donne imagines himself as 'righteous' and 'purged of evil', as his speaker 'leave[s] the world, the flesh, the devil': he exits the theatre of the world, with all its temptations.[10] This drama of salvation rehearses another 'play's last scene', one with a very different ending: the last scene of Marlowe's *Doctor Faustus*.[11] Here Faustus despairs, 'Now has thou but one bare hour to live, / And then you must be damned perpetually';

and at this moment of death when confession and repentance still seem possible, he too longs to ascend to 'leap up to my God!', while wondering, 'Who pulls me down?'[12] At the end of the play and the end of his life, Faustus wrestles with a dilemma that Marlowe presents as a divide between Catholic and Calvinist salvation theology: whether true repentance might earn Faustus forgiveness, or whether he is damned either way. Faustus ultimately encounters the angry face of God: 'My God, my God, look not so fierce on me!', he cries, recognizing divine judgment and the certainty that with his death will come damnation (5.2.112). Before then, he pleads with the 'stars that reigned at [his] nativity / whose influence [that] hath allotted death and hell' to draw him up and divide his body from his soul, sending his 'limbs' to hell 'so that [his] soul may but ascend to heaven' (5.2.81–7). In more radical terms, Faustus imagines liberation not from the body but from the soul itself. 'Why wert thou not a creature wanting soul? / Or why is this immortal that thou hast?', Faustus asks, reasoning that if 'Pythagoras' *metempsychosis* were [true] / This soul should fly from me and I be changed / Unto some brutish beast' if which 'all … are happy, for, when they die, / Their souls are soon dissolved in elements' (5.2.97–103). In 'This is my play's last scene', Donne likewise envisions the release of his body that presses him to 'hell' in order to free his soul to ascend to 'heaven', and elsewhere echoes Faustus' desire to forget the soul, or rather to be a creature without a soul to save: 'If lecherous goats, if serpents envious / Cannot be damn'd … / alas, why should I be?', he asks in 'If poisonous minerals', before turning, as Faustus does, to the problem of God's grace: 'mercy being easy, and glorious / To God, in His stern wrath why threatens He?' (9.3–4, 7–8). Donne answers his own question with another – 'But who am I, that dare dispute with thee / O God?' – and pleads for forgiveness as forgetting (9.8). 'O God, O! of Thine only worthy blood, / And my tears, make a heavenly Lethean flood, / And drown in it my sin's black memory', Donne demands, as if his salvation depends upon it: 'That Thou remember them, some claim as debt; / I think it mercy if Thou wilt forget' (9.10–14).

This plea for divine oblivion would seem to be the very inverse of Donne's aforementioned assertion in his 1618 sermon that 'the art of salvation is but the art of memory' (2.2.273), a phrase that bespeaks his reputation as a 'second St. Augustine' and his conversion from irreverent poet, Jack Donne, to devout preacher, Doctor Donne.[13] Nevertheless, remembering and forgetting are intimately connected in the *Holy Sonnets* through Augustine's *Confessions*. Donne's sermon is one in a series on the penitential Psalm 32, which describes David's confession of his sins, forgiveness from God, and the teaching of penitence, a lesson that Donne connects to Augustine's own confessions throughout: as the psalmist recounts, 'I said, "I will confess my / transgressions to the Lord", / and you forgave the guilt of my sin... / Therefore let all who are faithful offer prayer to you ... / I will instruct you and teach you / the way you should go.'[14] In this sermon, as Achsah Guibbory has demonstrated, Donne links Christian and Pagan forms of *anamnesis*: the soul's remembrance not simply of things past but rather of prior knowledge, forgotten and then recovered.[15] Significantly, *anamnesis* properly means 'to be reminded', to remember what has been forgotten. As Donne explains, '*Plato* plac'd *all learning* in the memory' and 'we may place *all Religion* in the memory too', for 'all knowledge, that seems new to day, says *Plato*, is but a remembering *of that* which your soul knew before ... the remembring you of the mercies of God' (2.2.274). Although Donne names only Plato, his references allude to Augustine's conversion of Platonic *anamnesis* for Christianity in the *Confessions*. Indeed, Donne's explanation of this phrase – from his injunction to remember that divine 'love will keep thee from sinning' and that 'love, which mis-placed, hath transported thee upon many sins', to his insistence even 'he that reads no Scriptures' nevertheless 'hath a *Genesis* in his *memory*' and 'cannot forget that God hath delivered him, from some kind of *Egypt*, from some oppression' – encapsulates Augustine's memoir (2.2.273–4). The *Confessions* begins as a love-letter to God and a confession of 'mis-placed' love, which Augustine recollects according to a place-based method of memory, and which ends with his interpretation of *Genesis*. Here, Augustine demonstrates how reading scripture allegorically is the ultimate form of *anamnesis* – the reminder that allows him to remember a priori divine love, beginning with creation and continuing throughout his life, and thereby to reform his fallen, forgetful soul. Yet Donne's sermon also emphasizes the role of forgetting: 'there may be enough in *remembering our selves*; but sometimes, that's the hardest of all', because 'many times we are farthest off from our selves; most forgetful of our selves' (2.2.274). The temptation to forget the divine and thus to be 'forgetful of our selves' is central to Augustine's conversion narrative in the *Confessions*, his journey from sin to salvation, from forgetfulness to remembrance. Augustine acknowledges that the temptations to forget rather than remember God are many, and perhaps the greatest temptation comes in the form of Faustus, the Manichean bishop who most represents Augustine's divided desires and loves, and who stands as an impediment to his conversion.

Augustine's *Confessions*: The Art of Salvation
as an Art of Memory

The art of memory – a method of mnemonic poetics – becomes an art of salvation through allegory, specifically Platonic allegories of love. Augustine's art of memory and its antecedents represent an allegorical poetics of memory, as I have argued elsewhere, a poetics exemplified by stories of ruin and recollection.[16] The origin story of the art of memory figures prominently in my understanding of it as a poetics: the tall tale of the ancient Greek poet Simonides, who supposedly discovers the art of memory when, after the collapse of a banqueting hall, he is able to identify the dead by recollecting their places within the hall. In *On the Orator*, Cicero uses this heuristic tale to teach the art of memory as a rhetorical tool, but ultimately gives the art of memory a far greater role in his dialogue: he plays the part of a new Simonides who memorializes the famous orators, now dead, and who recollects, partly as fact and partly as fiction, 'the ruins of [his] country', devastated by war.[17] Cicero's poetic use of the art of memory to construct *On the Orator* as a memorial space itself recalls Plato's treatment of *anamnesis* in the *Phaedrus*, which Cicero's dialogue explicitly re-enacts. In the *Phaedrus*, Socrates famously rejects artificial aids to memory, most notably writing, which he calls 'a recipe not for memory, but for reminder', which ultimately 'will implant forgetfulness [in] souls.'[18] His complaints about artificial memory extend to the use of mnemonics as a poetics, most explicitly in his derision of 'the inventor' of 'mnemonic verse' (267a, p. 512). Throughout the dialogue, Socrates criticizes the rhetorical and pedagogical uses of artificial memory and conflates their use with poetics as a method to remember and re-enact love stories: specifically, the tale of Troy's ruin and Helen of Troy's role therein. Nevertheless, he also appropriates for philosophy the method of the poets, though not their matter of memory. Playing the part of a poet, Socrates delivers a palinode of praise for the God of Love that serves as a teaching tale for philosophical *anamnesis*: a story of the soul's fall into forgetfulness and its remembrance when reminded of divine love (the love of wisdom, literally *philo-sophia*); a tale that Socrates himself admits was 'perforce poetical' (257a, p. 502). His allegory of divided loves, the right versus the wrong kind of love, is framed as a difference between the human and the divine, and symbolically, between poetry and philosophy. Through Socrates' storytelling, his allegory of love, Plato at once rebukes and remakes the poet's method in philosophy's image: as a process of retrieving prior memory, *anamnesis*, which turns all knowledge into self-knowledge rather than received wisdom. And although Socrates in the *Phaedrus* scorns writing as a mere 'reminder', it both plays a central part within the dialogue and offers a reminder of the irony that Plato himself memorializes Socrates through writing and, as a new Simonides, in order to remember the dead.

Like Plato, Augustine in his *Confessions* criticizes the poet's fictions and the centrality of their place in collective memory; yet also like Plato, Augustine adopts and adapts mnemonic poetics for his spiritual memoir. Augustine thereby tells the story of himself and his soul as an allegory for Everyman's journey from sin to salvation, as Christian mnemonic. Despite his regret for having once 'wept for Dido' and his desire to 'forget the wanderings of Aeneas and all that goes with them', Augustine neverthe-less reforms the poet's 'art of memory' into an 'art of salvation' in the *Confessions*, converting both Platonic anamnesis and Ciceronian mnemon-ics into a Christian poetics by which Augustine remembers himself from ruin.[19] Augustine asks, 'What, then, do I love when I love God?', and finds his answer in the step-by-step process of remembering. 'I rise by stages towards the God who made me', he writes, describing his memory accord-ing to mnemonic metaphors: 'a spacious palace, a storehouse of countless images of all kinds which are conveyed to it by the senses' (X.7–8.213–14). Drawing upon the rhetorical art of memory, Augustine describes the pro-cess of recollection by which 'some memories present themselves easily and in the correct order' and others he must 'shepherd [out] again from their old lairs', and he aligns memorial activity with cognition broadly, asserting that 'the mind and the memory are one and the same' (218–19, 220). Yet even as Augustine explores what he calls 'the vast cloisters of my memory', he also acknowledges the fundamental mystery of what it means to remember God within himself. 'Where and when did I experience a state of blessed happiness, so that I am enabled to remember and love it and long for it?', Augustine asks, a question that he answers through a ver-sion of Platonic-love-as-*anamnesis* (228). Yet even as he pursues the love of God in amorous and even erotic terms – 'You touched me, and I am inflamed with love of your peace' – he also emphasizes the need for divine grace to maintain his fidelity: 'Give me the *grace* to do as you command, and command me to do as you will!' (X.27.232, X.29.233). This plea for grace introduces the catalogue of temptations in Book X that continue to plague Augustine and prompt him to forget rather than remember, to embrace the diabolical rather than the divine. Such enticements include the love of 'praise' that tempts poets, with which Augustine identifies as an author of memoir, and implicitly, an allegory of himself (X.37.246).

Augustine's greatest temptation is represented by the Manichean Faustus, described as 'a great decoy of the devil', supposedly 'well versed

in all the higher forms of learning', who became a 'deadly snare' in which
Augustine was once 'caught' (V.3.92, V.7.99). Faustus' significance culminates with the conclusion to Book X, where, though unnamed, he
represents a Satanic figure who had once tempted Augustine to forget
God, implicitly juxtaposed with Augustine's Christianized art of memory. 'Whom could I find to reconcile me to you?', Augustine asks, as
he reflects upon the seduction of false mediators: 'Many men, so I have
heard, for lack of strength to return to you by themselves ... tried to
find you in all the conceit and arrogance of their learning' (X.42.250).
Augustine alludes to Faustus in this demonic role, whose diabolical
deceptions he connects to a condemnation of theatre: just as 'unhealthy
curiosity' leads some to 'put show in the theatre', he writes, 'for the same
reason men are led to investigate the secrets of nature ... which causes
men to turn to sorcery in the effort to obtain knowledge for the same
perverted purpose' (X.35.242). Augustine describes men (such as himself)
as being deceived by the 'fallen angels, the princes of the lower air', who
had 'tricked them, [by] using magic craft, for while they sought a mediator ... it was no mediator that they found' but instead 'the devil, passing
for an angel of light', and 'a potent lure for their proud flesh' (X.42.250).
Having fallen victim himself to such a devil in disguise, Augustine reasons that 'by the hidden pronouncements of your justice, you have given
the devil license to make a mockery of pride, he poses as a mediator', for
he is both 'like a man' because 'he is sinful' and he 'pretends to be like
God' (X.42.250). 'But', Augustine concludes, 'since *sin offers death for
wages*, in common with men he has this reason to be condemned to die'
(X.42.250, emphasis added). He alludes to Romans 6:23, 'For the wages
of sin is death', but omits what follows, 'but the gift of God is eternal life
through Jesus Christ our Lord.' Yet the implicit contrast between death
and immortality, the 'wages' of sin versus the 'gift' of God – that is,
grace – finds an answer in the conclusion of *Confessions*, where Augustine
interprets Genesis to demonstrate scripture-as-*anamnesis*: the ultimate
reminder of divine love.

Marlowe's re-enactment of Augustine's *Confessions* can be seen most
clearly in his response to this passage, which frames *Doctor Faustus* as a
perverse form of memory theatre. To be sure, Marlowe bases his play upon
the medieval Faust legend, but his version of Faustus is also profoundly
influenced by Augustine's writings. Indeed, the first scene of Marlowe's
play, like the 'play's last scene', turns on a dialectic of remembering and
forgetting in the vein of Augustine. From the start, Faustus decides to
forget God, reasoning that 'The reward of sin is death', and that 'If we say

that we have no sin, / We deceive ourselves, and there's no truth in us', and because 'we must sin', then 'we must die an everlasting death' (1.1.41–8). 'What doctrine call you this?', Faustus asks, '*Che sera, sera*', and with this chop logic, he bids 'Divinity, adieu!' in favour of the 'mighty god' of magic (1.1.49–50). Yet whereas Augustine omits what follows 'since *sin offers death for wages*' in order to expand upon the second part of the quotation – that grace or the 'gift' of God is 'eternal life' as mediated through Christ – Marlowe omits it in order to rewrite it, or rather, to write it off. In the play's last scene, Marlowe would seem to return to this quotation from Romans 6:23, in effect remembering what Faustus willfully forgets in the play's first scene: the possibility of redemption through divine mediation. In the end, Faustus looks to the heavens and envisions this possibility – 'See, see where Christ's blood streams in the firmament! / One drop would save my soul, half a drop' – and then ambiguously says, either wondering or resolving, 'Yet will I call on him' (5.2.70–3). This vision, itself invisible to the audience and thus explicitly theatrical, disappears to Faustus, who instead sees 'the heavy wrath of God' who, he finally realizes, 'wilt not have mercy on my soul', even though 'Christ's … blood hath ransomed me' (5.2.91–2). As Faustus initially dismisses the salvific possibility of penitential confession and contrition, accepting that 'the reward of sin is death', and then ultimately regards the 'gift of God [as] eternal life' through Christ as hopeless, Marlowe both remembers and misremembers Augustine in order to challenge the idea that an 'art' or method of salvation can exist after the theological cataclysm of the Reformation. Marlowe employs the medieval morality play as an anachronistic form in early modern England in order to highlight the problem of salvation: if seen in a Catholic context, then Faustus should be able to repent and redeem his soul, but if viewed in the context of Calvinism, then Faustus may be 'damned if he does and damned if he doesn't'. As Alan Sinfield elegantly puts it, we might 'regard Faustus not as damned because he makes a pact with the devil, but as making a pact with the devil because he is already damned'.[20] In this light, the apparent moral of the story – Faustus falls because he refuses God's grace and chooses Satan instead – may no longer apply if a reprobate Faustus never truly had a choice. Marlowe thus turns the morality play into a kind of amorality play that perversely remembers Augustine's *Confessions* in order to forget it and, in the end, to suggest that the 'art' or drama of salvation and the soul itself should be seen as memory theatre in a more literal and literary sense: as a matter of theatrical spectacle or even, Faustus suggests, a mere 'fable' (2.1.127).

The Holy Sonnets: Death and the Drama of Salvation

Returning to my earlier discussion of the *Holy Sonnets* as memory theatre, Donne re-enacts *Doctor Faustus* by recreating the mortal context, and
specific imagery, of its final scene. Like Marlowe's Faustus, Donne's persona in 'This is my play's last scene' is confronted with the imminence of
his death, fears the angry face of God, fantasizes about being freed from
having a soul altogether, and begs God to forget him – for 'a heavenly
Lethean flood' to 'drown … [his] sin's black memory', arguing 'That Thou
remember them, some claim as debt; / I think it mercy if Thou wilt forget'
(9.10–14). Here Donne would seem to sever the link between the art of
salvation and the art of memory, instead proposing something like an art
of forgetting and forgiving.[21] However, Donne's purpose here is not simply to re-en act or reject Marlowe's critique of Augustine. Rather, Donne
returns to the *Confessions* in order to fashion a persona and performance
at once Marlovian and Augustinian, producing a complex synthesis of
and dialectic between the two. The central question implicitly posed by
the *Holy Sonnets* is *how* to be a 'second Augustine' for a new time and
place, amidst the theological turmoil of Reformation. Donne reframes
Marlowe's stark binary between Catholic and Calvinist salvation theology, thereby returning to Augustine's *Confessions* in order to explore the
question of grace as just that: a question rather than an answer. To do so,
Donne emulates Marlowe's approach to the morality play by adapting
a form that he renders anachronistic: the Italian sonnet, originally and
intimately associated with Catholicism, confession, and conversion, and
with the 'art of memory' as both a poetics and a problem in relation to the
'art of salvation.' Indeed, the sonnet form develops directly in response
to Augustine's *Confessions*. Dante's and Petrarch's sonnet sequences at
once answer Augustine's criticism of poetry and appropriate his poetics of
memory, and both offer allegories of love-as-*anamnesis* which portray the
remembrance of the ruined, fallen soul (their own persona's) as a Christian
architectural mnemonic – albeit in strikingly different ways. In contrast
to Dante's poetics of confession and conversion, which begins with his
memoir-cum-sonnet sequence of a 'new life' in the *Vita Nuova* and culminates with his salvific vision at the end of *Paradise*, Petrarch's *Rime sparse*
or 'scattered rhymes' focus on time and death, forgetfulness and ambiva-
lence, ultimately separating the art of memory from the art of salvation so
that their aesthetic and eschatological ends cannot be reconciled for his
poetic persona.[22] With this incomplete if not failed conversion narrative,
Petrarch somewhat perversely severs the sonnet from salvation. Instead,

he represents a dividedness within himself and, allegorically, between the secular and sacred, within the ruined architecture of the sonnet. A playful, even parodic treatment of the sonnet tradition can be seen in 'The Canonization': Donne's desire to 'build in sonnets pretty rooms' in order to sanctify the memory of love constructs the sonnet as a space in which he irreverently couples the art of salvation with the art of memory. With the *Holy Sonnets*, however, Donne returns to this metaphysical conceit in all seriousness, adopting a Petrarchan form and persona for his allegory of divided loves and his complex response to Augustine. Like Marlowe, Donne exploits artistic anachronism by placing the Catholic sonnet in tension with Calvinist soteriology, juxtaposing a penitential art of memory with a performative art of salvation.

As in the sonnet tradition that answers Augustine, and in keeping with Marlowe's stage, Donne thus fashions his *Holy Sonnets* as a space in which to remember and re-enact the drama of salvation. Crucially, though, Donne's difference from Marlowe hinges on memory. Marlowe's Faustus remembers Augustine's *Confessions* in order to forget it: to dismiss the matter of sin and salvation, confession and conversion, with a '*che sera sera*', and in the end to exchange the soul for spectacle – that is, for theatre. Although Donne clearly reprises this role, to appreciate the complexity of his Faustian performance means to distinguish between Donne as poet and persona: whereas Donne-the-Persona seeks to forget his sin and his soul, Donne-the-Poet remembers them. As poet, Donne returns to the *Confessions* by representing his persona both directly as Faustus and indirectly as a pre-conversion version of Augustine, himself tempted by Faustus' art of forgetting: an Augustine who will discover the art of salvation as an art of memory – 'but not yet', to borrow Augustine's infamous prayer to God for 'chastity', or maybe not ever (VIII.7.169). By remembering himself as an earlier, divided Augustine, Donne asks whether such an 'art' of salvation is possible, a question that he poses through Marlowe's play, particularly its last scene. To play the part of a 'second Augustine' means, Donne suggests, playing through the part of Faustus: a version of Augustine's Faustian dilemma for a new time and place, necessarily mediated by Marlowe's Faustus.

In this way, Donne ironically frames his speaker's Faustian temptation to forget within the larger memorial and mnemonic structure of the *Holy Sonnets*, nesting memory theatre within memory theatre. Recall that Donne's persona begins by despairing of his state of his soul's ruin and need for reformation in the face of death – 'Thou hast made me, and shall Thy work decay? / Repair me now, for mine end doth haste' (1.1–2) – in terms that echo Augustine's Christianized architectural mnemonic: his depiction of his soul as a 'house … in ruins' that he 'remake[s]' and reforms as a house of God through the art of memory (1.5.24). God 'doth make his temple in thy breast', Donne's speaker says in 'Wilt thou love God, as thee he?', an edifice that he must remake (15.1–4). Like Augustine, who declares that 'I rise by stages towards the God who made me' and finds him through and within his memory (X.7–8.213–14), so Donne's speaker similarly attempts to rise towards God – 'when towards Thee / by Thy leave I can look, I rise again' – but is nevertheless divided by the Satanic temptation of 'our old subtle foe' (1.9–12). Like Augustine, Donne pursues the love of God in amorous as well as architectural terms: 'I, like an usurped town, to another due, / Labour to admit you … / "Yet dearly I love you, and would be loved fain, / But am betroth'd unto your enemy", Donne admits, confessing that "I … never shall be free, / Nor ever chaste, except you ravish me" (14.5–14). His speaker's Manichean divisions and torturous love story thus recalls Augustine's own temptation to forget the divine in favour of the dia bolical, figured by Faustus and the seductive temptation of his art. Augustine's demand, 'Give me the *grace* to do as you command, and command me to do as you will!' (X.29.233, emphasis added) – that is, remember and repent, and in so doing reform his ruined soul – is reiterated in part by Donne's poetic persona: 'Thy grace may wing me to prevent his art / And thou like ada-mant draw mine iron heart' (1.13–14). \The 'strange love' triangle of the *Holy Sonnets* – 'That Thou lovest mankind well, yet wilt not choose me, / And Satan hates me, yet is loth to lose me' – recalls Augustine's allegory of love and the temptation of Faustus as a figure of forgetting, if indirectly and ironically (2.13–4). Donne-the-Persona's desire to forget becomes a reminder of Donne-the-Poet's art of memory.

Donne places Marlowe and Augustine in a dialogical and dialecti-cal relationship throughout the *Holy Sonnets*, fashioning his persona as at once connected by, and divided between, these two figures. Donne's allegory of himself recalls an earlier Augustine in crisis – divided in his loves, secular and sacred, Pagan and Christian – yet one for whom, as for Marlowe, there would seem to be no 'art of salvation' in the wake of the Reformation. Instead, Donne's sermonic affirmation that 'the art of salvation is but the art of memory' becomes a problem that his poetry explores. Like Marlowe, Donne both demonizes and humanizes Faustus, turning his Manichean struggle between good and evil into an allegory of the central dilemma of Reformation salvation theology: *how* or *if* his soul might be saved, and still more pressingly, whether he can know either way.

In 'Show me, dear Christ, thy spouse so bright and clear', he portrays this theological dilemma as a sardonic, sexualized, and transparent allegory of divided loves-as-divided Churches, Roman Catholic and Reformed:

> What, is it she, which on the other shore
> Goes richly painted? or which robbed and tore
> Laments and mourns in Germany and here? …
> Doth she, and did she, and shall she evermore
> On one, on seven, or on no hill appear? …
> Betray, kind husband, thy spouse to our sights,
> And let mine amorous soul court thy mild dove.   (18.1–12)

Which church represents the right love and which the wrong, which the True Bride of Christ and which the Whore of Babylon, and more to the point, which might save his soul? Donne unveils his own allegory, laying naked a stark binary between churches and salvation theology that Marlowe's play dramatizes, and particularly in its nihilistic last scene. Like Marlowe's Faustus in the face of death and damnation, Donne's speaker despairs of his 'black soul, now … summoned / By sickness, Death's herald and champion', as 'damn'd and haled to execution', and thus seemingly incapable of redemption (4.1–2, 7). Yet Donne ultimately rewrites Marlowe's 'play's last scene' by returning to the question of salvation as more than a foregone conclusion; after all, his persona's drama of salvation hasn't ended yet.

Donne repeatedly returns to the question of grace in ways that echo but also exceed Marlowe's treatment of it. From a Marlovian perspective, Donne's question – 'Yet grace, if thou repent, thou canst not lack; / But who shall give thee that grace to begin?' – represents an insoluble paradox that leads to the question of whether his penitence is merely a performance (4.9–10). Yet Donne ultimately complicates the relationship between penitence and grace, reframing it in ways that return to Augustine's *Confessions*. Indirectly, Donne recuperates an Augustine more ambiguous and complex than the foundational authority for a Calvinist doctrine of predestination fundamentally at odds with free will, an Augustine who instead exemplifies the inextricability of grace and good works, who himself dramatizes salvation not as a static state but as an ongoing act or art of memory.[23] ''Tis late to ask abundance of Thy grace', Donne admits, but perhaps not too late, and he asks God to 'Teach me how to repent, for that's as good / As if Thou hadst seal'd my pardon with Thy blood' (7.13–14). The speaker's plea for God to teach him how to repent returns us to the ground of Donne's sermon, where Donne-the-preacher performs yet another version of Augustine-as-teacher. The Augustine of the *Confessions*, like the David of Psalm 32, confesses his sins to God, asks for forgiveness and receives it, and most importantly here, promises to teach the faithful how to do the same by remembering his life-story and struggle for salvation. Throughout the *Confessions*, the art of salvation and the art of memory are inextricably bound to one another, such that the ongoing desire for God's grace and the enactment and re-enactment of this desire ultimately are indistinguishable from one another. This is no simple lesson because it is God who 'teach[es] how to repent', thus teaching in this context is complexly imitative and performative, indeed, a form of memory theatre: Augustine re-enacts David's relationship to divinity, not directly but mediated through scripture, and this relationship is then doubly re-enacted by Donne in his sermon, mediated through Augustine's own allegory of *anamnesis* through scripture.[24] Yet the *Holy Sonnets*, in contrast to Donne's sermons, cannot 'teach' the reader 'how to repent' in order to be 'pardon[ed]' because, in the end, sonnets are not salvific; this follow's Augustine's distinction between the art of memory as an art of poetry and an art of salvation, fiction and scripture. Nevertheless, Donne treats the 'art of memory' as an 'art of salvation' in another crucial sense: as a 'method' of mnemonic poetics with which he stages the struggle for salvation, in the wake of the Reformation, as an ongoing dialogue with divinity. Throughout the *Holy Sonnets*, the relationship between grace and good works – here, penitence as poetry – does not represent a paradoxical futility but an irreducible complexity with which the soul must continue to grapple: an unending process of edification, of recollecting and reforming the ruins of the soul as a house of God, which Donne performs as a new Augustine within the space of Marlowe's memory theatre.

With the *Holy Sonnets*, Donne returns to the relationship between the soul's ruin and reformation as a form of confession – his poetic persona's autobiographical account of sin and salvation yet to be achieved. In the process, Donne challenges his own public conversions: Catholic to Protestant, courtier to confessor, sinner to saint, poet to preacher. Are his confessions ultimately more theatrical than theological? This question speaks to both Donne's secular and sacred poetry. In 'What if this present were the world's last night?', Donne questions his own sincerity, ruefully confessing that his *Holy Sonnets* attempt the same seductions of his earlier 'Songs and Sonnets': he repeats his 'idolatry … to all [his] profane mistresses' when he uses the sonnet's language of erotic love directed to both divinity and the devil (13.1, 8–14). Donne concludes by assuming the part of a Petrarchan lover in order to challenge the relationship between the art of salvation and the art of memory within, and as, the art of poetry:

Oh, to vex me, contraries meet in one…
… I change in vows, and in devotion.
As humorous is my contrition
As my profane love, and as soon forgot:
As riddlingly distempered, cold and hot…
… In prayers and flattering speeches I court God:
Tomorrow I quake with true fear of his rod.   (19.1–14)

Donne returns to the origins of the sonnet tradition with a Petrarchan division that mirrors the *Holy Sonnets'* Petrarchan form, but with an autobiographical twist: in Augustinian fashion, Donne confesses to the possibility that his secular and sacred love poetry are one and the same, that he writes love poetry to God as though a mere courtier of women and monarchs. Throughout, Donne suggests that he too may be one of the 'idolatrous lovers' who 'weep and mourn' and 'feign devotion', but who can take no pleasure in remembering his past: 'The itchy lecher, and self-tickling proud / Have the remembrance of past joys, for relief / Of coming ills. To poor me is allow'd / No ease' (3.5–12). Donne dangles the possibility that his *Holy Sonnets* are perhaps less than holy, more theatrical than theological, inspired not by God but by King James, who urged Donne to convert to Anglicanism in order to return, as it were, to grace. Indirectly, Donne ends by asking whether poetry's art of memory can represent an art of salvation. Can sonnets be salvific? In a literal sense, Donne suggests not, in effect dividing the sonnet from scripture as reminders of divine love that might reform the sinful soul. But in a literary sense, Donne's *Holy Sonnets* indeed depicts the art of salvation as an art of memory. As Donne returns to the sonnet, so he also returns to the dialectical relationship of remembering and forgetting in the *Confessions*, and to the question of what it means to be a 'second Augustine' within Anglican England. Such a dialectic also speaks to Donne's own memory. 'It may just be that Donne's acute anxieties over the cultural threats of forgetfulness, loss and erasure', Andrew Hiscock insightfully observes, 'are the very things which have ultimately ensured his survival among later generations.'[25]

Donne fashions the *Holy Sonnets* as a version of the *Confessions*, as his autobiographical memoir-cum-conversion narrative, by adapting an Augustinian persona and poetics of ruin and recollection, one mediated through Marlowe. In metatheatrical fashion, Donne remembers 'the art of salvation as an art of memory' but not as a simple assertion of faith. Rather, he constructs the *Holy Sonnets* as a memory theatre in a complex, ironic sense: as an 'art house' in which to remember earlier art that problematizes the relationship between 'the art of salvation' and 'the art of memory.' The sonnet, no longer simply the 'pretty room' within which Donne imagines building immortality, nevertheless remains a space in which to find a form of immortality, if only for a time. 'Death be not proud', his speaker asserts, for the time will come when time itself ends and death too 'shalt die' (10.1, 14). But until then, Donne, a microcosm of his island nation, must wrestle with what it means to remember God and to reform the ruins of the soul. His *Holy Sonnets* stands as such a space or place for the Poet's and Protestant's art of memory.

Notes

1 *Holy Sonnets*, 1.1–7, in John Donne, *The Complete English Poems*, ed. by A. J. Smith (New York: Penguin, 1996). Citations are by sonnet and line number.

2 On the art of death, see Sister Mary Catharine O'Connor, *The Art of Dying: The Development of the Ars Moriendi* (New York: Columbia University Press, 1942); and Nancy Lee Beaty, *The Craft of Dying: A Study in the Literary Tradition of the* Ars Moriendi *in England* (New Haven, CT: Yale University Press, 1970).

3 See David W. Atkinson's 'The English ars moriendi: Its Protestant Transformation', *Renaissance and Reformation*, 6.1 (1982): 1–10, which focuses on the continuities rather than discontinuities between Catholic and Protestant works of the art of death, despite doctrinal differences relating to predestination and penitence. Significantly in this context, he argues that the greatest 'distinction' between the two relates to their 'discussion of deathbed temptation', explaining that in contrast to extensive depictions of deathbed temptations by Catholic writers, that Protestant writers tended to 'reduc[e] deathbed temptation to a general and rather commonplace discussion of the devil, the world, and the flesh' (6, 1–10).

4 John Donne, *The Sermons of John Donne*, ed. by George R. Potter and Evelyn M. Simpson (Berkeley and Los Angeles: University of California Press, 1962), 2.2.273–4. Citations are by volume, number, and page. On the long shadow cast by the Augustinian conversion narrative, see Andrew Wallace, *The Presence of Rome in Medieval and Early Modern Britain: Texts, Artefacts and Beliefs* (Cambridge: Cambridge University Press, 2020), esp. pp. 128–59.

5 Anita Gilman Sherman, *Skepticism and Memory in Shakespeare and Donne* (New York: Palgrave Macmillan, 2007), p. ix.

6 Relatedly, see Lina Perkins Wilder's innovative study of mnemonics on the early modern stage, *Shakespeare's Memory Theatre: Recollection, Properties, Character* (Cambridge: Cambridge University Press, 2010).

7 William E. Engel, *Mapping Mortality: The Persistence of Memory and Melancholy in Early Modern England* (Amherst: University of Massachusetts Press, 1995), p. 11. On the art of memory, see Frances A. Yates, *The Art of Memory* (New York: Routledge and Kegan Paul), 1966; and Mary Carruthers, *The Book of Memory: A Study of Memory in Medieval Culture* (Cambridge: Cambridge University Press, 1990).

8 Donne, 'The Canonization' (lines 32–33), *The Complete English Poems*, pp. 47–8.

9 On the art of forgetting, see 'Introduction', in *Forgetting in Early Modern English Literature and Culture: Lethe's Legacies*, ed. by Christopher Ivic and Grant Williams (New York: Routledge, 2004), pp. 1–17.

10 See Ramie Targoff's compelling discussion of 'Donne's staging and resolving [of] devotional crises within the space of the sonnet', in *John Donne, Body and Soul* (Chicago: University of Chicago Press, 2008), p. 126.

11 Of course, this is not the only time that Donne responds to Marlowe. Donne's poem 'The Bait' also answers Marlowe's pastoral poem, 'The Passionate Shepherd to His Love', with an elaborate metaphysical conceit that reframes the earlier poem's idealized, prelapsarian representation of seduction as the eroticized struggle of the soul for salvation. On Faustus' 'end', see Chapter 4, 'Learn How to Die', by Scott Newstok.

12 Christopher Marlowe, *Doctor Faustus*, A-text, ed. by David Bevington and Eric Rasmussen (Oxford: Oxford University Press, 1998), 5.2.58–9. On Marlowe and the *ars moriendi*, see Maggie Vinter's illuminating *Last Acts: The Art of Dying on the Early Modern Stage* (New York: Fordham University Press, 2019), pp. 31–53.

13 Donne's biographer, Izaak Walton, writes that with Donne's conversion from Catholicism to Protestantism, 'the English Church had gained a second St. Austin'. Izaak Walton, *The Lives of John Donne, Sir Henry Wotton, Richard Hooker, George Herbert and Robert Sanderson* (London: Falcon Educational Books, 1951), p. 30.

14 Psalm 32.1–8, *New Oxford Annotated Bible*, ed. by Bruce Metzger and Roland Murphy (Oxford: Oxford University Press, 1994), pp. 698–9.

15 See Achsah Guibbory's seminal article, 'John Donne and Memory as "The Art of Salvation,"' *Huntington Library Quarterly*, 43.4 (1980): 261–74.

16 Rebeca Helfer, *Spenser's Ruins and The Art of Recollection* (Toronto: University of Toronto Press, 2012), esp. pp. 3–9.

17 Cicero, *De oratore*, III.iii.195 in *Cicero on Oratory and Orators*, trans. by J. S. Watson (Evanston: Southern Illinois University Press, 1970). Citations are by book, chapter, page number.

18 Plato, *Phaedrus, Critical Dialogues of Plato*, 275a, in *The Critical Dialogues of Plato*, ed. by Edith Hamilton and Huntington Cairns (Princeton, NJ: Princeton University Press, 1961), p. 520.

19 Augustine, *The Confessions of Saint Augustine*, trans. by R. S. Pine-Coffin (New York: Penguin, 1961), I.13.33–4. Citations are by book, chapter, page number. See also Augustine, *Answer to Faustus, A Manichean*, trans. by Roland Teske (Hyde Park, NY: New City Press, 2007).

20 Alan Sinfield, *Faultlines: Cultural Materialism and the Politics of Dissident Reading* (Berkeley and Los Angeles: University of California Press, 1992), p. 230. On the tropes of the medieval morality tradition in Elizabethan tragedy, see Rory Loughnane, 'The Medieval Inheritance', in *The Oxford Handbook of Shakespearean Tragedy*, ed. by Michael Neill and David Schalkwyk (Oxford: Oxford University Press, 2016), pp. 35–53.

21 Cf. Thomas Playfere's sermon *The Pathway to Perfection* (1593), where he argues for the art of salvation as an art of forgetting, in *The Memory Arts in Renaissance England*, ed. by William E. Engel, Rory Loughnane, and Grant Williams (Cambridge: Cambridge University Press, 2016), pp. 238–41.

22 Cf. Andrew Hui, *The Poetics of Ruins in Renaissance Literature* (New York: Fordham University Press, 2017), esp. pp. 111–17, on Petrarch's humanist rediscovery of ancient Rome through a Simonides-like exercise in memorial reconstruction of ruins through his 'Roman walks', and on Petrarch's *Rime sparse* seen in relation to the concept of 'vestiges', or 'footstep' traces of memory.

23 On Donne's complex engagement with Calvinism, see, for example, Barbara Kiefer Lewalski's classic study, *Protestant Poetics and the Seventeenth-Century Religious Lyric* (Princeton, NJ: Princeton University Press, 1979).

24 Compare this strategic 're-enactment' typically associated with the traditional memory theatre to Brian Chalk's discussion, 'Theatrical Monuments in Middleton's *Game of Chess*' in Chapter 7 of this volume.

25 Andrew Hiscock, *Reading Memory in Early Modern English Literature* (Cambridge: Cambridge University Press, 2011), p. 190.

CHAPTER 2

Spiritual Accountancy in the Age of Shakespeare

Jonathan Baldo

This world's a city full of straying streets,
And death's the market-place where each one meets.
            The Two Noble Kinsmen   (1.5.15–6)[1]

In what he calls the 'Age of Debt' – roughly, the three centuries leading up to the English civil wars – legal historian DeLloyd J. Guth demonstrates that the idea of debt had come to permeate late medieval and early modern culture: 'late medieval language and its metaphors were supersaturated with the imagery of debt'.[2] The concept of debt lay at the heart of morality as well as the understanding of mortality. It was one of the dominant metaphors by which medieval men and women lived, carrying with it 'the most personalized idea of contractual obligation, where it became primarily an internal matter of conscience, an external matter of morally right behavior and, of course, ultimately of salvation or damnation'.[3] In medieval texts like Langland's *Piers Plowman*, 'Words associated with commercial obligation, money-lending, and book-keeping had come to be applied directly to the business of heaven-seeking.'[4]

According to medieval church doctrine, nearly every human being accumulated a substantial debt of sin over the course of a lifetime on earth. Even if sins had been forgiven through absolution, they required penance, a temporal punishment or 'payment' for having sinned. Opportunities to pay down and eventually cancel one's debt took many forms, including pilgrimages, prayers, masses, indulgences, and acts of charity such as donations to a religious order. Late medieval theology held that it was impossible to do adequate penance in one's lifetime to fully 'satisfy' or pay off one's debt of sin.[5] The problem of incomplete penance was answered by the idea of purgatory, which became an official tenet of the Catholic Church in 1274. In this middle space between heaven and hell, one's spiritual debt could continue to be paid down, thereby improving one's chances of eventually achieving 'satisfaction' or remission of one's sins.

45

In both a material and a figurative sense, purgatory was connected to the ideas of debt and credit. For Annales School historian Jacques Le Goff, the prevalence of debt and the widespread practice of usury after 1200 created a need for the idea of purgatory: 'The birth of purgatory is also the dawn of banking.'[6] In other words, the invention of purgatory extended to usurers the hope of escaping eternal damnation and thereby, Le Goff claims, 'contributed to the birth of capitalism'.[7] In a spiritual sense, for the people of pre-Reformation England purgatory was itself a way station for the restitution of debts, in which souls would suffer a temporal punishment for sins that had been forgiven, but for which they still owed a debt. Indulgences sold by the Church, which became so repugnant to later reformers, as well as other interventions – prayers for the dead, tithes and other beneficence to the Church, masses – were designed to lessen if not free souls of the spiritual debts they had accumulated towards their Maker. Saints might be free of such obligations and go straight to heaven, but ordinary people died with a significant burden of sin upon their heads. As Carlos Eire writes, '[I]f one sinned with regularity, like most people, then penances could never be made up before one died. And this meant that penances had to be completed in the afterlife.'[8] Even sins that had been forgiven 'still had to be paid for either in this life or the next'.[9] The Church functioned as a massive spiritual accounting firm, and its 'accounting could be very precise',[10] according to Eire: 'By the late Middle Ages, certain acts and rites had been assigned a very specific value in terms of years to be shaved off one's sentence in purgatory, according to that formula that one day's suffering on Earth equalled ten thousand years in purgatory. These meticulously calculated partial indulgences were readily available everywhere.'[11]

The Reformation did away with this spiritual debtor's prison. It could afford to do so because it promoted a different idea of how the debt incurred by sin could be remitted. For reformers, Christ's sacrifice constituted a one-time payment to cancel or atone for the collective sins of mankind. One's debt could be paid down not in piecemeal fashion, through papal indulgences or acts of penance that would achieve 'satisfaction' of a portion of that debt, but rather all at once, through the believer's faith and God's grace. The Reformation, Guth argues, brought about a 'demoralizing of debt'. Moral obligations towards the dead diminished as the larger and related idea of debt became separated from moral categories, obligations, and judgements: 'Luther and later English reformers ... were appalled by purgatorial, debt-ridden beliefs that made God the Final Accountant.'[12] The age of debt, that of the late Middle Ages, was followed by the age of contract. Guth distinguishes them in these terms: 'Where the age of debt had moral duty and ultimately heaven-or-hell to enforce obligation, the new age of contract settled for formalized rules limited to the context of mundane "society". Social obligation would replace moral obligation as the rationale and force behind debt.'¹³ In post-Reformation England, debt obligations 'would be transplanted from moral conscience to self-interest, from a matter of the next world's eternal judgment to a matter of definable this-worldly benefit'.¹⁴ Historian Margot Finn similarly observes in her study of character and its relation to credit that, in the early modern period, debt tended to be represented as misfortune rather than as an indication of personal failure.¹⁵

Eliminating purgatory necessitated a new spiritual accountancy, one that, I shall argue, bears a curious resemblance to a pronounced change in bookkeeping practices in early modern England. In what follows I will explore a kinship between those practices and the language of debt and death in the plays of Shakespeare. Replete with punning on debt and death, the plays continually remind us of the confessionally contested relation between death and moral obligations. More often than not, those obligations were payable in the currency of remembrance: commemorative masses, for instance, or prayers for the dead. It is no accident that Shakespeare's chief figure of indebtedness, Falstaff, is also a master in the art of forgetting, or that Falstaff's original name was that of the Lollard Sir John Oldcastle, a prominent Protestant martyr.¹⁶ From a Catholic's perspective, the boastful, lecherous, lazy, thieving, selfish, and dishonest knight might have seemed a fit figure of the new faith: not because of any of the qualities I have just named, but rather by virtue of his prodigious skill in forgetting his debts.

'Til Debt Do Us Part: Or, a Debtor's (Mis)prision

The pun linking 'debt' to 'death' was not original with Shakespeare. It was proverbial in his day, but he seems to have been inordinately fond of it. Startled by the invisible Ariel's music, Stephano tries to bolster his courage with a proverb: 'He that dies pays all debts – I defy thee! – Mercy upon us!' (3.2.129–30). Prince Hal reminds Falstaff on the Shrewsbury battlefield, 'Why, thou owest God a death' (5.1.126).¹⁷ The pun in Hal's line would have been more audible to Elizabethan ears than it is to our own, since the digraph 'th' was pronounced like 'd'. Just after Hal's departure, Falstaff refers to the ultimate exit, one that he is reluctant to make: ''Tis not due yet. I would be loath to pay him before his day' (5.1.127–8). Unused to paying any of his numerous reckonings in a timely fashion,

Falstaff is not inclined to make an exception for God. The perennially indebted Falstaff incurs another debt in this scene: he borrows the Prince's wordplay, Falstaff's characteristic weapon against both death and the mountainous debts he has accumulated in the tavern. Like his famous rogue, Shakespeare himself was a lifelong borrower from a wide range of sources, even borrowing heavily from his own hugely successful *The First Part of Henry IV* while writing *The Second Part*. One of the many debts owed by the latter play to the former regards debt itself. A resigned Francis Feeble ruminates in the impressment scene before the very Falstaff who had dodged the mortal implications of the pun on Shrewsbury field, 'By my troth, I care not. A man can die but once. We owe God a death ...; and let it go which way it will, he that dies this year is quit for the next' (3.2.235–6, 238–9).[18] Death marks a double release, from debt as well as from life, and not the beginning of a lengthy incarceration in the spiritual debtor's prison that was purgatory.

Shakespeare does not limit the pun to places of death like battlefields. When Romeo, having fallen in love at the Capulets' ball, learns of Juliet's identity, he asks, 'Is she a Capulet? / O dear account. My life is my foe's debt' (1.5.116–17). 'Dear account' means terrible or heavy reckoning,[19] in addition to one that is 'dear' because it pertains to his beloved. Prior to becoming formally contracted to Juliet, Romeo has been contracted to his foe, and the debt he owes to the latter is 'dear' or 'heavy': namely, his own life. 'My life is my foe's debt' means 'I owe my life (in loving Juliet) as a debt to my foe'.[20] Romeo implies that his foe may choose to call in that debt at any time.

Like his medieval predecessors, Shakespeare frequently joins the languages of death, credit, and commerce in a more general way, not solely through the debt/death pun. Heroic death and commercial rhetoric mingle in *1 Henry IV* when, in response to his father's charge of degeneracy, a newly roused Prince Hal vows,

> I will redeem all this on Percy's head
> And in the closing of some glorious day
> Be bold to tell you that I am your son,
> When I will wear a garment all of blood
> And stain my favours in a bloody mask,
> Which washed away shall scour my shame with it.
> And that shall be the day, whene'er it lights,
> That this same child of honour and renown,
> This gallant Hotspur, this all-praised knight,
> And your unthought-of Harry chance to meet.
> For every honour sitting on his helm,

Would they were multitudes, and on my head
My shames redoubled, for the time will come
That I shall make this northern youth exchange
His glorious deeds for my indignities.
Percy is but my factor, good my lord,
To engross up glorious deeds on my behalf;
And I will call him to so strict account
That he shall render every glory up,
Yea, even the slightest worship of his time,
Or I will tear the reckoning from his heart.
This, in the name of God, I promise here,
The which, if He be pleased I shall perform,
I do beseech your majesty may salve
The long-grown wounds of my intemperance.
If not, the end of life cancels all bonds,
And I will die a hundred thousand deaths
Ere break the smallest parcel of this vow. (3.2.132–59)

Hal's self-defence is extraordinary on not only a personal level but a transpersonal one as well. It traces a major shift in cultural values from a warrior culture to a commercial one. He begins with language that projects a confrontation between a hybrid warrior-player and a throwback to medieval knighthood. Hal's 'garment all of blood' and 'bloody mask' perfectly capture his dual nature as cunning actor and valiant soldier. By contrast, the repetitive language he uses to describe his opponent, 'this same child of honour and renown, / This gallant Hotspur, this all-praised knight', deliberately lacks the tension inherent in the phrases he applies to himself. It mimics Hotspur's relative simplicity or self-sameness. Hal's language, however, soon modulates to that of a merchant. Like a cunning and adept merchant, he will force a dubious 'exchange' of glorious deeds for indignities, using Percy as a 'factor': that is, a buyer or agent of the merchant. Hal promises to be a hoarder of honours: like the hoarder Shakespeare himself when laying up stores of grain, malt, and barley, he plans to 'engross up' – that is buy up or accumulate – glorious deeds that his unknowing agent or 'factor', Percy, has been sent into the world to purchase on his behalf. The exchange will be as carefully watched as any financial transaction: 'I will call him to so strict account', Hal promises. Towards the end of the speech, the earlier warrior language merges with the merchant's, as if warrior and merchant had become one: if Hotspur does not 'render every glory up', he will 'tear the reckoning from his heart'. If he fails, then death will balance the books for him: 'If not, the end of life cancels all bonds.'

'Bonds' is an especially potent word in a speech designed to re-establish a broken filial bond.[21] Hal's word bears the same range of legal, economic, and affective meanings that it has in *The Merchant of Venice*. Hal's line is proverbial, meaning roughly 'Death pays all debts',[22] but in context it might remind us of the 'bonds' of loyalty, love, and devotion owed to a father and a king. Perhaps the word's greatest power for Shakespeare's early modern audiences, however, lies in its ability to recall a form of recent 'civil buffeting' (2.4.353): namely, that between Catholic and Protestant. Before the Reformation's elimination of purgatory, the end of life, rather than cancelling all bonds, multiplied obligations. These were reciprocal between the living and the dead, and of two kinds: the deceased could serve 'as intercessors in heaven or as souls in purgatory who needed one's help'.[23] In a general way, Hal's line evokes a post-Reformation world, one that rejected belief, in Eire's words, 'in any kind of interrelationship between the living and the dead'. For Luther and reformers who came after him, it was wrong '[t]o believe that those on earth could pray for the souls in purgatory or that the dead in heaven – the saints – could pray for anyone on earth'.[24] 'The end of life cancels all bonds' must have held a power to divide audiences, as Henry's kingdom was divided. Given the Reformation's cancellation of numerous obligations accruing with the death of a loved one, Hal's claim must have evoked sorrow in some audience members and relief in others. In the remote medieval world in which the play is set, the deceased person's spiritual debts were assumed by the living, who continued to pay them down through indulgences, prayers, masses, anniversaries, or, if one were wealthy, a perpetual chantry. Credits ultimately derived from Christ, 'who had no debt of sin to work off'. Consequently, His 'superabundant merits are now made available to sinners through the agency of the church, which dispenses the merits of saving grace through the sacraments – rather in the way that an automatic teller machine dispenses the cash laid up in our bank accounts'.[25]

Read against the obligations that traditionally bound the living to the dead, Hal's line looks ahead to a scene in *Henry V*. On the night before the great battle of Agincourt, Henry prays,

> Not to-day, O Lord,
> O not today, think not upon the fault
> My father made in compassing the crown.
> I Richard's body have interred anew,
> And on it have bestowed more contrite tears
> Than from it issued forced drops of blood.
> Five hundred poor I have in yearly pay,

Who twice a day their withered hands hold up
Toward heaven to pardon blood; and I have built
Two chantries, where the sad and solemn priests
Sing still for Richard's soul. More will I do,
Though all that I can do is nothing worth,
Since that my penitence comes after all,
Imploring pardon.   (4.1.289–302)

More often than not, chantries were provided for in wills to aid in atone-ment for sins committed by the deceased donor during his or her lifetime. The historical Henry V famously provided for a chantry chapel to be built in Westminster Abbey above his tomb so that prayers could be said in per-petuity in order to hasten the release of his soul from purgatory. Henry's ref-erence to chantry chapels where priests would say masses and daily prayers for the soul of Richard recalls a pre-Reformation world. The building and endowment of chantries drew particular scorn from reformers for contrib-uting to the church's amassing of great wealth, which was thought to have a corrupting influence on clerical lives. Parliamentary Acts of 1545 and 1547 under Henry VIII and Edward VI respectively closed the chantries, seized their assets, and transferred ownership to the Crown. Henry's speech also indirectly evokes a world in which the dead are segregated from the liv-ing. The speech is saturated with contrition as well as a self-concern for the future of his own soul; it is equally remarkable for its omission of any concern for his father's. Henry has pointedly built chantries for the release and repose of the soul of Richard, his father's cousin, but presumably it was Henry IV who stood in the greatest need of daily masses sung by chantry priests. Nowhere in King Henry's speech is there evidence of concern for his father's soul, only acknowledgement of the great crime, regicide, which was the ultimate cause of Henry V's possession of the crown. Prominently missing from Henry's prayer to the 'God of battles' is any confirmation of a 'bond' linking Henry to his father. 'The end of life cancels all bonds', indeed, for this updated, post-Reformation version of a late medieval king.

The speech therefore projects both a notable practice of pre-Reformation England and a prominent feature of post-Reformation England, which Eire characterizes as

> a segregated society in which the living and the dead could no longer min-gle, physically or spiritually. The dead were truly dead and gone: the saints in heaven could no longer be approached for favors, and the souls of the departed needed no prayers from the living, since there was no purgatory from which to be freed. For Protestants, death became the deepest abyss of all, an unbridgeable metaphysical and ontological chasm in time and space.

As Luther put it: 'The summons of death comes to us all, and no one can die for another. Every one must fight his own battle with death by himself, alone. We can shout into each other's ears, but everyone must himself be prepared for the time of death: I will not be with you then, nor you with me.'[26]

Or as Henry asserts in his dispute with the soldier Williams just moments before his contrite prayer, 'every subject's soul is his own' (4.1.175–6). The context is an argument over whether the king is responsible for the souls of his soldiers, 'if the cause be not good' (4.1.135). A man divided against himself, struggling with his own conscience and an apparently unredeemable guilt for retaining a crown that was obtained by spilling royal blood, Henry is a distant mirror of Elizabethan England, an early modern nation divided against itself, straddling a pre-Reformation world and a post-Reformation one in which the living were separated from the dead by an abyss, and in which, in Luther's words, 'every one must fight his own battle with death by himself, alone'.

In another play that famously straddles the tremendous divide that was the Reformation, Hamlet falls back on the language of indebtedness in his most famous meditation on death. Who, he asks, would bear the manifold burdens entailed by living 'When he himself might his quietus make / With a bare bodkin' (3.1.74–5)? The line alludes to the phrase ordinarily stamped on an account when it was paid in full: '*Quietus est*', 'It is at rest'. The stamp affirmed that an account was officially settled, and the debtor released from his obligation. In the play the Lord Chamberlain, Polonius, famously counsels his son to be 'Neither a borrower nor a lender' (1.3.74): a piece of advice well suited to an aristocracy that both required and sought to deny a burgeoning market economy that would soon challenge its power and influence. Hamlet's 'quietus', by contrast, implies that while living we exist in a perpetual state of debt. Death evens our account, a notion that Hamlet might have absorbed at Wittenberg, the city where the Reformation began, and that is decidedly at odds with pre-Reformation thinking about the vast majority of souls who die with a heavy burden of penance owed to God. Rather than settling an account and cancelling all debts or obligations, the death of a soul bound for purgatory opened up a whole new set of obligations.

Shakespeare's Ledger-Demain

Towards the beginning of Shakespeare's *Measure for Measure* Claudio is led off to prison. The offence, according to Mistress Overdone, is 'getting Madam Julietta with child', or as her pimp Pompey colourfully describes the trespass, 'Groping for trouts, in a peculiar river' (1.2.66–7, 83). Claudio faces the prospect of having his head chopped off 'within these three days', as punishment, you might say, for having previously lost his head (1.2.62–3). Later in the play the Duke, disguised as Friar Lodowick, attempts to console the condemned man in a lengthy speech that culminates in curious mathematical terms: 'Yet in this life / Lie hid moe thousand deaths: yet death we fear, / That makes these odds all even' (3.1.39–41). As numerous commentators have noted, the Duke's homily on death does not exactly hew close to the doctrine of Holy Church. Although its catalogue of life's vanities does reflect the tradition of the *ars moriendi*, the art of dying well, that in 1490 William Caxton initiated in England, the Duke's account of our common condition 'eliminates its spiritual aspect and is essentially materialist and pagan', according to Arden editor J. W. Lever.[27]

The mathematical terms that end the homily, like the disguised figure who utters them, conceal a decisive break with pre-Reformation thought about death and dying. The false friar projects this world as given over to the 'odd' – that is, not only to quirks and peculiarities but also to inequalities, asymmetries, incompleteness, remainders – with 'evenness' or equality in standing and fortune achievable only in death. In early modern English, 'odds' as a noun frequently referred to differences or inequalities, used chiefly in a phrase that was well established in sixteenth-century England, 'to make odds even', meaning 'to equalize or level inequalities, to adjust or eradicate differences; to cancel debts (sins, crimes, etc.) from a person's record; to do away with, atone for, remit, or forgive shortcomings and transgressions'.[28] Inequality of rank, fortune, and circumstance may mark nearly every aspect of living, but death evens everything. The Duke's words aiming at consolation indicate how odd and equivocal – both comforting and disenchanting – the term 'even' could be. In death all odds, in the senses of disparities, strife (being 'at odds'), and projections about future conditions (the odds that a particular outcome will transpire), disappear.[29]

In the disguised Duke's speech, death holds out the prospect of a world in which all is balanced and every account has been settled. Death amounts to calling it 'quits' in two senses – that is, marking a terminus but also cancelling all debts, or evening the score. The Duke's conceit implicitly casts death as a conscientious and honourable merchant who regularly balances books in a system of double-entry bookkeeping that gradually took hold in England in the course of the sixteenth and seventeenth centuries.

Double-entry bookkeeping, which came to be known as bookkeeping *alla viniziana* or the Venetian method, originated in the city-states of northern Italy in the fourteenth century and was widely and enthusiastically embraced by the merchants of Venice. It was common for Northern merchants during the period – for instance, members of the Hanseatic League – to travel to Venice to learn the new commercial arithmetic. The first treatise on the subject dates from 1494, approximately two hundred years after its invention. It was written by Luca Pacioli, a teacher of mathematics to Leonardo da Vinci and a Franciscan monk, like the false Friar Lodowick whom Isabella mistakes for a fellow Franciscan and therefore regards as a spiritual guide.[30] A half century later, in 1543, Londoners saw the first English treatise on double-entry: *A proftable treatyce to learne to knowe the good order of kepying of the famouse reconynge called in Latyn Dare and Habere and in Englyshe Debitor and Creditor* by Hugh Oldcastle, a schoolmaster, teacher of arithmetic and accounting, and the son of a shearman. That lengthy title is all that survives of Oldcastle's work, which was possibly a compilation and translation of earlier works, including Pacioli's. In 1588, a London schoolmaster John Mellis reworked and expanded Oldcastle's book in *A briefe instruction*.[31]

In this system each entry is recorded twice, once under credit to one account and again on a facing page under debit, representing another account. In this new system, the sum of credits for all accounts must equal the sum of debits, which were balanced on facing pages so as 'to makes this accompt even', in the language of a 1587 English ledger.[32] Jane Gleeson-White writes, 'Rather than mingling debt and credit entries under each other down a single column or page – as did the Florentine merchants before they began keeping their books *alla veneziana* – Venetian ledgers separate debits and credits.'[33] As Mary Poovey explains, 'To balance the sums on the facing pages, the accountant had to supplement records of actual transactions with numbers that had no referent in the company's business. To make the sums on the pages tally, the bookkeeper added a number to the deficient side sufficient to offset their difference.' Because the system's 'sign of virtue – the balance – depended on a sum that had no referent – the number added simply to produce the balance – the rectitude of the system as a whole was a matter of formal precision, not referential accuracy'.[34] As a result, although one could easily check the numbers' internal consistency as numbers were transferred from book to book, 'it was less easy to follow the course of an individual's transactions with the merchant, to tell exactly how a merchant stood with his creditors and debtors at any particular moment, or to tell whether the transactions initially recorded in the memorial were accurate'.[35] The function of the balance sheet, however, was at least as much rhetorical as it was practical. Its conclusion, writes James Aho, is 'not simply that such and such is the net worth of our business, but rather that such profit is morally legitimate. And it is so, because it arises from a fundamentally equitable and balanced transaction. 'We owe no more than what we have received and we have no more than what we have already given.'[36]

The implications of double-entry bookkeeping stretched far beyond accounting. For Grahame Thompson, double-entry bookkeeping bore theological implications, demonstrating the symmetry, proportion, and balance in God's design of the world.[37] According to Poovey, the spreading mercantile practice of double-entry bore epistemological as well as theological implications: in the history of wealth and society, it played a key role in developing our modern understanding of the fact. Double-entry's key idea of 'balance' – the appearance of equality between debits and credits – evoked 'both the scales of justice and the symmetry of God's world' and allowed 'the merchant to represent himself as solvent even if he was not *in order* to establish the credit necessary to make himself so'.[38] When the title character in Goethe's *Bildungsroman*, *Wilhelm Meister's Apprenticeship* (1795), tries to resist familial and class pressures to become a merchant, his long-time friend Werner, hoping to persuade Wilhelm to change his attitude towards a career in business, waxes eloquent on the subject of double-entry bookkeeping:

> What an overview we gain by the orderly fashion in which we conduct business. It permits us to survey the whole without being confused by the parts. What tremendous advantages accrue to the businessman by double bookkeeping. This is one of the finest inventions of the human mind, and every serious manager ought to introduce it into his business.[39]

In recent readings of *Othello* and *Cymbeline*, Patricia Parker has shown how debit and credit bookkeeping and its aims to produce faithful accounts had entered Shakespearean drama, which was staged in an area of London – namely, the theatre district – that was also thick with 'reckoning schools and accountants who taught arithmetic with double-entry'.[40] In his attempt to console Claudio – 'yet death we fear, / That makes these odds all even' – the would-be friar cancels the language of heavy indebtedness that for nearly everyone in England had once been an essential part of the rites of mourning and felt obligations towards the departed. He borrows instead the mercantile language of double-entry bookkeeping to represent death as a way of evening accounts, of balancing the books. Death has become a way of freeing those on either side of the gaping divide between the living and the dead from spiritual indebtedness, which had been paid for centuries in the currency of remembrance.

If, as the *OED* informs us, one of the meanings of the expression 'to make odds even' current in Shakespeare's day was 'to cancel debts (sins, crimes, etc.) from a person's record', then the statesman turned false friar may be said to offer Claudio a consolation that is decidedly post-Reformation. As Keith Thomas writes of the separation of the generations and the moral obligations they incur as a result of the Reformation,

> Whereas medieval Catholics had believed that God would let souls linger in Purgatory if no masses were said for them, Protestant doctrine meant that each generation could be indifferent to the spiritual fate of its predecessor. Every individual was now to keep his own balance-sheet, and a man could no longer atone for his sins by the prayers of his descendants.[41]

Vincentio's words of consolation carry this very implication: everyone keeps his or her own balance sheet, and is solely responsible for the satisfaction of debts and obligations that used to linger well beyond death. For Thomas, the severance of the welfare of the dead from the actions of the living 'implied an altogether more atomistic conception of the relationship in which members of the society stood to each other. No longer would they allocate so much of their resources to the performance of rituals primarily intended for the spiritual welfare of their dead ancestors.'[42] The increased atomism that Thomas sees as one consequence of the Reformation is certainly reflected in the Vienna of *Measure for Measure*, though it is also resisted in the fierce attempts by Claudio to muster his sister's intervention. The curious medievalism of *Measure for Measure*, a play featuring the deeply religious novice Isabella, the would-be saint Angelo, and a flawed ruler disguised as a friar, might very well have reminded many in the audiences of 1604 that what were until recently regular interventions on the part of the living for the welfare of the dead were now limited to interventions in the welfare of the living by and for the living, in order to prevent or delay death. Duke Vincentio's disguise as a friar might have reminded some in Shakespeare's audience of their remove from a Catholic England in which balancing one's spiritual books, making all these odds even, was a lengthy, multigenerational affair.

Though in a different spirit, Shakespeare's Cleopatra mourns the recent loss of her Antony in terms that also suggest that death, like a good merchant, holds the power to even the odd: 'young boys and girls / Are level now with men; the odds is gone, / And there is nothing left remarkable /

Beneath the visiting moon' (4.15.67–70). For Cleopatra, as for the disguised Duke, death may bring about an 'evened' world, one without 'odds' – that is, inequalities, singularities, difference – but on this side, not the far side, of death. Antony's death relegates her to a kind of death-in-life in which all odds, everything singular or remarkable, has been lost. Although Vincentio tries to console Claudio with the 'evening' powers of death, the prospect of a world without 'odds' is a woeful one for the Egyptian Queen. Death may still even all odds, but it is the living, Antony's survivors, who must endure the death-in-life of a fully evened world. Cleopatra's plaintive lines invert the values attributed to 'even' and 'odd' implied by the Duke's words of consolation. A figure of inequality and difference, of unevenness taken to the extreme, Cleopatra wants no truck with double-entry book-keeping and its merchant's morality. Other Shakespearean characters may busy themselves with evening spiritual accounts, but Cleopatra can be at home only in a world out of balance.

Notes

1 Unless otherwise noted, all quotations from Shakespeare's plays refer to individual Arden editions as follows: *The Two Noble Kinsmen*, Arden Third Series, ed. by Lois Potter (Walton-on-Thames: Thomas Nelson and Sons, 1997); *Antony and Cleopatra*, Arden Third Series, ed. by John Wilders (London: Routledge, 1995); *Hamlet*, Arden Third Series, rev. ed., ed. by Ann Thompson and Neil Taylor (London: The Arden Shakespeare, 2016); *King Henry IV, Part 1*, Arden Third Series, ed. by David Scott Kastan (London: The Arden Shakespeare, 2002); *King Henry IV, Part 2*, Arden Third Series, ed. by James C. Bulman (London: Bloomsbury Arden Shakespeare, 2016); *King Henry V*, Arden Third Series, ed. by T. W. Craik (London: Routledge, 1995); *Measure for Measure*, Arden Second Series, ed. by J. W. Lever (London: Methuen and Co., 1965); and *Romeo and Juliet*, Arden Second Series, ed. by Brian Gibbons (London: Methuen and Co., 1980).
2 DeLloyd J. Guth, 'The Age of Debt, the Reformation and English Law', in *Tudor Rule and Revolution: Essays for G. R. Elton from His American Friend*, ed. by DeLloyd J. Guth and John W. McKenna (Cambridge: Cambridge University Press, 1982), p. 70.
3 Ibid., p. 71.
4 Ibid., p. 73.
5 'Satisfaction' in the earliest sense represented the final stage in the process of religious penance, following 'contrition' and 'confession'.
6 Jacques Le Goff, 'The Usurer and Purgatory', in *The Dawn of Modern Banking* (New Haven, CT, and London: Yale University Press, 1979), p. 52.
7 Jacques Le Goff, *The Birth of Purgatory*, trans. by Arthur Goldhammer (Chicago: University of Chicago Press, 1984), p. 305.

8 Carlos M. N. Eire, *A Very Brief History of Eternity* (Princeton, NJ: Princeton University Press, 2010), p. 75.

9 Carlos M. N. Eire, *Reformations: The Early Modern World, 1450–1650* (New Haven, CT: Yale University Press, 2016), p. 136.

10 Eire, *A Very Brief History*, p. 74.

11 Eire, *Reformations*, p. 148.

12 Guth, 'The Age of Debt', pp. 69, 85. After the Reformation, Protestant ministers could no longer appeal to the idea of purgatory as a debtor's prison, but they sometimes transferred that idea onto either hell or the grave, as Laurie Throness, an historian recently turned politician, demonstrates. 'In the book of Matthew', he reminds us, 'Jesus styled Hell as a debtor's prison where tormentors would exact the entire payment for a debt from the unrighteous servant, so divines often used it in the same way, describing how the unrighteous would pay the "uttermost farthing" to all eternity.' Laurie Throness, *A Protestant Purgatory: Theological Origins of the Penitentiary Act, 1779* (Farnham: Ashgate Publishing, 2008), p. 100.

13 Guth, 'The Age of Debt', p. 86.

14 Ibid., p. 84.

15 Margot C. Finn, *The Character of Credit: Personal Debt in English Culture, 1740–1914*, Cambridge Social and Cultural Histories (Cambridge: Cambridge University Press, 2003), p. 29.

16 See Gary Taylor, 'The Fortunes of Oldcastle', *Shakespeare Survey*, 38 (1985), 85–100.

17 The connection between death and the quittance of debts was proverbial. See R. W. Dent, *Shakespeare's Proverbial Language: An Index* (Berkeley: University of California Press, 1981): 'To owe God a death' (G237), and 'Death pays all debts' (D148).

18 Cf. Dent, *Shakespeare's Proverbial Language*, 'He that dies this year is excused for the next' (D326.1).

19 G. Blakemore Evans, ed., *Romeo and Juliet*, The New Cambridge Shakespeare (Cambridge: Cambridge University Press, 1984), p. 87.

20 Ibid., p. 87. The equivalent line in Shakespeare source, Nicholas Brooke's narrative poem *The Tragicall Historye of Romeus and Juliet* (1562), reads, 'Thus hath his foe in choyse to geve him lyfe or death' (l. 325). Shakespeare alters the line by inflecting it with the language of ledgers, debts, and credits.

21 On the early modern language of oaths, vows, contracts, pledges, and other kinds of bonds in Shakespeare's plays, see John Kerrigan's excellent study *Shakespeare's Binding Language* (Oxford: Oxford University Press, 2016).

22 Dent, *Shakespeare's Proverbial Language*, D148.

23 Eire, *Reformations*, p. 720.

24 Eire, *A Very Brief History*, p. 73. On various ritual efforts to mend 'a relationship with the living that had been so painfully fractured by the abolition of purgatory and of the entire practice of intercession for the dead', see

Chapter 12, '"Superfluous Men" and the Graveyard Politics of *The Duchess of Malfi*', by Michael Neill.

25 Gerald Bray, 'Evangelicals, Salvation, and Church History', in *Catholics and Evangelicals: Do They Share a Common Future?*, ed. by Thomas P. Rausch (New York: Paulist Press, 2000), p. 86.

26 Eire, *Reformations*, p. 753. The quotation from Martin Luther is from his 'First Invocavit Sermon', in *Luther's Works*, ed. by Jaroslav Pelikan et al., 55 vols. (St. Louis, MO: Concordia Publishing House, 1955–1986), 51:70.

27 *Measure for Measure*, ed. by J. W. Lever, Arden Second Series (London: Methuen, 1965), p. lxxxvii.

28 *Oxford English Dictionary Online*, 2nd ed. (1989), 22 July 2009.

29 All three meanings were current in early modern usage. For instance, Shakespeare uses 'odds' in the sense familiar to gamblers in *2 Henry IV*, 5.5.103: 'I wil lay ods, that ere this yeere expire, / We beare our ciuil swords ... /As farre as France'. See *Oxford English Dictionary*, 2nd ed. (1989), 'odds', *n.* 2b, 3a, and 4. A radical levelling discourse may be harboured within the Duke's 'even'. David Norbrook has suggested that there are such hints in the Gardener's line from *Richard II*, 'All must be even in our government.' David Norbrook, '"A Liberal Tongue": Language and Rebellion in *Richard II*', in *Shakespeare's Universe: Renaissance Ideas and Conventions: Essays in Honour of W. R. Elton*, ed. by John M. Mucciolo et al. (Aldershot: Scolar Press, 1996), p. 47.

30 Isabella is joining the votarists of Saint Clare, an order of the Franciscans.

31 Jane Gleeson-White, *Double Entry: How the Merchants of Venice Created Modern Finance* (New York and London: W. W. Norton, 2011), p. 121.

32 Cited in Mary Poovey, *A History of the Modern Fact: Problems of Knowledge in the Sciences of Wealth and Society* (Chicago: University of Chicago Press, 1998), p. 55. See also p. 57: of a 'fictitious sum imported to make the entries balance: "more xxiii.li.xvii.s vi.d. due unto him upon this account, and to make it even, is born to balance in Creditor"'.

33 Gleeson-White, *Double Entry*, p. 93.

34 Poovey, *A History of the Modern Fact*, pp. 54, 55.

35 Ibid., pp. 55–6.

36 James Aho, 'Rhetoric and the Invention of Double Entry Bookkeeping', *Rhetorica: A Journal of the History of Rhetoric*, 3 (1985), 33.

37 Grahame Thompson, 'Early Double-Entry Bookkeeping and the Rhetoric of Accounting Calculations', in *Accounting as a Social and Institutional Practice*, ed. by Anthony G. Hopwood and Peter Miller (Cambridge: Cambridge University Press, 1994), pp. 40–66.

38 Poovey, *A History of the Modern Fact*, p. 64.

39 Johann Wolfgang von Goethe, *Wilhelm Meister's Apprenticeship*, vol. 9, *The Collected Works*, ed. and trans. by Eric A. Blackall in cooperation with Victor Lange (Princeton, NJ: Princeton University Press, 1989; repr. 1995), p. 18.

40 Patricia Parker, '*Cymbeline:* Arithmetic, Double-Entry Bookkeeping, Counts, and Accounts', *Sederi*, 23 (2013), 106. See also Parker, 'Cassio, Cash, and the "Infidel O": Arithmetic, Double-Entry Bookkeeping, and *Othello*'s Unfaithful Accounts', in *A Companion to the Global Renaissance*, ed. by Jyotsna G. Singh (Oxford: Wiley-Blackwell, 2009), pp. 223–41.

41 Keith Thomas, *Religion and the Decline of Magic: Studies in Popular Beliefs in Sixteenth and Seventeenth Century England* (New York: Oxford University Press, 1971), p. 603.

42 Ibid., p. 603.

CHAPTER 3

Recollection and Pre-emptive Resurrection in Shakespeare's Sonnets

John S. Garrison

Across Shakespeare's Sonnets, the speaker spends much of his time in a pre-emptive state of mourning, anticipating the loss of his own youth, the negative outcomes that follow romantic entanglements, and of course the possibility that the male beloved might not generate an heir before he ages and eventually dies. Viewed in this light, the poems can be seen as a prolonged meditation on what is missing or will soon be missing. Yet perhaps the most surprising presence of absence in the collection can be found in an apostrophe within Sonnet 39. In the third quatrain, the speaker pivots away from praising the absent friend in order to address a seemingly abstract concept when he says, 'O absence'.[1] This strange apostrophe, rather than following the tradition of addressing something missing, addresses the concept of missingness itself. Shakespeare is not the first poet to overtly consider this seeming-paradox and to address absence itself. Philip Sidney deploys a similar rhetorical move with his 'O absent presence' in the opening line of Sonnet 106 in *Astrophil and Stella* (1591).[2] Yet Shakespeare's sonnet collection will take a different tack to manage such absence in a strategy that wrestles with mortality itself. This chapter begins with this peculiar moment before examining other flashpoints for absence in his sonnets. What emerges is a pattern where the absent beloved becomes a present figure of pleasure because the speaker can manipulate the operations of memory in order to realize a form of psychic resurrection that obviates concern over loss.[3]

Before it deploys its unusual apostrophe, Sonnet 39 begins like many other sonnets addressed to the friend, with praise of his positive qualities: 'O, how thy worth with manners may I sing' (1). Note how the inverted syntax places the friend's 'worth' before the verb and the speaking subject. The structure of the line mirrors the operations of memory as the friend's outstanding qualities are recalled into the mind before the speaker can articulate them in song. The subsequent line emphasizes that, even when apart, the two men remain conjoined by the notion at the heart of the Renaissance friendship ideal: the friend-as-another-self. When the speaker declares, 'thou art all the better part of me', we hear echoes of Michel de Montaigne's famous formulation where friends 'intermix and confound themselves one in the other, with so universal a commixture, that they wear out, and can no more find the seam that had conjoined them together'.[4] Shakespeare's articulation of the two men's bond does not fully realize the ideal described by Montaigne as the speaker notes that the friend is still a divisible 'part' of him. However, the sonnet still seizes upon the logics that define such perfect amity when the poet describes himself as co-constituted with his beloved. In line 4's question, 'What is't but mine own when I praise thee?', we hear the speaker both hesitate around the narcissism inherent in praising the beloved and claim ownership over the beloved through intimate description. For the poet, to love himself at the level at which he praises the addressee is to risk the sin of self-love for which he admonishes himself in Sonnet 62 ('Sin of self-love possesseth all mine eye'). Yet, as Laurie Shannon has demonstrated, in the Renaissance friendship ideal, 'likeness, parity, equality, and consent present a thoroughgoing antidote to hierarchies'.[5] Thus, we might understand the discourses being deployed by the speaker to aspire towards this dynamic where 'likeness between friends radically cancels vertical difference'.[6] The lack of parity between the two men may not inhibit the speaker from claiming that he and his beloved share 'one mind and one heart' across two bodies as the friendship model entails.[7]

Given how the speaker claims his beloved is 'part' of him, we can understand the poet's recollection of his positive qualities to have a bodily dimension. To *remember* the absent friend is also to *re-member* him as the ego-collapsing formulation for idealized friendship means the two men cannot be fully disaggregated. Shakespeare repeatedly returns to the topic of the absent beloved and does so with such frequency that it implies that he derives pleasure from recollection in isolation. Such a dynamic finds expression in other Renaissance poetry. For example, in Donne's elegy 'Sappho to Philaenis', the beloved 'dwells with me still mine irksome memory / Which, both to keep and lose, grieves equally'.[8] These lines from Donne's poem express the dialectic energies that link memory, loss, and desire. In mourning, to forget the lost object is to finally acknowledge its permanent absence and to move towards acceptance of a world without the departed. To keep the lost object in the mind, though, acts as a constant reminder of the object's absence and may inhibit completion of the mourning process.[9] In either dynamic, recollection and forgetting operate in tandem to manage the catastrophic effects of loss.

Because the love between friends depicted in Sonnet 39 comes short of idealized friendship, it showcases the shortcomings of romantic relations more typically based in longing. Grappling with these shortcomings requires rethinking the problem of separation, and this perhaps spurs the poem's peculiar apostrophe:

> O absence, what a torment wouldst thou prove,
> Were it not thy sour leisure gave sweet leave
> To entertain the time with thoughts of love,
> Which time and thoughts so sweetly dost deceive. (39.9–12)

While 'absence' is admonished for causing torment, it is ultimately praised for the dialectical tension it fuels. The 'sour leisure' collides with 'sweet leave', and the intermingling of these unlike elements generates pleasurable 'thoughts of love'. These thoughts do not unite the two men physically. Instead, they ignite a creative process wherein the speaker conjures memories of past encounters or fantasies of future ones in order to derive erotic pleasure from the presence of absence. By contemplating such an operation, Sonnet 39 links to Sonnet 43, where the speaker describes 'my thought' and 'my desire' as 'present absent' (43.3–4)

Sonnet 39's shift from 'sour' to 'sweet' in line 7 hinges on the shift from 'leisure' to 'leave'. The *OED* informs us that, in Shakespeare's time as in our own, 'leisure' denoted 'the state of having time at one's own disposal; time which one can spend as one pleases; free or unoccupied time'.[10] In fact, the entry uses this line from Sonnet 39 as one of its examples for this definition. In contrast, 'leave', in its noun form, has had a primary meaning of 'permission asked for or granted to do something; authorization' since the thirteenth century and has denoted 'a period of time when a person has permission to be absent' since the middle of the sixteenth century. Intriguingly, then, it is not unencumbered free time but rather absence – bound by agreement and implied to be limited in duration – that makes possible the pleasurably sweet experience. The use of the noun 'leave' suggests that the beloved is expected to return and (when we consider its connotations as a verb) points to the fact that the beloved has left the speaker alone. So, to recall the beloved into present thoughts is to engage both anticipatory memory and recollective memory.

In the case of Shakespeare's speaker and his beloved, we know nothing concrete about the time they have spent together or whether they will spend time together in the future. The 'thoughts of love' may be left intentionally ambiguous because these thoughts' relationship to lived experience is largely irrelevant. Memory can generate positive – even idealized –

experiences that never occurred.[11] In his recent discussion of Sonnet 35, Stephen Guy-Bray has remarked that 'love is a particularly intense form of memory', and we can extend this formulation to apply to Sonnet 39 as well as to other moments in the collection which lament the beloved's absence. The poems dramatize how to love someone involves frequently recalling them into the mind. And this recall – motivated by a state of missing the friend and generative of fantasy – involves not only retrospective but also prospective mourning. Shakespeare's beloved is continually reconstituted in imagined scenes of union, parting, and subsequent reunion.[12] Derrida compellingly articulates how fantasy pre-forms lived experience: 'it has never been possible to desire the presence "in person", before this play of substitution and the symbolic experience of auto-affection'.[13] In other words, desire arises when we take material from memory and shape it to imagine what an erotic experience with someone might look like. After the actual physical encounter, we might long for a reunion as we charge the lived experience with meaning and re-narrate it in recollection.[14] A romantic relationship thus might be considered an ongoing process of forgetting and remembering someone. Such a process is imbued with an elegiac strain, showcased in Arthur Schopenhauer's notion that 'every parting gives a foretaste of death, every coming together again a foretaste of the resurrection'.[15]

From Mourning to Pleasurable Memory

Absence takes on a positive quality in the Sonnets as it is transformed from a driver of mourning to a driver of pleasure through the power of memory. And Sonnet 39's apostrophe to 'absence' leads to a culminating couplet where the speaker announces that the concept of absence has taught him how to obviate the problem of physical separation from the one he loves: 'And that thou teachest how to make one twain, / By praising him here who doth hence remain' (39.13–14). Although absence is the final addressee of the poem, the final thought is that the beloved is 'here' and will 'remain'. The adversarial relationship with absence as a tormentor in line 9 has given way to absence as a teacher in line 13. The heuristic power of the concept of absence is that it instructs the speaker how to split the addressee into two parts, and one of those parts can remain there with him. The dualities at the end of the poem echo language in Donne's poem quoted above where 'still mine' points to how the memory of the beloved allows the speaker to claim ownership over her even after she leaves him or dies. Odd as this dynamic might seem at first, we can understand it as an extension of a normative response to the knowledge that loss is inevitable and recovery from it will necessitate both planned and unforeseeable forms of mourning. In Shakespeare's Sonnets, such forms rely on extensive play with memory.

The use of 'one twain' in this sonnet's closing couplet nods once more to the friendship ideal, invoking a commonplace that a pair of true friends shares one soul between two bodies. It is this notion adapted from idealized friendship that allows Shakespeare's speaker to reconstitute the friend even when he is missing. 'Twain' is a particularly charged word here, as the *OED* notes that it functioned as a contranym in the early modern period denoting both 'separate, parted asunder; disunited, estranged, at variance' and 'consisting of two parts or elements; double, twofold'. This curious play of meaning throws into relief how the friend, like absence itself in this cryptic poem, seems to be neither absent nor present. Rather, he seems to occupy both states at once. This dynamic at the heart of desire is captured nicely when Roland Barthes remarks: 'But isn't desire always the same, whether the object is present or absent? Isn't the object *always* absent?'[16] If Shakespeare's friend were present, we can imagine that the friendship would still feel incomplete as the speaker fixates on their inequality. As the remembered friend, the absent friend then is one with whom the speaker can realize closer intimacy.

Absence remains the addressee of Sonnet 39 through the final couplet. Consequently, we realize that not only has the beloved been doubled but, evocatively, so has absence. There are now two absences: the abstract one that the speaker addresses at a distance and the absence that is palpably present with him in the moment of speaking. In his treatise on rhetoric entitled *The Garden of Eloquence* (1577), Henry Peacham describes apostrophe as 'a form of speech by which the orator turns suddenly from the former frame of his speech to another'.[17] Shakespeare does not follow the strict formal rules of address that Peacham avers, where this turning away is 'no other thing than a sudden removing from third person to the second'.[18] Shakespeare gives us a nuanced version of this, signalled by the use of second-person address for both the friend and absence. As we begin to see the ambiguous way that absence itself is arguably present in this and other sonnets, the collection stands out as a case study for Derrida's notion of 'hauntology', where the 'element itself is neither living nor dead, present nor absent: it spectralizes'.[19] In the poet's cry, 'O absence', the missing element is missingness itself and thus is present when addressed. Derrida suggests that hauntological states have direct ties to remembrance as the French term he uses repeatedly in his book, '*hauntise*', is translated in the standard English version as 'haunting' but more broadly means 'an obsession, a constant fear, a fixed idea, or a nagging memory'.[20] Sonnet 39 deploys apostrophe to render visible the hauntological underpinning of the speaker's pre-emptive mourning.

The turn in this poem to see the friend and absence together occurs at the volta (a term itself that indicates a turn in a sonnet), and indeed George Puttenham's *The Arte of English Poesie* (1589) entry on the apostrophe notes that 'the Greeks call such figure (as we do) the Turn-Way or Turnetale'.[21] Though the poem does celebrate the friend at the end, it does not turn the speech back to him as, for example, Sonnet 29 does ('Haply I think on thee'). Sonnet 39 (and, as we will see, other sonnets) exceeds the brief joy of memory pinpointed by Sonnet 29. The speaker of Sonnet 39 turns away from the missing friend to consider the friend that is present, the one in his memory now taking on palpable presence. Puttenham goes on to say that an apostrophe 'breedeth by such exchange a certain recreation to the hearers' minds'.[22] The call to absence may allow the speaker to recreate the addressee, even if that re-creation only assembled recollections of his own moments of remembrance.

Imagined Reunion as a Form of Revivification

While there are numerous instances when the speaker overcomes separation by conjuring memories of the beloved into the interior of the mind, the triptych of Sonnets 97–99 depicts a particularly intriguing strategy for addressing the problem of the absent beloved that involves instead the exterior world. These three poems connect to each other in theme and formulation, so much so that John Benson, in his 1640 volume of Shakespeare's poems, presents them as a single poem with the title 'Complaint for his Love's Absence'.[23] Benson makes a series of changes to Shakespeare's poems when he compiles his volume, yet the book does give us a sense of how early consumers of Shakespeare's work would encounter the poems. As Faith Acker observes, 'most seventeenth-century and eighteenth-century readers would have experienced Shakespeare's Sonnets not in their sequence from 1609 but in Benson's title arrangement'.[24] Indeed, the titles function to frame the poem(s) because they introduce themes or meanings before the reader's encounter with Shakespeare's actual lyric. Cathy Shrank notes that the titles in the volume 'offer a record of how someone has read – and how contemporary readers were being invited to read – the verses beneath'.[25] In this case, the triptych of poems gathered under the keyword 'absence' do not simply resemble each other but rather articulate a progression of thought. As the speaker fantasizes about the changing of the seasons while separated from his beloved, he comes to seize upon memory as a way to revivify the beloved in the form of constant, pleasing reminders present within the natural world.

Sonnet 97 opens what Benson presents as a conflated poem, and this particular sonnet is itself engaged in the operations of conflation. The present, past, and future collapse into each other within the speaker's memory. The first quatrain reads,

> How like a winter hath my absence been
> From thee, the pleasure of the fleeting year?
> What freezings have I felt, what dark days seen?
> What old December's bareness everywhere?   (1–4)

The use of past tense in line 3 puts us in the space of memory as the speaker recalls cold and darkness he has experienced, and the present-perfect tense in the first line informs us that these cold states in the past continue into the *now* of speaking. The speaker will later reveal that this viscerally felt winter is in fact only a resurgence of memory as the time of speaking is summer. In 'old December's bareness everywhere?', we hear the desolation that the speaker experiences during the time of loss. It is not simply that his internal emotional state resembles winter. Rather, he sees the world as a barren winter landscape which mirrors his feelings of despair. The use of the adjective 'old' to describe December points both to this being the recollection of a previous winter and to the present isolation fulfilling his own fears about the inevitable progression of his own mortality.

These opening lines also function as a recollection of previous poems. In Sonnet 6, we see a contrast similar to 97's conflict between the present season and the internal perceptions of the mind. Sonnet 6's opening plea, 'Then let not winter's ragged hand deface / In thee thy summer', suggests that the beloved embodies a season other than the impending one. The subsequent fantasy that the friend's essence can be 'distilled' into a 'vial' and released with summer's scent in the height of winter suggests further that memory can overpower the reality of one's current physical surroundings (2–3). More evocatively, and important for the discussion of Sonnets 98 and 99 later in this chapter, this fantasy suggests that memory of the friend can be transferred from his human body to a material substance. In Sonnet 6, the beloved can become glass; in Sonnet 2, the lover can embody leaves. Sonnet 97's reference to December as analogous to the speaker's aging further recalls Sonnet 73 ('That time of year thou mayst in me behold / When yellow leaves, or none, or few, do hang /

Upon those boughs which shake against the cold' [1–3]).[26] Across these examples, in order to make sense of loss, the speaker understands the world reflecting his emotional state and uses the metaphor of the natural world to describe this state.

The threat of mortality, as winter looms and the beloved's possible return is called into question, becomes a point of crisis for the speaker. The temporality of Sonnet 97 is unmoored as the speaker finds himself in a 'time removed' both from the beloved and from 'summer's time' (5). Like Sonnet 39, this poem contains a dual apostrophe. 'The pleasure of the fleeting year' functions as a possible appositive for 'thee', offering yet another instance where the speaker addresses an absent element that still resides in present memory. The poem is simultaneously addressed to the beloved, as Benson's title suggests. The beloved, the source of pleasure, is associated with the absent (but, in reality present) summertime. This association can be found throughout the collection, including in Sonnets 5, 6, and 18.

As we hear about the speaker's 'hope' and 'dread', we find present anxiety about the future being shaped by memory of past experience. That is, anticipatory memory informs emotion in the present. Paul Edmondson and Stanley Wells link this line to the sentiment found in Amiens' song in *As You Like It* that pines, 'Most friendship is feigning, most loving mere folly' (2.7.181).[27] Amiens' claim can refer either to retrospective assessment once these relations have ended or to anticipation if one needs to be warned when currently in such a relationship. If loving friendship is simply fleeting fantasy, then this only adds more importance to pre-memory and post-memory in terms of bringing the lover any tangible joy. If our actual experience of rewarding intimacy is brief and largely foolish, we need to reconstruct those experiences as more robust and more meaningful when we anticipate or recall them. As the poem closes, the speaker re-emphasizes that the natural world resembles his external state of lament, 'And thou away, the very birds are mute. / Or if they sing, 'tis with so dull a cheer' (12–13). We find that the lack of birdsong concerns not the present but rather anticipation of the return of a recalled season as 'leaves look pale, dreading the winter's near' (14). The multiple meanings of 'leaves' – including the undetermined amount of time that the beloved will be absent, the pages upon which the speaker writes, and the poet's lament about having been *left* alone – generates a lack of resolution at the end of the poem. That is, the speaker has not reached a new understanding of his problem or solved his problem as the volta transitions to the rhymed couplet. Perhaps that is why Benson senses that two more poems were needed to complete the arc and leave the speaker (and the reader) with a more positive revelation.

Sonnet 98 locates the speaker in springtime, and it remains unclear whether this is the spring previous to the season described in Sonnet 97 or the spring that follows it. Given the way that this sonnet shifts from one season to another, we can see why Benson would interpret a narrative arc to connect it to the previous one. The natural world observed in this sonnet reflects the speaker's somewhat ameliorated state because he can now acknowledge its beauty. However, the external world's bucolic pleasures only function to evoke recollections of the addressee: 'From you have I been absent in the spring, / When proud-pied April (dressed in all his trim) / Hath put a spirit of youth in every thing' (98.1–3) Yet neither 'the lays of birds' nor 'the sweet smell / Of different flowers' can excite the speaker enough to tell 'summer's story' (5–7). In a narrative universe where the beloved embodies summer, the speaker cannot generate enough optimism to imagine his return. And these bleak hopes of reunion foreshadow the beloved's death.

At its volta, the sonnet begins to tease out an increasingly complex relationship between the beloved and the natural world. The flowers 'were but sweet, but figures of delight / Drawn after you, you pattern of all those' (11–12). In the early modern period, the verb 'pattern' carried now-obsolete meanings of 'To match, parallel, equal' or 'To be a pattern, example, or precedent for; to prefigure'. Thus, we can begin to see the external, natural world as not just a reflection of the speaker's emotional state but also a double of the absent beloved. Marjorie Swann has traced how 'seventeenth-century people and plants were yoked together by an intricate set of correspondences', and this sonnet shows how such correspondences ignite an affective transference of the beloved's human qualities to the flowers' beauty.[28] Early modern readers would especially have seen such connotations in Shakespeare's choice of the word 'pattern', which resonates with the notion that one entity can be copied into other like forms.

Helen Vendler describes Sonnet 98 as a 'simpler version' of Sonnet 97, a claim that perhaps holds true in terms of the formalistic operations of the sonnet. However, a focus on the shifting uses of memory as bulwark against mortality across these poems suggests an interrogation of the relationship between longing and absence. Colin Burrow suggests that the 1609 collection overall is 'made up of readings and rereadings of its own poems'.[29] To re-read a text, and thus to resuscitate the ideas therein, offers a means to resist mortality. The coming of winter is tied to the separation from a beloved in the sonnet and thus offers the speaker a preview of the experience of mourning. Yet the act of re-reading underscores for us that recollection of the death of a loved one offers a way to return who and what is lost to the space of the mind. Sonnet 98 is striking for the way that it begins to reimagine the possibilities for the physical landscape that once only reminded the poet of the lack of this beloved.[30] As it closes, the poem makes clear that it is still very much the desolate landscape without a beloved but now that desolation is giving way to pleasurable interaction: 'Yet seemed it winter still, and, you away, / As with your shadow I with these did play' (98.13–14). The flowers, patterned after the beloved, now become playmates. Given how 'shadow' in the early modern period denoted both an outline created by light and also a ghost, we hear echoes of the elegiac mood that was made explicit in Sonnets 30 and 31. In the same breath, the use of the term 'play', punctuated by its placement as the final word, locates us in an erotically charged space. In Shakespeare's time, the term carried connotations of 'movement, exercise, and activity' as well as a now-obsolete meaning of 'to engage in amorous play, to make love; to have sexual intercourse *with*'. The absence of the beloved, made palpable in the figure of the shadow, has now become not only an object to be imagined but another subject with whom erotic activity is possible.

Sonnet 99 completes both Benson's conflated poem and a triptych that posits a doubling process in memory as a counterforce to physical death. It opens,

> The forward violet thus did I chide:
> 'Sweet thief, whence didst thou steal thy sweet that smells,
> If not from my love's breath? The purple pride,
> Which on thy soft cheek for complexion dwells,
> In my love's veins thou hast too grossly dyed.'   (1–5)

Here, the invocation of 'sweet' twice in the second line signals how, as Jeffrey Masten suggests, '*sweet* indicates the fungibility of male friends'.[31] Here, though, the term is not used to suggest a trans-subjective bond between two loving individuals. Instead, the poet's desire for his friend allows him to transfer the other man's qualities to the surrounding flowers. That is, the terms of early modern friendship allow the speaker to locate his friend already as part of him (as we saw in the discussion of Sonnet 39), and this gives the lover the power to project the beloved where he likes: in the mind, in a shadow, in flowers. Dympna Callaghan chooses the intriguing term 'plagiarism' to describe the 'theft of the friend's beauty' in Sonnet 99.[32] While my focus on memory places the active work in the poet's mind, Callaghan's choice of term points to the *copying* at work here, especially in terms of how this concept is central to Shakespeare's urging of the young man to bear a child before death.

Sonnet 99 evocatively reconceives of one of the common techniques in the early modern memory arts, one that Mary Carruthers helpfully terms 'the architectural mnemonic'.[33] In this technique, the practitioner memorizes an inventory of items by associating each of them with a separate room in an imagined building through which one walks in the mind. Rather than an internal, fantasized architectural space, Shakespeare uses an external, real-world sensorium. By experimenting with this alternate model, Sonnets 97–99 parse elements of the beloved into living things whose lifetimes are fleeting yet whose essences evoke richly erotic bodily responses. The violets' 'sweet' smell here both recalls the distillation of the beloved into glass where he will 'sweet some vial' in Sonnet 6 and points to what Holly Dugan has found to be 'perfume's "curious" materiality'.[34] Dugan observes that smell connects to embodied erotic experience in these sonnets given that perfume is derived from flower essences (which are likened to the beloved) and is also a means by which to attract a beloved. The notion that the physical experience of smell links to powerful internal thoughts would not be surprising to early modern readers. Peacham's *The Garden of Eloquence* (1593) specifically notes that smell 'is commonly used to signify the pleasure of the mind'.[35]

Absence and the Elegiac Mode

Tracing the prominent and multivalent role of memory in Shakespeare's Sonnets helps us see how they recall another genre where mourning and desire collide: the love elegy. Francis Meres, in his assessment of the state of English poetry in *Palladis Tamia* (1598), equates classical poets 'famous for elegie' with a list of English poets that includes Shakespeare.[36] He describes these writers as 'the most passionate among us to bewail and bemoan the perplexities of love', suggesting that the most powerful of love poets were those composing elegies.[37] We can detect the crossing of the funeral elegy and the love elegy in 'bewail and bemoan'. The single genre term denotes two apparently different classes of poetic expression, but Meres' choice of phrase here underscores how outpourings of grief can appear similar to articulations of pleasure. Indeed, Meres might have had in mind the shared element of absence that connects mourning and unrequited love. John Harington's *A Brief Apology of Poetry* (1591) defends the erotic elegy by stating that while it might contain 'lewdnesse', its meditation is 'still mourning'.[38] The close proximity between death and

eroticism – a proximity that leads Shakespeare to declare 'desire is death' in
Sonnet 147 – lies at the heart of the love elegy and resonates in the genre's
influence on Shakespeare's Sonnets.

Yet the absence associated with mourning and unfulfilled romantic
longing should not be taken as entirely negative. Meres' volume notes elsewhere that 'the memory of dead friends doth bite the mind, but not without pleasure'.[39] Meres' point about the pleasure of memorializing deceased
friends finds powerful expression in Sonnet 30, where the speaker draws
upon the capacities of memory to reimagine an isolated state as an opportunity for connection. The poem begins with a fall into memory: 'When
to the sessions of sweet silent thought / I summon up remembrance of
things past' (1–2).[40] He will at first recall 'precious friends hid in death's
dateless night' (6). Yet he will balance the calculus of friends who have
died by turning to recollection of his living friend: 'But if the while I think
on thee, dear friend, / All losses are restor'd, and sorrows end' (13–14). The
poem does not simply recall past pleasure; it recalls friends to life.

Recollection, Reunion, and Resurrection

The strategy for revivifying the absent beloved depicted in Sonnets 97–99
suggests an innovation regarding the early modern memory arts, especially
in terms of how recollection was typically associated with sexuality. Several
early modern memory handbooks suggest that interpolating sexual fantasies into the work of recollection can increase the retention of memories.
Pietro da Ravenna, in the popular and subsequently reprinted *Memoriae
ars quae Phoenix inscribitur* (1491), describes how the author describes how
instead of rooms in his mind he 'put beautiful women since they greatly
excite my memory'. Giovanni Battista della Porta's *L'arte del ricordare* (1566)
similarly describes using the details of a beautiful woman's body or images
'ten to twenty beautiful women whom we have enjoyed, loved, or revered'
as powerful visual associations with facts to be memorized.[41] Shakespeare
deploys the obverse of the system delineated in such examples. Rather
than using desirable bodies to remember a series of names or qualities in
the plant kingdom, he uses the details of the natural world to remember
the elements of the beloved. In this way, his strategy ties to poetic creation
as it takes the blazon and utilizes it not just to praise the addressee but to
assuage his feelings of being separated. The sonnet's speaker goes on to
liken the lily to the beloved's hand and the marjoram to his hair, thereby
re-membering him by parsing the most desirable bodies into surrounding
nature. The rich homoeroticism of the memory in these sonnets breaks

with da Ravenna's assertion that his method will be of no use to those men who spurn women because '*sed isti fructus difficilius consequentur*' ('they will have much more difficulty in obtaining good results').[42]

At the poem's end, it is left interestingly ambiguous just how successful this strategy has been for overcoming absence.[43] The final couplet could imply either that the poet is sated or that he is overwhelmed when the world becomes engulfed in memories of the beloved: 'More flowers I noted, yet I none could see / But sweet or colour it had stol'n from thee' (14–15). This is the sole poem in the collection with only 15 lines and thus signals a site of excess. Lina Bolzoni notes that in the early modern period it was 'commonly believed that the intensity of amorous desire causes the *phantasma* – that is, the image of the beloved–to concentrate within itself all the vital forces of the lover [because] it feeds on recollection'.[44] She goes on to describe rather unpleasant sounding medical treatments, which include applying hot substances to the areas of the brain associated with memory in order to disperse the persistent image of the beloved. It is thus open to interpretation whether the incessant recollection in Shakespeare's Sonnets is a situation that seems to be demanding intervention or is a situation designed as an intervention for the beloved's absence. However, if the goal of the poet is to reconcile threat of the beloved's death by keeping him alive in his memories, he does seem to be adapting a variety of tactics lionized by the memory arts.

Perhaps it is memory's capacity for control through repetition that situates it as a viable weapon with which to combat mortality. Thomas Wilson, in a section titled 'The Division of Memory' in his sixteenth-century treatise on rhetoric, writes 'the best art of memory that can be, is to hear much, to speak much, to read much, and to write much'.[45] This list could certainly describe Shakespeare's project in writing his sonnets both in terms of how they serve his memory and attempt to influence the memory of others. Bradin Cormack has posited that 'Shakespeare's representation of desire and the failed promise of love' suggests that 'repetition might be thought to emerge from desire's incompleteness'.[46] The analysis presented in the present chapter would support this claim, and I would suggest that Shakespeare uses repetition to stir his own memory – rather than to summon a response from the beloved – in order to satisfy his desires. The promise that one might overcome absence through strategic recollection would certainly appeal to a speaker whose thoughts so frequently turn to death and loss.

In fact, Shakespeare's chosen genre for his meditation on memory may simply obviate the possibility of a response. Vendler argues

> Since the person uttering a lyric is always represented as alone with his thoughts, his imagined addressee can by definition never be present. The lyric (in contrast to the dramatic monologue, where there is always a listener present in the room), gives us the mind alone with itself.[47]

Vendler's description helps us make sense of Grant Williams' recent assertion that 'the sonnets enshrine doubt concerning love's noble code over and over again to the point that they lay bare its flimsy pretence and arbitrariness'.[48] Agreeing with these claims need not necessarily lead us to assess the Sonnets as a sustained contemplation of the speaker's failure to fulfil his desires or as a sequence about an increasing sense of mourning the inescapability of loss. Rather, we can think of this sometimes-clustered collection as a layered meditation on new possibilities both for love and for memory to proffer means by which to shore up against the impending weight of mortality, especially at those points of intersection where we find love and memory co-constituted. It is not simply that recollecting a lost loved one can bring them to life in the mind. Asserting a more tantalizing link between memory and mortality, Shakespeare's Sonnets contemplate recollection as an art to be managed towards the end of constituting forms of pleasure only possible when the beloved is absent and mourning can be reconfigured as an occasion for fantasy.

Notes

1 Unless otherwise noted, all citations of Shakespeare's Sonnets come from William Shakespeare, *Complete Sonnets and Poems*, ed. by Colin Burrow (Oxford: Oxford University Press, 2002).
2 Philip Sidney, *The Poems of Sir Philip Sidney*, ed. by William A. Ringler, Jr. (London: Clarendon, 1977), p. 235.
3 While the term 'resurrection' would have carried strong religious connotations in the early modern cultural context, I use the term in this chapter in the broader, more modern sense of revivification after death.
4 Michel de Montaigne, *The Essayes of Michael Lord of Montaigne, Translated by John Fiorio, The First Booke* (London, 1603), p. 94.
5 Laurie Shannon, *Sovereign Amity: Figures of Friendship in Shakespearean Contexts* (Chicago: University of Chicago Press), p. 11.
6 Ibid., p. 11.
7 The early modern commonplace takes up a classical definition of ideal friendship seen in, for example, Cicero, *On Friendship*, sec. 1.25, in *Laelius, On Friendship (Laelius de Amicitia) and The Dream of Scipio*, trans. by J. G. F. Powell (Warminster: Aris and Phillips Ltd., 1990).
8 John Donne, *The Complete English Poems*, ed. by A. J. Smith (London and New York: Penguin, 1996), p. 127, lines 13–14.

9 Freud suggests that we complete the process of mourning when we transfer our affection from a lost beloved to a new individual. However, this formulation overlooks the ways that we may still possess a version of the beloved lingering in our memories or how we ourselves might change to resemble the lost beloved. This is surely only part of the story of how we are affected by our relations with the dead. Judith Butler argues that while Freud 'suggested that successful mourning meant being able to exchange one object for another [...] Perhaps, rather, one mourns when one accepts that by the loss one undergoes one will be changed, possibly forever.' Judith Butler, *Precarious Life: The Powers of Mourning and Violence* (London and New York: Verso, 2004), pp. 20–21.

10 All word meanings and etymologies are drawn from the *Oxford English Dictionary* online, www.oed.com.

11 By not revealing the details of his fantasies about the beloved, the speaker underscores the intimacy of whatever interaction he imagines. 'Sex may be good to think with', Valerie Traub remarks, 'Not because it permits access, but because it doesn't.' Valerie Traub, *Thinking Sex with the Early Moderns* (Philadelphia: University of Pennsylvania Press, 2016), p. 4.

12 Stephen Guy-Bray, 'Remembering to Forget: Shakespeare's Sonnet 35 and Sigo's "XXXV"', in John S. Garrison and Kyle Pivetti, eds., *Sexuality and Memory in Early Modern England: Literature and the Erotics of Recollection* (London and New York: Routledge, 2015), p. 43 (pp. 43–50).

13 Jacques Derrida, *Of Grammatology*, trans. by Gayatrie Spivak (Baltimore, MD: Johns Hopkins University Press, 1976), p. 154.

14 This operation resembles the one articulated by the speaker in Barthes' *A Lover's Discourse*, who states that 'The being I am waiting for is not real. [...] "I create and re-create it over and over, starting from my capacity to love, starting from my need for it": the other comes here where I am waiting, here where I have already created him/her.' Roland Barthes, *A Lover's Discourse: Fragments*, trans. by Richard Howard (New York: Hill and Wang, 2010), p. 39.

15 Arthur Schopenhauer, *Studies in Pessimism*, trans. by T. B. Bailey Saunders (Whitefish, MT: Kessinger Publishing, 2010), p. 65.

16 Barthes, *A Lover's Discourse*, p. 15.

17 Henry Peacham, *The Garden of Eloquence* (London, 1593), p. 116.

18 Ibid., p. 116.

19 Jacques Derrida, *Specters of Marx*, trans. by Peggy Kamuf (London and New York: Routledge, 1994), p. 63.

20 Ibid., p. 224n2.

21 George Puttenham, *The Art of English Poesy: A Critical Edition*, ed. by Frank Whigham and Wayne A. Rebhorn (Ithaca, NY: Cornell University Press), p. 323.

22 Ibid., p. 323.

23 While presented as a single poem, the indentation of the rhymed couplets makes visible the embedded sonnets. Shakespeare, *Poems: Written by Wil. Shake-speare. Gent.* (London, 1640), D8ᵛ–E1ʳ.

24 To emphasize how widely Benson's versions would have shaped readers' receptions of the Sonnets, Acker notes that Benson's versions of the poems were reprinted in 1710, 1714, 1725, 1726, 1728, 1760, 1771, 1774, and 1775. Faith D. Acker, 'John Benson's *Poems* and Its Literary Precedents', in Emma Depledge and Peter Kirwan, eds., *Canonising Shakespeare: Stationers and the Book Trade, 1640–1740* (Cambridge: Cambridge University Press, 2017), p. 91 (pp. 89–106).

25 Cathy Shrank, 'Reading Shakespeare's *Sonnets*: John Benson and the 1640 *Poems*', *Shakespeare*, 5.3 (September 2009), 279 (271–291).

26 Maurice Charney notes that this sonnet's image of a tree in winter resonates with Cymbeline's description of his state after the departure of his beloved Belarius, a separation which 'shook down my mellow hangings, nay, my leaves, / and left me bare to weather' (*Cymbeline*, 3.3.63–64). Charney, *Wrinkled Deep in Time: Aging in Shakespeare* (New York: Columbia University Press, 2009), p. 17.

27 Paul Edmondson and Stanley Wells, *Shakespeare's Sonnets* (Oxford: Oxford University Press, 2004), p. 88.

28 Marjorie Swann, 'Vegetable Love: Botany and Sexuality in Seventeenth-Century England', in Jean E. Feerick and Vin Nardizzi, eds., *The Indistinct Human in Renaissance Literature* (New York: Palgrave Macmillan, 2012), p. 141 (pp. 139–158).

29 Shakespeare, *Complete Sonnets and Poems*, p. 116.

30 Lauren Berlant, *Desire/Love* (Brooklyn, NY: Punctum Books), p. 14.

31 Jeffrey Masten, 'Towards a Queer Address: The Taste of Letters and Early Modern Male Friendship', *GLQ*, 10 (2004), 376 (367–384).

32 Dympna Callaghan, *Shakespeare's Sonnets* (Malden and Oxford: Wiley-Blackwell, 2007), p. 134.

33 For a description of how this ancient practice was reintroduced in the late medieval period as part of the memory arts, see May Carruthers, *The Book of Memory: A Study of Memory in Medieval Culture*, 2nd ed. (Cambridge: Cambridge University Press, 2008), pp. 43–47. An example of an early modern text that describes the technique in terms of a contemporaneous 'large edifice or building', see Hugh Plat, *The Jewell House*, N1ʳ. An excellent resource for more context on the early modern arts – as well as for excerpts from exemplary treatises including the ones by da Ravenna, Peacham, Plat, and Wilson mentioned in this essay – is William E. Engel, Rory Loughnane, and Grant Williams, eds., *The Memory Arts in Renaissance England: A Critical Anthology* (Cambridge: Cambridge University Press, 2016).

34 Holly Dugan, *The Ephemeral History of Perfume: Scent and Sense in Early Modern England* (Baltimore, MD: Johns Hopkins University Press, 2011), p. 58.

35 Peacham, *Garden of Eloquence*, p. 6.

36 On the popularity of the love elegy in Shakespeare's time, see Victoria Moul, 'English Elegies of the Sixteenth and Seventeenth Century', in T. S. Thorsen, ed., *The Cambridge Companion to Latin Love Elegy* (Cambridge: Cambridge University Press, 2013), pp. 306–319.

37 Francis Meres, *Palladis Tamia, Wit's Treasury* (London, 1598), Oo4ᵛ.

38 John Harington, *A Preface, or rather a Briefe Apologie of Poetrie*, preface to the translation of *Orlando Furioso* (London, 1591).

39 Meres, *Palladis Tamia*, R3^{r-v}.

40 Tracing this pattern across Shakespeare's Sonnets, as well as in Donne's and Surrey's poems mentioned here in this chapter, may suggest opportunities for future study that examines the intersected themes of memory and desire as a much broader early modern preoccupation. See Henry Howard, Earl of Surrey, 'Complaint of the absence of her lover, being on the sea', in Marie Loughlin, Sandra Bell, and Patricia Brace, eds., *The Broadview Anthology of Sixteenth-Century Poetry and Prose* (Peterborough, ON: Broadview Press, 2011), p. 192, lines 8–9.

41 Giovanni della Porta, *L'Arte del ricordare* (Naples: Marco Antonio Passaro, 1566) and Pietro da Ravenna, *Memoriae ars quae Phoenix inscribitur* (Vienna: Mathias Bonhome, 1541). These and other examples are quoted and described in Lina Bolzoni, *The Gallery of Memory: Literary and Iconographic Models in the Age of the Printing Press*, trans. by Jeremy Parzen (Toronto: University of Toronto Press, 2001), pp. 146–149.

42 Bolzoni, *Gallery of Memory*, p. 147.

43 On assessing the relative success (or failure) of this trope involving presence and absences to resolve the larger issue at stake in a poetic exercise, see Chapter 11, 'The Many Labours of Mourning a Virgin Queen' by Andrew Hiscock.

44 Bolzoni, *Gallery of Memory*, p. 146.

45 Thomas Wilson, *The Arte of Rhetorique* (London, 1560), 7^{v}.

46 Bradin Cormack, 'Shakespeare's Narcissus, Sonnet's Echo', in Leonard Barkan, Bradin Cormack, and Sean Keilen, eds., *The Forms of Renaissance Thought: New Essays on Literature and Culture* (New York: Palgrave Macmillan, 2009), p. 137 (pp. 127–149).

47 Helen Vendler, 'Formal Pleasure in the Sonnets', in Michael Schoenfeldt, ed., *A Companion to Shakespeare's Sonnets* (Oxford: Blackwell, 2007), p. 28 (pp. 27–44).

48 Grant Williams, 'Monumental Memory and Little Reminders: The Fantasy of Being Remembered by Posterity', in Andrew Hiscock and Lina Perkins Wilder, eds., *The Routledge Handbook of Shakespeare and Memory* (New York: Routledge, 2017) p. 298 (pp. 297–311).

CHAPTER 4

Learn How to Die

Scott Newstok

... teach me how to hope, / Or tell me how to die
Tennyson, 'The Skipping Rope'

The End of Study

Renaissance readers like Antonfrancesco Doni were overwhelmed by 'so many books that we do not have time to read even the titles.'[1] Seeking refuge from 'too much to know' (*Love's Labour's Lost* 1.1.94), they made all kinds of shortcuts to knowledge: anthologies, commentaries, compendia, dictionaries, chrestomathies, encyclopedias, epitomes, florilegia, glossaries.[2] As Colin Burrow has reminded us, writers lifted from these digests, in turn creating their own commonplaces in a mutual process of contraction and expansion.[3] Shakespeare seems to have cribbed extensively from Thomas Cooper's *Thesaurus* (1565), aka treasury of words. These shortcuts were *manuals*, guidebooks designed to be 'handy': practical (for handwork), portable (in the hand), memorable (to hand). As James Sanford's translation of *The Manuell of Epictetus* (1567) glosses his title:

> This booke (gentle Reader) is entituled a Manuell, which is deriued of the Latin word *Manuale*, and in Greeke is called *Enchyridion*, bicause he may be contained ε υ χ ε ι ρ ι that is, in the hand. It is a diminutiue of *Manus*, as it were a storehouse, & which ought always to be had in hand, as the handle in the sword.[4]

Yet as Renaissance educational handbooks were revised, they had a tendency to proliferate. (Little has changed in the business of textbook publishing!) For instance, the first edition of Erasmus' *Adagia*, or 'sayings,' gathered 818 proverbs and glosses; its final edition had swollen to 4,151. To paraphrase Pascal, it's harder to compose something short than something long.[5]

I have myself recently struggled to write a very short handbook called *How to Think Like Shakespeare*. In spite of the immodest title, my goal was

78

rather modest: to help us think through 'the end of study,' as Berowne casually jests at the outset of *Love's Labour's Lost* (1.1.55). Marlowe's Faustus similarly opens with a restless challenge to educational orthodoxy, ringing changes on that very word 'end' (1.1.1–4). As we hear in both Berowne and Faustus, 'end' can mean a kind of 'goal' or 'culmination' (as in the Latin *finis*); 'end' can resonate with a philosophical sense of 'purpose' or 'function' (as in the Greek *telos*); and 'end' can invoke the more ominous undertones of 'limit,' or even 'destruction.'[6] You can sense Faustus (overtly) and Berowne (if more tacitly) chafing at the consensus surrounding this 'end.'[7] Faustus' soliloquy hastens from abandoning the liberal arts to a nihilistic end, blasphemously concluding: '*Consummatum est*; this bill is ended.' I worry that we've made our own kind of Faustian bargain with education, resorting to inoffensively aimless nostrums like 'the end of education is self-education.'[8] Not to pick on John Dewey,[9] but his oft-cited claim that 'the aim of education is to enable individuals to continue their education' is the phrase that launched a thousand mission statements. Perniciously, the evacuation of ends leads to what theologian Paul Tillich characterized as the 'vicious circle of production of means as ends which in turn become means without any ultimate end.'[10] To cite Berowne, again:

> So study evermore is overshot:
> While it doth study to have what it would
> It doth forget to do the thing it should,
> And when it hath the thing it hunteth most,
> 'Tis won as towns with fire, so won, so lost.   (1.1.40–44)

Focusing narrowly on educational targets might be the self-destructive end of study.

Of Craft

In contrast to the corrosive regime of 'assessment,' I propose that 'craft' better describes (and celebrates) the elusive heart of education, whether in Shakespeare's era or ours. And I think that considering playwriting as part of the long 'craft of dying' tradition (and its self-help manuals) is one way to revivify our teaching. I'm aware that invoking 'craft' as a conceit for the work we do risks appearing hopelessly precious at a moment when far more daunting challenges press upon our classrooms – from outbursts of terrorizing violence to continued inequity in access to education. And, as design theorist David Pye quipped, 'craft is a word to start an argument with.'[11] Nowadays, 'craft' tends to evoke either products (beer, soap, cheese) targeted for niche markets, or projects made by hand at home (knitting, children's activities). The former can be abused for marketing ends by corporations whose methods of distribution resemble nothing like artisanal practices; the latter conveys a diminutive, often dismissively gendered sense of isolated production. Yet neither connotation adequately captures the scope of the collective practices that suffused labor in urban early modern Europe, where craft was not merely a *mechanical* process but also communal, intellectual, physical, and emotional. Craft entailed discipline (enforced by people as well as the object itself), and its practitioners habituated themselves into effective yet ever-evolving patterns. While playmaking was never formalized as a recognized London guild, 'theatrical apprenticeship was much like apprenticeship in more traditional trades, and the similarities became more notable as the professional theatre became more stable and structured.'[12]

'Craft' has often been posed in tension with (purportedly) 'higher' intellectual pursuits, whether in ancient Greek philosophy, or in the eighteenth-century emergence of 'fine arts' discourse, or in disdain for indigenous cultural practices. Frequently, an anti-craft bias has entailed an elevation of the mind over the body, as in the debate between W. E. B. Du Bois and Booker T. Washington. George Puttenham's rhetorical handbook sought to help sixteenth-century students navigate the path 'from the cart to the school, and from thence to the court'; having at last become a courtier, the student must not risk exposing himself as *a craftsman*, who would then be disregarded 'with scorn [and] sent back again to the shop.'[13] Yet the 'skills' versus 'theory' binary (a rough if contested translation of Aristotle's *techne* vs. *episteme*) is more honored in the breach than the observance. Happily, doing and thinking are reciprocal practices. Plato often resorted to craft metaphors to describe intellectual pursuits (such as statecraft), and Aristotle readily acknowledged that *techne* could involve theoretical reflection upon its own practices. One of Socrates' interlocutors once scoffed at him: 'you simply do not stop speaking about shoemakers, fullers, cooks, and doctors, as if our discussion were about them.'[14] Well, they *were* about them: thinking is as much of a craft as any physical trade. In short, 'making is thinking,' and 'making' does constitute 'knowing.'[15] And this kind of *making* capaciously applies to everything from a physical object to the kind of rhetorical labor we undertake in our classrooms.

The etymology of the English word 'craft' reminds us that centuries before it was a *trade* or *profession*, it was a *strength*, a *power*, a *force*. As Alexander Langlands reminds us, Alfred's translation of Boethius deploys 'craeft,' rather unexpectedly yet tellingly, as one of the words to translate *virtus.*[16] In other words, craft involved a laudable transformation of some material, as in the earliest instances of resourceful toolmaking. Eventually this capacity to transform becomes isolated as a *skill* or *art*, a dexterous ingenuity. Only later does 'crafty' come to mean full of guile – thereby, as Virginia Woolf put it, yoking 'two incongruous ideas': 'making something useful out of solid matter' and 'cajolery, cunning, deceit.'[17] Shakespeare deploys 'craft' almost exclusively in the sense of being *wily*; in fact, the only time he uses the word 'craftsperson' appears in King Richard II's scornful dismissal of Bolingbroke's 'Wooing poor *craftsmen* with the *craft* of smiles' (1.4.24–28). One of Robert Armin's quips upon questions similarly played upon these overlapping senses: '*Craftsmen*, whose *craft* in cleanly covering | Is to be *crafty* in your kindest cunning.'[18] This *cunning* sense of 'craft' still hints at the cognitive dimension to *making* – that is, an intimate, immersive relationship to *material*, whether physical or conceptual. The material resists, pushes back. There is a reciprocal, mutual shaping between the maker and the made. The crafter transforms a common object into her or his own artifact. She or he has made something public private, 'the way a block of stone ceases to belong to nature and becomes the sculptor's as [s]he works on it.'[19] In doing so, a recurrent set of physical habits become apparent, and with them, habits of mind, to which the crafter can return. In this sense, craft becomes both empirical and cumulative. Over time, these skills become consolidated as a kind of 'grammar' of strategies, shared within a community and communicated across generations. Experienced members of the community initiate novices. While its tacit patterns can be made into formulas, 'craft' resists verbal description; even when its 'secrets' are published, the practice itself usually requires – well, *practice*.

Ben Jonson depicted Shakespeare hammering out words like Hephaestus, the ur-craftsperson:[20] 'he, | Who casts to write a living line, must sweat, | ... and strike the second heat | Upon the muses' anvil' (lines 58–61). Moreover, in his *Discoveries*, Jonson provides a definition of poesy that harkens back to the word's Greek roots: 'A poem, as I have told you, is the work of the poet; the end and fruit of his labour and study. Poesy is his skill or craft of making.'[21] 'Craft of making' – that's what we teach, in the arts of language, in the craft of thought. Or, even better, 'craft of will,' that elliptical phrase from *A Lover's Complaint* that cunningly distils the maker's mark with both aim and name (line 126). The more craftily we can convey this, the more likely we will be able to sustain our end of study. And returning to the 'craft of dying' might, I hope, help us attend to the *active* elements of the cultures of mortality in which Shakespeare would have been educated and apprenticed.

Crafting Death

Many printers of early English books chose 'craft' when translating titles
of continental treatises, whether rhetorical handbooks, or horticultural
guides to planting and grafting trees. In particular, the late medieval *ars
moriendi* was typically Englished by Caxton as *The Arte & Crafte to Know
Well to Dye* (1490) or *The Craft for to Deye, for the Helthe of Mannes Sowle*
(1491).[22] Scholars have heard the echoes of the craft of dying in Macbeth,
or John of Gaunt, of the Duke of Gloucester, or in Vincentio's counsel
to Claudio, or through the deathbed stage picture in *Othello*.[23] Maggie
Vinter sees *Volpone* as a farcical sendup of this same deathbed tradition.
Hamlet might allude to the very first words Christopher Sutton's 1600
Disce Mori. Learn to Die: 'That religion is somewhat out of joynt.'[24] Even
more intriguing are the *formal* homologies between the craft of dying –
what Kathrine Koller terms 'the art of arts' and dramaturgical practice
itself.[25] The *ars moriendi* manuals, often framed in the theatricalized form
of a series of dialogues, were deeply performative, calling to mind Robert
Herrick's 'The Plaudite, or end of life': 'The first Act's doubtfull, (but
we say) / It is the last commends the Play.'[26] While these handbooks had
their roots in the medieval manuscript tradition, the sixteenth-century
expansion of the book trade 'continued and amplified' this genre, making it 'one of the popular self-help topics in the Elizabethan publishing
industry.'[27]

   As Alec Ryrie has observed, 'the early modern Protestant deathbed' was
'a highly structured cultural site. Dying was too important a business to
be improvised. The dying were plentifully provided with scripts to follow.'[28] In other words, the craft of dying was *scripted*, then *practiced*, then
performed behavior, with actors and audiences, chiming with the arts of
dramatic performance. The deathbed was 'the centre of a moral theatre';
even a kind of stage for 'theatrical conventions of the Renaissance art of
dying.'[29] Arnold Stein, who long ago helped initiate these lines of inquiry,
noted how the *ars moriendi* genre's 'affinities to a dramatic action'

> brought into use other potentialities. Those assisting the protagonist,
> *moriens* – his friends, counselors, and witnesses – took part in dialogues
> and were alternately an immense audience who could also represent a larger
> audience of readers. The sequence of conflicts and temptations instructed
> the living, added suspense to the plot, and could furnish vivid scenes ....
> The dramatic elements produced their own sense of participation, but the
> form also kept and exploited the dramatic advantage of being able to move
> readers attending an imagined action.[30]

Christopher Sutton even invokes the *theatrum mundi* conceit:

> The interlude is the same, we are but new actors upon the stage of this world … all are actors of several parts: they which are gone, have played their parts, and we which remain are yet acting ours: only our epilogue is yet for to end.[31]

Thus, like the anatomy theater and the rhetorical *quaestiones* tradition, the craft of dying entailed one of the many cultural practices that shaped early modern drama's staging of death.

Erasmus contributed to this literature with two treatises on the craft of dying, which (as F. G. Butler argued) may have informed the death scenes in *King Lear*.[32] Erasmus' *Preparation to Deathe* (1538) dramatizes demonic strife through what Kristin Poole terms 'a striking move [:] a long third-person excursus on how to address the devil spontaneously transforms into a heated second-person dialogue':[33]

DYUELL:	Thou shalt be haled downe to hell.
MAN:	My heed is in heuen.
DYUELL:	Thou shalt be damned.
MAN:	Thou art a barratour, and a fals harlot, no judge, a damned fende, no damnour.
DYUELL:	Many legions of dyuels wayte for thy soule.
MAN:	I shoulde despaire, yf I had not a protectour, which hath ouercome your tyranny.[34]

As Poole notes,

> the deathbed dialogue … resonates, in very powerful ways, with the actual theater … [which was] part of the fiber of the *ars moriendi* texts. Sixteenth-century *ars moriendi* literature frequently relies upon, is framed by, exploits and extols a theatrical vocabulary.[35]

For Erasmus, death 'is of mans lyfe the last part (as it were) of the playe.'[36] Erasmus' earlier (1509) dialogue on death was eventually included in his manual on letter-writing, which became a staple of Tudor pedagogy. As Leonard Barkan asserts, 'Whether Shakespeare read Erasmus or not, he certainly had an Erasmian education.'[37] And one can point to the school-room as another workshop where Shakespeare, in the words of Orlando, 'stud[ied] how to die' (*As You Like It*, 4.3.66).

We know that Tudor rhetorical training was suffused with imitation, oscillating from the strict reproduction that Ascham's double translation demanded, to the profusion that Erasmian *copia* licensed. Strikingly, many of the examples that Tudor schoolboys were meant to emulate were 'rife with first-person speeches uttered at moments of death … Hecuba mourns the ruin of her city, Niobe and Medea mourn over the bodies of their children, and Achilles grieves for his dead friend.'[38] While the intent of such pedagogy was to produce fluent civil servants, such rehearsals of death were an inadvertent creative apprenticeship for a generation of tragedians. My students are sometimes disappointed to learn that Hamlet's own meditations upon mortality are often little more than commonplacing of Montaigne, who himself called study 'a kind of apprentisage and resemblance of death,' and who asserted 'The continuall worke of your life, is to contrive death.' We all know this continual work is difficult – difficult enough that we spend much of our lives evading it! Goethe asserted that 'It is quite impossible for a thinking being to imagine nonbeing, a cessation of thought and life.'[39] Freud concurred, and resorted to the theatrical conceit to explain why: 'it is indeed impossible to imagine our own death; and whenever we attempt to do so we can perceive that we are in fact still present as spectators.'[40]

Imagine Your Death

Yet perhaps literature *can* help us imagine the unimaginable. When asked how one faces death, Allen Ginsberg once suggested:

> I think poetry helps because you imagine your death, and you begin to blueprint and plan and realize mortality and then after a while you become consciously aware of the fact that mortality is limited and then you begin to appreciate living more, as well as appreciate the great adventure of dying, and then realize that it is part of the vast process and an occasion for lamentation and rejoicing and everything. The whole thing comes together. It's the great subject. Because, you know, without death there's no life. Without life, there's no death.[41]

Speaking of one's self in the past tense, or of one's death in the present tense, entails the imaginative scope of fictive work: crafting absent things to appear present; making the dead legible to us again. Recall Cicero's grisly account of Simonides, who was fabled to have invented the art of memory and its method of *loci* in response to identifying unrecognizable deceased bodies by their spatial placement. Today's cognitive science validates what memory practitioners already knew in Shakespeare's era: physical configurations reinforce recollection, whether on the page of a book or the stage of a theater.

This coincidence of time and space through the deictic center (I-ME-HERE) would later be elaborated in the mnemonic theater of Giulio Camillo – a tool of inventorying, thinking, and recovering lost objects. Drama helps us question whether we can say with certain knowledge: 'I know when one is dead and when one lives' (*King Lear* 5.3.234). In this sense, it is akin to John Amos Comenius' 'school of death,' the last of his stages of life, the putative 'end' of learning of 'universal education.' As Jan Habl proposes,

> Comenius realized the need for lifelong formation of humanity only in the emendation phase of his work, as seen for example in *Pampaedia*, where, unlike in the Didactics, he supplements individual 'schools' with 'the school of adulthood, the school of old-age and the school of death,' because in the General Meeting he already knew that 'all life is a school.'[42]

But Comenius might shudder with our era's techno-commercialization of the 'school of death'; nowadays, you can 'get random reminders of [your] own mortality from WeCroak, an app with notifications that don't mince words: "Don't forget, you're going to die,"' or purchase *memento mori* coins from the Daily Stoic website.[43] Essayist Sallie Tisdale cavalierly claims that 'we cannot practice death,' instead enjoining a 'practical perspective' on mortality.[44] Yet while 'The spiritual work of dying is hard … This kind of work is best not engaged in by scientists but by artisans; a *scientia mortis* is inferior to an *ars moriendi*.'[45]

Today's accounts of how to face death have, quite strikingly, featured passages from early modern literature. Roy Scranton's decidedly bleak *Learning to Die in the Anthropocene* (2015) recurrently meditates upon Montaigne's Ciceronian dictum 'to philosophize is to learn how to die,' reassuring us that 'We will always be practicing, failing, trying again and failing again, until our final day. Yet the practice itself is the wisdom.'[46] Paul Kalanithi's memoir *When Breath Becomes Air* (2016) derives its very title from Fulke Greville:

> You that seek what life is in death,
> Now find it air that once was breath.
> New names unknown, old names gone:
> Till time end bodies, but souls none.
>   Reader! then make time, while you be,
>   But steps to your eternity.[47]

In Kalanithi's yearning words: 'I was searching for a vocabulary with which to make sense of death, to find a way to begin defining myself and inching forward again.'[48] Robert Pinsky praised how Kalanithi's vocabulary was 'inspired to plainness by poetry – the closest possible thing to silence, defying silence.'[49] Indeed, Kalanithi invokes a host of writers, most notably Thomas Browne, as Sherwin Nuland did before him.[50] On the last page of his narrative, Nuland invokes *Julius Caesar*:

> Of all the wonders that I yet have heard,
> It seems to me most strange that men should fear;
> Seeing that death, a necessary end,
> Will come when it will come.[51]

Shakespearean elegiac verse remains a favorite in these contemporary guides, most notably the elegiac lines recited by Guiderius and Arviragus in *Cymbeline*:

> Fear no more the heat o'th' sun,
> Nor the furious winter's rages.
> Thou thy worldly task hast done,
> Home art gone and ta'en thy wages.
> Golden lads and girls all must,
> As chimney-sweepers, come to dust.
>
> Fear no more the frown o'th' great,
> Thou art past the tyrant's stroke.
> Care no more to clothe and eat,
> To thee the reed is as the oak.
> The sceptre, learning, physic, must
> All follow this and come to dust.　　　　　　(4.2.257–69)[52]

Stephen P. Kiernan cites them, as does Katy Butler.[53] In fact, Butler explicitly returns to the *ars moriendi* tradition to ground her analysis – just as Simon Critchley, Lydia Dugdale, and Thomas Pfau have recently done.[54] The endurance of this tradition is remarkable – even Martin Luther revised his own version of it.[55]

But poignant as they are, these gestures are comparatively fleeting. As we face an era of climate crisis and declining faith in institutions, can the early modern period's own confrontation with death provide resources for our own quandaries? Jan Zwicky thinks that the answer is the same as it has always been: 'We should approach the coming cataclysm as we ought to have approached life.'[56] Reminding us that the performance of Athenian tragedy was followed by a satyr play (much as Elizabethan tragedies would be followed by a festive jig[57]), Zwicky urges us to revive a Socratic 'lightness of touch that comes from not taking one's self too seriously. We will sense it as a smile: the absence of fear and the refusal of despair. Even in the face of death.'[58]

Zwicky's sage counsel recalls what Samuel Johnson urged, a kind of 'pre-hearsal' of death, occasioned by every time we recognize the last time we do something:

> It is very happily and kindly provided that in every life there are certain pauses and interruptions, which force consideration upon the careless, and

seriousness upon the light; points of time where one course of action ends and another begins; and by vicissitude of fortune, or alteration of employment, by change of place, or loss of friendship, we are forced to say of something, 'this is the last.'[59]

In the last issue of *The Idler*, Johnson ponders: why does the last occasion of *anything* (even something despised!) make one just a little melancholy? He posits that it's because this last occasion offers an anticipatory glimpse of the last time we do *everything* – that is to say, a premonition of our own finitude: 'to life must come its last hour, and to this system of being its last day.' One need not be Christian to find the sentiment compelling. Indeed, you can point to Johnson's Stoic sources, which encourage us to think on death every day, as in Epictetus: 'Let death and exile, and all other things which appear terrible, be daily before your eyes, but death chiefly; and you will never entertain any abject thought, nor too eagerly covet anything.'[60]

Think Here

This constant confrontation with death – a repeatedly rehearsed performance – marks John Donne's *Second Anniversary*. Donne's insistence on '**think**'ing about death tolls an anaphora that creates from within the poetry an internal, echoic refrain that draws attention time and again – and yet differently and more poignantly – with each repetition:

> **Thinke** thy selfe labouring now with broken breath,
> And **thinke** those broken & soft Notes to bee
> Diuision, and thy happiest Harmonee.
> **Thinke** thee laid on thy death-bed, loose and slacke;
> And **thinke** that but vnbinding of a packe,
> To take one precious thing, thy soule, from thence.
> **Thinke** thy selfe parch'd with feuers violence,
> Anger thine Ague more, by calling it
> Thy Physicke; chide the slacknes of the fit.
> **Thinke** that thou hear'st thy knell, and **thinke** no more,
> But that, as Bels cal'd thee to Church before,
> So this, to the Triumphant Church, cals thee.
> **Thinke** Satans Sergeants round about thee bee,
> And **thinke** that but for Legcies they thrust;
> Giue one thy Pride, to'another giue thy Lust:
> Giue them those sinnes which they gaue before,
> And trust th'immaculate blood to wash thy score.
> **Thinke** thy friends weeping round, and **thinke** that thay
> Weepe but because they goe not yet thy way.
> **Thinke** they confesse much in the world, amisse

> Who dare not trust a dead mans eye with that,
> Which they from God, and Angels couer not.
> **Thinke** that they shourd thee vp, and **thinke** from thence
> They reinuest thee in white innocence.
> **Thinke** that thy body rots, and (if so lowe,
> Thy soule exhalted so, thy thoughts can goe.)
> **Thinke** thee a Prince, who of themselues create
> Wormes which insensibly deuoure their state.
> **Thinke** that they bury thee, and thinke that right
> Laies thee to sleepe but a Saint Lucies night.[61]

Identity has always entailed a shuttling back and forth between the physical body and how it is conceived – in Nigel Llewellyn's terms, the natural
body and the social body, the former being mortal, the latter potentially
enduring through ritual and other memorial practices.[62] This interplay
between the actual and the created requires imaginative memory to put
the vanished past in touch with the living present. While all writing enacts
this tension between the real and the imagined, epitaphs epitomize it, by
giving voice to the body that lies 'here.'

   Deixis consists of features of language that are *situational*, in that they
refer directly to personal, temporal, or locational characteristics.[63] While
I find the word 'here' to be particularly beguiling, deixis applies to any
context-specific utterance used to provide discursive *specificity*: *I, you, we*;
my, thy; *now, then*; *this, that*; *here, there*. The temporality of the 'future
imperfect' is ingeniously dramatized in Sonnet 81:

> Or I shall live your epitaph to make,
> Or you survive when I in earth am rotten;
> From hence your memory death cannot take,
> Although in me each part will be forgotten.
> Your name from hence immortal life shall have,
> Though I, once gone, to all the world must die:
> The earth can yield me but a common grave,
> When you entombed in men's eyes shall lie.
> Your monument shall be my gentle verse,
> Which eyes not yet created shall o'er-read,
> And tongues to be your being shall rehearse,
> When all the breathers of this world are dead;
>   You still shall live (such virtue hath my pen)
>   Where breath most breathes, even in the mouths of men.

An initially balanced set of outcomes – either the speaker or the addressee
will die first – soon tip into asymmetrical destinies: for the addressee, *an
epitaph, memory, an immortal name, lying entombed in men's eyes in my*

(this!) verse monument; for the speaker, *decay, oblivion, an unmarked grave, culminating in the aggressively buried absence of the speaker in the sestet* (but for 'my pen').

Both plays and epitaphs depend upon the problematically deictic reference to something 'Here.' The recourse to a declarative 'here' across print and stage media has as its common reference point the body – a body that is in a peculiar way *not quite present*, and thus needing proclamation of its presence. Shakespearean characters acknowledge their ghastly semi-absence onstage, where there is no 'here' *here*. When Romeo avers '*I have lost myself; I am not here; / This is not Romeo, he's some other where*' (1.1.184–85), or when Othello laments 'That's he that was Othello. *Here I am*' (5.2.290), or when Peter Quince declares 'We are not here' (5.1.115), we sense Shakespeare intuiting a subtle insight about performed presence. He took the Epicurean solace – 'When we exist, death is not present, and when death is present, we do not exist' – and sought to step outside of it, making Hamlet's death sentence 'I am dead' (5.2.316) possible, albeit within quotation marks.

Yet another mode of craft characterizes the staging of the statue scene in *The Winter's Tale*, one that traverses arts, time, and geography. Here he worked not only with the named 'rare Italian master' Giulio Romano for the multimedia extravaganza of sculpture, painting, music, words, and faith. There's been much speculation about which 'Giulio Romano' Shakespeare meant to invoke as the artist who painted (and/or sculpted) Hermione. I concur with those who suspect that Shakespeare was familiar with Giorgio Vasari's 1550 *Lives*, which asserts that 'Jupiter saw sculpted and painted statues breathe … by the skill of Julio Romano.'[64] But what of that other Giulio – Giulio Camillo, whose *Idea of the Theatre* inspired much of Frances A. Yates' work on *The Art of Memory*?[65] As William Uricchio holds,

> Camillo's aptly invoked theatre metaphor suggests a different configuration and dynamic – a space of performance – that would, in his words, render 'scholars into spectators' … this performance without an audience is the act of scholarly-spectatorship itself. The stage-bound spectator 'performs' by contemplating the rich array of data that constitutes the theatre …. The transformational act requires performance.[66]

The work that Paulina enjoins upon Leontes in this final scene is a laborious (16-year!) forgetting of the narcissistic male self, in order to project him into the subject position of others. This was impossible for Leontes in the first three acts; but now he seems at last able to imagine himself in her place, imagine him there, along the lines of the *ethopoeia* habituated in the Tudor classroom.

Leontes' guilty fixation upon the death of his wife and son, his daily exercises of mourning, his 'shame perpetual' publicly announced through their grave's mutual epitaph – all culminate in the final scene, where we don't quite know whether the figure of Hermione is a statue, or a person, or maybe even some kind of philosophical ghost.[67] As R. S. White puts it: 'Such a mode of living art prevents us from extracting any abstract statement of theme, for we too are ones in this interlude.'[68] We are left, wondering:

> is (was) this Pygmalion's statue?
> is (was) this a resurrection?
> does (did) the figure move?
> does (did) it breathe?
> is (was) it dead?
> is (was) it alive?
> is (was) it flesh?
> is (was) it stone?
> is (was) it as she?
> is (was) it an *it*?

There's a productive overlap to memory and mortality, from craft of pre-hearsing the *ars moriendi* to the verbal tenses we find ourselves drawn into using when issues of death are in play.[69]

Notes

1 Geoffrey Nunberg, 'The Organization of Knowledge,' *History of Information i218* (January 4, 2022). https://courses.ischool.berkeley.edu/i218/s10/SLIDES/HOFIknowl2-22GN.pdf.
2 See Ann Blair, *Too Much to Know: Managing Scholarly Information before the Modern Age* (New Haven, CT: Yale University Press, 2010).
3 Colin Burrow, *Shakespeare and Classical Antiquity* (Oxford: Oxford University Press, 2013).
4 *The Manuell of Epictetus*, trans. by Ja[mes] Sanford (London, 1567), A4ʳ.
5 'I have not made this longer than the rest [of my letters], but that I had not the leisure to make it shorter than it is.' Blaise Pascal, Letter 16, in *Les Provinciales, or, The Mystery of Jesuitisme*, 2nd ed. (London, 1658), p. 292.
6 Jacques Derrida played these intonations off one another in his 1968 lecture 'The Ends of Man,' in *Margins of Philosophy*, trans. by Alan Bass (Chicago: University of Chicago, 1972), pp. 111–36; today, polemics about *The End of School* or *The End of College* levy apocalyptic language to dismantle public institutions. See Zachary Slayback, *The End of School: Reclaiming Education from the Classroom* (Coldwater, MI: Remnant Publishing, 2016) and Kevin Carey, *The End of College: Creating the Future of Learning and the University of Everywhere* (New York: Riverhead Books, 2015).

7 For a convergent critical treatment of Faustus, 'at the end of the play and the end of his life,' see Chapter 1, 'Death and the Art of Memory in Donne' by Rebeca Helfer.

8 Russ McDonald, 'Planned Obsolescence or Working at the Words,' in *Teaching Shakespeare: Passing it On*, ed. by G. B. Shand (Chichester: Wiley, 2009), p. 27.

9 John Dewey, *Democracy and Education* (New York: The Macmillan Company, 1916), p. 117. Because his opaque prose unfortunately obscures his often subtle insights, Dewey gets unfairly blamed for a lot of nonsense; even during his own (long) career he often found himself having to correct dogmatic applications of his own meditations; for a thoughtful reappraisal, see R. W. Hildreth, 'What Good Is Growth? Reconsidering Dewey on the Ends of Education,' *Education & Culture*, 27.2 (2011), 28–47.

10 Paul Tillich, *Theology of Peace*, ed. by Ronald H. Stone (Louisville, KY: Westminster John Knox Press, 1990), p. 132.

11 David Pye, *The Nature and Art of Workmanship* (Cambridge: Cambridge University Press, 1968), p. 20.

12 David Kathman, 'Players, Livery Companies, and Apprentices,' in *The Oxford Handbook of Early Modern Theatre*, ed. by Richard Dutton (Oxford: Oxford University Press, 2009), p. 413.

13 George Puttenham, *The Art of English Poesy: A Critical Edition*, ed. by Frank Whigham and Wayne A. Rebhorn (Ithaca, NY: Cornell University Press, 2007), 3.25.378–79.

14 Callicles to Socrates (Plato, *Gorgias*, in *Collected Dialogues of Plato Including the Letters*, ed. by Edith Hamilton and Huntington Cairns (New York: Pantheon, 1961), p. 491).

15 Richard Sennett, *The Craftsman* (New Haven, CT: Yale University Press, 2008), p. ix. Pamela H. Smith, 'Making as Knowing: Craft as Natural Philosophy,' in *Ways of Making and Knowing: The Material Culture of Empirical Knowledge*, ed. by Pamela H. Smith, Amy R. W. Meyers, and Harold J. Cook (Ann Arbor: University of Michigan Press, 2014), p. 40.

16 Alexander Langlands, *Cræft: An Inquiry into the Origins and True Meaning of Traditional Crafts* (New York: W.W. Norton, 2018), p. 18.

17 Virginia Woolf, 'Craftsmanship' (broadcast April 20, 1937), in *Selected Essays*, ed. by David Bradshaw (Oxford: Oxford University Press, 2009), p. 85.

18 M. C. Bradbrook, *Shakespeare the Craftsman* (London: Chatto & Windus, 1969), p. 54.

19 David Lowenthal, *The Past is a Foreign Country – Revisited* (Cambridge: Cambridge University Press, 2015), p. 85, citing the sixteenth-century educator Johannes Sturm, *De imitatione oratoria*, who in turn was citing Horace: '*publica materies privati iuris erit*'.

20 Jonas Holst points out that Homer describes Hephaestus as 'famous for his skill.' Holst, 'The Fall of the *Tektōn* and The Rise of the Architect: On the Greek Origins of Architectural Craftsmanship,' *Architectural Histories*, 5.1 (2017), 3. http://doi.org/10.5334/ah.239.

21 Ben Jonson, *Timber, or Discoveries*, ll. 2375–76, in *Ben Jonson, Vol. 8: The Poems; The Prose Works*, ed. by C. H. Herford, Percy Simpson, and Evelyn Simpson (Oxford: Oxford University Press, 1947), p. 636.

22 Among the substantial library on the *ars moriendi*'s influence on literature are Sister Mary Catharine O'Connor, *The Art of Dying Well: The Development of the Ars Moriendi* (New York: Columbia University Press, 1942); Nancy Lee Beaty, *The Craft of Dying: A Study of the Literary Tradition of the Ars Moriendi in England* (New Haven, CT: Yale University Press, 1970); David William Atkinson, ed., *The English Ars Moriendi* (Bern and New York: Peter Lang, 1992); Robert Watson, *The Rest Is Silence: Death as Annihilation in the English Renaissance* (Berkeley: University of California Press, 1994); Amy Appleford, *Learning to Die in London, 1380–1540* (Philadelphia: University of Pennsylvania Press, 2015); Maggie Vinter, *Last Acts: The Art of Dying on the Early Modern Stage* (New York: Fordham University Press, 2019); and D. Vance Smith, *Arts of Dying: Literature and Finitude in Medieval England* (Chicago: University of Chicago Press, 2020). Peter Carlson provides a helpful overview: Carlson, 'The Art and Craft of Dying,' in *The Oxford Handbook of Early Modern Literature and Religion*, ed. by Andrew Hiscock and Helen Wilcox (Oxford: Oxford University Press, 2017), pp. 634–49; see also the recent dissertation by Simon Fortin, 'Dying to Learn, Learning to Die: The Craft of Dying in Early Modern English Drama and the Cultivation of Dying-Voice Literacy' (unpublished doctoral dissertation, CUNY, 2016).

23 See Bettie Anne Doebler, 'Othello's Angels: The *Ars Moriendi*,' *ELH* 34.2 (June 1967), 156–72; Phoebe S. Spinrad, '*Measure for Measure* and the Art of Not Dying,' *Texas Studies in Literature and Language*, 26.1 (1984), 74–93; Claire Saunders, '"Dead in His Bed": Shakespeare's Staging of the Death of the Duke of Gloucester in *2 Henry VI*,' *The Review of English Studies*, New Series, 36.141 (February 1985), 19–34; Harry Berger, Jr., '*Ars Moriendi* in Progress, or John of Gaunt and the Practice of Strategic Dying,' *Yale Journal of Criticism*, 1.1 (1987), 39–65; and Todd Borlik, '"The Way to Study Death": New Light on a Variant in F2 *Macbeth*,' *The Explicator*, 70.2 (2012), 144–48.

24 On *Hamlet*'s commonplacing, see Vanessa Lim, '"To be or not to be": Hamlet's Humanistic *Quaestio*,' *The Review of English Studies*, 70.296 (2019), 640–58.

25 Kathrine Koller, 'Falstaff and the Art of Dying,' *Modern Language Notes*, 60.6 (June 1945), 386.

26 Robert Herrick, '225. The Plaudite, or end of life,' in *The Complete Poetry of Robert Herrick: Volume I*, ed. by Tom T. Cain and Ruth Connolly (Oxford: Oxford University Press, 2013), p. 90.

27 Aaron T. Pratt, 'A Conversation on "Dying Well in Early Modern England,"' *Ransom Center Magazine* (October 30, 2018); Simon Palfrey and Emma Smith, *Shakespeare's Dead* (Oxford: Bodleian Library, 2016), p. 24.

28 Alec Ryrie, *Being Protestant in Reformation Britain* (Oxford: Oxford University Press, 2013), p. 464. Beaty earlier noted the 'quasi-dramatic form' of treatises like Thomas Becon's 1561 *The Sick Man's Salve* (*The Craft of Dying*, p. 135).

29 David Cressy, *Birth, Marriage, and Death: Ritual, Religion, and the Life-Cycle in Tudor and Stuart England* (Oxford: Oxford University Press, 1997), p. 392; Dennis Kezar, *Guilty Creatures: Renaissance Poetry and the Ethics of Authorship* (Oxford: Oxford University Press, 2001), p. 140.

30 Arnold Stein, *House of Death: Messages from the English Renaissance* (Baltimore, MD: Johns Hopkins University Press, 1986), p. 12.

31 Christopher Sutton, *Disce mori. Learne to die. A religious discourse, moouing euery Christian man to enter into a serious remembrance of his ende. Wherein also is contained the meane and manner of disposing himselfe to God, before, and at the time of his departure* (London, 1600), p. 17; previously mentioned in the Introduction, n.5.

32 F. G. Butler, 'Erasmus and the Deaths of Cordelia and Lear,' *English Studies*, 73.1 (1992), 10–21.

33 Kristin Poole, *Supernatural Environments in Shakespeare's England Spaces of Demonism, Divinity, and Drama* (Cambridge: Cambridge University Press, 2011), p. 71.

34 Desiderius Erasmus, *Preparation to deathe: A booke as deuout as eloquent, compiled by Erasmus Roterodame* (London: 1538), F6^{r-v}.

35 Poole, *Supernatural Environments*, p. 77.

36 From the preface 'to the ryght noble lorde Thomas, Erle of wylteshyre, and of Drmanie, sendeth gretynge,' n.p., in Erasmus, *Preparation to deathe*.

37 Leonard Barkan, 'What Did Shakespeare Read?' in *The Cambridge Companion to Shakespeare*, ed. by Margreta de Grazia and Stanley Wells (Cambridge: Cambridge University Press, 2001), p. 36. Emrys Jones put it even more bluntly: 'without Erasmus, no Shakespeare': Jones, *The Origins of Shakespeare* (Oxford: Oxford University Press, 1977), p. 13.

38 Lynn Enterline, *Shakespeare's Schoolroom* (Philadelphia: University of Pennsylvania Press, 2012), p. 113.

39 Attributed to Goethe by Johann Peter Eckermann, in *Conversations with Goethe* (1852) and cited by Shaun Nichols, 'Imagination and Immortality: Thinking of Me,' *Synthese*, 159 (2007), 215.

40 Sigmund Freud, 'Thoughts of the Times on War and Death,' in *The Standard Edition of the Complete Psychological Works of Sigmund Freud*, vol. 14 (London: Hogarth Press, 1957), p. 289.

41 Allen Ginsberg, 'An Interview by Gary Pacernick' (1997), in *First Thought: Conversations with Allen Ginsberg*, ed. by Michael Schumacher (Minneapolis: University of Minnesota Press, 2017), p. 351.

42 Jan Habl, '"Only that man who governs himself may govern others": Jan Amos Comenius and His Anthropological Assumptions of Moral Politics,' *Pro Rege*, 43.4 (2015), 13. See also John Edward Sadler, *J. A. Comenius and the Concept of Universal Education* (London: Routledge, 1966; repr. 2013).

43 Virginia Heffernan, 'The Beautiful Benefits of Contemplating Doom,' *Wired* (April 2019). www.wired.com/story/the-beautiful-benefits-of-contemplating-doom/.
    In an interview with the Daily Stoic website, James Romm, 'How to Die: What Author James Romm Learned From Seneca's Writings on Death'

(https://dailystoic.com/james-romm/), points out that *memento mori* was a phrase spoken by a general's slave during a triumphal procession. It was never discussed by Seneca in the extant works, to my knowledge, but one does find the phrase *Meditare mortem* – 'Rehearse death' – used several times.

44 Sallie Tisdale, *Advice for Future Corpses (and Those Who Love Them): A Practical Perspective on Death and Dying* (New York: Simon & Schuster, 2018), p. 1.

45 Jeffrey P. Bishop, '*Scientia Mortis* and the *Ars Moriendi*: To the Memory of Norman,' in *Health Humanities Reader*, ed. by Therese Jones, Delese Wear, and Lester D. Friedman (New Brunswick, NJ: Rutgers University Press, 2014), p. 401.

46 Roy Scranton, *Learning to Die in the Anthropocene* (San Francisco, CA: City Lights Publishers, 2015), p. 90.

47 Fulke Greville, *Poems and Dramas of Fulke Greville: First Lord Brooke, Volume 1*, ed. by Geoffrey Bullough (Oxford: Oxford University Press, 1945), p. 131.

48 Paul Kalanithi, *When Breath Becomes Air* (New York: Random House, 2016), p. 148.

49 Robert Pinsky, 'How a 16th-Century Poem Inspired the Clarity of the Prose in *When Breath Becomes Air*,' *Slate* (September 9, 2016). https://slate.com/culture/2016/09/paul-kalanithis-when-breath-becomes-air-became-a-best-seller-for-a-nearly-unheard-of-reason-the-quality-of-its-prose.html.

50 Sherwin B. Nuland, *How We Die: Reflections on Life's Final Chapter* (New York: Random House, 1995), pp. 62–63.

51 Ibid., p. 262.

52 As in Sonnet 73, Shakespeare likes to take us to that morbid brink of thought, then pulls us back. (Here, Innogen is only *mostly* dead, and soon awakens.) As Wendell Berry enjoins: 'Practice resurrection.' Berry, 'Manifesto: The Mad Farmer Liberation Front,' in Wendell Berry, *Collected Poems* (San Francisco, CA: North Point Press, 1985), p. 151.

53 Stephen P. Kiernan, *Last Rights: Rescuing the End of Life from the Medical System* (New York: St. Martin's Press, 2006), p. 177; Katy Butler, *The Art of Dying Well: A Practical Guide to a Good End of Life* (New York: Scribner, 2019), p. 196.

54 Simon Critchley, 'To Philosophize Is to Learn How to Die: Facing Death can be a Key to Our Liberation and Survival,' *New York Times* (April 11, 2020); Lydia S. Dugdale, *The Lost Art of Dying: Reviving Forgotten Wisdom* (New York: HarperOne, 2020); Thomas Pfau, 'The Lost Art of Dying,' *Hedgehog Review* (Fall 2018). https://hedgehogreview.com/issues/the-evening-of-life/articles/the-lost-art-of-dying.

55 Volker Leppin: 'he did nothing else than write a new *ars moriendi*.' Leppin, 'Preparing for Death: From the Late Medieval *Ars Moriendi* to the Lutheran Funeral Sermon,' in *Preparing for Death, Remembering the Dead*, ed. by Jon Øygarden Flæten and Tarald Rasmussen (Göttingen: Vandenhoeck & Ruprecht, 2015), p. 14.

56 Jan Zwicky, 'A Ship from Delos,' in *Learning to Die: Wisdom in the Age of Climate Crisis*, ed. by Robert Bringhurst and Jan Zwicky (Regina, Saskatchewan: University of Regina Press, 2018), p. 45.

57 See Roger Clegg, and Lucie Skeaping, *Singing Simpkin and Other Bawdy Jigs: Musical Comedy on the Shakespearean Stage* (Exeter: University of Exeter Press, 2014).

58 Ibid., p. 71. Clegg and Skeaping, *Singing Simpkin*.

59 Samuel Johnson, *The Idler*, no. 103 (Saturday, April 5, 1760), in *Yale Digital Edition of the Works of Samuel Johnson*. www.yalejohnson.com/frontend/sda_viewer?n=107591.

60 Epictetus, *The Enchiridion*, trans. by Thomas Wentworth Higginson, in *The Works of Epictetus* (Boston: Little, Brown, and Company, 1865), p. 383.

61 John Donne, *The Variorum Edition of the Poetry of John Donne, Vol. 6: The Anniversaries and the Epicedes and Obsequies*, ed. by Gary A Stringer (Bloomington: Indiana University Press, 1995), p. 27; emphasis added.

62 Nigel Llewellyn, *Art of Death: Visual Culture in the English Death Ritual, c.1500–c.1800* (London: Reaktion Books, 1991).

63 See Heather Dubrow, *Deixis in the Early Modern English Lyric: Unsettling Spatial Anchors Like 'Here,' 'This,' 'Come'* (Basingstoke: Palgrave, 2015).

64 B. J. Sokol, *Art and Illusion in The Winter's Tale* (Manchester: Manchester University Press, 1994), p. 85.

65 See William West, 'The Idea of a Theater: Humanist Ideology and the Imaginary Stage in Early Modern Europe,' *Renaissance Drama*, 28 (1999), 245–87.

66 William Uricchio, 'A Palimpsest of Place and Past: Location-Based Digital Technologies and the Performance of Urban Space and Memory,' *Performance Research*, 17:3 (2012), 47. See also Kathleen George: 'Is it too much to think the story of Camillo was nudging [Shakespeare] as he wrote *The Winter's Tale*?' George, *Winter's Tales: Reflections on the Novelistic Stage* (Newark: University of Delaware Press, 2005), p. 21.

67 As Hans Jonas' speculates: 'metaphysics arises from graves.' Jonas, 'Tool, Image, and Grave: On What Is Beyond the Animal in Man,' in Hans Jonas, *Mortality and Morality: A Search for Good after Auschwitz* (Evanston, IL: Northwestern University Press, 1996), p. 84.

68 R. S. White, *Let Wonder Seem Familiar: Shakespeare and the Romance Ending* (London: Bloomsbury 2000), p. 155.

69 See Lydia Davis' searching 'Grammar Questions,' a meditation upon the pronouns and verbs that are accurate for her dying, soon to be dead, father:

> When he is dead, everything to do with him will be in the past tense. Or rather, the sentence 'He is dead' will be in the present tense, and also questions such as 'Where are they taking him?' or 'Where is he now?' Actually, then I won't know if the words 'he' and 'him' are correct, in the present tense. Is he, once he is dead, still 'he,' and if so, for how long is he still a 'he'?

Lydia Davis, 'Grammar Questions,' in *110 Stories*, ed. by Ulrich Baer (New York: New York University Press, 2002), p. 72.

Grounding the Remembrance of the Dead

Preface to Part II

Grounding the remembrance of the dead refers to the acts of establishing a place of burial and interring the corpse in that place. Where one was buried mattered greatly for early moderns. Despite being prohibited during the early medieval period by church councils, intramural interment – for those who could pay for it – gradually became more accepted.[1] Memorials within cathedrals and chapels held greater prestige than churchyard graves, and, before the Reformation, a memorial's placement within the church gained higher social value according to its proximity to altars, as well as the relics and images of saints, all of which were thought to confer spiritual benefit upon the dead and to ensure the dead's remembrance by the living.[2]

The importance of the burial place is structured into the art of memory. Images are recollected on the basis of their association with well-defined loci belonging to an overall architectural scheme. In societies that revere the memories of ancestors, the dead are the most privileged of images, as suggested by the origin story of how Simonides stumbled upon the invention of the art of memory.[3] By recalling each place at the banquet table, Simonides was able to identify the unrecognizable corpses crushed by the hall's collapsed roof. Does not Simonides's story explain the underlying principle of every cemetery or tomb? To keep the dead alive in one's memory, the living must be able to visit a distinct site, which they can associate with the dead and where they can ritualize their commemoration. The idea that the ultimate locus is one's final resting place is not lost upon Thomas Wilson, when, during his discussion of the art of memory, he raises a tale replete with grim overtones of the *memento mori*. At the time of the Norfolk rebellion, a priest condemned to hang with fellow rebels realized that his gibbet had been erected on the very spot where fourteen years earlier, while 'wallowing … down on the grass',[4] he declared, with merriment, to a friend: 'This is my resting place for ever and ever, here shall be my dwelling, because I have chosen it' (Psalm 132:14).

Figure Pr2.1   Mausolaeum, Philip Galle, *The Tomb of Mausolus at Halicarnassus*, Netherlands, *c.* 1572. National Gallery of Art, Washington. Accession Number: 2011.139.96.

Survivors create a burial place to secure the permanence of the dead in the memory of the individual and his or her community. The prohibition against cremation and the stigma of being drowned or buried at sea[5] – dramatized, for example, by the play *Pericles* – betray the fear of one's body having no anchored site. Without locating remains, there can be no remembrance and, for Christianity, no resurrection. And so burial places sponsored by the wealthy and powerful aim for a secure grounding with ontological heft as though the dead's fading presence needed a geographical foundation to bear it into the future. During the early modern period, the *locus classicus* of such heft was none other than the legendary tomb of Mausolus at Halicarnassus, Caria (see Figure Pr2.1). Erected on the edge of the sea, the Mausoleum stood in defiance against the impermanence of a watery burial. Because of the magnificence of the tomb, one of the seven wonders of the ancient world,[6] Mausolus's name – a monumental eponym – was given as a general term for any stately commemorative edifice.[7] Capitalizing on this grounded commonplace, a short pamphlet of epitaphs written on the death of Prince Henry was entitled 'Mausoleum', printed in bold capitals.[8] The stark contrast between the two elemental resting places – a grounded place and a fluid 'no place' – would have been perceived by early modern Londoners in the enduring legacy of Westminster's imposing royal memorials and the anonymity of the plague pits.[9]

But burial places, fabricated out of physical and linguistic materials, have been built up over time and are thus subject to the erosion that comes from the destruction of matter and the decay of memory. Henry VIII's dissolution of the monasteries would have thrown a long shadow over the efforts of Tudor and Stuart tomb designers. John Weaver, who, staunch Protestant though he may have been, wrote the first major catalogue of England's funeral monuments, bears witness to the fact that burial places can be effaced from history: in his book he beholds not just the 'lively statues and stately monuments Westminster Abbey' but 'the mournful ruins of other religions houses, although their goodly fair structures be altogether destroyed, their tombs battered down, and the bodies of their dead cast out of their coffins'.[10] Weaver's tome serves as a surrogate necropolis to those who have lost their mortuary homes, replicating on a national scale what Simonides did ages ago on the local.

Part II's four chapters consider the literary, climatic, philosophical, and religious ramifications of the place of the dead in seventeenth-century England. Patricia Phillippy's Chapter 5 puts a contemporary spin on the axiomatic principle that how we remember the dead depends upon where they are interred. Phillippy focuses her examination on two monuments of the Dudley women, one located in a parish church in Stoneleigh, Warwickshire, the other in a parish church of St Giles in the Fields, Middlesex. For Phillippy, however, a burial place is not just defined by its geographic coordinates, a point named on a map; it belongs to a set of relationships between the local and the global such that any act of commemoration operates in an ecosystem or ecological network that interconnects a monument with a complex of 'social, somatic, and climatic conditions'. Phillippy thus has no interest in determining a top-down causal link between meteorological trends and the degradation of buildings, but rather situates the monuments in the wider horizon of the two parish communities of Alice Dudley, a gentry woman, whose early abandonment by her husband left her and her five daughters' status uncertain until Charles I created her a duchess for her own lifetime. Both communities, as exposed as they were to the extreme weather crises of the Little Ice Age, shaped the bodies, lives, and deaths of the Dudley women so much so that their bequests and monuments respond in subtle ways to the climate challenges faced by their parishioners. What emerges from this study of the Dudley women's ecosystem is a gender analysis of how their monuments, commemorating an all-women household, do not base femininity upon bearing children and promote instead female autonomy and agency, troubling patriarchy's 'ecology of dominance'.

During the period, physical tombs did not always receive admiration and approval, especially from humanists mindful of Horace's oft-quoted dictum on writing outlasting bronze and withstanding the vagaries of weather.[11] Even Weaver explicitly favours paper memorials over marble ones.[12] With *A Game at Chess*, Brian Chalk's chapter examines the way in which Middleton's stagecraft sacrifices the ambition of pursuing long-term monumentalization for short-term popularity and profitability. Middleton theatricalizes his play's stakes by means of a chess match that allegorizes the real politic of diplomacy, the White side representing the Stuart court and the Black representing the former's Spanish rivals. Although, superficially speaking, England stands to win everlasting glory in its victory over Spain, the parameters of the game itself underscore the transience of making one's mark in the immediate political and dramatic arenas. The board does not offer any piece the security of a fixed place, for each piece, no matter how monumental it may appear, is subject to strategic and aleatory movements, its own and those of the pieces around it. And finally, the captured pieces are removed from the board and thrown into the bag, which, indiscriminately jumbling them together, symbolizes the levelling power of death. When all is said and done, the villainous characters on the Black side, despite their loss, possess a theatrical charisma that outshines their less memorable White counterparts. The chessboard thus becomes a metaphor for the play as a vehicle of commercial topicality in opposition to a lasting literary legacy. Middleton knows that he banks upon contemporary political intrigue to win over the audience – and win over audiences the play did, running for nine days straight, becoming the period's greatest box-office success, until it was shut down for its scandalous depictions.

Chapters 6 and 8, by Philip Schwyzer and Claire Preston, respectively, examine how the ground becomes much more than just a receptacle for the dead. The place of burial could unsettle remains, for interment in the earth sparked religious controversy and philosophical meditation during the period. Milton's Sonnet 18, Schwyzer argues, poses a confessional crux through its treatment of the 1555 massacre of the Waldensians in Piedmont. While explicitly disparaging idolatry, the poem values the martyred remains of the Waldensian community, leaving Milton the staunch Protestant surprisingly open to accusations of relic veneration. In order to make sense of this issue, Schwyzer examines the work of earlier poets, playwrights, and preachers who use the same trope of scattered bones. Post-Reformational writers were preoccupied with this trope, which they interpolated into Ezekiel's vision of the valley of the dry bones, because, as Schwyzer contends, the ungathered remains of the dead put an 'impossible demand' upon Protestant England. The Reformation's closure of the charnel houses meant that people were no longer permitted to collect the bones disinterred from churchyard graves to make room for new corpses. Burial practice enforced an eventual dispersal that only God could overcome with a miracle. To resolve the problem of honouring the scattered bones of the Waldensians without turning them into relics, Milton cleverly associates their scattering with the act of sowing and thereby renews the fertile ground of memory by leading to the proselytization of Italians.

Preston's chapter fittingly rounds out Part II, not only because of Thomas Browne's authorship of *Urne-Buriall*, the seventeenth century's most grandiloquent statement on death and the grave, but also because of Browne's *memento mori* deductions from the premise of humanity's microcosmic constitution. Preston reads *Urne-Buriall* alongside a much lesser-known work, Browne's *A Letter to a Friend*, which, dating from the same period, discusses one of his patients who suffered at length and eventually died of consumption. From his particular medical descriptions of a single clinical case, Brown develops eschatological ruminations about humanity's ultimate disintegration into detritus and dust. The wasting disease afflicting his patient literally burns up his body from within and, as sounded out by Browne's lexically rich commentary, reproduces at the level of the individual the final apocalyptic conflagration of the world. As the burial service in the Book of Common Prayer reminds us, the dead have affinities with the place of interment itself, the ground to which they are commended. Preston finds in the *Letter*, then, an illuminating complement to *Urne-Buriall*: while the latter studies how the dead body reverts to its constitutive state of ashes, the former contemplates how the living person 'a grave in preparation' displays the signs of returning to the basic element of earth – the ultimate point of *mortality* between microcosm and macrocosm.

Notes

1 Ralph Houlbrooke, *Death, Religion, and the Family in England, 1480–1750* (Oxford: Oxford University Press, 1998), p. 331.

2 Ibid., p. 331. Peter Marshall, *Beliefs and the Dead in Reformation England* (Oxford: Oxford University Press, 2002), p. 21.

3 Cicero, *De oratore: Books I and II*, trans. by E. W. Sutton and H. Rackham, 2 vols. (Cambridge, MA, and London: Harvard University Press, 1996), 2.86.351–8.

4 See entry II.2 on Thomas Wilson in *The Memory Arts in Renaissance England*, ed. by William E. Engel, Rory Loughnane, and Grant Williams (Cambridge: Cambridge University Press, 2016).

5 See Chapter 8, 'Thomas Browne's Retreat to Earth' by Claire Preston; and Christopher Daniell, *Death and Burial in Medieval England 1066–1550* (London: Routledge, 2005), pp. 75–6.

6 The canonical list of the seven wonders of the ancient world was established in the Renaissance. See Peter A. Clayton and Martin J. Price, 'Introduction', in *Seven Wonders of the Ancient World*, ed. by Peter A. Clayton and Martin J. Price (London: Routledge, 1988), pp. 5ff. 'Queene Artemisia made for her husband, that famous tombe mausoleum, famous ouer the world', says Church of England clergyman Andrew Willet, *An Harmony upon the First Book of Samuel* (London, 1607; STC 25678), R6ʳ.

7 Thomas Elyot, *The Dictionary of Sir Thomas Eliot Knight* (London, 1538; STC 7659), N3ʳ.

8 See anon., *Mausoleum or, The Choicest Flowers of the Epitaphs, Written on the Death of the Never-Too-Much Lamented Prince Henry* (London, 1613; STC 13160).

9 Historical geographers have devoted considerable attention to the challenges of remembering those carried away by the plague in earlier times; see especially in this regard Mary J. Dobson's study of the south-east of England which presents demographic data for over five hundred parishes, *Contours of Death and Disease in Early Modern England* (Cambridge: Cambridge University Press, 2002).

10 See entry IV.5 on John Weaver in *Memory Arts*, ed. by Engel, Loughnane, and Williams, p. 207.

11 Horace, *Horace: The Odes and Epodes*, trans. by Charles E. Bennett (Cambridge, MA; London: Harvard University Press; Heinemann, 1964), 3.30.1–5.

12 See entry IV.5 on John Weaver in *Memory Arts*, ed. by Engel, Loughnane, and Williams.

CHAPTER 5

Memory, Climate, and Mortality
The Dudley Women among the Fields

Patricia Phillippy

Doomes-day Booke

By 1624, 'through the injury of time and weather', George Montaigne, Bishop of London, reported, 'there had a general wrack befallen the ancient parish church of St Giles in the Fields'.[1] Founded in 1101 as part of a hospital for lepers, situated in the countryside beyond London, St Giles became a parish church in 1542, with the land and buildings of the hospital conveyed to John Dudley, Lord Lisle, after the dissolution.[2] Registering the threat of time's wrack that besets all monuments, Montaigne echoes a common early modern theme, but his indictment of weather's ill-effects suggests an awareness of the singularly brutal period of climatic change now known as the Little Ice Age (LIA). The years surrounding the demolition and rebuilding of the church, from 1623 to 1630, marked one of the coldest periods of the LIA: 'the Grindelwald Fluctuation, or Hyper-LIA' brought a global drop in temperature of 1.5 degrees Celsius.[3] Geoffrey Parker captures the effects in Europe: '1627 was the wettest summer recorded for the past 500 years, and 1628 saw a year without summer, with temperatures so low that crops never ripened. Between 1629 and 1632 much of Europe suffered excessive rains followed by drought.'[4] Montaigne suggests his mindfulness of the cold when he directs clergy to encourage donations 'with all possible expedition, for that the winter coming on, the parishioners (to the number of two thousand souls) would be utterly destitute and deprived of spiritual comfort'. He adds, 'all monies collected should be entered in a vellum book … as a perpetual memorial'.[5] The *Liber Domus Dei Anglice, or Doomes-day Booke* survives in the parish today. Its first entry celebrates 'the munificence of the most pious Lady Alice Dudley', transcribing the inscription of a marble tablet mounted above the North Gate of the churchyard.[6]

I begin with his episode not to argue that climatic conditions determined the fate of the church building, but to invoke an interconnection,

subtler than simple cause and effect, between memory, climate, and mortality as it is played out in the memorial network created by Alice, Duchess
Dudley, and her five daughters between 1621 and 1674. This chapter recov-
ers a web of material and memorial connections joining the Dudley wom-
en's acts of commemoration in an ecology that sees the church building
and its monuments as intermeshed with the social, somatic, and climatic
conditions in which these women lived and died. Mobilising climate, as an
agent in rather than a mere a backdrop to their memorial activities, brings
into focus aspects of the Dudley women's project that redirect familiar
devotional and monumental gestures towards a wider field of social values
that both led and responded to environmental changes on a global scale.
Duchess Dudley's donation of a chancel screen in St Giles, for instance,
reveals the 'complex entanglements of human and natural histories'
implicit in negotiations with climate change.[7] Dudley's eulogist and rector
of St Giles, Robert Boreman, tells us:

> When the former Church … lay in Rubbish, there being a Void space at
> the upper end of the *Chancel*, which was stored with Lumber as the Boards
> of Coffins and Dead-mens Bones, She, being offended by that unhandsome
> prospect, erected a decent *skreen*, to divide the said *Chancel* from the fore-
> named place, to hide it from the beholders eyes.[8]

When the church was rebuilt, this utilitarian shroud was replaced by 'a
beautiful *Skreen* of Carved Work, which was placed where the former in
the Old Church stood': a donation prompted by Laudian belief in the
divinity of the *sanctum sanctorum*.[9] The second screen, 'being found superstitious', was taken down by Parliamentary ordinance in 1643 and 'sold for
fortye shillings … given to the poore on Christmas eve following'.[10]

This ecology of the Dudley women's memorial project studies a literal
network of artefacts and charitable donations, and situates these women's
artefactual remains among the intertwined environmental forces influenc-
ing memory, climate, and mortality in their lifetimes. Viewing memory as
at once somatic and social, as Garrett A. Sullivan, Jr. has argued, inextricably binds the remembering body to its environment.[11] The iterative arts of
memory occur internally within humoral mind-bodies – vulnerable to the
influences of climate and sex – and embed themselves externally in 'cognitive artifacts' and socially approved performances.[12] While considering the
unified memorial project pursued by all six Dudley women, I focus on two
monuments joining two parish churches, St Mary the Virgin in the village of Stoneleigh (Warwickshire) and St Giles in the Fields (then in rural
Middlesex, now in Central London). The Dudley women's memorials are

intertwined with the materiality of these sites and their environmental and climatic conditions, and equally entangled with the legacy of their subjects' embodied experience of gender. By insisting on the material conditions of body and place, and carrying their traces forward in commemorative and charitable acts, these works trouble the patriarchy supporting both the gendering of memory and the practices contributing to climate change in this period of nascent globalisation.

Elizabeth M. DeLoughrey writes that 'to parochialize the Anthropocene is to uncover its place-based allegories'.[13] The second section of this chapter, 'Fatal Synergy', mines the 'natural [and] human archives' informing the LIA, locating this evidence within two parishes to sketch an allegory of vulnerability and resilience in the Dudley women's works.[14] This discussion reframes the Dudley women's conventional acts of charity within the growing pressures exerted by the shift in population from rural to urban places – a shift that contributed to the survival of the Stoneleigh monument and the ruin of those in St Giles. The third section, 'The Chancel and the Cage', explores the specific vulnerabilities of women in the LIA to argue that the Dudley women's memory work reimagines commemorative conventions to destabilise and displace the patriarchy that 'redistributes' natural creatures within an ecology of dominance.[15]

Fatal Synergy

If dynasty is a site which redistributes nature's agents – where the body is defined by cultural affiliation – the Dudley women's claim to dynastic identity involved fraught engagements with this 'natureculture'.[16] Alice Leigh, daughter of Sir Thomas Leigh of Stoneleigh, married Sir Robert Dudley, the natural son of Lady Douglas Sheffield and Robert Dudley, 1st Earl of Leicester in 1596. She gave birth to five daughters before, in 1605, Dudley lost a Star Chamber case to establish his legitimacy.[17] By 1611, Dudley had permanently left England for Italy, styling himself Duke of Northumberland, a title recognised by Emperor Frederick II. Dudley converted to Catholicism and married Elizabeth Southwell, who had journeyed with him from England. Until Dudley's death in 1649, Alice occupied an uncertain status; not maid, widow, or wife, she was neither definitively entitled to dynastic benefit nor excluded from it. She raised her daughters at Dudley House in the parish of St Giles in the Fields, where, in 1669, she died, aged 90, having outlived all but one daughter. William Dugdale reports, 'The corps lyes now in great state at her house in Holburne; the roome wherein it is, being hung with velvet, and a chayre

of state, cushion and coronet, according to her degree, and a great ban-
ner of Armes empaled with her husband ... as is proper in such cases.'[18]
This pomp was mandated not by Alice Dudley's status as the widow of
a duke but by a grant of title in her own right. '[P]artly for the services
done by [Dudley's sons-in-law] Sir Robert Holburne and Sir Ric. Leveson
to the King in his great distresses', Dugdale confirms, 'did the late King
by his letters patent ... grant that this lady should enjoy the title of a
Dutchesse during her life, and her daughter to have place as ye daughters
of a Duke.'[19] Dudley's funeral occurred ten days after her death, her corpse
accompanied by 'Fourscore and ten Widows (according to the Number
of the years, She lived)', each receiving a gown, a white kerchief, and one
shilling for the funeral supper.[20] The same day, Dugdale recalls, 'March.
16. I came out of London wth the corpse of the Dutchess Dudley ... to
St Alban's. 17. To Layton in Bedfordshire. 18. To Northampton. 19. To
Dunchurch. 20. To Stoneley, where the sayd Corps was interred'.[21] In her
will, Dudley 'appointed five pounds to be given to every Place or Town
where Her *Corps* should rest in it's Passage from *London* unto *Stoneley*[;]
where She hath a Noble Monument long since prepared by Her selfe'.[22]

The half-century of Alice Dudley's residence St Giles in the Fields was
one of pervasive and radical changes entangled with, if not resulting from,
the climate change of the LIA. From the fifteenth to the eighteenth centuries, a period of global cooling occurred, within which episodes of extreme
cold have been identified based on natural evidence (ice cores, pollen and
spore deposits, tree rings) and human archives (written texts, oral tradition, visual representations, and, after 1650, instrumental data).[23] A combination of factors contributed to the LIA: around 1500, the sun entered the
'Hallstatt millennial solar minimum', marked by three episodes of unusu-
ally low solar activity, the 'Spörer Minimum' (1440–1530), the 'Maunder
Minimum' (1645–1720), and the 'Dalton Minimum' (1780–1820). By
1609, telescopes existed in Europe capable of observing sunspots, which
index solar activity: 'while 100 sunspots were observed each year between
1612 and 1614, virtually none were visible in 1617–18'.[24] Exacerbating the
effects of solar minima were volcanic eruptions, which released sulphuric
dioxide clouds that spread worldwide, obscuring the sun and cooling
oceans. The interactions of these phenomena were particularly severe in
the seventeenth century, which began in the midst of the Grindelwald
Fluctuation (1560–1630), coincident with high solar activity and a series of
'catastrophic volcanic eruptions at tropical latitudes'.[25] The frigid Maunder
Minimum followed, when, as Parker tells us, 'astronomers around the
world made over 8,000 observations between 1645 and 1715 [yet] the grand

total of sunspots observed in those 70 years scarcely reached 100, fewer than appear in even a single year in the twenty-first century'.[26] Influenced by these interconnected phenomena, much of the earth in the seventeenth century 'experience[ed] the coldest weather recorded in over a millennium', during which an estimated one-third of the population died.[27]

While climate historians agree on these two root causes underlying the LIA, a third factor contributed to the global climate change in the period. European colonial expansion in America, the so-called 'Columbian Exchange', intermingled goods, people, plants, and pathogens, resulting in 'a swift, ongoing, radical reorganization of life on Earth without geological precedent'.[28] Basing their argument on stratigraphic evidence, geographers Simon Lewis and Mark Maslin collate a 'suite of changes' to trace the origins of anthropogenic climate change to European colonial expansion and its biological and cultural drivers and outcomes. The introduction of Eurasian pathogens into the New World, along with the mass extinction ancillary to the process of colonisation, decimated the Amerindian population: by 1650, the native population had declined from 61 million to just 6 million. Since Amerindians had used fire to clear forests, the reforestation following their genocide produced a decline in CO_2 in the earth's atmosphere. This, Lewis and Maslin argue, corresponds to the coldest period of the LIA (1594–1677). At the lowest point of the CO_2 dip, the 'Orbis spike' in 1610, they locate the beginning of the Anthropocene, an epoch boundary 'between Earth's last globally synchronous cool period before the long-term global warmth of the Anthropocene Epoch'.[29]

Inserting human agency into early modern climate change expands our view of the period's responses to the challenges of extreme weather, encouraging 'a more effective lineage of the deeper socio-cultural conditions which led to the Anthropocene'.[30] 'The Orbis spike', Lewis and Maslin argue, 'implies that colonialism, global trade and coal brought about the Anthropocene. Broadly, this highlights social concerns, particularly the unequal power relationships between different groups of people, economic growth, the impacts of globalised trade, and our current reliance on fossil fuels.'[31] As Dipesh Chakrabarty observes, 'anthropogenic explanations of climate change serve to collapse [the] distinction between natural history and human history'.[32] The ecology of global exchange redistributes natural memory and its artful technologies, dissolving distinctions between them.

Alice Dudley's two parishes, St Mary the Virgin in Stoneleigh and St Giles in the Fields, confronted the extreme weather crises of the LIA in different ways, but their histories are intertwined. The church of St Mary the Virgin was built in the twelfth century near a Cistercian abbey which passed into the hands of the Leigh family in 1561. The heavily wooded landscape was gradually converted by the monks to arable lands. Six mills served the medieval community, but a decline in population in the fifteenth century coincided with the Spörer Minimum, when cold temperatures and heavy rains shortened the growing season, leading to devastating losses and consequent famine. Conditions worsened with outbreaks of plague (in 1471 and 1479–80) and the repurposing of arable land to pasture. By the mid-sixteenth century, the village was largely depopulated: of forty-four houses, only ten were left occupied. In 1616, Sir Thomas Leigh, Alice Dudley's father, 'had license to impark 700 acres', further reducing an already diminished population.[33] Alice Dudley was one of eleven parishioners buried in St Mary's in 1669, while six baptisms and two marriages took place that year.[34] *The Great Frost*, a dialogue between a Countryman and a London Citizen, captures the desperation of the rural population suffering through 1608, a year so cold that the Thames froze:

> The poore Plough-mans children sit crying and blowing their nayles, as lamentably as the children and seruants of your poore Artificers. Hunger pinches their cheekes as deepe into the flesh, as it doeth into yours here. You cry out here, you are vndone for want of coale, and wee complaine, wee shall dye for want of Wood. All your care is to prouide for your Wiues, children and seruants, in this time of sadnesse … wee greeue as much to beholde the miserie of our poore Cattell (in this frozen-hearted season) as it doeth to looke vppon our owne affliction.[35]

'The ground is bare', the Countryman concludes, 'and not worth a poore handfull of grasse. The earth seemes barren, and beares nothing, or if shee doeth, most vnnaturally she kills it presently, or suffers it through cold to perish.'[36]

When Dugdale accompanied Alice Dudley's corpse from St Giles to Stoneleigh, the weather 'appears to have been notably cold'.[37] Her monument (see Figure 5.1), dominating the chancel of St Mary's church, was erected before 1655 by the London tomb sculptor William Wright.[38] The Latin epitaph, probably provided by Dugdale after the Duchess's death, recalls Charles I's letters patent and enumerates Dudley's charitable acts. Alice Dudley's shrouded effigy is joined on the monument by that of her unmarried daughter, Alicia, who died in 1621 at the age of 23: a casualty of the spike in mortality during an 'intensely cold winter' just before an outbreak of plague.[39]

Dudley's return to Stoneleigh places her in the role of gentry landowner, aligning her, perhaps with the 'prodigall landlords' who enslave poor tenants, as *The Great Frost* complains.[40] Yet her charity – £20 annually forever

Figure 5.1   Monument to Frances Kniveton by Edward or Joshua Marshall (*c.* 1663),
St Giles in the Fields. Photo Credit: Patricia Phillippy.

to augment 'the poor Vicaridges' of Stoneleigh and surrounding parishes, £100 per annum forever to the poor of the same parishes, and £50 to the poor on the day of her funeral – responds to the desperation of these rural communities.[41] While conventional, her donations become intertwined with the vulnerability and resilience attending responses to climate crises. These 'interlinked concepts', as Georgina Endfield states, illuminate 'the complexity between human and natural systems', building communal experiences which may 'become inscribed into memory in the form of oral history, ideology, custom, narrative [or] artifact'.[42] The shrouded effigies of Duchess Dudley and her daughter transfer the somatic vulnerability of the sleeping female body to a social performance: a memorial presence ensuring the resilience of the communities it feeds and the monument that marks its source.

The intimate role that memory plays in negotiations with environmental change is displayed vividly in *The Great Frost*, when the Countryman

recites a climatic history stretching back to Edward III's reign and concluding in Elizabeth's:

> There was one great Frost more in England, (in our memorie,) ... in the
> seuenth yeere of Queen Elizabeth, which began vpon the 21. Of December,
> and held on so extremely, that vpon New yeeres eue following, people
> in multitudes went vpon the Thames from London Bridge to Westmin-
> ster ... This Frost began to thaw vpon the third day of Ianuary ... which
> sudden thaw brought forth sudden harmes, for houses and bridges were
> ouer-turned by the Land-floodes [with] many numbers of people perishing
> likewise by those waters.[43]

'You haue a happy memorie Father', the Citizen replies, 'your head I see
is a very storehouse of antiquitie: you are of your selfe a whole volume
of Chronicles.'[44] Intertwined with orality, textuality, time, and weather,
the iterative act of memory speaks to living vulnerabilities and enduring
resilience. The repetitive experience of climate itself is embodied in the
reprinting of the dialogue six years later, as *The Cold Year 1614*.[45]

Duchess Dudley employs the heraldic and monumental machinery
available to her to commemorate her restorative gestures in Stoneleigh and
to assert her privilege to dispense charity. Yet she also initiates a memorial
network that joins her two parishes and unites all of the Dudley women in
more intimate, personal memory work. *The Great Frost* displays the different aspects of the climate crisis experienced in country and city, but also
the interconnected fates of these two sites. Migrations to urban centres
following enclosure is a familiar story, in which the damages of pastur-
age were deepened by the marginal or non-arable land left by the LIA.
The pressures of growing numbers of the poor, increasingly concentrated
in London's outer parishes, away from wealthier central boroughs, were
exacerbated by climate.[46] On the frozen Thames, the Citizen complains,
'neither could coale be brought vp the Riuer, neither could wood be sent
downe', a condition imperilling especially the poor, whose 'care for fier
was as great as for food'.[47] Throughout the seventeenth century, St Giles
in the Fields experienced an influx of poor, and with them came shortages
of food and fuel, malnutrition, and high mortality. While parishioners in
St Giles number 2,000 in 1623, more than twice as many burials (4,457)
occurred in 1665, 3,216 of them due to plague.[48] So 'overburthened with
poor' was the parish that 'the first outbreak of sustained mortality crisis
[in late 1664] occurred in St Giles in the Fields'.[49] Yet this was only the
most virulent of recurring constellations of cold weather, pestilence, and
death embodying the 'fatal synergy' of global climate and local crises.[50]
Elizabethan proclamations in 1592 and 1602 prohibiting building within

the parish, perceived as restraining agriculture and engendering pestilence, align with periods of extreme cold (1594–7 and 1601–3) and outbreaks of plague, 1592–3 and 1603).[51] The Dudley women, though insulated by class from the most profound crises in their parish, cannot have been blind to the ills of the changing urban landscape. Duchess Dudley's conventional bequest to ninety 'poore old women' of funeral garments and supper takes on new resonance in this context. Her more substantial donations, as at Stoneleigh, work to build the resilience of the communities she influenced through 'little reminders' or precise interventions.[52] 'Six pence should be given to every poor body that should meet Her *Corps* on the Road' from St Giles to Stoneleigh, and 'For the placing out for ever of poor Parish Children of St Giles' Apprentices, two hundred pounds to purchase a piece of Land at ten pounds per ann. And two to be put out every year.'[53]

'The Lady Ann Duddelye' and 'The Lady Frances Duddelye' appear with their mother in the *Doomes-day Booke*, youthful contributors to the rebuilding of St Giles in 1623, and, decades later, both were buried in the church.[54] In 1708, Edward Hatton noted the features of 'an extraordinary spacious Monument' for Frances Dudley, Lady Kniveton. It was 'mostly Marble, adorned with Cartouches, Cornish, Pediment, Mantling, Festoons; on the Pediment [are] two Boys, supporting a large Mantling, supposed to let down and cover the whole Monument; as also her Effigies lying at full length finely carved'. The inscription recorded that 'The Right Honourable Lady Ann Holbourne, Sister of the said Lady Frances … did will this Monument … to be erected to the memory of her sister near to whom she herself (which died August 1663) lies also interred and is placed here for want of convenient room in the Chancel'.[55]

Nothing remains of the monument now except Frances's reclining, shrouded effigy and an inscription echoing that in Stoneleigh, memorialising the letters patent conferring her mother's title (see Figure 5.2). Frances married Sir Gilbert Kniveton in May of 1634, but was widowed by November of the same year. She returned childless to Dudley House, where she lived until her death in 1641. By 1647, her sister Anne, who married Sir Robert Holborne in 1633, was also widowed and childless. Anne's will, written in 1663, documents the provenance of the monument that Hatton saw fifty years later: 'I desire my body may be privately and decently buried in the Chancell of St Giles Church in the ffeilds, as near the body of my dear sister the Lady Frances Kniveton as it can be laid'. Further, she charges her sister Katherine, 'to see … the Lady Kniveton's tomb set up in St Gyles church as I have agreed with one Mr. Marshal a Stonecutter, which if … my estate will hold out, I desire my owne figure

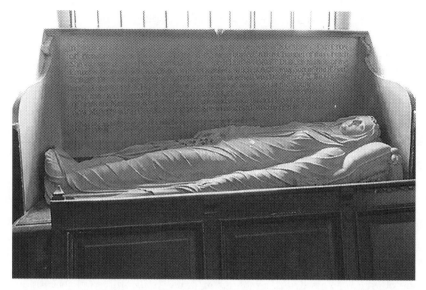

Figure 5.2   Monument to Alice, Duchess Dudley, and Alicia Dudley by William Wright (*c.* 1655), St Mary the Virgin's, Stoneleigh (Warwickshire). Photo Credit: Patricia Phillippy.

may be added to hers in a winding sheet as my deare sister's is'. She adds that she has agreed to pay Mr. Marshall, 'a Stonecutter in Shoe Lane' (Edward or Joshua Marshall) to have the tomb finished and set up 'beside the South window in St Gyles', as Hatton transcribes, 'for want of convenient room in the Chancel'.[56]

The remaining monument, unremarkably placed near the church entrance, is a fragment of Anne Holborne's project, which was clearly intended to emulate the monument in Stoneleigh. Duchess Dudley may have devised the two monuments to mirror each other, and the St Giles tomb remained incomplete. In large part, the monument fell victim to 'the urban graveyard effect' in very literal terms.[57] The unsustainable population growth in the parish occurred alongside 'climatic activity [which] promoted sickness' and increased the lethality of diseases.[58] The heavy burden of the poor extended to their burial: in 1592, 597 parishioners died, while the number of burials in St Giles's churchyard was 894; in 1625, 947 died, and 1,333 were buried.[59] So overwhelming was the rate of mortality in the parish that by the end of the century it was resolved again to rebuild the church from the ground up: the swollen churchyard caused 'the floor or body of the church [to] lay lower than the street by eight feet, at least, and thereby (and by the great number of burials within it) is become very damp and unwholesome'.[60] Frances Kniveton's monument was dismantled when the church was demolished in 1731, as an additional inscription confirms: 'Since the rebuilding of this Church this Monument was reset up by the Hon. Charles Leigh of Leighton in Bedfordshire, 1738'.

The monument in St Giles in the Fields works to continue Duchess Dudley's presence in the parish by memorialising the lives and deaths of her daughters. The vulnerability of this project is everywhere evident; Frances's displaced effigy and Anne's absent image – perhaps because her estate would not 'hold out' – embody the fragility of memory and the vulnerability of memorialisation. Yet Alice Dudley's contributions to the resilience of the parish participate in a wider social project of poor relief mobilised by the churchwardens: while the vestry records list monies disposed 'for putting forth of poor parish children apprentices' in 1646, an entry in 1670 locates Duchess Dudley's bequest in a nascent welfare state: '1670 (June 30) This day appeared in the vestry 20 boys, placed out apprentice by the gift of her grace the late dutchess Dudley'.[61] In their entanglements with their parishes, the Dudley women's memorial arts and acts mirror their subjects. 'In divers accidents and things relating to our Parish, I oft appeal'd to [Duchess Dudley's] stupendous *Memory*, as an ancient Record', Boreman confesses. 'Her vast *Memory* was the Storehouse and Treasury' of the parish: 'She was a *Living Chronicle* bound up with the *thread* of a long-spund Age'.[62]

The Chancel and the Cage

Confronting the climatic extremes of the LIA, many believed that 'an Arme from Heauen hath ... shaken Whips ouer our Land, sometimes scourging vs with strange Inundations of Flouds; then with mercilesse Fires then with intollerable and killing Frostes' – justly deserved punishments for sins.[63] Yet against the 'peccatogenic worldview', a developing scientific project began to explore predictive if not preventive responses to these natural phenomena, hinting at a human capacity to influence, rather than merely endure, climate change.[64] Acknowledging the social values promoting anthropogenic climate change in the period of colonial expansion encourages us to recognise 'unequal power relationships between different groups of people' and the means by which 'nature' and the bodies aligned with it were redistributed to advance patriarchal interests and assets.[65] Linda Williams has explored the ecology of mastery implicit in

Figure 5.3   Monument to Sir Richard and Katherine Leveson, attributed to Thomas Burman (*c.* 1661), St Michael's, Lilleshall (Shropshire). CC Attribution-Share Alike 3.0 Unported.

colonialism, arguing that the biological assumptions enabling the subjugation of naturally inferior 'tribal people' also inform the subordination of 'naturally inferior' women.[66] Although Chakrabarty's blending of human and non-human histories accords with the intertwining of body and environment in humoral framings of climate and gender, the political deployment of humoral theory is troubled by an essentialising dualism, in spite of the non-dualist materialism humoral theory implies. Humoral physiology separates Europeans from Amerindians, and sets men against women: in the phlegmatic mind-bodies of women, as Lina Perkins Wilder points out, memory can only 'repeat and valorize patriarchal hierarchy'.[67]

The Dudley women deploy the technologies of natural and cultural production – monumental and procreative, dynastic and charitable – to trouble the patriarchal redistribution of women as nature's agents. Their programme memorialises a strictly female household which includes two additional members. In 1661, Katherine Leveson was widowed without children. Her husband willed the creation of a joint monument in St Michael's, Lilleshall (Shropshire), where Katherine was buried in 1674 (see Figure 5.3). Katherine appears shrouded, like her mother and sisters, but posed in the toothache position mirroring her husband's.[68] Although Katherine shares her monument with her husband, her epitaph remembers the letters patent making her mother a duchess. The final link in this familial chain, Douglas Dudley, married William Dansey, to whom she bore three sons before her death in 1649. She is buried in St George's, Brinsop (Herefordshire) below a mural monument. Without a shrouded effigy, her epitaph nonetheless connects her to the Dudley matriarchy: 'Here lyeth the body of the Rt Hon. Ladie Douglas Dudley, wife unto Captain William Dansey ... who departed this life the 11 day of August, Anno Domini 1649.' In death, as in life, she remained a Dudley woman.[69]

We might imagine that the accidental fates of the Dudley daughters as mothers – one dying single, three widowed without children – accounts for the feminine household they construct in their shared afterlife. Situating their lives in the material conditions of the parish where they were raised, however, reveals that, despite their class, the Dudley daughters were influenced by the changing conditions of marriage and maternity that affected poor and middling women living through climate change. As Parker puts it, 'women, whether free or unfree, suffered disproportionately in most parts of the world'.[70] A fall in temperature of 1 degree Celsius, he demonstrates, corresponds to an equal decline in fertility, while malnutrition, scarcity, and disease contributed to high rates of maternal and infant mortality and stillbirths. 'Periods of adversity', Parker writes, 'produced both biological and behavioural responses that dramatically reduced fertility: more spontaneous abortions and fewer conceptions (sometimes because ovulation has ceased), decreased libido, a rise in age of menarche, and a fall in age of menopause'.[71] Socially, later marriages, often due to financial constraints, decreased the number of births: the average age of marriage for women increased from 20 in the sixteenth century to 27 a century later. Amid the economic challenges that attended the LIA, fewer women married: by the 1630s, one in four women remained single.[72]

The great majority of recipients of poor relief in the parish of St Giles in the Fields were women. Without the advantage that apprenticeship may have afforded men, poor women were often without any means of support. Some ended up in 'the Cage', a semi-permanent prison, 'and to judge from the churchwarden's accounts', John Parton writes, 'with no great lenity'. Support extended to women in the Cage included:

1641. Pd. To a poor woman who was brought to bed in the cage ... 2 s. od.
_____. For a shroud for a poor woman that dyed in the cage ... 2s. 6d.
1648 (July 9.) To Ann Wyatt in the cage, to relieve her and buy her a truss
    of straw ... 1s. 6d.
1648 (July 12.) Paid for a shroud for Ann Wyatt ... 2s. 6d.[73]

Although the Cage was replaced by almshouses in 1656, churchwardens reported fifty years later that poor relief cost the parish £3,300 annually.[74]

The Dudley women's rank shielded them from the brutalities of poor women's lives in the parish. Yet their marital careers parallel those of poorer women. Of the four Dudley daughters who married, only one was under 30: Frances was 31, as was Katherine. Anne married at 27. In 1637, Katherine Leigh bequeathed £100 to her granddaughter 'Douglas Dudley', suggesting Douglas was still single. If so, she married in her late thirties and bore three children before her death at 49.[75] These circumstances may reflect the financial hardship besetting Alice Dudley after her husband's departure from England. When her single daughter Alicia made her will at the age of 21, two years before she died, she bequeathed most of her legacy, £3,000, to her mother's management, precisely forbidding 'my said honourable ffather, hys Executors, nor assignee, nor any persons whatsoever that shall, or may, henceforth ... clayme any interest or pretend any right' to her estate.[76] Alicia and her mother must have had cause for concern. As Dugdale reports, the king's letters patent two decades later were granted 'partly in consideration of the greate losses which Sir Robert Dudley had, by his departure out of England (for he sold Kennillworth-Castle and other great possessions to Prince Henry, and never received anything of moment for it)'.[77] By Act of Parliament, three months before Alicia's death, Alice sold her jointure of Kenilworth woods for £4,000.[78]

These are sizeable amounts, yet during negotiations of Katherine's marriage in 1629, she was called upon to defend herself and her mother against charges that they had inflated her dowry. Lands to the value of £32,000, she writes to Leveson, are pending the outcome of lawsuits in the Chancery court. Katherine claims she is promised 'a thousand pound in preasent' by 'my La: grandmother', Katherine Leigh, as 'a token of hir loue, allthough not worth the naming for a porsion'.[79] If Katherine is to be believed, money was not at issue in the Dudley daughters' courtships, yet cash in hand seems tentative and may have delayed their marriages. A second obstacle may have been reputation: the vexed admixture of blood and rank that conferred nobility.

The Dudley monuments reimagine the traditional iconography of women's memorial sculpture to move away from rooting femininity in procreation, advancing instead autonomous female subjects who destabilise the ecology

Figure 5.4   Monument to Rachel Gee by William Wright (1649/50), All Saints, Bishop Burton, East Riding. Photo Credit: David Ross/Britain Express.com. Used by permission.

of mastery. The shrouded effigy most often appeared on women's monuments, commemorating the separation of wives and mothers from family, particularly young children, left behind.[80] The Dudley women both exploit and depart from these conventional associations. William Wright's monument for Rachel Gee (see Figure 5.4), created just before he carved Dudley's Stoneleigh tomb, poignantly depicts a mournful toddler at the head of his shrouded mother: Rachel died aged 18 leaving behind a 2-year-old son.[81] The Dudley women's commissions unsettle this model of maternal commemoration, eliding marriage and motherhood to memorialise instead the resonant connections between single women – affiliations so infrequently memorialised in the early modern period. The two shrouded effigies planned for St Giles immortalise sisters, while Stoneleigh presents mother and daughter in Christian sisterhood; two Alices joined in sleep. The toddlers on these monuments are putti, holding back the mantle to discover the scene, trumpeting their subjects' fame. By repurposing the imagery of maternal mortality, the Dudley women redefine the somatic as a social performance.

The monument for Sarah Latch, erected in 1644 (see Figure 5.5), strikingly illustrates the family values that the Dudley women refuse.[82] Sarah's impenetrable stone shroud is disturbed only by her husband's lifting the

Figure 5.5   Monument to Sarah Latch (*c.* 1644), St John the Baptist, Churchill
(Somerset). © Mike Searle, CC BY-SA 2.0.

winding sheet to reveal her face to his eyes alone. Sarah remains concealed and confined, even in death, by the protection of the patriarchal household that the monument commemorates. The Dudley women, denied this protection in their lifetimes, evade its confinement in death. By lying prone and vulnerable before the viewer, the Dudley women boldly exclude themselves from the home economics of patriarchy to create an alternative household ruled by women. Their finely carved effigies are portraits, refusing the erasure that death – or marriage – may demand.

The Dudley women's monuments defy the economics of women's lives and deaths and the ecology of dominance that so reduced their fortunes. They offer the vulnerability and resilience of memorialisation as an allegory for communal responses to climate change, and they indict, rather than valorise, the unequal power relations of colonial prerogative to shape continents, parishes, households, or tombs. Exploiting visual iteration and textual repetition – strategies central to memorialisation – the Dudley women perform powerful, autonomous acts of memory, precisely embedded in body and place. Their ecology weaves together the politics of colonialism and climate, gender and memory, dynasty and devotion.

The Dudley women's memory work, like the Anthropocene – and like climate itself – is local and global, retrospective and anticipatory. Parochialising the fatal synergies of climate, memory, and mortality reveals how easily the Anthropocene maps onto Christian teleology, from Eden to the Apocalypse, and unearths the eschatology informing both early modern and twenty-first-century views of climate change and its apocalyptic futures. Embraced by this narrative, at ease and at rest, the Dudley women memorialise the female body in its somatic integrity and social agency. They ask us to remember a female family, lingering between the mortal climates of earth and the universal calm where they will awaken, and together rise.

Notes

1 George Montaigne (or Mountain), quoted in John Parton, *Some Account of the Hospital and Parish Church of St Giles in the Fields* (London: Luke Hansard, 1822), p. 193. Parton erroneously attributes the letter to George Abbot: for correction, see Rowland Dobie, *History of the United Parishes of St Giles in the Fields and St George Bloomsbury* (London: printed for the author, 1829), pp. 94–5.
2 See Parton, *Some Account*.
3 Dagomar Degroot, 'Climate Change and Society in the 15th to 18th Centuries', *Wiley Interdisciplinary Reviews: Climate Change*, 9.3 (May/June 2018), 2. https://doi.org/10.1002/wcc.518.
4 Geoffrey Parker, *Global Crisis: War, Climate Change and Catastrophe in the Seventeenth Century*, abr. and rev. (New Haven, CT, and London: Yale University Press, 2017), p. 3.
5 Montaigne, quoted in Parton, *Some Account*, p. 194.
6 Camden Local Studies and Archives, P/GF, St Giles in the Fields 'Minutes of the Vestry, 1618–1900', quoted in Parton, *Some Account*, p. 195.
7 Linda Williams, 'The Anthropocene and the Long Seventeenth Century, 1550–1750', in Tom Bristow and Thomas H. Ford, eds., *A Cultural History of Climate Change* (London: Routledge, 2016), p. 99.
8 Robert Boreman, *A Mirror of Christianity and a Miracle of Charity* (London: E. C. for Robert Royston, 1669), p. 21.
9 William Laud, as Bishop of London, consecrated the church in 1630.
10 Quoted in Parton, *Some Account*, p. 202.
11 Garrett A. Sullivan, Jr., *Memory and Forgetting in English Renaissance Drama* (Cambridge: Cambridge University Press, 2005), pp. 1–25.
12 John Sutton, 'Spongy Brains and Material Memories', in Mary Floyd-Wilson and Garrett A. Sullivan, Jr., eds., *Environment and Embodiment in Early Modern England* (Basingstoke: Palgrave, 2007), p. 16. On climatic humoralism, see Mary Floyd-Wilson, *English Ethnicity and Race in Early Modern Drama* (Cambridge: Cambridge University Press, 2003). On women's limited cognitive capacity due to their phlegmatic natures, see Sullivan, *Memory and Forgetting*, pp. 26–47.

13 Elizabeth M. DeLoughrey, *Allegories of the Anthropocene* (Durham, NC: Duke University Press, 2019), p. 36.

14 Parker, *Global Crisis*, pp. xiv–xv.

15 See Bruno Latour, *Politics of Nature: How to Bring the Sciences into Democracy*, trans. by Catherine Porter (Cambridge, MA: Harvard University Press, 2004), p. 21: 'Nature is not in question in ecology: on the contrary, ecology dissolves nature's contours and redistributes its agents'.

16 Donna Haraway, *The Companion Species Manifesto: Dogs, People, and Significant Otherness* (Chicago: Prickly Paradigm Press, 2003), p. 1.

17 Simon Adams, 'Sir Robert Dudley (1574–1649)', in *ODNB*, https://doi .org/10.1093/ref:odnb/8161.

18 William Dugdale, 'Dugdale's Account of Duchess Dudley', *The Gentleman's Magazine* (April 1820), 311.

19 Dugdale, 'Dugdale's Account', p. 310.

20 Boreman, *Mirror of Christianity*, p. 25; and Add MS 12514, fol. 277, 'Order of the proceeding to the funerall of the Lady of the Lady Alice, Dutchesse Dudley, 16 Martii, 1668'. TNA PROB 11/329/325, 'Will of Lady Alicia Duches Duddeley', 9 March 1669, calls these mourners 'poore old women'.

21 William Dugdale, *Diary*, in William Hamper, ed., *The Life, Diary and Correspondence of Sir William Dugdale, Knight* (London: Harding and Lepard, 1827), p. 131.

22 Boreman, *Mirror of Christianity*, p. 26; and TNA PROB 11/329/25, 'Will of Lady Alicia Duches Duddeley'. Dugdale, 'Dugdale's Account', p. 310, says the monument was built twenty years before the Duchess's death and cost 'neare four hundred pounds'.

23 Parker, *Global Crisis*, pp. xiv–xv.

24 Parker, *Global Crisis*, p. 11.

25 Degroot, 'Climate Change', p. 2.

26 Parker, *Global Crisis*, p. 11.

27 Parker, *Global Crisis*, p. xv.

28 Simon L. Lewis and Mark A. Maslin, 'Defining the Anthropocene', *Nature*, 159 (March 2015), 174. Alfred W. Crosby, *Ecological Imperialism* (Cambridge: Cambridge University Press, 1986) coined the term 'Columbian Exchange'.

29 Lewis and Maslin, 'Defining the Anthropocene', pp. 174–6.

30 Williams, 'The Anthropocene', p. 100.

31 Lewis and Maslin, 'Defining the Anthropocene', p. 176.

32 Dipesh Chakrabarty, 'The Climate of History: Four Theses', *Critical Inquiry*, 35 (2009), 201.

33 'Parishes: Stoneleigh', in L. F. Salzman, ed., *A History of the County of Warwick: Volume 6, Knightlow Hundred* (London: Victoria County History, 1951), pp. 229–40. See *British History Online*, www.british-history.ac.uk/vch/ warks/vol6/pp229-240.

34 Warwickshire Record Office, 'Warwickshire, England, Church of England Baptisms, Marriages, and Burials, 1535–1812: Stoneleigh, 1616–1699', fols. 9, 16, and 19, 'Lady Alice Dutchesse Duddeley was bur. March 20'.

35 Thomas Dekker (attrib.), *The Great Frost. Cold Doings in London* (London: Henry Gosson, 1608), B4^v.

36 Dekker, *The Great Frost*, C1^r.

37 *Weatherweb, Weather in History, 1650–1669 AD*, https://premium.weatherweb .net/weather-in-history-1650-to-1699-ad/.

38 See Shakespeare Birthplace Trust, Cat. DR18/2/82, 'Acquittance of William Wright of London, March 27, 1655'.

39 See Neil Cummins, Morgan Kelly, and Connor Ó Gráda, 'Living Standards and Plague in London, 1550–1665', *Economic History Review*, 59 (2016), 12–13.

40 Dekker, *The Great Frost*, B4^v.

41 Dugdale, 'Dugdale's Account', p. 310.

42 Georgina H. Endfield, 'Exploring Particularity: Vulnerability, Resilience, and Memory in Climate Change Discourses', *Environmental History*, 19.2 (April 2014), 305–6.

43 Dekker, *The Great Frost*, C1^v–C2^r.

44 Dekker, *The Great Frost*, C2^r.

45 Thomas Dekker, *The Cold Year 1614* (London: W. W. for Thomas Langley, 1615).

46 See Cummins, Kelly, and Ó Gráda, 'Living Standards'.

47 Dekker, *The Great Frost*, B3^r.

48 Parton, *Some Account*, p. 265.

49 Dobie, *History*, p. 112; and Cummins, Kelly, and Ó Gráda, 'Living Standards', pp. 18–19.

50 Parker, *Global Crisis*, pp. xxi and 73.

51 Dobie, *History*, p. 42; and Mike Hulme, 'Climate', in Bruce R. Smith, ed., *The Cambridge Guide to the Worlds of Shakespeare, Shakespeare's World, 1500–1660*, 2 vols. (Cambridge: Cambridge University Press, 2016), I:33.

52 Grant Williams, 'Monumental Memory and Little Reminders: The Fantasy of Being Remembered by Posterity', in Andrew Hiscock and Lina Perkins Wilder, eds., *The Routledge Handbook of Shakespeare and Memory* (London: Routledge, 2018), pp. 297–311.

53 Boreman, *Mirror of Christianity*, pp. 25–6.

54 Quoted in Dobie, *History*, p. 99. Ann donated £6; Frances £4.

55 Edward Hatton, *A New View of London*, 2 vols. (London: R. Chiswell and A. and J. Churchill, 1708), II:283.

56 TNA PROB 11/312/122, 'Will of Anne Holburne', 27 August 1663.

57 Parker, *Global Crisis*, p. 51.

58 Parker, *Global Crisis*, pp. 72–3, shows that a fall of 1 degree C coincides with a 2 per cent increase in mortality, attributable to cardiovascular disease caused by cold temperatures, ill-effects of smoke from coal fires on cardiac and respiratory systems, and weakened bodily defences against disease.

59 Dobie, *History*, p. 128.

60 Dobie, *History*, p. 112.

61 Quoted in Parton, *Some Account*, pp. 313–14.

62 Boreman, *Mirror of Christianity*, pp. 10–11.

63 Dekker, *Cold Year*, B1ʳ.
64 See Degroot, 'Climate Change', p. 7; and Parker, *Global Crisis*, pp. 9–12.
65 Lewis and Maslin, 'Defining the Anthropocene', p. 176.
66 Williams, 'The Anthropocene', p. 102.
67 See Lina Perkins Wilder, 'Veiled Memory Traces in *Much Ado About Nothing*, *Pericles* and *The Winter's Tale*', in Hiscock and Wilder, eds., *Routledge Handbook*, p. 239.
68 On this 'toothache' pose, which reflected both the funeral decorum and aesthetic predisposition of such monuments during the early modern period, see Chapter 9 'The Unton Portrait Reconsidered' by Peter Sherlock, and Chapter 12 '"Superfluous Men" and the Graveyard Politics of *The Duchess of Malfi*' by Michael Neill.
69 Jackson Joseph Howard, *Miscellanea Genealogica et Heralidica*, 3rd series, vol. 4 (London: Hamilton, Adams, and Co., 1902), p. 283.
70 Parker, *Global Crisis*, p. 498.
71 Parker, *Global Crisis*, pp. 77–8.
72 Parker, *Global Crisis*, p. 78.
73 Parton, *Some Account*, p. 228.
74 Parton, *Some Account*, p. 310.
75 TNA PROB 11/182/163, 'Will of Dame Katherine Leigh', dated 10 February 1637; proved 8 February 1640.
76 TNA PROB 11/138/369, 'Will of Alicia Dudley', 7 November 1621.
77 Dugdale, 'Dugdale's Account', p. 310.
78 George Adlard, *Amye Robsart and the Earl of Leycester* (London: John Russell Smith, 1870), pp. 239–40.
79 Staffordshire and Stoke on Trent Record Office, Cat. D868/2/4, Katherine Dudley to Richard Leveson, c. 1628. In 1640, Katherine Leigh bequeathed £3,100 to her daughter and £100 to each granddaughter: see TNA PROB 11/182/163, 'Will of Dame Katherine Leigh'. Thomas Leigh died in 1626, leaving his estate to male heirs while his daughter received 'the best Bason and Ewer ... as a token of [his] love for hir'. See TNA PROB 11/149/258, 'Will of Sir Thomas Leigh', 24 May 1626.
80 Judith W. Hurtig, 'Seventeenth-Century Shroud Tombs: Classical Revival and Anglican Context', *The Art Bulletin*, 64.2 (July 1982), 217–28.
81 Joseph Foster, ed., *The Pedigrees of the County Families of Yorkshire*, 3 vols. (London: W. Wilfred Head, 1874), III:n.p.
82 Sarah and Thomas Latch were married for thirty-five years: see Edward Dwelly, ed., *Dwelly's Parish Records* (London: E. Dwelly, 1864), p. 284.

CHAPTER 6

Scattered Bones, Martyrs, Materiality, and Memory in Drayton and Milton

Philip Schwyzer

My starting point is John Milton's 18th sonnet, 'On the Late Massacre in Piedmont'. Written in May or June 1655, the poem responds to the slaughter of more than a thousand members of the Waldensian religious community in April of that year. Milton, echoing the graphic reports in newsbooks, denounces the appalling acts of violence committed by the Catholic forces of the Duke of Savoy; his attention is more closely fixed, however, on the human remains that, a month after the massacre, he pictures still scattered on the mountainside.[1]

> Avenge O Lord thy slaughter'd Saints, whose bones
>   Lie scatter'd on the Alpine mountains cold,
>   Ev'n them who kept thy truth so pure of old
>   When all our Fathers worship't Stocks and Stones,
> Forget not: in thy book record their groanes
>   Who were thy Sheep and in their antient Fold
>   Slayn by the bloody Piemontese that roll'd
>   Mother with Infant down the Rocks. Their moans
> The Vales redoubl'd to the Hills, and they
>   To Heav'n. Their martyr'd blood and ashes sow
>   O're all th'Italian fields where still doth sway
> The triple Tyrant: that from these may grow
>   A hunder'd-fold, who having learnt thy way
>   Early may fly the Babylonian wo.[2]

The sonnet propounds a familiar opposition between the 'pure' religion of Protestants and a corrupt Catholicism distracted and preoccupied by material objects and images. The Waldensians, whose distinctive religious beliefs and practices were understood to date back at least to the twelfth century (and were regarded by some as preserving the genuine apostolic faith), are credited with having 'kept thy truth so pure of old / When all our Fathers worship't Stocks and Stones'.[3] The 'Stocks and Stones' connote medieval images of saints, fashioned of wood and stone, to which Milton's English readers' ancestors bowed down in the blindness of their superstition; they may also suggest pagan idols worshipped in Britain in the distant apostolic era. Echoing denunciations of idol-worship in the Books of Jeremiah and Ezekiel, the phrase works here as in many Protestant polemics as shorthand for the errors of both Catholics and Gentiles who seek the sacred in material forms.

Yet in Sonnet 18, the conventional opposition between Protestant purity and Catholic idolatry and backsliding is troubled from the start by the poem's fascination with the material remains of the slaughtered Waldensians. The rhyme scheme of the first quatrain, introducing the haunting series of long o'es that runs throughout the sonnet, sets up an association between the scattered 'bones' of the victims and the 'Stones' venerated by Catholic idol-worshippers. Protestant readers would not have been surprised to find 'Stocks and Stones' paired with 'bones' in a rhyming list, but some would certainly have been taken aback at Milton's handling of the pairing. The different objects frequently appeared together in denunciations of Catholic idolatry: 'to giue ... honour to Angels and Saints, to Idols and Images, to stocks and stones, to blockes & Bones'; 'Angels, Saints, stocks, stones, and rotten bones'; 'to pray to stocks and stones, reliques and bones, as the Papists do'.[4] Towards the end of the century Thomas D'Urfey wrote mockingly of 'Your Worshiping of Stocks and Stones, / And bringing Life back with Saints Bones'.[5] In verse and even in prose, the irresistible rhyme of 'stones' and 'bones' works easily to confirm their equivalency as 'dead things', hollow idols resounding with long o'es in their spiritual emptiness. Milton's apparent determination to set the rhyme words in opposition, privileging poignant 'bones' over superstitious 'stones', runs athwart a powerful current in Protestant literature.

The sonnet's opening lament that the bones of the 'Saints ... Lie scatter'd' similarly seems to set itself at cross-purposes with Protestant tradition. Scattering the bones of saints was nothing short of a foundational Reformation activity. Reporting on the destruction of St Swithin's shrine at Winchester in 1538, commissioner Thomas Wriothesley declared his intention 'to sweep away all the rotten bones that be called relics; which we may not omit lest it should be thought we came more for the treasure than for avoiding of the abomination of idolatry'.[6] Scattering rotten remains might be a dirty job, but it was necessary as a rebuke to the idolaters, those worshippers of stocks, stones, and bones. While the actual fate of the relics of St Thomas Becket remains a mystery, the report that his bones had been burnt 'and the ashes scattered to the wind' became a defining image of the Henrician Reformation.[7] Nor was the work of scattering finished with the destruction of saints' shrines in the early years of the Reformation.

Precisely 114 years after Wriothesley's visit to Winchester, Parliamentary forces ransacked several tombs in the Cathedral, 'scatter[ed] their bones all over the pavement of the Church', and, by report, used 'the bones of Kings, Queens Bishops, Confessors and Saints' as missiles to break the offending picture windows.[8] Extreme and distasteful as such actions might be, they were in line with and affirmed the fundamental Protestant understanding that bones were not people, and that sympathy with dead human matter could mark the perilous first step on the path to idolatry. Catholic writers who throughout the period expressed horror at such 'Cruell Graverooters' for 'disparsing the bones and reliques of holie sainctes' were responding just as the emptiers of shrines and coffins anticipated and hoped.[9]

The octave of Milton's sonnet thus presents a cluster of images which are entirely at home and conventional in Protestant polemics against idolatry and the cult of saints. Yet rather than letting these images work in concord, he makes them poles of opposition. Rather than serving as emblems of superstition, the scattered bones of the saints (relics in all but name) represent the victims of and an enduring rebuke to the sin of idolatry. Later in the sonnet, Milton effectively weaponizes human remains and grants them sacred force in the form of 'martyred blood and ashes' to be sprinkled over Italy. This ostensibly anti-Catholic poem thus veers brazenly and repeatedly towards the language of Catholic relic veneration.[10]

Has Milton somehow lost his way? Critics are generally agreed that Milton in this sonnet never veers into outright papistry – any lapses from Protestant orthodoxy, if they exist, lean instead towards the doctrines of Mortalism and perhaps Traducianism, as Timothy Burbery argues.[11] But what prompted Milton to write in terms so intensely redolent of Catholic practice? Does Milton here, as Kathryn Gail Brock suggests, deploy 'language and imagery shared by Catholic and Protestant polemicists' in order to set the reader the faith-affirming challenge of sorting the Protestant truth from the lexically identical Catholic heresy?[12] Building on Brock's argument, is it possible to read the sonnet as a sort of *Paradise Lost* in miniature, leading the reader from the initial attraction of sin (aren't martyrs awfully poignant, and aren't their bones worthy of reverence?) to a recognition of its foulness?

Though such a reading is attractive, it doesn't seem to me that the poem's intense engagement with blood, bones, and ashes can be dismissed as merely a test or a feint, a step towards a clearer (more allegorical) understanding in which bones, *qua* matter, can never really matter. Milton, I will suggest, is genuinely concerned with unburied human remains, both as objects arousing pity, and as capable of a kind of material efficacy.

Moreover, he is aware of writing in a Protestant poetic tradition that acknowledged scattered bones as things of power, capable of soliciting both human and supernatural action. This essay will seek to contextualize Milton's sonnet alongside earlier poems which deal with the veneration of relics and the wider problem of loose and disarticulated bone in a post-Reformation context, focusing in particular on agricultural images of the 'scattering', 'gathering', and 'sowing' of human remains.

Michael Drayton and the Martyrs' Scattered Bones

Problematic as it was, reverence towards the physical remains of Protestant martyrs was not unprecedented in English poetry. A passage with intriguing resemblances to Milton's sonnet occurs in Michael Drayton's *Englands Heroicall Epistles*, first printed in 1597. Modelled on Ovid's *Heroides*, the *Heroicall Epistles* are verse letters imagined to have been sent between men and women from English history, ranging from the mid-twelfth century to the mid-sixteenth. The majority of these lovers, having died before the Reformation, are quite naturally Catholics, and it is arguably with an eye to historical verisimilitude that Drayton gives some of them a keen interest in holy relics, saints, and shrines.[13] The collection concludes, however, with two undoubted Protestants, Lady Jane Grey and her husband Guildford Dudley, whose letters are exchanged shortly before their execution in 1554, in the reign of Mary. Having acknowledged that she neither sought nor had a rightful claim to the throne, Jane Grey thanks heaven for granting her and her husband 'glorious martirdome' before they are forced to witness the revival of 'all Idolatry, and sinne' under Mary and the persecution of the faithful:

> When tiranny, new tortures shall inuent,
> Inflicting vengeance on the innocent.
> Yet heauen forbids, that Maries wombe shall bring,
> Englands faire Scepter to a forraine King,
> But vnto faire Elizabeth shall leaue it,
> Which broken, hurt, and wounded, shall receaue it:
> And on her temples hauing plac'd the Crowne,
> Roote out the dregs Idolatry hath sowne;
> And Syons glory shall againe restore,
> Layd ruine, wast, and desolate before:
> And from black sinders, and rude heapes of stones,
> Shall gather vp the Martirs scattered bones,
> And shall exterpe the power of Rome againe,
> And cast aside, the heauy yoake of Spaine.[14]

The resemblances between this passage and Milton's Sonnet 18 include many of the conventional tropes and manoeuvres of anti-Catholic polemic (hints of strange tortures; the slaughter of innocents; charges of idolatry and tyranny; nationalization of the conflict through reference to Italy; calls for and expectation of divine intervention), but they go well beyond these. Both poems refer to the scattered bones of Protestant martyrs; both look forward to redemption arising from the martyrs' ashes or cinders; both also include distinctive images of sowing, botanic growth, and failed or foiled motherhood. They share a similar temporal situation and movement, looking forward from a present characterized by persecution and slaughter to a future in which the martyrs' remains will play a role in the fight-back against Catholic oppression. Although my wider argument does not rest on Milton having read and remembered this passage in *Heroicall Epistles*, the resemblances are strong enough to warrant the suspicion that he did.

There are also some significant differences between the passages. Whereas Milton, as we have seen, aligns his images of sowing, growth, and motherhood with the pure faith of the Waldensians, for Drayton these are all associated with Catholicism, a confession of perverse and failed fertility. Writing in the reign and in the praise of a virgin queen, Drayton's Protestantism is more chastely associated with images of cleansing, gathering, and ordering. Furthermore, where Milton's poem conveys a steady centrifugal movement, with the remains that have already been scattered on the mountains finally being sown still further across the Italian fields, in Jane Grey's epistle the movement is centripetal: that which has been scattered will be gathered together, that which has been sown will be weeded out. Drayton, outlining a policy programme within the capacity of a human monarch, describes victory in terms of restoration and curation, rather than the miraculous, transformative harvest brought forth by Milton's God.

In Drayton's epistle, as in Milton's sonnet, the clear opposition between Protestant purity and Catholic idolatry is troubled if not undermined by the reverential reference to the relics of Protestant martyrs. The promised gathering of the 'Martirs scattered bones' is all the more surprising given that nothing of the kind seems to have taken place in Elizabeth's reign. Protestant thought on martyrdom and relics offers essentially no backing for the consummation anticipated by Jane Grey. As Susannah Brietz Monta has shown, John Foxe's understanding of martyrs and martyrdom had much in common with Catholic models but departed from them entirely on the matter of relics.[15] At no point does there seem to have been an organized or sanctioned effort to gather up the bones of Marian martyrs such as Cranmer,

Latimer, and Ridley. There were, to be sure, stories of pieces of their burnt
bodies being seized by Protestant onlookers as relics at the scene of execution, but the fact that these accounts were swiftly seized upon by Catholic
polemicists as evidence of Protestant hypocrisy can only have served as an
additional deterrent to any subsequent attempt to gather up the bones of the
martyrs.[16] As for Jane Grey herself, she was known to have been buried along
with Guildford Dudley in the chapel of the Tower of London in 1550, in an
unmarked grave; her bones were not scattered or in need of regathering, nor
were they moved or interfered with in Elizabeth's reign. Although the rest
of Jane Grey's prediction is reliably prophetic of the Elizabethan present in
which it is written – and could be compared to numerous similar prophecies
in history plays by Shakespeare and others – her expectations regarding the
reassembly of martyrs' remains seem to have gone unfulfilled.

   Where Drayton seems to lapse into confusion or self-contradiction,
critics do not automatically leap to the assumption that he is really doing
something awfully clever. Coming from the hand of a Spenser or a Milton,
Jane Grey's talk of martyrs and their bones might be interpreted as a deftly
ironic touch, signalling to the reader that for all her zeal and innocence,
she has not fully grasped the tenets of the reformed faith. Drayton was
certainly capable of such irony, yet in this case it seems likely that Jane's
muddled hopes for a Protestant relic collection are his as well. Drayton
saw himself as a militant Protestant, not least as a point of national and
political honour, but much of his work is suffused with nostalgia for the
medieval world. He had an enduring interest in and attachment to the
relic cults of medieval England, especially where the saints in question
were also English heroes, and pilgrimage could be interpreted as an expression of patriotic devotion. His *Poly-Olbion* features a number of laments
for lost tombs and shrines, including two instances where he recycles Jane
Grey's rhyme of 'bones' with 'heapes of stones':

> This King, even in that place, where with rude heapes of stones
> The *Britains* had interr'd their Proto-martyrs bones ....

> So that the earth to feele the ruinous heapes of stones,
> That with the burth'nous weight now presse their sacred boanes ...[17]

These multiple reworkings of the same rhyming couplet seem to indicate a
certain stubborn fixation on an idea, if not an outright failure of original-
ity. Set beside each other, the two couplets from *Poly-Olbion*, both referring to St Albans, suggest a cycle of gathering and loss. Rescued from 'rude
heapes of stones' to be enshrined by King Offa in a newly constructed

monastery, Alban's bones and those of other English worthies find themselves again concealed under 'ruinous heaps of stones' when the monastery is dissolved during the Reformation. Similarly, in the case of Jane Grey, Drayton looks forward to a future turn of the wheel, when the martyrs' bones dispersed under heaps of stones will be regathered and installed in some sort of national shrine. This vision arguably has less to do with the sacred qualities of human remains than with a pragmatic understanding of how victors – great monarchs like Offa, Henry VIII, and Elizabeth – make use of old bones to signal the tone of a new regime. From antiquity to Drayton's era, and indeed our own, casting out the bones of the unworthy and enshrining those of the regime's heroes and putative antecedents serve as a way of marking both territory and time, equivalent to issuing a new coinage.

One way of reading Jane Grey's call for a gathering of the bones of the Protestant martyrs is as a response, even a riposte, to the Jesuit poet and martyr Robert Southwell. Southwell had been executed just two years before Drayton published *Heroicall Epistles* – and, as the martyr had foreseen, his reputed relics were already finding their way into the hands of recusants.[18] Several years earlier, in his *Epistle of Comfort*, Southwell had looked forward to a gathering in of the scattered bones of England's Catholic martyrs, very much along the lines of Jane Grey's prediction in Drayton's poem, though naturally with the sides reversed:

> I doubte not but eyther they or theyre posteritye shall see the verye prisons and places of execution, places of reuerence and great deuotion, and the scattered bones of these that in this cause haue suffered, which are now thoughte vnworthye of Christian burial, shrined in gold: when the prophane carcases of hereticks, now so costly enbalmed, shalbe esteemed more worthy of the martyrs present disgrace, & farr more vnworthy of such funerall solemnyties.[19]

Like Drayton's various pairings of 'bones' with 'heapes of stones', this passage hints at a potentially endless cycle of human remains shuffling in and out of honour as one confessional regime gives way to another. Yet while Southwell and Drayton both lament the abhorrent fact of the martyrs' bones being 'scattered', they don't seem to mean exactly the same thing by this term, or look forward to the same solution. For Drayton, on the one hand, 'scattered' means disaggregated and dispersed, a situation to be redeemed when the bones are 'gather[ed]' together, presumably for honourable burial. Southwell, on the other hand, looks forward to the relics being 'shrined in gold', which need not imply their being gathered in one place, and might rather suggest enshrinement of individual bones in separate golden reliquaries. As he makes plain in the same treatise, the power of relics is only enhanced by their dispersal: 'everye quarter, and parcell, yea everye dropp of bloode, is able to doe as much, and somtymes more forcible effectes, then the martyr himselfe, if he had remayned alyve'.[20] For Southwell, then, 'scattered' does not mean disaggregated so much as 'cast aside'; it bears on the honour or lack of it accorded to the bones, rather than their proximity to one another, and the solution to scattering may involve a still wider dispersal. In this respect, it is Southwell's quintessentially Catholic response to scattered bones rather than Drayton's Protestant one that finds the closer echo in Milton's sonnet.

Although the gathering of the bones in Jane Grey's epistle is clearly linked in some way to the triumph of true religion, the bones themselves are not described as relics or explicitly hailed as worthy of special veneration. This point holds true at least for the six editions of *Heroicall Epistles* printed in the reign of Elizabeth (1597, 1598, 1599, 1600, 1602, 1603), all of which refer to the 'martirs scattered bones'. In 1605 and after, however (that is to say, in the several editions published in the reign of James), Drayton revises the phrase to 'the martyrs sacred bones'.[21] On the face of it, the shift from 'scattered' to 'sacred' (the softer disyllable seeming to hatch from the longer word's hardened shell, in which it had lain nestled all along) makes the Catholic resonance of the passage even more difficult to ignore, as if Drayton were encroaching further on Southwell's territory and attributing real spiritual efficacy to the bones. Yet if the change in wording heightens the passage's rather queasy religiosity, it simultaneously robs it of a certain specific moral urgency. The revised phrase conveys a mood of sentimental nostalgia, rather than operating as a call to action, a call which Elizabeth ultimately did not (and could not) heed. As I shall argue in the next section of this chapter, 'The Valley of Dry Bones', the trope of scattered bones carries a peculiar force in early modern English literature, invoking at once the sacred and the sacrilegious, encapsulating an intolerable circumstance and an impossible demand.

The Valley of Dry Bones

In his Easter Day sermon of 1629, John Donne invoked the image of scattered bones when speaking of the types of resurrection:

> We celebrate this day, the Resurrection of our Lord and Saviour Christ Jesus, Blessed for ever; and in His, all ours; All, that is, the Resurrection of all Persons; All, that is, the Resurrection of all kinds, whether the Resurrection from calamities in this world, *Ezechiels* Resurrection, where God saies

to him, *Putasne vivent?* Son of man doest thou thinke, these scattered Bones can live againe?[22]

References to far-flung human remains and scattered dust are frequent in Donne's sermons and poems, irresistibly drawn as he was to the theme of corporeal recomposition on 'the last busy day'.[23] 'Where be all the splinters of that Bone, which a shot hath shivered and scattered in the Ayre? ... In what wrinkle, in what furrow, in what bowel of the earth, ly all the graines of the ashes of a body burnt a thousand years since?' '[L]egions of Angels, millions of Angels shall be employed about the Resurrection, to recollect their scattered dust, and recompact their ruined bodies.'[24] In this Easter sermon, however, his focus is not on the Last Day, but on an earlier example of bodily resurrection, the vision of the prophet Ezekiel in the valley of dry bones. The text is worth quoting at length in order to see how it was interpreted and augmented by Donne and other English preachers and writers of the seventeenth century:

> The hand of the Lord was upon me, and carried me out in the spirit of the Lord, and set me down in the midst of the valley which was full of bones,
>
> 2 And caused me to pass by them round about: and, behold, there were very many in the open valley; and, lo, they were very dry.
>
> 3 And he said unto me, Son of man, can these bones live? And I answered, O Lord God, thou knowest.
>
> 4 Again he said unto me, Prophesy upon these bones, and say unto them, O ye dry bones, hear the word of the Lord.
>
> 5 Thus saith the Lord God unto these bones; Behold, I will cause breath to enter into you, and ye shall live:
>
> 6 And I will lay sinews upon you, and will bring up flesh upon you, and cover you with skin, and put breath in you, and ye shall live; and ye shall know that I am the Lord.
>
> 7 So I prophesied as I was commanded: and as I prophesied, there was a noise, and behold a shaking, and the bones came together, bone to his bone.
>
> 8 And when I beheld, lo, the sinews and the flesh came up upon them, and the skin covered them above: but there was no breath in them.
>
> 9 Then said he unto me, Prophesy unto the wind, prophesy, son of man, and say to the wind, Thus saith the Lord God; Come from the four winds, O breath, and breathe upon these slain, that they may live.
>
> 10 So I prophesied as he commanded me, and the breath came into them, and they lived, and stood up upon their feet, an exceeding great army.[25]

God's work here is indeed miraculous – yet it is worth asking, in what exactly does the miracle consist? The vision begins in a valley full of bones which are exceedingly 'dry'; God probes Ezekiel's faith in asking whether such bones can 'live'. The larger miracle is accomplished in three steps:

firstly the joining of bone to bone (37:7), secondly, the restoration of muscle and flesh (37:8), and finally the restoration of life through divine breath (37:9–10). Taken together these wonders signify God's intention to reunite his people in the land of Israel (37:11–14). This surely, is miracle enough; yet it is worth emphasizing that nowhere does the biblical text specify that the bones in the valley are, as Donne puts it, 'scattered', in the sense of individual skeletons being dispersed over a wide area or intermixed with others. What is emphasized about the bones is simply that they are very numerous and 'very dry' – indicating that they have lost all connective tissue and are fully disarticulated. For St Jerome, this was compatible with an understanding of the valley as a cemetery where Ezekiel 'joins bones to bones and brings them forth from their sepulchres'.[26] Sixteenth and seventeenth-century artists on the Catholic continent reflected Jerome's understanding in representing the valley as a relatively orderly burial site. Thus in Giorgio Ghisi's engraving (1554) the bones awaiting enfleshment are neatly arranged, either as complete skeletons, or in rows of skulls and decorative clusters of long bones, as found in continental ossuaries; Francisco Collantes' *Vision of Ezekiel* (1630) likewise depicts the valley as an ancient cemetery, wherein the revived dead emerge from beneath tomb slabs or out of the earth itself.[27] The bones in these artworks are both dry and anonymous, but they are not disordered or out of place.

Even as he quotes the Vulgate, Donne smuggles an unwarranted English word into the third verse. '*Fili hominis putasne vivent ossa ista*': 'Son of man doest thou thinke, these *scattered* Bones can live againe? [emphasis added]'.[28] Donne's insertion augments and shifts the focus of the miracle, making it not only a matter of joining, enfleshment, and revivification, but also, perhaps even more importantly, a miracle of sorting and gathering. Numerous other English preachers and commentators in the seventeenth century did precisely the same. For these writers, the question posed and answered in the valley of dry bones was not only whether the dead can live, but whether what has been scattered may be gathered again. Calling upon the House of Lords to bring order and discipline to the Church, John White reminded them of 'the Prophet Ezechiel, in a vision of a Field full of dryed bones scattered all about, every bone out of his place, and sodainly, by a Word of the Prophets mouth, comming together'. Lamenting divisions within the Church on whether Christmas should be celebrated, John Reading complained 'we now seem like those dry and scattered bones in the Prophets vision, Ezek. 37'. The catechist Edward Boughen taught children to recite, 'We have Ezek. 37.1. where the dead, dry, scatter'd bones come together, bone to his bone'.[29] In the torn and fractious middle decades of the seventeenth century, the passage's perceived theme of miraculous gathering and binding undoubtedly held a powerful attraction. Yet as Donne's 1629 sermon among others demonstrates, well before the Civil War English Protestants were already conditioned to imagine the dry bones as strewn haphazardly across the valley.

Though English writers of the seventeenth century were not the first to imagine the dry bones of Ezekiel 37 as widely scattered, the remarkable consensus and undue emphasis on this interpretation demands some contextual explanation.[30] Writers and preachers like Donne and White fixated on the idea of scattered bones, I suggest, because such bones presented an unprecedented moral and practical problem in post-Reformation England. Both before and after the Reformation, the spectacle of 'bones ... scattered at the grave's mouth' (Ps. 141:7) would have been a common sight in English churchyards, whenever the preparation of a new grave entailed the disturbance of older remains. Yet whereas in the past such loose and anonymous fragments would have been transferred to an ossuary or charnel house, where they would remain in a consecrated setting and benefit from prayers said for the dead, this practice was widely abandoned when prayer for the dead was itself forbidden. In the short term, the Edwardian closure of charnel houses produced some brutal spectacles of performative disregard; in the longer term, it led to painful, recurring dilemmas over how to deal with superfluities of unhoused bone.[31] Although there is ample evidence that human instinct shuddered at the mistreatment or obvious neglect of human remains, even in fragmentary and anonymous form, powerful religious considerations militated against any form of reverence or ritual in dealing with them. The action that writers such as Donne ascribed to God in Ezekiel's vision, the sorting and gathering of bones into a meaningful order, came to be seen as miraculous because it was something English Protestants could no longer do for themselves.

For Shakespeare and Edmund Spenser, in a pair of strikingly similar passages, the spectacle of scattered bone resonates with themes of despair, spiritual vertigo, and isolation from God. Dreaming of drowning on the eve of his own death, Clarence in Shakespeare's *Richard III* describes a phantasmagoric vision of bones and treasure 'All scattered in the bottom of the sea' (1.4.28).[32] Gemstones twinkling in the empty eye sockets of skulls 'wooed the slimy bottom of the deep / And mocked the dead bones that lay scattered by' (1.4.32–33). In this nightmarishly lonely inversion of Ezekiel's vision, no God arrives to ask if these wet bones can live. The scattered bones, no less than the jewels, cry out to be gathered, but Clarence is powerless to comply, to turn away, or even to die. A strikingly similar tableau involving scattered bones, great wealth, and a powerless observer is presented in the second Book of Spenser's *Faerie Queene*. Entering the first chamber in the Cave of Mammon, Sir Guyon finds a room full of locked caskets containing (it is assumed) inestimable wealth:

> But all the grownd with sculs was scattered,
> And dead mens bones, which round about were flong,
> Whose liues, it seemed, whilome there were shed,
> And their vile carcases now left vnburied.   (2.7.30)[33]

Among the many temptations Guyon must face in Mammon's Cave, these scattered bones are perhaps the strangest and most haunting. The bones are the only visible temptation in the room, since the iron chests are barred and impossible to open. At first glance, these foul remnants of 'vile carcases' seem a world away from the glittering treasures Guyon will encounter further on in his journey through Mammon's underground realm. Yet the temptation they offer is the same: to sin by imputing transcendent value to earthly matter of no spiritual worth. If Guyon were to succumb to the human impulse to gather and honour the scattered skulls and bones, there is every reason to think that the fiend that stalks behind him throughout this episode would rend him instantly limb from limb, adding to the scattered spectacle.[34]

Neither in Clarence's dream nor in the Cave of Mammon do the bones of the dead belong to martyrs. Nevertheless, their scattered condition sets up a sense of poignancy, of frustrated desire, the simultaneous imperative and inability to do *something*. In both passages the observer is clearly prevented from intervening by strong external forces. In other circumstances we can only imagine that they would rush to aid the fallen – but what kind of aid could be offered to scattered bones that would not ensnare the doer in superstitious veneration of dead matter? As it is, they must leave redress in the hands of a deity who is conspicuously absent from the fantasized milieu.

Shakespeare and Spenser employed the trope of scattered bones to convey the agony of inaction in the face of an impossible demand. A more complex and challenging use of the trope involved combining the trope with an additional problem or challenge, one capable of resolution, to heighten the moral urgency of the latter. This would be one way of interpreting what happens in Jane Grey's epistle, where the unfulfilled longings stirred by the call to gather the martyrs' bones spill over into next couplet and heighten the imperative to extirpate the power of Rome. A further example occurs in one of Richard Crashaw's earliest poems, 'Upon the

Ensuing Treatises' (1635), written in praise of the Laudian campaign to restore the beauty of holiness to English churches:

> No longer shall our Churches frighted stones
> Lie scatter'd like the Burnt and Martyr'd bones
> Of dead Devotion; nor faint Marbles weep
> In their sad Ruines ...   (ll. 30–33)[35]

At first glance the poem seems to propose a simile between the stones of a damaged church and the burnt and scattered bones of martyrs. Yet in reading over the passage the remains of the dead seem to flicker and almost vanish before our eyes, as we note that these are not after all 'martyr's bones' but rather 'martyr'd bones'. If at first 'dead Devotion' strikes us as simply another way of saying 'dead martyrs', on closer inspection the phrase participates rather in a metaphor of the physical church as the body of devotion. The lines thus hover between the subordinated simile, 'the stones of a desecrated church are like the scattered bones of martyrs', and the dominant metaphor, 'the church is a body which may endure martyrdom and the scattering of its parts'. Only the simile, which emerges with immediate clarity in line 31 before blurring and partially dissolving into the metaphor in line 32, really involves the image of human remains; only fleetingly are the scattered bones of martyrs made present in the reader's imagination. The ambiguity preserves a measure of deniability, since the direct comparison of church masonry with martyrs' bones would involve Crashaw in the dangerous claim that the renovation of churches was a moral good akin to gathering and venerating relics. Yet even this tenuous reference to scattered bones serves to introduce a sense of intolerable scandal and an imperative which the beauty of holiness is able to respond to and resolve.

From Scattered to Sown

As the preceding discussion indicates, the opening reference in Milton's Sonnet 18 to 'saints, whose bones / Lie scatter'd' resonates with a history of English poets and writers grappling intently, and sometimes awkwardly, with the moral and theological problem of scattered bone. Milton could not fail to be aware that his references to saints' bones and martyred blood veered towards the language of Catholic relic veneration in a way that was bound to provoke the anxiety of the Protestant reader. More to the point, he was aware of how a series of English poets whose work he intensely admired had summoned images of scattered bone to crystallize problems at once incomparably urgent and difficult if not impossible of solution. Like Spenser, Shakespeare, and Crashaw, Milton introduces the trope of scattered bone precisely to summon a sense of insufferable scandal and moral imperative. Like Drayton and Southwell, he goes on to insist that the problem can only be resolved through regime change: in this case, the conversion of Italy. Like Donne, he knows that scattered bone is a matter for God alone. The specific brilliance of the solution Milton finds in Sonnet 18 lies in the way he sets the moral urgency of scattered bone at the service of a larger issue whilst refusing to allegorize away the specific poignancy of human remains, achieving a resolution in which dead matter is simultaneously venerated and made to disappear.

Gordon Teskey has described Milton's treatment of the corpses of the massacred Waldensians as 'cold and efficient', arguing that the poet is 'instinctively disinclined to linger on the pathos or the outrage of the scene because it is, after all, over …'.[36] In different ways this strikes me as both right and wrong. Milton does seem to be moved less by the deaths of the Waldensians than by the hope that God will be moved by them. Their remains are introduced not as objects of human pity but as a rhetorical device addressed to the divine being who alone has the authority to resolve the problem of scattered bone, as he did with Ezekiel in the valley.[37] The task must be left in God's hands, for any human effort to bring order and meaning out of a scattering of bones risks falling into the same idolatry, the worship of 'Stocks and Stones [and bones]', that animates the enemy. Yet whilst Milton's rhetorical plea to the deity is expertly and efficiently crafted, it does not entirely exhaust his poetic interest in the remains of the Waldensians. Having seen the likes of Drayton and Crashaw pull off similar manoeuvres with scattered bones, deploying their insistent pathos for rhetorical effect to serve a larger cause, Milton grasps the point that when human remains are used in this way, they still persist as an unresolved remainder. (Yes, some part of the reader's mind will whisper, true religion has triumphed – but the bones are still scattered on the mountainside.) He resolves the problem of the remainder by choosing to hear the silent plea of scattered bones – traditionally understood as a demand to be 'gathered up', reunited, joined together – as a plea instead to be scattered still more widely, to be sown.

Milton's closing injunction to God, 'Their martyr'd blood and ashes sow / O're all th'*Italian* fields', echoes the Tertullian maxim often translated as 'the blood of the martyrs is the seed of the church'.[38] The sentiment appealed powerfully to early modern Catholics and Protestants alike, though of course the latter would claim to understand the wonder-working capacities of blood in purely figurative terms.[39] Milton's assertions about blood and ashes in this sonnet are, of course, primarily metaphorical. He is not saying that hearts and minds will be changed when particulate human matter falls over Liguria and Tuscany in a light rain, but that the example of the Waldensians' martyrdom will hasten the conversion of Italy. Yet while we know it is a figure of speech, it is remarkably difficult not to imagine the blood and ashes in physical terms. We are apt to do so for at least two reasons: firstly, because the poem has already required us to dwell on the image of the actual material remains of the Waldensians (their scattered bones), and secondly because the trajectory involved in this sowing of blood and ash, from a higher altitude to a contiguous lower one, is exactly what might be accomplished through the natural forces of wind and rain. The blood and ashes, then, are metaphors that we cannot help imagining as real. And by this point in the poem, the scattered bones of the Waldensians, that at the start of the sonnet seemed irreducibly real and physical, have taken on the same hybrid quality. Their scattering now strikes us as a prefiguration of the greater sowing, and in the final lines they are caught up in the centrifugal rush, travelling out over the Italian fields. At the close of Milton's sonnet, the mountainsides are clean.

Notes

1 On echoes of news reports in the sonnet, see Elizabeth Sauer, *Milton, Toleration, and Nationhood* (Cambridge: Cambridge University Press, 2013), pp. 71–72.

2 John Milton, 'On the Late Massacher in Piemont', in *The Complete Works of John Milton, Vol. 3: The Shorter Poems*, ed. by Barbara Kiefer Lewalski and Estelle Haan (Oxford: Oxford University Press, 2012), p. 245.

3 On the disputed antiquity and continuity of the Waldensian communities, see Stefano Villani, 'The British Invention of the Waldenses', in *Remembering the Reformation*, ed. by Alexandra Walsham, Brian Cummings, Ceri Law, and Karis Riley (London: Routledge, 2020). On Milton's interest in and knowledge of them, see William B. Hunter, Jr., 'Milton and the Waldensians', *Studies in English Literature, 1500–1900*, 11:1 (Winter, 1971), 153–64.

4 Simon Harward, *Two Godly and Learned Sermons* (London, 1582), D6^r; Mathew Sutcliffe, *A True Relation of Englands Happinesse* (London, 1629), p. 24; Samuel Smith, *Moses his Prayer* (London, 1656), p. 402.

5 Thomas D'Urfey, *Collins Walk through London and Westminster* (London, 1690), p. 133.

6 *Letters and Papers, Foreign and Domestic, Henry VIII, Volume 13 Part 2, August–December 1538*, ed. by James Gairdner (London, 1893), *British History Online*, p. 55, www.british-history.ac.uk/letters-papers-hen8/vol13/no2.

7 Margaret Aston, *Broken Idols of the English Reformation* (Cambridge: Cambridge University Press, 2015), pp. 374–78.

8 Mercurius Rusticus [Bruno Ryves], *Angliæ ruina: or, Englands ruine* (London, 1648), pp. 232–33; Stanford E. Lehmberg, *Cathedrals under Siege: Cathedrals in English Society, 1600–1700* (University Park, PA: Pennsylvania University Press, 1996), p. 28.

9 Petrus Frarinus, *An Oration against the Unlawfull Insurrections of the Protestantes of our Time* (1566), n.p.; Thomas Heskyns, *The Parliament of Chryste* (Antwerp, 1566), K3^r.

10 Milton's understanding of the term 'relics' in the context of Sonnet 18 bears comparison to Andrew Marvell's use of the word in his description of Archibald Douglas' death (in *Last Instructions*), as a kind of calculated rhetorical extravagance; see Chapter 10 of this volume, 'Andrew Marvell's Taste for Death', by Anita Gilman Sherman.

11 Timothy J. Burbery, 'From Orthodoxy to Heresy: A Theological Analysis of *Sonnets XIV and XVIII*', *Milton Studies*, 45 (2006), 1–20.

12 Kathryn Gail Brock, 'Milton's "Sonnet XVIII" and the Language of Controversy', *Milton Quarterly*, 16:1 (1982), 3–6, esp. 5.

13 See, e.g., 'Mortimer to Queen Isabel', ll. 63–64, 139–44, 'King John to Matilda', ll. 83–84, *Englands Heroicall Epistles*, in *The Works of Michael Drayton, Volume 2*, ed. by J. W. Hebel (Oxford: Shakespeare Head, 1933).

14 Michael Drayton, *Englands Heroicall Epistles* (London, 1597), 73^v.

15 Susannah Brietz Monta, 'Representing Martyrdom in Tudor England', in *Oxford Handbooks Online* (2016), https://doi.org/10.1093/oxfordhb/9780199935338.013.71.

16 See Alexandra Walsham, 'Skeletons in the Cupboard: Relics after the English Reformation', *Past & Present*, 206, supplement 5 (2010), 132–33. Perhaps the closest equivalent of the gathering imagined by Drayton lies in the small handful of cases of bodies which had been disinterred and abused under Mary being reburied in university churches. None of these cases involved martyrs, however. See Peter Marshall, *Beliefs and the Dead in Reformation England* (Oxford: Oxford University Press, 2002), pp. 122–23.

17 Michael Drayton, *Poly-Olbion*, in *The Works of Michael Drayton*, vol. 4, ed. by J. W. Hebel (Oxford: Shakespeare Head, 1933), 11.359–60, 16.79–80.

18 Robyn Malo, 'Intimate Devotion: Recusant Martyrs and the Making of Relics in Post-Reformation England', *Journal of Medieval and Early Modern Studies*, 44:3 (2014), 531–48; Arthur F. Marotti, 'Southwell's Remains: Catholicism and Anti-Catholicism in Early Modern England', in *Texts and Cultural Change in Early Modern England*, ed. by C. C. Brown and A. F. Marotti (London: Palgrave, 1997).

19 Robert Southwell, *An Epistle of Comfort to the Reverend Priestes* (London, 1587), 212^v–13^r.

20 Ibid., 149^r.

21 Michael Drayton, 'The Lady Jane Gray to Gilford Dudley', in *Works of Michael Drayton, Volume 2*, ed. by Hebel, l. 180. (Hebel's text follows the 1619 edition.) This is the same phrase Drayton would apply repeatedly in *Poly-Olbion* to the bones of martyrs and heroes lost in the dissolution of monasteries such as St Albans and Glastonbury (3.308, 16.80, 24.111).

22 John Donne, 'SERMON XXIV. Preached upon Easter-day. 1629', in *LXXX Sermons Preached by that Learned and Reverend Divine, John Donne* (London, 1640), p. 233. Compare this treatment of 'scattered bones', with reference to post-Reformation anxieties about corporeal recomposition on the Day of Judgement, to the argument adduced about Donne's *Holy Sonnets* in Chapter 1 of this volume, 'Death and the Art of Memory in Donne'.

23 John Donne, 'The Relic', in *The Complete English Poems*, ed. by A. J. Smith (London: Penguin, 1986), l. 10.

24 John Donne, 'A Sermon Preached at the Earl of Bridgewaters house … November 19, 1627', in *John Donne: Selected Prose*, ed. by Evelyn Simpson, Helen Gardner, and T. S. Healy (Oxford: Oxford University Press, 1967), p. 326; 'A Sermon Preached upon Easter Day [1622]', p. 215.

25 Ezek. 37:1–10 KJV.

26 Jerome, 'To Pammachius against John of Jerusalem', trans. by W. H. Fremantle, in *Nicene and Post-Nicene Fathers, Series 2, Volume 6*, ed. by Philip Schaff (Grand Rapids, MI: Wm. B. Eerdmans Publishing Company, nd.), www.ccel.org/ccel/schaff/npnf206.vi.viii.html.

27 Giorgio Ghisi, *The Vision of Ezekiel* (1554) engraving after a design by Giovanni Battista Bertani, British Museum V, 8.93; Francisco Collantes, *Vision of Ezekiel* (1630), oil on canvas, Museo del Prado, Madrid.

28 In another place Donne similarly inserts the unwarranted 'scattered' into a paraphrase of Philip Melancthon on the resurrection of the dead; see 'Sermon 8: Preached at S. Pauls, June 21. 1626', in *The Sermons of John Donne, Vol. 12: Sermons Preached at St Paul's Cathedral, 1626*, ed. by Mary Ann Lund (Oxford: Oxford University Press, 2017), p. 135.

29 John White, *The troubles of Jerusalems restauration* (London, 1646), p. 6; John Reading, *Christmass Revived* (London, 1660), pp. 18–19; Edward Boughen, *The Principles of Religion* (London, 1646), p. 32.

30 Although his works were not widely known in England in this period, the fourth-century church father Gregory of Nyssa had envisioned 'vast heaps of bones flung at random, some this way, some that'; see 'On the Soul and the Resurrection', in *Nicene and Post-Nicene Fathers, Series 2, Volume 5*, ed. by Philip Schaff (London, 1893), p. 461. A landscape of widely scattered bone would fit well with the vision's prophetic significance, both in its immediate context (as a promise to reunite the children of Israel in their homeland) and as a prefiguration of the final resurrection of bodies.

31 In a notorious incident in 1549, up to 1,000 cartloads of bone were removed from the charnel of St Paul's Cathedral and dumped unceremoniously in Finsbury Fields; see Thomas J. Farrow, 'The Dissolution of St. Paul's Charnel: Remembering and Forgetting the Collective Dead in Late Medieval and Early Modern England', *Mortality* (2021), https://doi.org/10.1080/13576275.2021.1911976. In the seventeenth century, according to John Aubrey, old bones from London's graveyards were shipped out of the city for use as fertilizer. See Vanessa Harding, *The Dead and the Living in Paris and London, 1500–1670* (Cambridge: Cambridge University Press, 2002), p. 65; Ralph Houlbrooke,

Death, Religion and the Family in England, 1480–1750 (Oxford: Oxford University Press, 1998), pp. 334–35; Philip Schwyzer, *Archaeologies of English Renaissance Literature* (Oxford: Oxford University Press, 2007), pp. 108–50.

32 William Shakespeare, *King Richard III*, ed. by James R. Siemon (London: Methuen, 2009).

33 Edmund Spenser, *The Faerie Queene*, ed. by A. C. Hamilton et al., rev. 2nd ed. (London: Longman, 2007).

34 In Krier's reading of the Mammon episode, the scattered bones exemplify what she terms 'the problem of heaps', profusions of detail that defy mental sorting or allegorical interpretation. In other words, Guyon cannot make the necessary connections here. Theresa M. Krier, 'Psychic Deadness in Allegory: Spenser's House of Mammon and Attacks on Linking', in *Imagining Death in Spenser and Milton*, ed. by E. J. Bellamy, P. Cheney, M. Schoenfeldt (London: Palgrave, 2003).

35 Richard Crashaw, 'On a Treatise of Charity', in *The Poems of Richard Crashaw*, ed. by L. C. Martin, 2nd ed. (Oxford: Oxford University Press, 1957). The poem initially appeared as preface to Robert Shelford's *Five Pious and Learned Discourses* (Cambridge, 1635), A1^{r-v}.

36 Gordon Teskey, *The Poetry of John Milton* (Cambridge, MA: Harvard University Press, 2015), pp. 225, 224.

37 On echoes of Ezekiel 37 in this sonnet, see in particular Ryan Hackenbracht, *National Reckonings: The Last Judgment and Literature in Milton's England* (Ithaca, NY: Cornell University Press, 2019), pp. 40–41.

38 Additional resonances noted by the poem's editors include the parable of the sower (Matt. 13: 8) and the myth of Cadmus sowing dragons' teeth.

39 '[W]hen you persecute vs … you doe but sowe seed that will spring with a more plentifull haruest', Southwell, *Epistle of Comfort*, 196^v; 'The Church is sowen with the Martyrs blood, and made fruitfull', John Carter, *The Nail and the Wheel* (London, 1646), p. 69.

CHAPTER 7

Theatrical Monuments in Middleton's
A Game at Chess

Brian Chalk

In August 1624, towards the end of his long and versatile career as a professional author, Thomas Middleton produced the biggest theatrical success not only of his playwriting life but of the early modern period. Outduelling the work of rivals such as the long-deceased Christopher Marlowe, the more recently departed William Shakespeare, and an ageing and bitterly jealous Ben Jonson, Middleton's *A Game at Chess* ran for nine consecutive days in front of capacity crowds and provoked more testimonials than any other play of its era.[1] Rather than recreating classical models of theatre or drawing upon the innovations of his contemporaries, Middleton boldly utilizes chess as an allegorical vehicle to dramatize recent events surrounding England's tumultuous relationship with Spain, with the White House representing the English and the more sinister Black standing for the Spanish. As Gary Taylor points out, whereas 'other history plays worked to familiarize the far-away to make the past present; Middleton's play sets out instead, to re-present the present to itself'.[2] The run might have continued indefinitely were it not for Don Carlos Coloma, the outraged Spanish Ambassador who demanded that performances of the 'scandalous' and 'impious play' be stopped and that the 'vile persons' responsible be 'publicly punished as an example'. According to one report, he insisted specifically that 'Middleton the poet' must be 'sought after' and 'clapt in prison'.[3] Paradoxically combining fame with infamy, Middleton found himself a fugitive from justice, with the outrageous success of his creation serving as evidence against him.

The irony of the situation was not lost on the dramatist. In addition to the brazen topicality that Taylor and others have observed, the play's scandalous potential emerges from the long-standing trope connecting chess and death at the heart of Middleton's allegory.[4] In a brief poem, 'To the King', that he may have written in prison, Middleton consolidates this connection by inserting himself into the drama as a means of arguing for his release:

> A harmless game, raised merely for delight,
> Was lately played by the Black House and White.
> They changed the game and put me in the bag –
> And that which makes malicious joy more sweet,
> I lie now under hatches in the Fleet.
> Use but your royal hand, my hopes are free;
> 'Tis but removing of one man – that's me.   (1–8)

Referring to the play as 'a harmless game' intended to please rather than offend, Middleton is at pains to minimize the importance of *A Game at Chess*. Citing the action of the plot while also making his allegiances clear, he slyly points out that if matters remain as they are, then the Black House will have prevailed rather than the White, unlike in the play itself. The speaker's plea that James use his 'royal hand' to remove him from the bag, moreover, takes the king off of the board and returns Middleton there in his stead, putting the King in charge of the pieces rather than among them. In terms of the allegory the play develops, granting this request would be tantamount to reviving Middleton from the symbolic death to which the bag consigns him. In either scenario, the speaker admits, 'the removing of one man' is no great matter, even if that man happens to be the author himself.

This chapter argues that the interest Middleton shows in the levelling power of mortality in *A Game at Chess* reveals a consistent attitude towards fame and the eternizing powers of theatre. Rather than transcending the cultural practices and preoccupations of his own time, Middleton's works in general, and *A Game at Chess* in particular, demonstrate an insistent effort to immerse themselves within them. Instead of setting the play apart from the plays for which he is best known, I suggest Middleton furnishes *A Game at Chess* with similar theatrical and thematic interests, many of which bring issues involving memorialization to the surface.[5] While the allegorical surface of the play seems to indulge the eternizing designs of the White House, the more theatrically compelling characters of the Black House, like the moving monuments they resemble, pursue the approbation of the moment over the possibility of a more enduring legacy. Representing the pursuit of fame as a game, *A Game at Chess* appears designed to gain Middleton the immediate notoriety of the public stage rather than the eternizing admiration of posterity, even at the cost of the future of his career.

All Things Draw to an End

More than a mere artistic phenomenon, the tombs, skulls, and funeral imagery that Middleton and his contemporaries frequently incorporate into their works emerged from a culture-wide preoccupation with memorialization. As Peter Marshall and other scholars have pointed out, in addition to more subtle transformations, the transition from Catholicism to Protestantism in the post-Reformation England from which Middleton emerged eliminated both purgatory and the role of intercessory prayers. 'The new dispensation', in Marshall's words, 'threw up questions that were matters of concern well beyond the boundaries of academic theology', such as 'Did the dead know or care about the state of living friends? In what sense would human bonds or affection be articulated or enacted in the next life'?[6] This newfound chasm between the living and the dead inspired Protestants to seek alternative avenues of memorialization that were not implicated in Catholicism's economy of intercession.

Given that religious strictures forbade early moderns from communicating with the dead through prayer and, by extension, rendered their relationships to their posthumous selves less direct and more ambiguous, the popularity of monuments in the period suggests that they were seeking some form of compensatory consolation. John Weever's *Ancient Funeral Monuments* (1631) is one of many texts from the period that testifies to this fixation. Weever's primary objective, as William E. Engel, Rory Loughnane, and Grant Williams of *The Memory Arts in Renaissance England* observe, is to strike a balance between upholding Protestant values that avoid 'valorizing the usage of images' while also decrying 'the dissolution of the monasteries under Henry VIII and Edward VI'.[7] To achieve this goal, Weever emphasizes that monuments are morally edifying as well as visually appealing. Monuments, in Weever's words, provide 'a sight which brings delight and admiration' while also inspiring 'a religious apprehension in the minds of the beholders'.[8] Even the many monuments that have been compromised by iconoclasts never fail to put 'us in mind of our mortality, and consequently bring us to unfeigned repentance'.[9]

While Weever emphasizes lessons on mortality consistent with the logic that underpins *memento mori* objects, however precarious, the sight of monuments clearly also put early modern viewers 'in mind' of the *immortality* sought by those who constructed them. One popular method of assuaging anxieties involving the afterlife, in which the playwrights of the era took particular interest, was the growing practice of the living commissioning monuments to themselves in advance of death.[10] According to Nigel Llewellyn, one third of monuments from this era were constructed while their subjects were still alive and able to inspect them.[11] Pre-emptive monuments, then, offered a sort of compromise in which their subjects could take part in shaping their posthumous existence without sliding fully into Catholic territory. Middleton, for his part, embraces this trend in his tributary poem to Webster's *The Duchess of Malfi*, where he congratulates his fellow playwright for 'raising' his monument in his lifetime, 'for every worthy man / Is his own marble' (1–3).[12] On behalf of his colleague, Middleton withholds the scepticism which, we shall see, characterizes his own approach towards the eternizing powers of theatre.

For further encouragement to participate in this practice, on both a literary and statuary level, the subjects of Jacobean England could always look to the king. The construction and rearrangement of funeral monuments was among King James's primary means of projecting his image.[13] In *Basilikon Doron*, for example, a political treatise furnished with self-consciously literary qualities, James embraces the practice of pre-emptive monument-making by imagining instructing his son and heir, Prince Henry, on the principals of monarchy from beyond the grave. 'I leave it as my Testament and latter unto you', the king tells his son, 'Chargeing you in the presence of GOD, and by the fatherly authoritie I haue over you, that yee keepe it euer with you as carefully, as Alexander did the Illiads of Homer'.[14] Likening his work to that of Homer, with Prince Henry as a reincarnation of Alexander the Great, James generously offers his son his inheritance in advance, positioning himself as both beyond and centrally involved in his formation as future king. The conceit of addressing Prince Henry as if from beyond the grave proved tragically ironic, while also demonstrating the perils of pre-emptive memorialization that Middleton's plays warn against. In 1612 Prince Henry predeceased his father and inspired the sort of outpouring of grief that James anticipated he would receive when Henry replaced him on the throne.

James's reign as monarch parallels strikingly Middleton's career as a mature writer; contributing a pageant to the new king's procession into London in 1604 along with Jonson and Thomas Dekker was one of the dramatist's first big breaks. Whereas Jonson seizes the opportunity to advertise his erudition, Middleton seems characteristically attuned to the demands of the moment. At this early stage, Middleton unequivocally embraces the narrative the Jacobean regime sought to impose upon the succession. In Middleton's arch, Astraea, the goddess of justice, perpetuates the perspective James promotes by promising an easy transition from the 'funeral pile' of the former queen to 'Th'attractive wonder of man's majesty' (2122–2124):

> Mirror of times, lo where thy fortune sits
> Above the world and all our human wits,
> But thy high virtue above that. What pen,
> Or art, or brain can reach thy virtue then?   (2142–2145)

Taking full advantage of the opportunity to endear himself to the new monarch, Middleton shrewdly represents James as the king represents himself in *Basilikon Doron*. While the death of the queen appeared to move England 'backward', Middleton assures us that the 'pen', 'art', and 'brain' that James possesses has replaced those mournful feelings with a sense of optimism while also, of course, suggesting that the writers he inspires will play a part in glorifying his era.

As I have argued elsewhere, early modern dramatists were in a unique position to comment on the paradoxes inherent in this process of pre-emptive commemoration.[15] Writing in a medium that foregrounds its relationship to ephemerality as a matter of course, dramatists were able to forge self-conscious relationships with conceits of memorialization and to convey, to differing degrees, their confidence or lack of faith that plays can provide a stable vehicle for posterity. Middleton, who makes dramatic use of *memento mori* themes and objects as inventively as any writer of his notably death-focused era, seems acutely aware of these cultural fixations, the king's interest in them, and, most especially, the self-serving distortions that they inevitably engender.

If Middleton's arch celebrates straightforwardly James's efforts at memorializing his reign, his plays tend to travesty the idea that we can control and manipulate our posthumous identities in implicit and explicit terms. As critics have noted, Middleton's most consistent response to the inevitability of death and the possibility of controlling one's posthumous existence is mockery.[16] Middleton's position, in and of itself, is unremarkable; mockery is in many ways fundamental to the *ars moriendi* visuals that Middleton and others put on stage, with the image of the skull providing a sobering reminder of what death has in store for us.[17] Compare, for example, Hamlet's address to the 'chopfallen' Yorick that takes place shortly before his own death (5.1.181).[18] More unique to Middleton, I suggest, is the way in which this sense of mockery comes to engulf not only characters who fall victim to his tragic protagonists but also the protagonists themselves, especially those who believe they can exert shaping power over the worlds in which Middleton places them. In *The Revenger's Tragedy*, to offer another well-known example, Vindice sees Hamlet and raises him by using the skull of his murdered love Gloriana as a *memento mori* device, a stage prop, and a murder weapon at various points in the play. His mortal mistake is his assumption that his mastery of the revenge genre exempts him from the consequences of his actions. Sentenced to death after bragging to the new monarch that he has murdered the former one, Vindice concedes that "Tis time to die when we are ourselves our foes' (5.3.130). In keeping with the play's title, Vindice's only legacy is that of a 'revenger', a collective rather than individualized fate.

In *The Changeling*, as Michael Neill has argued, Beatrice-Joanna follows a similar path as she gradually becomes indistinguishable from De Flores, who occupies the role of despised nemesis, lover, and mutual destroyer over the course of the play. 'Look but into your conscience', De Flores grimly orders his partner in crime, 'You'll find me there your equal' (4.1.131–132). The 'unsettling consequence', in Neill's words, 'is that De Flores becomes the real hero of the play', and 'his re-enactment of Othello's eroticized murder and suicide enforces, by its half-contemptuous self-satisfaction, the only claim to distinction that Middleton and Rowley's degraded world will allow'.[19] Similar to Vindice's, Beatrice-Joanna's drive to separate herself from her darkest urges while also indulging them results in those urges subsuming her identity and overtaking the world of the play she inhabits. When De Flores announces that he and Beatrice-Joanna are 'left in hell' even prior to their deaths, Vermandero responds tellingly by assuring him that 'we are all there' (5.3.164–165).

Middleton most closely anticipates the stagecraft of *A Game at Chess* in *Women, Beware Women*, where Livia's game of chess parallels the unscrupulous seduction of Bianca by the Duke. Seeking a diversion to 'drive out time till supper', Livia suggests 'chess or draughts' to Bianca's mother-in-law, whose desire for social advancement easily distracts her from her obligation to protect Bianca (2.2.187–188). Livia, who aptly plays with the black pieces, enables the Duke's plan to move forward by encouraging Guardiano to show Bianca the 'monument', a 'thing everyone sees not' (2.2.276–277). Combining the thematic interests of Middleton's previous tragedies while also foreshadowing *A Game at Chess*, the lure of the monument tricks Bianca, whose name translates to 'white', into playing the Duke's 'game' and results in her conversion to 'black'. As Livia steadily discards the white pieces of her opponent, rendering the board increasingly black, the Duke replaces Guardiano in theatrical fashion and quickly rapes Bianca. Surprised at her sudden reappearance with the game still in process, her mother-in-law unwittingly predicts Bianca's transformation when she asks if Bianca has 'seen all'. 'That have I, mother', she answers sardonically, 'The monument and all' (2.2.49–50). For Livia, the conversion experience Bianca undergoes, from innocence to experience and, in terms of the game, from white to black, mirrors the *memento mori* messages she sees enacted in chess. 'The games e'en at the best now', she remarks, noting how the experience of playing reminds us 'How all things draw to an end' (2.2.410). No one in Middleton transcends the game or its inevitable conclusion, not even, as the author readily admits in the poem with which I began, Middleton himself.

The Game of Fame

A Game at Chess has long been understood as a contemporary success but not a timeless one. Most notably, T. S. Eliot called the play 'a perfect piece of literary political art', with the latter inevitably overshadowing the former.[20] Nowhere in Middleton's works, however, are the seemingly contradictory impulses between the drive towards memorialization and the inevitability of theatrical ephemerality more evident. Examining Middleton's complex manipulation of monumentalization and theatricality in *A Game at Chess* suggests that Middleton purposely embraced the transience of the theatrical medium with the play, eschewing ambitions to hold interest for posterity. The relationship between Middleton's art and James I's ambitions can be refracted through *A Game at Chess* to illuminate the value of dramatic effect in narratives of political power, and, by extension, the playwright's commitment to a theatrical world that self-consciously mocks the eternizing ambitions of both kings and writers.

As the 'Persons and Pieces of the Play' in the *Oxford Middleton* edition of the later form describes, the 'whole play is a chessboard'.[21] On the level of plot, the play, or 'game', dramatizes the Black House and White House's pursuit of the 'fame' of victory, a word that recurs suggestively throughout and activates different interpretive registers depending on which side uses it. Rejecting the ephemeral delights that the Black Kingdom offers, the White Kingdom seeks glory that transcends the context of the game. After the White Knight foils a plot of rape against the Virgin White Queen's Pawn, the King, who provides a mouthpiece for his side, pre-emptively assures him that 'This fair delivering act virtue will register / In that white book of the defence of virgins, / Where the clear fame of all preserving knights / Are to eternal memory consecrated' (3.1.163–166). To King James, the 'clear fame' the White House champions distinguishes them from the 'infamy' of the Black.

If we consider the action on stage from the allegorical surface the rules of the game provide, interpreting the plot proves deceptively simple. At the play's climactic moment, the White Knight, Prince Charles, allows the

Black Knight to lure him, along with the White Duke of Buckingham, towards his side, only to entrap the Black Knight into 'checkmate by discovery', a move that, according to a 1614 chess guide, 'occurs when one piece moves out of the lines of its fellow piece and thereby delivers an inescapable check'.[22] On stage, the movement of the White Knight creates a path for the White Duke to place the Black King in check. Reinforcing the relationship between chess and death that Middleton develops throughout the play, the 'bag' for discarded pieces opens in the form of the stage's trapdoor and consumes the Black House entirely. The White King James presides over their descent into the 'hell-mouth', which, he assures the audience, is 'greedily gaping for increase of fellowship / In infamy' (5.3.175–177). The 'infamy' White King James describes is tantamount to the indistinguishability that so often subsumes Middleton's tragic protagonists. Within the confines of the bag, the status that distinguishes the Black Knight from the non-essential pieces he discards throughout the game disappears along with the Knight himself.

In addition to different sides of the board, the White and Black represent different modes of theatricality. The Black Kingdom, in the words of the Virgin White Queen's Pawn, revels in 'sin's glorious ostentation', pointedly bringing to mind Protestant critiques that denounce Catholic ritual as theatrical rather than substantive (2.2.170). Similar to Marlowe's *Doctor Faustus*, however, from which *A Game at Chess* borrows its conclusion, the excitement that the descent into hell generates derives from the experience of witnessing the fall of the Black House rather than revelling along with the victors. Unlike the White characters, the Black characters possess theatrical charisma that transcends the play; the White Characters, despite their victory, remain entrapped within it.

While the White House wins the game, then, the scandalous potential of the play emerges from how easily the Black House prevails in the more important task of holding the interest of the audience, thus gaining theatrical fame that, I suggest, redounds negatively on the White by calling attention to the transience of their victory. Before the 'chess-play' begins, the prologue purposefully removes any suspense involving the winner. As in any game, the prologue reminds the audience, some characters will be 'entrapped and taken, to their shame'. In the end, the prologue promises reassuringly, 'You shall see checkmate given to virtue's foes'. Ultimately, however, despite the outcome of the game the play dramatizes, 'the fair'st jewel that our hopes can deck / Is so to play our game t'avoid your check' (1–2; 6–10). The prologue and, by extension, the playwright, yield power of the board to the audience. Given that the outcome of the game is predetermined, the challenge of the play is to produce a response worthy of another game, or performance. The White House wins the game, and wrongly considers itself the victor of the play. The Black House, which produces ephemeral effects over enduring ones, wins the audience.[23]

Despite the ultimately straightforward nature of the White House's victory, moreover, the comparison of the two kingdoms that the play invites, Middleton was surely aware, illuminates negative aspects of the English court even while targeting the Spanish. In addition to widespread anti-Spanish sentiment, fomented in part by propagandist pamphlets Middleton used as sources for the play, Buckingham and Charles's covert trip to Madrid in 1623 served as Middleton's primary inspiration for forming the plot. Frustrated by endless marriage negotiations, and spurred on by Buckingham, the prince made the dangerous decision to travel to Spain in disguise and seduce the Spanish infanta in person. Reversing the action Middleton depicts on stage, the mission was an unequivocal failure. After six months of being outmanoeuvred by Philip IV, represented on stage by the Black King, Charles and Buckingham returned to London to a relieved but increasingly decrepit King James. Given their humiliating failure in Spain, contemporary reports that Prince Charles and the Duke 'laughed hartely' at a performance of *Game at Chess* and were 'loth to have it forbidden' should come as no surprise. James, however, when he finally learned of the play and the Spanish Ambassador's angry reaction to it, was furious that no one had alerted him of its controversial potential.[24]

Similar to his contribution to James's procession, in which Middleton perpetuates a narrative pleasing to the Jacobean regime, *A Game at Chess* ostensibly dramatizes the version of events that Charles and Buckingham concocted to gloss over their lack of success in Spain. Whereas Middleton's arch predicts a glorious future to mark the auspicious beginning of the Jacobean dynasty, the play takes on the more difficult task of reconfiguring or, to use language appropriate to Middleton's conceit, 'whitewashing', actions that called the future of the dynasty into question. The 'romance tale' that Charles and Buckingham created, with Charles moving from 'starstruck' to 'spurned' lover, was one of the last stories James's regime created about itself to perpetuate its waning ambitions.[25] These two works, as I mentioned earlier, bookend the careers of both men. The king was dead less than a year after *A Game at Chess* premiered, and Middleton, who died in 1627, seems never to have written another play. The arch, similar to the monuments discussed, creates the illusion of permanence pleasing to the Jacobean regime. Theatrical performances, in contrast, insist on their transience. Paradoxically, the qualities that generated the play's popularity reduced its value for posterity. In keeping with the ethos that drives his plays, this seems to have been a trade-off that Middleton was willing to make.

Death Knows No Difference

While the major figures of the White House transparently represent members of the Jacobean court, the play's ability to blur and even collapse the difference between theatre and reality comes through most vividly in the Black Knight (Gondomar), whose real-life counterpart's well-known struggles with anal fistula were aided by Middleton's use on stage of his actual clothing and treatment chair. Along with associations with the historical Gondomar, the boastful soliloquies and Machiavellian machinations of the Black Knight generate interest by recalling earlier Shakespearean playwriting characters such as Richard III and Iago. Similar to the comparison discussed earlier of Hamlet and Vindice, Middleton distinguishes the Black Knight by making this tendency towards self-dramatization more extreme. The Black Knight, in one editor's words, 'is a chessman so intoxicated by the intricate possibilities open to him that he plays for the sake of the play rather than for victory'.[26] Throughout the play, the Black Knight mirrors on stage the asymmetrical movements of a knight on a chessboard. When the Black Knight's Pawn Gelder warns his master that his 'plot's discovered', he responds by dispassionately asking for more specificity: 'Which of the twenty thousand and nine hundred / Fourscore and five? Canst tell' (3.1.127–130). Like many of Middleton's heroes, the play ultimately punishes the Black Knight for his pre-emptive claims of ownership over the narrative. Gondomar's tendency to revel in his virtuosic movements around the board generate much of the action on stage while also blinding him to the countermoves from the White that doom the Black House to the bag in act 5.

In contrast to the Black Knight, the linguistically exuberant and morally ambivalent Fat Bishop Spalato generates interest by ignoring the game in favour of satisfying his enormous appetites. Whereas the Black Knight develops plots to entrap his White competitors, Spalato generates pamphlets, or 'scripts', that he wields as weapons against both houses over the course of the play (1.1.244).[27] Although Spalato provokes the Black Knight's anger by mockingly promising a cure to his ailment, it is the speed with which he generates texts that proves most bothersome to his nemesis. 'Look, more books yet!' he exclaims when he spots the Fat Bishop on stage, 'Yonder greasy gormandizing prelate / Has wrought our house more mischief by his scripts, / His fat and fulsome volumes, / Than the whole body of the adverse party' (2.2.48–52). Spalato's pamphlets, like the play itself, call attention to their ephemerality in a manner that weaponizes it. Despite their capacity to cause damage, Spalato cheerfully admits that the texts themselves have no enduring value. When convenient to his self-serving purposes, he quickly switches sides: 'It is but penning / Another recantation against the White House / And then I'm in o't'other side again / As firm as e'er I was, as fat and flourishing' (3.1.52–56). Spalato's dismissive attitude towards his own output – 'It is but penning' – belies the damage his pamphlets produce.

Similar to the meta-theatrical commentary that Middleton features throughout the play, the pamphlets that Spalato produces slyly call attention to the precarious business of being a professional writer in early modern London. Thomas Nashe, no stranger to the ups and downs of his craft, describes 'fiddling his pamphlets door to door like a blind harper for bread and cheese'.[28] Elsewhere, more pointedly, he refers to pamphlets as 'dung papers'.[29] As a prolific writer of pamphlets himself, Middleton would have understood Nashe's frustrations well. At the same time, his use of source material makes clear that he also realized that ephemeral texts have the capacity to make an outsize impact on the subjects they target. Along with contemporary reports of Charles's journey to the 'Black' kingdom of Spain, pamphlets featuring anti-Spanish propaganda comprise Middleton's primary source for the play. In keeping with the precedent Spalato's pamphlets set, *A Game at Chess* itself would go on to become the most troublesome script of the era.

With *A Game at Chess*, Christina Marie Carlson has recently argued, Middleton 'warns against easy and unthinking acceptance of the dictum that providentialism suggests the possibility of continued divine favour and memorializes instances of divine intervention to reinforce the idea that God favours England and Protestantism exclusively'.[30] The play perpetuates this perspective by subtly undercutting the grandiose claims of the White King at every opportunity. As Middleton was obviously aware, in chess, the king is a relatively ineffectual figure in terms of determining a game's outcome. In keeping with this practice, the role of White King James is primarily to provide self-aggrandizing commentary in response to the actions of more transformative characters. Tellingly, when the White King arrives on stage, his first act is to receive a book from Spalato that contains evidence against the Black House. Seeking to appeal to the King's erudition and susceptibility to textual persuasion, the duplicitous Bishop's text features language 'Writ like a Ciceronian in pure Latin' (2.2.91). The scholarly acumen which, as we saw in the section 'All Things Draw to an

End', the king advertises in works such as *Basilikon Doron*, renders him a less rather than more dynamic character in a theatrical context.

The temptation scene the Black Knight prepares for the White Knight (Charles) and the White Duke (of Buckingham) collapses theatrical spectacle with the Catholic ritual it seeks to criticize. Taking advantage of the resemblance between chess pieces and monuments, the scene's effects include an altar *richly adorned with tapers* as Black pieces disguised as statues that come to life and dance in an attempt to seduce and convert the White Knight (5.1.33). Given that the outcome is predetermined, when the White Knight (Charles) reassures the delighted King that "twas a game, sir, / Won with much hazard, so with much more triumph', the audience experiences the excitement of the theatrical effects, but none of the 'hazard' the Knight describes (5.3.173–174). Similar to earlier in the play, the King quickly consigns his enemies to the fate he fears most:

> Obscurity is now the fittest favour
> Falsehood can sue for. It well suits our perdition.
> It's their best course that have so lost their fame
> To put their heads into bag for shame.   (5.3.175–178)

Pairing the loss of 'fame' with 'shame', White King (James) revels over a victory he did nothing to secure. Appropriately, Bishop Spalato upstages the King even in the bag by refusing to yield space to the Black King. 'I'm not so easily moved when I'm once set', he insists, 'I scorn to stir for any king on earth' (5.3.201–202). Although the White Knight confirms the win, Middleton retains Spalato to spare the audience the banality of the King's commentary.

Of the members of the White House, the Virgin White Queen's Pawn, whose plot line Middleton interweaves with that of the White Knight, is the most theatrically compelling precisely because she comes closest to yielding to the temptations of the Black and, by extension, participates in the world of the play in a manner the other White characters do not. Recalling Livia in *Women, Beware Women*, the Jesuit Black Queen's Pawn uses the illusion of 'fate' in conjunction with 'magical glass' to tempt the Virgin White Queen's Pawn into an encounter with the Jesuit Black Bishop's Pawn. In this instance, unlike in his earlier play, Middleton merges the game with the attempted seduction. The Virgin White Queen's pawn, the first character of her house to appear alone on stage, understands that she is *always* on the 'board'. At the play's conclusion, Middleton even subverts the King's right to the play's concluding lines by having the Virgin White Queen's Pawn speak an epilogue after the King has ordered the bag closed:

> My mistress, the White Queen, hath sent me forth
> And bade me bow thus low to all of worth
> That are true friends of the White House and the cause,
> Which she hopes most of this assembly draws.
> For any else – by envy's mark denoted,
> To those night glow-worms in the bag devoted –
> Where'er they sit, stand, and in corners lurk,
> They'll be soon known by their depraving work.
> But she's assured, what they'd commit to bane
> Her White friends' hands will build up fair again.   (Epilogue, 1–10)

Rather than the King, the Virgin White Queen's Pawn takes orders from the White Queen, the most powerful figure on the chessboard. To generate applause, she subjects the audience to the inspection that she undergoes throughout the play at the hands of the Black House. Borrowing a conceit from the morality play tradition, she warns that failure to respond with enthusiasm will expose audience members as potential supporters of the wrong side.[31] Regardless of where in the theatre they 'sit, stand', or 'lurk', their inner blackness will ultimately reveal itself. Simultaneously implanting the hidden desires it seeks to detect, the epilogue echoes the strategy of the Black House rather than rejecting it.

Closing the thematic circle I have sketched out in this essay is the connection discussed, which Middleton forges among chess, death, and the loss of identity in the play. Although he is not alluding to *A Game at Chess*, George Strode's *Anatomy of Mortalitie* brings the conclusion of Middleton's play vividly to mind. Emphasizing the arbitrary nature of the pieces' identities, the author imagines death as the ending of a chess game in which 'the men are tumbled together, and put into the bag'.[32] Recalling the *memento mori* objects in Middleton's other plays, the conclusion of the game provides a reminder that, regardless of their status in life, the dead are ultimately indistinguishable from one another. 'There is a great difference in men', Strode continues, 'and greater respect had to some than to others … but when death cometh … then there will be no such difference in the grave, neither doth Death know any such difference for he spareth none.'[33] The differences between men, in Strode's metaphor, parallels the differences among pieces on a chessboard. The role the game assigns each piece generates and delimits various movements while guaranteeing a conclusion that effaces the hierarchy that distinguishes them. From this perspective, which Middleton's plays consistently endorse, revelling in the victory of any individual game ignores that we are all ultimately destined for the same destination. As the Black Knight reminds us, unwittingly predicting his own fate as well as the pieces he targets, 'The bag is big enough; 'twill hold us all' (3.1.313–314).

Topicality and Posterity

Despite the scholarly enthusiasm Middleton has generated in recent decades, *A Game at Chess* is, to reformulate Jonson's praise of Shakespeare, not of all time but purposely and insistently of its age. As Lukas Erne points out, 'despite its huge success in 1624, when its explosive topicality was immediately recognized and embraced', the 'modern stage history' of *A Game at Chess* is 'almost a blank'.[34] The paradoxical nature of Middleton's triumph is in keeping with the perspective towards posterity that, I have suggested, he consistently projects in the play. Rather than transcending the context in which it was produced, *A Game at Chess* calls attention to the play's topicality in a manner that withholds from future readers the features that contributed so vitally to its initial success. Indeed, as Taylor and others have noted, the play seems to anticipate and even court its own censorship.[35] Over and over again, early contemporary responses to the play emphasize the boldness of its author. One gets the sense that the overriding reaction from the audiences that packed the Globe for nine days running was incredulity.

In keeping with the effect that Middleton seeks to produce elsewhere in his works, *A Game at Chess* revels in its own transience. Although Taylor argues that the play 'transformed ephemera into art', I would suggest that its value emerges from Middleton's insistence on challenging the distinction between the two.[36] Middleton seemed to realize that the play's commercial success depended upon its capacities to track the vagaries of the public's consumer appetites, a tracking that potentially diverges from and compromises the timelessness of tragic art. The title page of the 1625 quarto printed during Middleton's lifetime reinforces this effect with the promise that the edition includes a version of the play 'as it was acted nine days at the Globe' (see Figure 7.1). The promise that a printed version offers an exact replica of what was performed is a common advertising strategy among early modern plays. Here, however, the emphasis on the 'nine days' in which performing *A Game at Chess* was permissible conveys the sense of dangerous transience that contributed to its remarkable appeal. Indeed, the title page, which does not include Middleton's name, reads as if the remarkable stretch of time that play ran for is a part of the title itself. More successfully than any other work of its era, the play seemed able to harness its sense of its own ephemerality and deploy it as a theatrical effect. The prologue, in this way, anticipates the poem 'To the King' that Middleton would write in his defence; the prologue describes his modest ambitions for the play before the actors take the stage: 'the fairest jewel that our hopes can deck, / Is so to play our game to avoid your check' (9–10). The

Figure 7.1   Title page, *A Game at Chæss as it was Acted Nine Days to Gether at the Globe* (London: Ian Masse, 1625). STC 17883. Image used courtesy of The Huntington Library.

pieces, like the moving monuments they resemble, provide a false assurance of permanence. In the end, as Middleton seemed acutely aware, all that remains is the game itself.

Notes

1 'In 1626', Gary Taylor reports, 'Jonson coupled Middleton with another object of his contempt, the radical satirist George Wither, and imagined the "poor English play" ("*The Game at Chess*") being used as toilet paper'. See Gary Taylor, 'Thomas Middleton: Lives and Afterlives', in Thomas Middleton, *Thomas Middleton: The Collected Works*, gen. ed. by Gary Taylor and John Lavagnino (Oxford: Oxford University Press, 2007), p. 49. On the play's popularity, see Gary Taylor, 'A Game at Chess: A Later Form', in *Thomas Middleton: The Collected Works*, gen. ed. by Taylor and Lavagnino, p. 1825. All quotations from Middleton's works are taken from the Oxford edition.
2 Gary Taylor, 'A Game at Chesse: An Early Form', in *Thomas Middleton: The Collected Works*, gen. ed. by Taylor and Lavagnino, p. 1775.

3 Gary Taylor and John Lavagnino, eds., *Thomas Middleton and Early Modern Textual Culture* (Oxford: Oxford University Press, 2007), p. 829. Taylor's work, from which I profited greatly, includes a detailed account of the Spanish Ambassador's complaint to James, the play's incredible success, and its complicated textual history.

4 William Engel observes that 'The image of Death as the Leveller, heedless of distinctions in gender, class, or station, was so common in the early modern period that it hardly requires further commentary'. William E. Engel, *Mapping Mortality: The Persistence of Memory and Melancholy in Early Modern England* (Amherst: University of Massachusetts Press, 1995), p. 188.

5 As Richard Dutton notes, the way in which *A Game at Chess* 'sits at the intersection of theatre history and politics has inspired critics to separate it from his other works, and distracted them' from the fact that it is 'one of the finest plays by one of the most skilled dramatists of the period' (p. 448). Richard Dutton, 'Thomas Middleton's *A Game at Chess*: A Case Study', in J. Milling and P. Thomson, eds., *The Cambridge History of British Theatre*, vol. 1 (Cambridge: Cambridge University Press, 2004), pp. 424–438.

6 Peter Marshall, *Beliefs and the Dead in Reformation England* (Oxford: Oxford University Press, 2002), p. 188. In addition to Marshall, see David Cressy, *Birth, Marriage, and Death: Ritual, Religion, and the Life Cycle in Elizabethan and Stuart England* (Oxford: Oxford University Press, 1997) and Peter Sherlock, *Monuments and Memory in Early Modern England* (Aldershot: Ashgate, 2008).

7 See William E. Engel, Rory Loughnane, and Grant Williams, eds., *The Memory Arts in Renaissance England: A Critical Anthology* (Cambridge: Cambridge University Press, 2016), p. 206.

8 Ibid., p. 207.

9 Ibid., p. 207.

10 I explore how Marlowe, Jonson, Shakespeare, and John Fletcher react to the question of whether their works would endure for posterity in *Monuments and Literary Posterity in Early Modern Drama* (Cambridge: Cambridge University Press, 2015).

11 Nigel Llewellyn, *Funeral Monuments in Post-Reformation England* (Cambridge: Cambridge University Press, 2000), p. 57.

12 Thomas Middleton, 'In the Just Worth of that Well-Deserver, Mr. John Webster, and Upon this Masterpiece of a Tragedy', quoted in John Webster, *The Duchess of Malfi*, ed. by Michael Neill (New York: W.W. Norton & Company, 2015).

13 See Chalk, *Monuments*, pp. 26–28.

14 James Stuart, *King James VI and I: Political Writings*, ed. by Johann P. Somerville (Cambridge: Cambridge University Press, 1994), p. 3.

15 Chalk, *Monuments*, p. 4.

16 'Middleton's tragedies', in Paul Budra's words, 'are at once too violent, frightening, self-referential, funny, and sexual' for the relative 'delicacy' that Shakespeare's tragedies feature'. Paul Budra, 'The Emotions of Tragedy:

Middleton or Shakespeare?', in Gary Taylor and Trish Thomas Henley, eds., *The Oxford Handbook of Thomas Middleton* (Oxford: Oxford University Press, 2012), p. 493.

17 In *The Honest Whore, Part One*, which Middleton co-authored with Thomas Dekker, the Duke muses at 'mad mortals' who attempt to 'rear great names / On tops of swelling houses!' (10.67–69). In *The Lady's Tragedy*, the sight of the Lady's monument fills the Tyrant with necrophiliac lust. 'The monument woos me', he insists, 'I must run and kiss it' (4.3.9). Owing to his devotion to monuments, the latter character experiences a degree of disgrace beyond even what the former one predicts.

18 William Shakespeare, *Hamlet*, ed. by A. R. Braunmuller (New York: Penguin Books, 2001).

19 Michael Neill, *Issues of Death: Mortality and Identity in English Renaissance Tragedy* (Oxford: Clarendon Press, 1997), p. 171. On the political and cultural dynamics of theatrical 're-enactment' as it is being discussed here, see also Chapter 1 in this volume by Rebeca Helfer, 'Death and the Art of Memory in Donne', with special reference to Augustine re-enacting 'David's relationship to divinity, not directly but mediated through scripture, and this relationship is then doubly re-enacted by Donne in his sermon, mediated through Augustine's own allegory of anamnesis through scripture'.

20 T. S. Eliot, *Selected Essays*, 3rd ed. (London: Faber and Faber, 1951), p. 166.

21 Thomas Middleton, *A Game at Chess*, in *Thomas Middleton: The Collected Works*, gen. ed. by Taylor and Lavagnino, p. 1830.

22 Quoted in Thomas Middleton, *A Game at Chess*, ed. by J. W. Harper (London: Ernest Benn Limited, 1966), p. 89.

23 As Gary Taylor points out, 'the play was sometimes referred to as "Gondomar"' by contemporary audiences, collapsing the title with its most popular character. Taylor, 'A Game at Chess: A Later Form', p. 1827.

24 See Taylor, 'A Game at Chesse: An Early Form', p. 1777.

25 Mark Kishlansky, *A Monarchy Transformed: Britain, 1603–1714* (London: Penguin Books, 1997), p. 104.

26 Middleton, *A Game at Chess*, ed. by Harper, p. xviii.

27 The fear that he activates is not only that White pieces can be taken by the Black side but also converted into one of them. After traitorously delivering intelligence to the Black Knight, the White King's Counsellor Pawn realizes this subversive possibility when he insists on his inner-blackness: 'You see my outside, but you know my heart, knight; / Great difference in the colour' (1.1.116–117).

28 See Taylor, 'Thomas Middleton: Lives and Afterlives', p. 36.

29 Thomas Nashe, quoted in Engel, Loughnane, and Williams, eds., *Memory Arts*, p. 321.

30 Christina Marie Carlson, 'The Rhetoric of Providence: Thomas Middleton's *A Game at Chess* (1624) and Seventeenth-Century Political Engraving', *Renaissance Quarterly*, 67 (2014), 1226.

31 I am grateful to Rory Loughnane for pointing out to me Middleton's use of this device.

32 Cited in Engel, *Mapping Mortality*, p. 189.

33 Ibid., p. 14.

34 Lukas Erne, '"Our Other Shakespeare": Thomas Middleton and the Canon', *Modern Philology*, 107.3 (February 2010), 499.

35 Taylor, 'A Game at Chess: A Later Form', p. 1775.

36 *A Game at Chess*, in this way, invites comparison with *The Roaring Girl*, another play that purposely anchors itself in its time by representing a figure from Jacobean England on stage. In a discussion of the latter play that can be usefully applied to *A Game at Chess*, Jeffrey Knapp argues 'against the detractors of mass entertainment' by suggesting that 'the ambition to please a mass heterogenous audience can have a complicating rather than a reductive effect on entertainments'. Jeffrey Knapp, *Pleasing Everyone: Mass Entertainment in Renaissance England and Golden-Age Hollywood* (Oxford: Oxford University Press, 2016), p. 52.

CHAPTER 8

Thomas Browne's Retreat to Earth

Claire Preston

In *New Atlantis* (1627), Francis Bacon describes Bensalem's splendid government-sponsored laboratories. There, among a dazzling array of experimental equipment, scientists have 'lakes, both salt and fresh' used for 'the burials of some natural bodies, for we find a difference in things buried in earth, or in air below the earth, and things buried in water'.[1] Things buried were intensely interesting to early modern natural philosophers and antiquarians: What are fossils? they asked. What happens to bodies in the earth? What is the planet's subterranean geology? How many kinds of soils are there?[2] Why are trees and boats found deep underground? Why are there marine remains on and under dry land? Why do some stones look a lot like existing species? Did earthquakes alter the geography of the world? These were all questions addressed by Thomas Browne. With William Dugdale he discussed buried forests and even underground harbours as evidence of ancient inundations, some perhaps caused by catastrophic tectonic events.[3]

Fossils were perplexing enough as creatures known and unknown, but even more so when apparently pelagic animals were discovered far from the sea and even on mountaintops. That they were petrified (or, as Browne says, had become 'Gorgons of themselves'[4]) made it difficult to determine if they were natural objects or shaped stones; if the latter, what hand had fashioned them? If the former, what was their relation to extant species? The underground was full of disconcerting puzzles. The interior of the earth itself seemed to Thomas Burnet like an enormous, ruined edifice with crumbling rooms and passageways,[5] and to Athanasius Kircher like a gigantic physiological system that replicated parts of human anatomy.[6]

Human remains come into these discussions: they are a 'morsel for the Earth, whereof all things are but a colonie', says Browne in *Urne-Buriall* (1658), his magisterial disquisition on cremation and interment (*UB* III.109).[7] The earth itself is an empire of dust, beginning with Adam: our first parent was no more than 'an extract of the Earth', fashioned of dust by

159

his maker (*UB* I.89). *Urne-Buriall*, on post-mortem burning, is animated by the *earthiness* of humankind, a quality rendered in the circularity of creation and cremation, a dust-to-dust autopoiesis that he likens elsewhere to the hieroglyphic ouroboros, the snake swallowing its own tail (*LF* 182).[8] That dusty circularity in *Urne-Buriall* is something he also thinks about in another work of the mid-1650s, *A Letter to a Friend* (*c.* 1656), in considering the combustibility of humans in disease and death, and the incendiary fate of the planet on the last day.

What does Browne mean when he asserts that man is a 'colony' of earth? As a physician and as a reflective Christian, he links dust, ashes, and earth to disease, destruction, and resurrection, a medico-theological analogy or compaction of cosmology and of symptomology. In *Urne-Buriall* he is thinking about the disposal and commemoration of the ashes of the dead; in *A Letter to a Friend*, about disease as a kind of cremation, and of a particular disease that afflicts not only his patients but also the earth itself. His medical eschatology of ultimate destruction makes bodies, and the earth from which they emerge and to which they retreat, finally the same thing.

Soft Death

Urne-Buriall was probably written in 1656 and published, with *The Garden of Cyrus*, in a small octavo volume in 1658. These two works, respectively on death and life, on burial and florescence, have generally been read by modern critics as companion pieces, *Cyrus* (an odd and various tract) representing resurrection and 'the delightful world [that] comes after death' in its celebration of gardens and verdancy, where 'Paradise succeeds the grave' (*The Garden of Cyrus* Epistle 87). That traditional critical pairing probably is correct – by the 1650s Browne was in full control of his manuscripts and their presentation by the press – so we can be fairly certain that it was deliberate.[9]

Less obvious is the relation, equally strong, of *Urne-Buriall* to the posthumously published *A Letter to a Friend*, a brief medical-moral account of the death of a young man by consumption. Although there is a good deal of uncertainty about its date, recipient, and the identity of its subject, internal and other evidence suggests that it too was composed in 1656; moreover, *A Letter to a Friend* and *Urne-Buriall* share some important rhetorical and thematic features in their elaboration of dust, ashes, earth, and the fires that produce them. This essay reads the two as a very different pairing from that fertile year.

Urne-Buriall, a worldwide survey of mortuary customs and a meditation on the failure of cultural and historical memory, is too well known to
require much description. The more obscure *Letter to a Friend*, an epistolary essay, describes to a mutual friend the recent death of one of Browne's
patients, convincingly identified as Robert Loveday of Chediston in
Suffolk, the translator of La Calprenéde's *Cleopatre*.[10] We know from
Loveday's surviving letters that he had suffered from consumption (pulmonary tuberculosis) for some years before his death, and that he died
at about the age of 33 in 1656. The *Letter* discusses the final stage of his
life, when Browne was called to attend Loveday, and makes post-mortem
observations on the case. This first part of the *Letter*, an essay on the disease
and the young man himself, is cast in the form of a medical *consilium*, the
learned doctor's conventional, Hippocratic format for giving account of
his observations, diagnosis, and treatment. The *Letter*'s second phase is
very different and stylistically almost unrelated, a somewhat Polonian set of
maxims inspired by Loveday but directed to the recipient friend.[11] Because
the medical phase shares with *Urne-Buriall* some identical allusions,[12] and
the striking concern with the post-mortem state of bodily remains, the two
works seem compositionally related to each other, as closely linked in their
way as *Urne-Buriall* is to *The Garden of Cyrus*. If they are indeed coeval, the
mid-1650s is a period of compositional brilliance in Browne's career almost
equal to the early 1640s when he was revising *Religio Medici* and composing *Pseudodoxia Epidemica*.[13]

Browne's treatment of Loveday in the *Letter* is both highly personal
and strictly disinterested. He oscillates between the vast corpus of learned
medicine that informed pre-modern practice, and a kind of spiritual
biography in which the young man's grievous symptoms are elaborated
into general truths about human mortality and the pathology of dying,
but simultaneously developed as a moral anatomy of his character. It's a
mixture of thinking about the disease in general, and the particular symptoms of this patient, mingling the medical and the moral to highlight
Loveday's retiring and ascetic virtue. Although, we are told, consumptives often refuse to recognise that they are dying (apparently a common
psychological symptom), Loveday had been spiritually prepared for a
death long-expected during the years since his first diagnosis. Along with
good health, Browne tells us, he had shed all expectation of marriage and
fatherhood,

> willing to quit the World alone and altogether, leaving no Earnest behind
> him for Corruption or Aftergrave, having small content in that common
> satisfaction to survive or live in another, but amply satisfied that his Disease

> should dye with himself, nor revive in a Posterity to puzzle Physick, and make sad *Memento*'s of their parent hereditary. (*LF* 187)

Loveday also resisted another 'stupid symptom' of the dying, that of becoming narrow-minded, tenacious, and miserable (*LF* 188). This young man resists the usual psycho-symptomatic compromises of the ebbing life, having lived in unblemished, abstinent renunciation and humility informed by the controlling illness that would have earmarked his brief future. Browne says in *Religio Medici* that

> it is a brave act of valour to contemne death, but where life is more terrible than death, it is then the truest valour to dare to live ... Men that looke no further than their outsides thinke health an appertinance unto life, and quarrell with their constitutions for being sick .... (*RM* I.43)[14]

Loveday, we come to understand, has all along contemned life in his stoic endurance of a dreadful illness. Consumption is no ordinary disease, however: it has a well-known array of effects on personality, later Romantically enshrined in John Keats, Helen Burns, Little Eva, and various opera characters, an evolution from the saintly, even martyr-like, *contemptus mundi* of Loveday, whose personal life is desiccated by the expectation of consumptive death, who was much contented that he would not exceed the years of his saviour. He is for Browne a fascinating example of one who could predict and lived much of his life with the certainty of his own early death, something he lingers on in the *Letter* when he discusses various historical figures who died on their birthdays (as Browne himself would do in 1682). To die of consumption is in some sense holy; the moral anatomy of this particular consumptive is a kind of martyrology. Loveday becomes emblematic, for Browne the doctor, of his disease, and for Browne the moralist, of the art of dying in undiminished faith.

As an *ars moriendi* tract, the *Letter* moves back and forth between the general and the particular, in medicine, in history, and in moral meditation, so that Loveday's status wavers between an individual with a specific character, story, and symptomology, and an exemplar of a dreaded pathology, of a pious life, and of a good death. The odd shift from elaborated medical *consilium* to a series of moral maxims two-thirds of the way into the *Letter* is thus in keeping with a diagnostic tract that cannot resist generating universal truths from the grisly particulars of one man's illness.[15]

A decade earlier in *Religio Medici* Browne had marvelled:

> I, that have examined the parts of man, and know upon what tender filaments that Fabrick hangs, doe wonder that we are not always [sick]; and

considering the thousand dores that lead to death, doe thanke my God that we can die but once. (*RM* I.43)

During his long professional career Browne must have treated hundreds, perhaps thousands, of patients; and yet early modern medicine was almost completely ineffectual in curing or even managing most illness, a calamitous fact that would certainly have been foremost in the mind of any learned physician, who mainly watched his patients suffer or die. And a great many of those doomed souls would have been consumptives: the Bills of Mortality for the late 1650s show that a quarter of all London deaths were consumptions. It was nothing if not routine.[16] Why did Browne, more often beguiled by the unusual and the strange, choose to write meditatively about a consumptive patient, one who, like so many others, suffered from a very common, utterly unremarkable, essentially hopeless complaint that offered nothing rare or extraordinary in its grim progression. Why not write about, say, epidemics of plague or smallpox or typhus or any of the more violent or sudden afflictions, the mass casualties of early modern England, or about some more clinically unusual illness? He wrote his doctoral dissertation at Leiden on smallpox, and we have medical notes and formally composed consultative correspondence with medical colleagues discussing the great variety of a doctor's clinical experience, as well as his epistolary conversations with his son Edward, also a doctor, which provide fascinating insights into his medical interests and diagnostic and therapeutic regimes. Even in *A Letter to a Friend* he briefly mentions a strange infantile disease of the Languedoc called the morgellons,[17] as well as what may have been progeria. Elsewhere he described what sounds like *myasthenia gravis*, anorexia, and various depressive and delusional illnesses.[18] But no patient prompted him, as Loveday did, to write philosophically about these other, more notable examples. Undoubtedly Loveday was personally interesting to Browne; but more than that, consumption itself convened several themes that mightily and consistently influenced his thinking about the human condition.

In his medical capacity Browne discusses the *marasmus* or wasting characteristic of the disease, also known as phthisis (Greek, 'wasting'; by extension, tuberculosis):

In his consumptive Condition and remarkable Extenuation he came to be almost half himself, and left a great part behind him which he carried not to the Grave ... an Aruspex might have read a Lecture upon him without Exenteration, his Flesh being so consumed that he might, in a manner, have discerned his Bowels without opening of him. (*LF* 183)

In other words, no formal anatomy (exenteration) was necessary in this emaciated ('extenuated') condition, where the innards of the body were virtually visible from the outside; but Browne appears to have opened him anyway – still a relatively unusual occurrence in an era when forensic anatomies were by tradition reserved for hanged criminals and would have dishonoured anyone else; moreover, the operation could only have been done to satisfy curiosity when the cause of death was obvious. In any case, the course of Loveday's illness is marked in the formal observations of anatomical dissection: Browne finds the usual evidence of the caul or fatty membrane around the intestines wholly consumed, the bowel itself empty, the lungs blue-grey and blotchy, the pericardium withered, the pulmonary lobes adhering to the pleura. The corpse, he says, is 'exuccous', his own neologism for 'juiceless' which he uses in *Urne-Buriall* also; all these symptoms are presented in the lexis of the dry, the sapless, the used-up, the devoured. The disease, understood medically as a kind of febrile scorching, yields appropriate adjectives – what Browne sees in his post-mortem examination is evidence of consumption by heat. The curious and distressing claim that his entrails can be examined from outside the withered phthisical body emphasises that desiccation, which is a favourite palimpsestic idea of Browne's, revisited several times in his works: he notes the latent buried visage of forebears revealed in the emaciated faces of the dying; and even the oxidized implements of brass discovered in long-buried cinerary urns, when exposed to the air, 'begin to spot and betray their green entrals' (*UB* III.104). It is as if consumption is a kind oxidisation of the flesh.

An important feature of this account is Browne's literal lexical application of *consume/consumption*: the disease is so-called because it seems to eat up or devour its victim, and that in consequence 'his Inwards and Flesh remaining could make no Bouffage, but a light bit for the Grave' (*LF* 183). He has already produced 'exuccous', and this French word *bouffage*, meaning a satisfying meal, or 'cheek-puffing' repast, is likewise only recorded in English in this one instance.[19] It's absolutely typical that Browne introduces an unusual, foreign word for meatiness as a precise antithesis of leanness to suggest that this consuming disease is a hearty eater, and that the grave also possesses an appetite that will be unsatisfied by so meagre a corpse, this 'light bit'. The body as the repast of the disease and of the grave is a step along the way in that inevitable retreat to earth that all lives follow. The shift here from the sickbed to the grave moves the field of consideration from life to afterlife, and the body itself from the world above ground to the subterranean arena that occupies him in *Urne-Buriall*. That semantic and thematic retreat to earth generates more images of death's ability to reveal interior or abstract realities in this particular disease: Browne says that Loveday's was 'a mortal visage and last Face', 'a Face of Earth' (*LF* 183) – in other words, Hippocrates's specification of the sharp nose and hollow eyes that signal the approaches to death – and then to a more mystical signature in the dying face that likens it to the earth itself from whence we all came.[20] There is 'no sigil … to cure an extreme Consumption or *Marasmus*' (*LF* 181), no occult amulet or preparation that works by magical sympathy. Instead, Loveday's face is itself the sigil of his own mortality.

The 'Firy Principle'

Burning and conflagration constitute the most obvious connection between *Urne-Buriall* and the *Letter*. Almost from the beginning of *Urne-Buriall* Browne reminds us that ritual incineration restores us to the condition of earth from which mankind sprang: fire is the one solvent that returns us to that pre-Adamic state as a type of mere dust. Dust, earth, and ashes are all cognate substances, and *Urne-Buriall* commences with 'the subterranean world', the place where the buried, ash-filled urns that inspired it were found near Little Walsingham, not far from the ruins of a Roman pyral oven (*UB* I.89).[21] Although cremation prevented disease and preserved the body from vengeful enemies and grave-robbers, he is more intrigued that 'it was most natural to end in fire, as due unto the master principle … according to Heraclitus' (*UB* I.91), who wrote that fire is the primary material of creation, that all things are manifestations or modifications of it, and will be resolved into it again.[22] Cremation purifies by 'refining the [body's] grosser commixture', he explains, 'and firing out the Ætheriall particles so deeply immersed in it' (*UB* I.91). Literal and metabolic cremation are entwined in the *Letter*.

The diagnostic system of early modern medicine detected in consumption a signature of the end of the world, 'the final pyre of all things' (*UB* I.91). Browne says in the *Letter*, even before Loveday's complaint is identified, that 'they who shall live to see the Sun and Moon darkned, and the Stars to fall from Heaven, will hardly be deceived in the Advent of the last Day' (*LF* 179), as if the connection between the consuming fire of this disease and the consuming flames of apocalypse were already understood. The consumptions that accounted for 25 per cent of all deaths in contemporary London could be not only the pulmonary variety but also lymphatic tuberculosis (or scrofula); all consumptions, characterised by chronic fever, were imagined as the literal combustion by heat of the body's resources, especially its fatty and fleshy parts.[23] Thomas Nashe described consumption as a devouring flame that 'drinks up *Life*'s moisture ... till all its oile [is] spent, / [and] glimmers i'th'socket' like a candle guttering, or a 'roast[ing] to death', to 'melt away little by little'.[24] Robert Boyle considered his own feverish ague as a flame burning a tallow candle.[25] Fever as a signature of the last day is of course familiar from John Donne's poem about the death of a young girl, where the 'wrangling schools, that search what fire / Shall burn this world' fail to recognise that 'this her fever might be it'.[26] Consumption is a condition, Browne explains,

> which if other diseases fail, will put a period unto long Livers, and at last make dust of us all. And therefore the *Stoicks* could not but think that the firy Principle would wear out all the rest, and at last make an end of the World. (*LF* 181)

It is thus regularly aligned, and not just by Browne, with what he calls 'the last and generall fever' (*RM* I.43), the destruction of the world as predicted in Revelation.

In *Religio Medici*, following Aristotle and Galen, he imagines the body and its metabolism as a burning lamp,[27] and ascribes early death to the lack of 'vital oyle' (*RM* I.42). In *Urne-Buriall* he muses 'that the bulk of a man should sink into so few pounds of bones and ashes, may seem strange unto any who considers not its constitution, and how slender a masse will remain upon an open and urging fire of the carnall composition' (*UB* III.108). But, he concludes, 'the body compleated proves a combustible lamp, wherein fire findes flame even from bones, and some fuell almost from all parts' (*UB* III.108), a quality proven by tallow candles and the fact that animals make 'good burning lights' (*UB* III.108). Domestic necessity in the form of candles becomes a signature of the wasting of hectic or phthisical fevers as a kind of pyral combustion.

Unlike the incinerated dead in *Urne-Buriall*, however, Loveday was not cremated, nor could he have been: the practice was illegal, suspect among the Christian sects as being pagan and as interfering with the resurrection of the whole body by atomising it.[28] Cremated ashes, moreover, seemed to allude to a troubling annihilation. Nevertheless, in one of the more stupendous passages of *Religio Medici* Browne declares that he is not especially concerned about the possible resurrectionary impediments in cremation:

> I beleeve that our estranged and divided ashes shall unite againe, that our separated dust after so many pilgrimages and transformations into the parts of mineralls, Plants, Animals, Elements, shall at the voyce of God returne into their primitive shapes; and joyne againe to make up their primary and predestinate formes. (*RM* I.46)

What a scientist can do in the laboratory in the way of revivifying destroyed specimens, God can easily do among the dead. Browne likes images of resurrection and spends some time in *Urne-Buriall* imagining the reconvening of bones and body-parts in everything from the dream of Ezekiel to the burial of Theseus. In other words, for Browne cremation is a natural and unproblematic topic because resurrection is unconnected with the precise state of our remains – God can resurrect anything he wants in whatever state, even dust and ashes. However, although he was the first to discuss the practice of cremation seriously in England, and in doing so triggered a long debate about it over the next two centuries, it did not become legal until the 1870s.[29] Loveday didn't require cremation in any case: the patient had in a sense already undergone pyral combustion in the course of his long dying. 'Life', Browne says, 'is a pure flame, and we live by an invisible Sun within us' (*UB* V.123), and this is one of several analogies that poses human metabolism itself, whether in health or in hectic fever, as a system that uses up the body as fuel.[30]

Theories and types of fever were legion in the Galenic/Hippocratic medical tradition, and although pulmonary tuberculosis itself was thought to be caused by corrosive phlegm moving from the brain to the lungs, the hectic or wasting fever symptomatic of the disease was associated by Galen with a damaging superabundance of yellow bile, the choleric or hot humour.[31] The learned term for fever was *pyrexia*, from the same Graeco-Latin root of *pyre*, and like so many Brownean words, this root seems to make him think of the close relationship between the heated phthisical or wasting illness, cremation in mortuary disposal, and the apocalyptic fires of theological doctrine. If consumption, by ritual fire after death and by disease in life, figures social practice and medical reality, it also signifies, for Browne, a spiritual truth: like James Shirley, who moralised consumption as a disease that lightens the garment of flesh and turns the sufferer to pure spirit, 'nothing but angel now',[32] in the *Letter* Browne also discovers Loveday's spiritual refinement by metabolic fire and imagines his illness as a trial that converts flesh not only into spirit, but also into moral emblem.

He is ironic about those Christians who, although they 'abhorred ... [and] detested' cremation, yet 'stickt not to give their bodies to be burnt in their lives' (*UB* 92), and praises the valour of martyrs who died by fire (*UB* IV.117). Martyrdom by fire haunts the *Letter* physiologically: Loveday's pyrexical combustion is converted into a medical emblem of his pious life and good death, a kind of immolation in which phthisis with pyrexia becomes virtually a holy complaint, a kind of pathogenic sacrifice and trial by fire. In this one ordinary disease endured by a somewhat extraordinary patient, the figurative cremation by fever is a fiery consumption of the body's tallow that bares Hippocrates's last face as well as a spectrum of other signatures of the world's end: as Loveday lost weight the hidden visage of his relations and ancestors was exposed, a morbid phenomenon of pyrexical withering and melting of flesh that Browne explains as revealing 'the community of seminal Originals ... before latent in us' (*LF* 180), or hereditary likenesses to our forebears. Such pathogenic and crematory effects fascinate him: buried bones allow 'no impossible physiognomy to conjecture at fleshy appendencies; ... handsome formed sculls, give some analogie of fleshy resemblance ... Physiognomy outlives ourselves, and ends not in our graves' (*UB* III.110–111).

Residues of Fire

Dust and ashes would have been related terms in a seventeenth-century ear: Abraham refers to himself as 'dust and ashes' (Genesis 18:27), as does Job, twice (Job 30:19; 42:6); above all, the order for burial of the dead in the Book of Common Prayer makes one thing of the body, dust, ashes, and earth.[33] Although Browne seems to mingle burial and cremation in the dedicatory epistle of *Urne-Buriall* when he asks 'Who knows the fate of his bones? ... who hath the oracle of his ashes?' (*UB* Epistle 83), he is normally very exact in distinguishing the two. 'Time which antiquates Antiquities ... hath an art to make dust of all things' (*UB* V.118), he says in chapter 5: ashes are always the product of cremation, whereas dust is made by the action of time.[34] God specified that we be returned to dust, and thus Christians 'affect[ed] rather a depositure than absumption' in order to comply (*UB* I.93). These two terms are curious and unusual: 'depositure' (burial) is used here for only the second time in English; and 'absumption' (by which he means burning or cremation) usually means 'wasting away' (for example, in evaporation) or 'gradual destruction' – in other words, something more like the effect of phthisical consumption and even decay than like pyral cremation. Browne's unique use of the rare 'absumption' elides the two kinds of mortuary practice, the atomisation or gradual destruction of decay in grave-burial, and the more sudden dissolution of the pyre.

In *A Letter to a Friend*, that conflation is more marked when the concept of 'dust' seems to be transferred to the idea of ashes, as when 'an extreme Consumption or *Marasmus*, ... if other Diseases fail, will put a period unto long Livers, and at last make dust of all' (*LF* 181). Curiously, perhaps, for a discussion of consumption that he imagines as implicitly pyral, he does not use the word 'ash' or 'ashes' at all in the *Letter*, much as the word 'dust' hardly appears in *Urne-Buriall*. The two ideas are, however, mingled in the 'retreat to earth'; and here the word 'earth' retains a characteristic Brownean wordplay: it refers simultaneously to the planet, the ground, the grave, the soil, dust, and the residue of human remains of all varieties – all these are 'earth' and all are comprehended in the word. Two sections of the *Letter* discuss 'malevolent Places on Earth' – that is, local or 'endemial' health hazards associated with geographical location. For example, Portugal does not favour the tabid (tubercular) patient; Austria is risky for the colical, as is Rome for the weak-legged (*LF* 180); England promotes rickets (*LF* 185). Such places, he explains, 'single out our Infirmities, and strike at our weaker Parts' (*LF* 180). East Anglia, though commonly thought healthful for consumptives because of the nitre (volatile potassium nitrate) in the air, did Loveday little good: in its 'endemial and local Infirmities proper unto certain Regions' (*LF* 180) the earth itself is an antagonist to health; earth practises upon the human subject as do diseases. Our earthiness, our earthy origin, our subjection to earth, is inherent in us and an augury of the place and substance to which we will all return, just as the hectic fever reduces us to our nascent earthy condition. Browne's notion of dust and of earth is inflected by his antiquarian and natural-philosophical interest in the subterranean, from the archaeology of the East Anglian substrate to grave-wax, the hard jellied substance found in burials in certain earths.[35] In the *Letter*, that interest settles on a complex and layered signature of the world itself as a resting place, an adversary, the site of our final conflagration, dust and ashes being ultimately indistinguishable. Thus, when he describes Loveday's as a 'face of earth' he seems to mean that it displays the many sigils of death: fingernails, the muscle of the thumb, a spot behind the ear, the depth of the jugular notch or throat-pit, and the Hippocratic indications of hollow eyes and a sharp nose, the infallible indicators of the great medical authorities – all are finally collapsed into a metaphor of earth. If *Urne-Buriall* anatomises the ways our bodies in death are returned to the earth as ashes, the *Letter* tells us how bodies in life begin to *be* the earth itself in previously hidden signs that remind us we are all mere extracts and colonies of it, that the body is a grave in preparation and that the earth itself is our 'seminal original'. This personal cycle in which we first arise from earth into a life of earth-like symptoms, and return to earth at last as ashes or dust, is a microcosm of the great conflagration that will turn earth itself to powder.

A Letter to a Friend, although it never names its subject, is nevertheless concerned with a particular individual who is memorialised in it.

Urne-Buriall, also about a kind of burning, also declines to name its subjects – but only because the persons whose remains lie in the anonymous
urns found near Walsingham can never be identified; they are emblematic
of the general anonymity of humankind, of whom far more have lived
and died than will ever be known or remembered. *Urne-Buriall*'s attention to general, nondescript mortality produces a strangely crowded tract,
one full of notable examples that lead us to the nothing, the anonymity, of death which, as Hamlet reminds us, is 'common'. Like Loveday
in the *Letter*, these urns are nameless; their ashes contain nothing at all
notable; and they have long since been further effaced by grave-robbers.
Browne says that he was impelled to write about them because 'they arose
as they lay, almost in silence among us ... [and] we were very unwilling
they should die again, and be buried twice among us' (*UB* Epistle 84).
Thus *Urne-Buriall*, like the *Letter*, is a memorial act that insists we try
to remember, or at least honour, the unknown dead. Even the place of
burial, 'in a field of old Walsingham', is only vaguely specified as being
about five miles from Brancaster to the north-west. Where, exactly, forty
or fifty supposedly Roman but in fact Saxon urns were discovered in 1656
is lost to us.[36] We are still searching for those urns and those anonymous
dead.

At the beginning of this essay, I noted seventeenth-century science's
keen interest in the subterranean world – in fossils, earthquakes, petrifica-
tion, and the nature of soils. The noise of all these questions and debates
is humming away in the background of *Urne-Buriall*, and it is important
to recognise that if Browne's antiquarian knowledge of mortuary customs
through the ages is powerfully on display in the essay, he actually is much
more concerned with the way that 'singular contrivances of ... corporall
dissolution', in the form of burying and burning, elaborate on these more
scientific, geological themes. 'We are coldly drawn unto discourses of
Antiquities', he says in the dedication of *Urne-Buriall*, 'who have scarce
time before us to comprehend new things, or make out learned Novelties'
(*UB* Epistle 84). Thus, although the work appears to be solely concerned
with antiquities, it is in fact animated by the various dissolutions, both
physical and memorial, that interment either of bodies or of ashes creates.
We see this in the way he pieces together what he can of the remains found
in the Norfolk urns much as a palaeontologist might piece together an
ancient skeleton. Some of the urns included among their ashes as much as
two pounds of bones – skulls, ribs, jaws, thighbones, and teeth – with signs
of incineration; nearby were the remains of the sunken *ustrinum*, the pyre
or place of burning that must have supplied these contents.

Browne's analysis of all this is almost like a site report: the depth and composition of the soil noted, the variety of urns and their weight of ash recorded, the sex and age surmised of the persons whose random bones survive, even the archaeology of place names adduced from nearby Saxon Burnham back to Brancaster and Branodunum, the Roman name for the garrison there. Browne surely knew that these urns were not Roman but Saxon; yet in his longing to identify them as more gloriously imperial he obviously chose to forget that, from their shape and decoration conjecturing that these were either Roman urns, or else those of Britons Romanised by their colonial masters. His learned excavation here ranges from the anatomical and the mineralogical to the onomastic, the mythical, and the historical. He reads these urns as almost corporeal in design, with ears and long necks: 'the common form with necks was a proper figure, making our last bed like our first; nor much unlike the Urnes of our Nativity, while we lay in the nether part of the Earth, and inward vault of our Microcosme' (*UB* III.102). Here, in a wonderful medical metaphor, he draws on his expertise in embryology to suggest that the urns are uterine, their handles the fallopian tubes, and thereby makes another one of his circular figures in which the earth of the grave is prefigured in the 'earth' of our gestation in the womb, the 'urn' of our nativity, perhaps with the subterranean pun on the biological *matrix* or uterus, and Mother Earth.

What is most striking about these uterine urns, however, is that, like the evacuated innards of Loveday observed in dissection, they have very little in them, or at least very little of note – they are mainly described in terms of what they lack. When he refers to the tomb of the fifth-century Frankish King Childeric (discovered in Tournai about three years before he wrote *Urne-Buriall*) and to an antique urn in the collection of the sixteenth-century Cardinal Farnese in Rome he can offer a rich and enticing list of their gorgeous contents: Childeric's tomb contained his golden sword, two hundred rubies, many imperial coins, and three hundred golden bees 'according to the barbarous magnificence of those dayes in their sepulchrall Obsequies' (*UB* II.99); the Farnese urn yielded carved gems, animals made of amethyst and agate, crystals, and silver implements. Compare this with the extraordinary set of absences that characterise the Norfolk urns, discussed mainly in terms of what they are not or what they might be. Beyond the anonymity of the cremated individuals, their ashes contain little of interest, only 'substances *resembling* Combes, Plates *like* Boxes ... long brass plates ... *like* the handles of neat implements, brazen nippers ... a *kinde* of Opale' (*UB* II.95; emphasis added), which he mentions almost listlessly; there are none of the coins which are normally so helpful in establishing dates, no lamps, wines, lachrymatories, rings, chalices, bay leaves, or any of the hundred items he knows to have been discovered in Roman urns; in short, little on which he can exercise his active imagination in recreating the customs and emotions of the final farewells that probably accompanied their depositure in earth. He tells us that contemporaries who have examined these urns suspect that the bone fragments in each urn come from more than one source, although Browne himself concludes that there is no evidence to support this either way, nor to determine whether they were from adults or children, male or female. 'The earth had confounded the ashes of these ossuaries' (*UB* III.104), and basic distinctions of sex and age made impossible to adjudicate securely. These urns, excavated and then evacuated in the cause of enquiry, are almost devoid of items and identity, making the pyral burning of the grave an almost exact replica of the pyrexical combustion that left Loveday's insides desiccated and nearly destroyed. Both investigative operations, of excavation and of anatomy, yield exactly the same result.

In his 'deliberate and creeping progress to the grave' (*LF* 188) Loveday modestly declined to compose his own epitaph, insisting on his own anonymity after death. Likewise, the featureless urns of an obscure Saxon burial site in Norfolk bear no marks of identity. Browne's lifelong fascination with erasure and forgetfulness, so brilliantly on display in the *tour de force* that is *Urne-Buriall*, is equally if more subtly present in *A Letter to a Friend*. The urns that he would not wish to see buried in oblivion *twice* are rescued from the earth by the remarkable essay that supplies in its riches of information all that they themselves lack, from names to grave goods. And the second part of *A Letter to a Friend* works similarly. This is the series of advisories, moral maxims, that Browne appends to the discussion of Loveday, a gift of good advice to the recipient of the letter in the form of lapidary adages. 'Be charitable before wealth makes thee covetous'; 'trust not the omnipotency of gold'; 'Persons lightly dip'd, not grain'd in generous Honesty, are but pale in Goodness, and faint hued in Sincerity' (*LF* 192) – such aphorisms and directives go on for several pages, piling up treasures of wisdom almost like the pompous wealth of ancient tombs. These sententious offerings function as the epitaph Loveday never wrote and as precious interments that accompany him in the grave. *A Letter to a Friend* is itself a memorial to one who is otherwise nearly lost in the oblivion that has swallowed the urns. Loveday and those urns, together, rest in the earth of East Anglia.

Dust and ashes, the deep discoveries of the subterranean world, the inflections in mortuary custom, even the grisly symptoms of disease – all these speak to a notion of universal interment, of a world emerging from and declining back to earth. 'The earth is still in the urn to us', Browne remarks at the start of *Urne-Buriall* (*UB* 89). That insistent sense of circularity should therefore end this essay, in words that Browne and all English persons would have known well – the order for the burial of the dead in the Book of Common Prayer, and the words with which the priest commits the body to the earth:

> I commend thy soule to God the father almighty, and thy body to the grounde, earth to earth, asshes to asshes, dust to dust, in sure and certayne hope of resurreccion to eternall lyfe, through our Lord Jesus Christ, who shall chaunge our vile body, that it may be lyke to his glorious body, accordyng to the myghtie workyng wherby he is hable to subdue all thynges to himselfe.[37]

These ringing words must have offered Browne a profoundly resonant verbal palette for painting the idea of en-urnment, the change of the vile body into something quite unlike itself, 'all angel now', and of the world itself awaiting the purifying flame of a final, pyral conflagration.

Notes

1 Francis Bacon, *The Advancement of Learning and New Atlantis*, ed. by Arthur Johnston (Oxford: Clarendon Press, 1974), p. 240.
2 According to John Evelyn, precisely 170,001,060 (*A Philosophical Discourse of Earth* (London, 1676)), p. 11.
3 On underwater properties, see Thomas Browne, *Pseudodoxia Epidemica*, ed. by Robin Robbins, 2 vols. (Oxford: Clarendon Press, 1981), I.5.6; on underground properties and fossils, see II.5.7, II.1.80–81, III.13.210, III.23.258, III.24.263; on marine creatures underground, see Dugdale to Browne, 17 November 1658 (BL MS Sloane 1911–13, fol. 104) and Dugdale to Browne 24 February 1658–9 (BL MS Sloane 1911–13, fol. 101); on tectonic shifts, see Browne to Dugdale, 16 November 1659 (in Keynes IV, 320).
4 Browne, *Pseudodoxia Epidemica*, II.i.82.
5 Thomas Burnet, *The Theory of the Earth* (London, 1684), pp. 110–121.
6 Athanasius Kircher, *The vulcano's: or, Burning and fire-vomiting mountains* (London, 1669), [a3^r]–2.
7 Unless otherwise indicated, all references to Browne's works are to Thomas Browne, *Religio Medici and Other Works*, ed. by L. C. Martin (Oxford: Clarendon Press, 1964); chapter and/or page numbers appear within the text. Citations of *Urne-Buriall* (1658) appear as '*UB*'.
8 Citations of *A Letter to a Friend* (1690/1712) appear as '*LF*'.
9 His first work, *Religio Medici* (1643), had been pirated and published in an unauthorised form in 1642, much to his distress.

10 Frank Livingstone Huntley first proposed that the subject was Loveday, and less convincingly that the friend was Sir John Pettus, a patient and friend of Browne's living near Norwich (Huntley, *Sir Thomas Browne: A Biographical and Critical Study* (Ann Arbor: University of Michigan Press, 1962; pbk 1968), pp. 184–203).

11 Some of these maxims appear in yet another work, *Christian Morals* (London, 1716; *op. post.*).

12 To Dante and to the churchyard of St Innocent's in Paris.

13 *Christian Morals* likely also belongs to 1656.

14 Citations of *Religio Medici* appear as '*RM*'.

15 This movement is unusual: learned medicine was much more likely to derive individual prognoses from general principles.

16 The Bills of Mortality list 12,157 deaths by consumption in London in the years 1655–9, the period in which *LF* was written ('Table of Casualties', in John Graunt, *Observations on the Bills of Mortality*, in *The Economic Writings of Sir William Petty*, vol. 2, ed. by Charles Henry Hull (Cambridge: Cambridge University Press, 1899), table facing p. 406). That this figure amounts to 25 per cent of mortalities relies on the arithmetic of R. Y. Keers, *Pulmonary Tuberculosis* (London: Baillière Tindal, 1978), p. 23.

17 The morgellons was first described by Browne in *LF*; it is currently thought to be psychogenic (delusional parasitosis).

18 Browne to Samuel Bave, 24 April 1642 (BL Add. MS 46378 (B)); to John Maplet to B, 27 August 1668 (BL MS Sloane 4062, fol. 168); to Edward Browne, 18 May 1679 (BL MS Sloane 1847, fol. 219).

19 Randle Cotgrave, *A Dictionarie of the French and English Tongues* (London, 1611), [L4^v].

20 Hippocrates, *Prognostic*, trans. by W. H. S. Jones (Cambridge, MA: Harvard University Press/Loeb Classical Library, 1923), p. 2.

21 Browne was sent a few of these urns, probably by an antiquarian friend, although the nature and source of the donation is not known.

22 Carl Huffman, 'Pythagoreanism', in *The Stanford Encyclopedia of Philosophy* (Fall 2019), ed. by Edward N. Zalta, https://plato.stanford.edu/archives/fall2019/entries/pythagoreanism/ [accessed 1 December 2019].

23 It is the reduced oxygen to the tissues that causes wasting, not the fever itself.

24 Thomas Nashe, *The Terrors of the Night* (London, 1594), F3[^{r}].

25 Robert Boyle, 'Accidents of an Ague', in Robert Boyle, *Occasional Reflections* (London, 1665), 2:10, 220.

26 John Donne, 'A Feaver', in John Donne, *Poems by J.D.* (London, 1633; *op. post.*), p. 210.

27 See, for example, Thomas Cogan, *Haven of Health* (London, 1588), AA4^r–BB1^r. I thank Grant Williams for this reference.

28 In *Urne-Buriall*, Browne explains that Christians 'properly submit[ed] unto the sentence of God, to return not unto ashes but unto dust againe, conformable unto the practice of the Patriarchs' (*Hydriotaphia, Urne-Buriall …. Together with The Garden of Cyrus* (London, 1658), 1.92–3); that penalty, levied

upon Adam and Eve after their transgression, is in Genesis 3:19: 'In the sweat of thy face shalt thou eat bread, till thou return unto the ground; for out of it wast thou taken: for dust thou art, and unto dust shalt thou return'.

29 The booming urban population's funerary needs required too much space.

30 'Hectic' is the medical term for consumptive fever; its metaphorical use (excitement or busy activity) was Rudyard Kipling's.

31 Galen, *Methodus Medendi [Method of Medicine]*, ed. and trans. by Ian Johnston and G. H. Horsely (Cambridge, MA: Harvard University Press/Loeb Classical Library, 2011), 10.5.

32 James Shirley, 'Upon Mr Charles Beaumont who died of a Consumption', in James Shirley, *Poems* (London, 1646), 65.

33 [Thomas Cranmer], *The Book of Common Prayer* (London, 1549), fol. cxxvi.

34 Indeed, in *Urne-Buriall* he uses the word 'dust' only one other time (I.93).

35 He was the first to discuss the phenomenon of adipocere (*UB* III.110).

36 It may be site 2030 as identified by Norfolk Heritage Explorer, www .heritage.norfolk.gov.uk/record-details?MNF2030-Walsingham-Early-Saxon-cremation-cemetery&Index=2&RecordCount=1&SessionID=43225fa2-a701-4f52-b02f-7d248f16124c [accessed 13 June 2022].

37 [Cranmer], *The Book of Common Prayer*, fol. cxxvi.

The Ends of Commemoration

Preface to Part III

The essays in this part, each in their own way, are indicative of the sea change marking approaches to early modern visual and literary studies as regards the ends to which commemoration figures into the critical discussion of cultural thanatology. All four essays take into account a key aspect of how and the extent to which distinctive expressions of Protestant commemoration put the focus on secular life, tending to serve the living rather than the dead.[1] Catholic rites of burial and related ends of commemoration served principally the dead rather than the living although, of course, the living very much were involved in acts and rites of 'postmortem intercession'.[2]

As will be discussed later in this preface, Peter Sherlock (Chapter 9) explores what was gained and what ends were being served (and for whom) with the building of a knight's tomb and then, later, with a portrait depicting, among other things, this very tomb – clearly motivated by a different prefigured end than was the case with the *in situ* memorial. Anita Gilman Sherman (Chapter 10) points out the trace of a shift in aesthetic no less than religious and scientific sensibilities in the mid-seventeenth century that allowed for a reconceptualization of the ends of the traditional *memento mori*. No longer was this admonitory device, whether textually conveyed or as a symbolic token, used exclusively to help one prepare for their death (see Figure Pr3.1); for Andrew Marvell it became a kind of poetic *jeu d'esprit*. A new sense of enjoyment in and of itself of the ends of commemoration becomes possible with the aestheticization of the *memento mori* while, at the same time, self-consciously pointing out the paradoxes of commemoration. Andrew Hiscock (Chapter 11) and Michael Neill (Chapter 12) bring to light the political ends of monumentalization with recourse to the visual and textual record of outpourings of grief upon the death of Queen Elizabeth and of Prince Henry respectively.

Figure P13.1   Death's head, Henry Peacham, *Minerva Britanna*, 1612, C4^r.

Each of these essays engages in a thoughtful remapping of the well-travelled cultural terrain that shifted by virtue of events associated with the English Reformation, including the rise of nationalism and spread of print culture. Relations between the living and the dead were being altered steadily if incrementally in Tudor–Stuart England. Mourners no longer were enjoined to think of themselves as being able actively to intervene in the lives of their dead loved ones, which left open the option of new approaches to actively remembering – or passively forgetting – their forebears. The old mechanisms for keeping the dead alive in both thoughts and actions quietly were being dismantled and diminished, and so the memory arts and the death arts, once close partners, entered a phase in which their relations were fraught with complications that merit closer scrutiny.[3]

Dying and recollection still were both seen as 'arts', and recollection was crucial to understandings of a 'good death' because fame offered early moderns their best chance at some version of immortality through carefully curated commendation. Thus to study the 'art of dying' and 'the art of memory', along the lines undertaken by the four essays in this part, is to consider the concepts as they were treated in the Renaissance: as being absolutely and inextricably interlinked. These four essays on the ends of commemoration examine different aspects of the shifting early modern ideas about the body and those cultural – which is to say, those interlinked political, social, religious, and aesthetic – practices immediately concerned with mortal corporality. Each of the essay's findings bring to our attention intriguing histories that shed important light on how future studies of the works considered here, and along these lines, might well proceed.

More specifically, Peter Sherlock (Chapter 9) argues that the frequently discussed Unton Memorial Portrait deserves to be reconsidered not primarily as a narrative of the Elizabethan knight's life and death, but as a more profound statement about early modern memory and mortality. The key to recognizing this is in the portrait's spatial arrangement: a third devoted to Unton's birth, life, and death; a third to the rituals of death; and a third to memory and the afterlife. Detailed analysis of the architecture and image of Unton's monumental tomb (included as a vignette in the portrait), and in comparison with those of late sixteenth and early seventeenth century monuments, suggests that this depiction – perhaps a fantasy or a design or an image of the actual Faringdon monument – is most unlikely to have been created earlier than 1600. This enables the picture to be re-dated to the period 1600–1606, and thus distanced from the immediate circumstances of Unton's death. Its creation may be seen as part of an attempt to develop a complex visual, literary, and even musical memorial tradition imitating that of Unton's more famous contemporary Philip Sidney. Central to Sherlock's analysis is the Unton monument's use of a reclining effigy, a powerful and influential trope in English sepulchral imagery in the period and the subject of contemporary comment by the playwright John Webster. What emerges is an even more compelling glimpse into early modern concepts of memory and mortality, and the role commemoration played after the immediate rituals of death were completed. The chapter contributes not only to a reappraisal of the Unton Memorial Picture, but also to developing a theory of memory and commemoration authentic to the English Renaissance. Along the way, this chapter discusses the same play as analysed more fulsomely by Neill (Chapter 12); and, the memorial's work in the world to commemorate and perpetuate has affinities with the essays by Phillippy (Chapter 5), Chalk (Chapter 7), and Hiscock (Chapter 11).

In Chapter 10, Anita Gilman Sherman addresses Marvell's long-noted fascination with memory and mortality, so as to bring to the fore larger questions of decorum and taste in the *ars moriendi*. Marvell returns time and again in his poetry to the moment of death, staging sometimes heroic conduct,

sometimes youthful vulnerability, sometimes the precariousness of beauty
and thereby ringing changes on the *carpe diem* motif.[4] These poems achieve
their peculiar tonality, Sherman argues, by testing the conventions of the *ars
moriendi* and occasionally breaching the porous boundaries between good
and bad taste. Marvell's interest in the aesthetics of the *ars moriendi* demonstrates the gradual secularization of the death arts at the end of the seventeenth century, as the preoccupation with dying a good death turns into a
desire for a tasteful death. This chapter analyses Marvell's sustained concern
with the problematics of tasteful dying in two ways: his own remarks about
decorum and rhetoric in his satirical prose, and by way of European neo-
classicism and its reception in England. Because Marvell's work has lately
been contextualized with few exceptions (exemplarily, the work of McDowell
and Pertile, as discussed in Sherman's chapter) either in terms of English
politics or in terms of his literary forebears and sources, Sherman's effort to
place his poetry within contemporary French and Italian theorizations of
style breaks new ground. For Marvell's stylistic experiments and forays into
a range of dying poses not only interrogate neo-classical canons of taste and
beauty, but also evince scepticism about preparations for death and the project of memorialization. Sherman's insightful treatment of Marvell's taste for
death charts key aspects in the aestheticization of the art of memory and connects in significant ways to the larger theoretical concerns about the arts of
dying which variously are brought out in the critical interpretations of 'artful
dying' by Neill on Webster (Chapter 12), Helfer on Donne (Chapter 1), and
Hiscock on 'The Many Labours of Mourning a Virgin Queen' (Chapter 11).

Indeed, Andrew Hiscock's discussion takes as its focus the multifarious
ways in which the passing of the last Tudor monarch was formulated in
manuscript, correspondence, and printed texts, taking as its particular focus
Elizabethan iconography's response to the forces of Fortuna and Chronos.[5]
While much critical discussion thus far has focused upon the varying gov-
ernmental strategies involved in the growing corpus of iconography surrounding Elizabeth during her lifetime, much more neglected has been the
study of the significant corpus of texts (in English, Latin, and continental languages) emanating from home and abroad invested in discourses of
grief and remembering in the years following her death. Hiscock's chapter explores how Elizabeth in fact emerges as a deeply conflicted cultural
battleground: if reviled by Catholic antagonists, her political legacy is often
unsettled and problematized by loyal Catholic subjects, political hagiogra-
phers, and accounts circulating in popular culture. Elizabeth thus is situated during and after her life not only in the visual arts of the period, but
also in the symbolic discourses associated with her sovereignty, which are

compared and contrasted with other contemporary sovereigns, especially the king of France. Finally, due consideration is given to the cultural imperatives of the new Jacobean age where figures like Francis Bacon and James VI and I, sought both to exploit and reconfigure the mythologies of nation and belonging associated with the late queen. Insofar as this chapter is concerned with rituals surrounding dying and the public and private spheres of mourning, it dovetails aptly with the contributions to this volume by Phillippy (Chapter 5), Chalk (Chapter 7), Sherlock (Chapter 9), Sherman (Chapter 10), and, as will be discussed in what follows, Neill (Chapter 12).

Michael Neill (Chapter 12) casts a critical eye on Webster's *The Duchess of Malfi*, the play of the period perhaps best known for its steady preoccupation with death and memorial artifice. Most striking in this regard are three episodes involving the Duchess herself, including, in the first scene, the wooing of Antonio coloured by oddly disturbing references to 'a winding sheet' and to 'the figure cut in alabaster / Kneels at my husband's tomb' (1.1.380, 442–3); and in Act 4, her murder prefaced by a piece of grotesquely macabre theatre, when Bosola enters in the guise of an old man announcing himself a 'tomb-maker' whose 'trade is to flatter the dead' (ll. 135–6). But the tomb he promises never appears, becoming instead a conspicuous absence at the centre of the action.[6] And this is an absence, Neill argues, that is closely bound up with contemporary events (namely, the death from typhoid of King James's eldest son, Henry, Prince of Wales), and thus with the dissident politics on which Webster's famous tragedy is grounded. As a result, Henry's passing was the occasion for an unprecedented exhibition of public grief. A flood of mourning publications included accounts of his life, descriptions of his funeral,[7] and more than fifty elegiac volumes from leading poets of the day – among them Webster himself, who must have put aside work on *The Duchess of Malfi* to compose the first of his tributes to the dead prince, *A Monumental Columne* (1613). And so, appropriately, a primary focus of this chapter is the 'echo episode' in *The Duchess of Malfi* (5.3), in which Neill astutely explores the ways the scene's vividly imagined prospect of monastic ruins and decaying funeral monuments resonates not simply with the play's recurrent graveyard imagery,[8] but also with the preoccupations of two of Webster's better-known non-dramatic works – *A Monumental Columne* (1613) and *Monuments of Honour* (1624). Neill thus links Webster's monumental tragedy to its immediate historical context. This chapter's treatment of *The Duchess of Malfi* and the play's fascination with rites and practices of monumentalizing has important points of overlap with the issues attending commemoration as raised by both Chalk (Chapter 7) and Sherlock (Chapter 9).

Taken together, these four chapters on the ends of commemoration reveal stunning insights into how the death of the body came to be seen less as a definitive moment than a crossing of a porous threshold joining, rather than dividing, the living and the dead in a new kind of relationship than what was experienced in earlier Tudor times.[9] Each essay situates itself with respect to this liminal space, offering insights into early modern England's creative engagements with, preparations for, memorializations of, and meditations on the complexities of death, dying, and commemoration. In all, this part presents a rich sampling of the aesthetic, affective, creative, and political responses of early modern men and women to the end of life and the cultural and spiritual afterlives of the departed.

Notes

1 See Elizabeth Tingle, 'Changing Western European Visions of Christian Afterlives, 1350–1700: Heaven, Hell, and Purgatory', in *A Companion to Death, Burial, and Remembrance in Late Medieval and Early Modern Europe, c. 1300–1700*, ed. by Philip Booth and Elizabeth Tingle (Leiden: Brill, 2021), p. 36: 'Protestants faced judgement alone, clothed solely in faith, and God's decision was independent and absolute.'

2 On 'perpetual masses by or for an individual … to help free a soul from its time-limited resting place in purgatory', see Elizabeth Tingle, 'The Counter Reformation and Preparations for Death in the European Roman Catholic Church, 1550–1700', in *A Companion to Death*, ed. by Booth and Tingle, p. 192.

3 See John S. Garrison, *Shakespeare and the Afterlife* (Oxford: Oxford University Press, 2018), p. 78: 'Though the Reformation may have dismissed Purgatory, neither could its long history be elided nor its symbolic power assuage longing to connect with the dead.'

4 See entry IV.16 on Andrew Marvell in *The Death Arts in Renaissance England*, ed. by William E. Engel, Rory Loughnane, and Grant Williams (Cambridge: Cambridge University Press, 2022).

5 Cf. Roy Strong, *The Elizabethan Image: An Introduction to English Portraiture, 1558–1603* (New Haven, CT: Yale University Press, 2019), pp. 28–59.

6 By comparison, Shakespeare likewise dealt dramaturgically with such 'theatrical transmediation' involving the interruption of the figure of Death in the midst of life; see, for example, with reference to *Love's Labour's Lost*, Stuart Sillars, *Shakespeare and the Visual Imagination* (Cambridge: Cambridge University Press, 2015), p. 128.

7 Elaborately staged processions in later state funerals, in which 'death imitates art', came to follow the pattern of the dramatic *topos* of the 'dead march', which itself mimics religious ritual; see Brian Cummings, '"Dead March": Liturgy and Mimesis in Shakespeare's Funerals', *Shakespeare*, 8.4 (2012), 368–85.

8 On the post-Reformation commonplace motif of tombs left to decay in recently obsolete monastic churches, see Peter Sherlock, *Monuments and Memory in Early Modern England* (Aldershot: Ashgate, 2008), p. 102.

9 As regards the historical contexts underlying the living's relation to the dead in the later fifteenth century, with special reference to rituals and representation, see Clifford Davidson and Sophie Oosterwijk, *John Lydgate, 'The Dance of Death', and Its Model, the French 'Danse Macabre'*, ed. by Clifford Davidson and Sophie Oosterwijk (Leiden: Brill, 2021), pp. 1–75, esp. pp. 5–62.

CHAPTER 9

The Unton Portrait Reconsidered

Peter Sherlock

The portrait of Sir Henry Unton is one of the most striking images of memory and mortality in early modern England (Figure 9.1). It commemorates Sir Henry Unton (*c.* 1558–1596), a man who, if not for the portrait, would be largely forgotten today outside the pages of the *History of Parliament* or the *Oxford Dictionary of National Biography*. Nevertheless, to his contemporaries, Unton was the real deal: a provincial gentleman of high birth who, through his education, service on the battlefield, and ambassadorial career, embodied early modern ideals of masculine virtue and honour. He was even knighted on the battlefield by the Earl of Leicester, and fought alongside that other Elizabethan hero, Sir Philip Sidney.[1]

Both the portrait and its subject have been the objects of considerable scholarly curiosity and popular fascination since 1884, when it was acquired by the National Portrait Gallery and put on public display in London. Painted on a wood panel, measuring 1632 mm by 740 mm, the work foregrounds a central portrait bust of Henry Unton seated at his desk, poised to commence writing on a blank sheet of paper. The central image is surrounded by an intricate narrative sequence composed of scenes that illustrate Unton's journey from birth through education, marriage, military service, and diplomatic missions, as well as scenes of his domestic life at home in Wadley, Berkshire. The bulk of the portrait's narrative, however, depicts the elaborate funerary rituals that took place following Unton's death in France, including the transportation of his mortal remains across the English Channel and his burial and commemoration in his home parish of Faringdon, Oxfordshire.

The portrait has been a visual source for myriad studies, from the rituals of birth and marriage, through transport, musical technique, and the consumption of food, to the elaborate social order, heraldry, and costumes of early modern funerals. The final element in the panel's narrative sequence is an image of Unton's tomb and monument at Faringdon. Although this

Figure 9.1   Portrait of Sir Henry Unton by unknown artist. © National Portrait Gallery, London.

detail is one of the earliest English depictions of a church monument on a painted panel, it has been largely unexamined. Is it an accurate reproduction of the actual monument, which was destroyed in the Civil Wars? Or is it an artist's fantasy, reflecting how contemporaries imagined monumental art? This chapter attempts the first detailed analysis of the image, arguing that Unton's monument (or at least its depiction in the Unton Portrait) was on the leading edge of stylistic developments in late Elizabethan and early Stuart commemoration.

Roy Strong's 1965 study remains the definitive account of the Unton Portrait's creation, contents, and provenance.[2] The portrait first appears in an inventory of the estate of Unton's widow Dorothy, and was almost certainly created at her behest. Strong assumed that the picture dates from shortly after Unton's death in 1596. Close examination of the portrait and its fabric by the National Portrait Gallery in recent years has not questioned this assumption, and the National Portrait Gallery's current label records it as 'circa 1596'.[3] This chapter instead proposes a later date of 1606 – the date Unton's monument at Faringdon was completed.

Nigel Llewellyn argues persuasively that the picture is representative of early modern understandings of death: Unton is dying throughout his life, while the rituals of death and memory extend well beyond the day, month, and even year of his decease.[4] Clare Gittings instead frames the portrait as the last gasp of a formal Elizabethan cult of death, soon to be displaced by the more emotional world of Donne, Van Dyck, and Digby.[5] In this chapter, I extend Llewellyn's interpretation to emphasise how the Unton

Portrait perpetuates not only the memory of the dead but also remembrance of the rituals of death themselves, in ways that are well attuned to the language of love and grief.

The Unton Portrait is a compelling case study for investigating the themes of memory and mortality in early modern England. It is a highly successful memorial, perpetuating Unton's memory to posterity and attracting the attention of modern-day visitors no longer familiar with the arts of death. The portrait therefore allows us to pursue two of the major questions of the historical study of memory, in this case with reference to the premodern context of early seventeenth-century England. First, how did this society conceive of the nature and function of memory? Second, how did memory (as we would understand it today) operate in that time and place? Put another way, how was memory described, and how was it performed in early modern England?

Judith Pollmann argues that a significant new practice of early modern memory was to draw on the past in order to learn from historical examples. According to Pollmann, 'Rather than thinking of the history of memory as a linear process in which the rise of new forms of engagement with the past implies the fall of all that came before, it is much more useful to conceive of it as a cumulative process.'[6] This observation is exemplified by the Unton Portrait. It builds up a complex picture of Unton's deeds and attributes through its narrative format, overlaying one idea on another. At the same time, its place within a larger commemorative plan shows how the central principle of the medieval arts of death – *memento mori*, remember to die – survived the Protestant Reformation to be propagated anew in Elizabethan and early Stuart England.

The Unton Portrait: Life, Death, and Afterlife

When we look at the Unton Portrait, what are we meant to see? Most striking is the body of Sir Henry Unton. The central image is reminiscent of a demi-portrait or of a monumental bust mounted on a church wall, like those produced for preachers and poets contemporary with Unton.[7] This image establishes Unton's physical presence. Closer examination of the portrait reveals at least twenty further depictions of Unton's body. Half of these are crowded into the story of Unton's life: his body is present in birth, marriage, education, war, and diplomacy, and in places as diverse as Oxford, Padua, Zutphen, and the French court. He may even be represented as a member of musical groups performing at his home in Wadley. Five bodies illustrate Unton's death and burial, including the moment of death in France, the passage of his mortal remains first across the Channel and then the English countryside, and the final funeral procession from Wadley to Faringdon Church. There is a depiction of Unton's coffin and urn in the grave under his monument where his body literally dissolves into dust. Three more bodies figure Unton's memory: the main portrait bust itself (disconnected from the narrative of his life and death), the effigy on his funeral monument, and a wailing figure lying against his tomb.

The journey of Unton's many bodies is reminiscent of earlier Christian traditions of saints' lives, which depict the saint's deeds in life as well as miracles performed after death, transcending the ultimate barrier between the living and the dead, between mortal decay and eternal life. In this new hagiography, Unton is not a saint, nor is he holy. Indeed, once buried, Unton's body disappears from view; there is no incorrupt, resurrected body able to deliver spiritual benefits to the believer. But Unton's presence still has the power of an icon. His memory is able to deliver spiritual benefits for a Protestant kingdom. The portrait's viewer is reminded to imitate the good life of earnest study, honourable actions, and virtuous living, and to reap the benefits of music, masques, marriage, and merriment. The focus on the rituals of death and burial further remind the viewer to remember to die, and in so doing, to acknowledge that death undoes all.

The large image of Unton provides further clues to the picture's composition and its messages. He is angled towards the left side of the picture (the right side from Unton's point of view), with Death leaning to whisper into his left ear. Unton turns away from the narrative of his mortal existence, even away from Death himself (who has already done his worst) to the contemplation of the afterlife. This posture points to the spatial arrangement of the picture: one third is devoted to Unton's birth, life, and death, another third to the rituals of death, and the final third to memory and the afterlife.

Accounts of the Unton picture tend to focus almost exclusively on the first third of the image, behind Unton's left shoulder, because of the fascinating detail it presents of its subject's life and acts, especially his ambassadorial travels and the image of his wedding banquet and masque. Yet the overarching themes of the picture are memory and mortality. Fully two-thirds of the space is given over to mortality, afterlife, and posterity. The strongest narrative movement in the image is not the winding course of Unton's life through Europe, but is instead the funeral procession leading inexorably from one side of the picture to the other, from his house at Wadley to his burial and monument at Faringdon.

Unton's destination is that of all mortal flesh. On arrival at the final third of the portrait, dominated by Faringdon Church, Unton's being is divided into three parts, and shared between the earth, the heavens, and posterity. His body is interred in a coffin in the ground where it will decay. His soul is not depicted, but surely awaits entry to the afterlife which is shown in the upper left quadrant. In stark contrast to the intricate details of education and travel, the afterlife is a blurry, empty realm. The unknowable quality of this afterlife indicates how Unton – like all the virtuous dead – must await the resurrection, when the mortal remains of his body shown under his monument will be raised and reunited with his soul.

In-between earth and heaven is the mortal present and future. Here, Unton's memory is perpetuated to posterity by the monument itself, and in the heraldry which decorates the funeral procession and ritual. These provide the means for future generations to recall his name. The portrait therefore shows Unton's bust contemplating not only his mortality but also the hope of eternal salvation and the perpetuation of his fame.

This reading is supported by a range of gendered oppositions: birth and death, sun and moon, Death and Fame. Sir Henry's birth is presided over by his mother, Anne Seymour, portrayed as a larger-than-life figure in her bedchamber with her coat of arms and its ducal coronet prominently displayed, rather than those of Unton's father who was lower-born than his wife. The birth-chamber is carefully paralleled by the depiction of Unton's monument. Here, however, Unton's widow, Dorothy, presides above her husband, and the arms are those of Unton and Wroughton, representing their marital union. The message seems deceptively simple. Yet, rather than merely conveying the moral truth of the biblical text 'for we brought nothing into this world, and it is certain we can carry nothing out' (1 Timothy 6:7 KJV), the analogy of cradle and grave also illustrates that the death of one man, in this case a man who had no children to inherit his name and estate, does not terminate the power and magnificence of honour and lineage. The show must go on, and so the sun shines on the scenes of Unton's life journey, while death and the afterlife is the domain of the moon. Death stands behind Unton, reminding him of his mortality, though he has already struck the fatal blow. In contrast, Fame flies down with a laurel wreath ready to crown Unton and to blow her trumpet to announce his arrival into the heavenly country.

The portrait conveys a theological understanding not only of death, which comes to all, but also of memory. Even posterity, the memory of the dead, is also mortal, as the rituals of death will end and even monuments crumble into dust. The true nature of eternal life is yet to be revealed; the trumpet shall sound, and the dead shall be raised, but what comes next is known only to God. Thus, the heavenly realm shown above Faringdon Church is sketchy in its appearance, devoid of living creatures or of mortal bodies. The mortal viewer is led instead to contemplate the memory of dying, the rituals of death, holding in tension grief for the dead with consciousness of one's own mortality. Strikingly, there are no images of angels, God, or Jesus. This is a classic Protestant response to the problem of death in a post-Reformation world, in which the dead could not reach out to the living, and the prayers of the living could give no benefit to the dead, in which God's salvation was available through a theological principle of justification by grace, but could only be represented in words, not images.

Unton's Monument

The portrait's spatial organisation reflects contemporary understandings of the operation of death upon body, soul, and memory found in hundreds of Elizabethan and Jacobean epitaphs. The standard formula might go something like, 'he left his soul to God, his body to the tomb, and his fame to posterity'.[8] As such, the portrait functions exactly like a contemporary funeral monument.

It is all the more surprising then that almost no attention has been paid to the image of Unton's monument in the bottom left corner of the portrait. This is one of the earliest, if not *the* earliest, surviving painting of an English church monument (Figure 9.2). Numerous images of saintly shrines and royal or aristocratic tombs may be found in medieval and early modern manuscripts. There are also several late sixteenth-century and early seventeenth-century monuments that take the form of a painting on canvas or wood hung in a church, usually mimicking stone memorials.[9] There are also a few paintings that present a fictional monument – a monument that should have been. The most notable of these is the 1567 memorial picture of the unfortunate Henry Stuart, Lord Darnley, which shows his parents and infant son kneeling at prayer by his tomb. The Darnley picture creates an imaginary monument to compensate for the loss of opportunity to mourn his death and of his end.[10]

Unton's actual monument in Faringdon Church was largely destroyed in 1646 during the Civil Wars. The few surviving remnants were collected together by Unton's nephew, George Purefoy, in 1658, and the inscription was recorded in Elias Ashmole's collections on Berkshire. The epitaph states that the monument was erected in 1606 by Unton's widow Dorothy, some ten years after his death.[11] Roy Strong, assuming that the

Figure 9.2   Unton Portrait (detail of tomb), Sir Henry Unton by unknown artist.
© National Portrait Gallery, London.

Unton Portrait was created shortly after his death, asserts that the image of
the monument in the portrait is most likely an early design for the tomb,
rather than a painting of the completed sepulchre at Faringdon.[12] Drawing
on the last fifty years of research into English church monuments, I argue
that the portrait does indeed contain a picture of the completed or near-
completed monument. As a result, the portrait itself must have been completed no earlier than 1606.

As depicted in the portrait, the Unton monument appears to the modern eye to be a typical example of an Elizabethan or Jacobean tomb. The
monument presents a sarcophagus bearing an effigy, surmounted by a
triumphal arch, and sumptuously decorated with classical architecture,
allegorical statues, and heraldry. This basic form was in widespread use
in England from the 1580s, introduced and then propagated at influential
sites such as Westminster Abbey and St Paul's London. Monuments of
this type were created by the London and Southwark tomb workshops led
by continental masons such as the Cures.[13]

Careful comparison of the portrait image with contemporary monuments reveals that Unton's monument was at the cutting edge of early seventeenth-century English sepulchral fashion. It adopts three features first introduced into English monumental sculpture on the tomb of John, Lord Russell (d. 1584), erected shortly after his death by his widow Elizabeth Cooke Hoby Russell at Westminster Abbey.[14] First is the elegant sarcophagus on which Unton's effigy rests, replacing the more common rectangular tomb chest or flat panels. Second is the appearance of allegorical figures on the rear wall of the Unton monument on either side of the inscription panel, one bearing a palm and the other a wreath to represent Fame and Victory. These parallel figures in the spandrels of the Russell tomb are themselves imitations of antiquity and of Renaissance monuments from continental Europe.

Foremost in the imitation of Russell's monument, however, is Unton's effigy, turned on its side and propped on one elbow. This was a form that became highly popular from about 1606 – precisely the year in which Unton's monument was completed – but prior to this date it was found on only a handful of examples, three of which were at Westminster Abbey.[15] By 1612/13, the style had become so common that it was the butt of a joke in John Webster's play *The Duchess of Malfi*, in which the tomb-maker Bosola tells the Duchess that the dead do indeed affect fashion in the grave, for

> Princes' images on their tombs do not lie, as they were wont, seeming to pray up to heaven, but with their hands under their cheeks, as if they died of the toothache. They are not carved with their eyes fixed upon the stars, but as their minds were wholly bent upon the world, the self-same way they seem to turn their faces.[16]

The Unton Portrait image shows in tiny painted detail that Unton's effigy was somewhat more sophisticated than its predecessors, who wore their robes of estate and were turned stiffly on their sides. Unton was clothed in his armour, his legs stretched out, his head and hands shown bare, with helmet and gauntlets removed. His sword lies in front of him, and his head is supported under the left cheek by his left hand. There is a marked resemblance to the effigy of Sir Edmund Uvedale (d. 1606) at Wimborne Minster, probably erected by Uvedale's widow shortly after his death (Figure 9.3). Like Unton, Uvedale was a veteran of the Netherlands campaigns, and was similarly shown in armour with his bare right hand supporting his head and his left hand resting on his gauntlet.

Figure 9.3   Recumbent tomb effigy of a gentleman, monument of Sir Edmund Uvedale
in Wimborne Minster, Dorset, England. John Hopkins / Alamy Stock Photo with
license.

Another innovative feature of Unton's monument was the effigy of his widow, kneeling behind him at a prayer desk. This is one of the few surviving parts of the Unton monument in Faringdon Church today, showing Dorothy in her widow's hood, with her (probably reconstructed) hands clasped in prayer. While the use of a kneeling effigy was very common in the sixteenth century, monuments and monumental brasses of this period tended to pair kneeling images of husband and wife, or widow and widower, facing each other across a prayer desk. The specific combination of one effigy kneeling and the other reclining or recumbent is rare prior to the 1620s. The nearest comparable monument of the same period to Unton's is that of Mary Thornhurst (d. 1609), erected at Canterbury Cathedral between 1609 and 1616 – although in this example it is Thornhurst who reclines on her elbow and one of her three husbands who kneels behind (Figure 9.4).[17]

A further piece of evidence is the architecture and decoration of Unton's tomb. The arch above the effigy is freestanding, without the usual square frame of the late sixteenth century. The upper storey of the monument presents familiar additions in the form of two large black obelisks and four flaming urns. Less common at this date are two

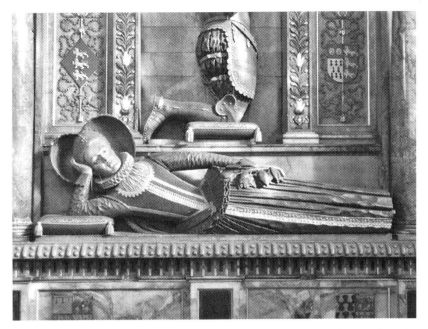

Figure 9.4   Recumbent tomb effigy of Lady Mary Thornhurst, Canterbury Cathedral, Chapel of St Michael's Warriors. Photo credit © Canterbury Cathedral Library and Archives.

cherubs who crouch on top of the arch on either side of Unton's heraldic crest, clutching implements of some kind. Finally, the monument presents four allegorical figures. These were common elements of English monumental sculpture by 1631, when John Weever famously complained of those who 'garnish their Tombes, now adayes, with the pictures of naked men and women; raising out of the dust, and bringing into the Church, the memories of the heathen gods and goddesses, with all their whirligiggs'.[18] Again, such figures were common from the 1610s but are less often found on Elizabethan monuments. On Unton's monument, Fame and Victory stand either side of the inscription under the arch, in a style not dissimilar to the figures in the spandrels of the Russell monument at Westminster. Faith with her staff on the left and Hope with her anchor stand in niches to either side of the sarcophagus. The closest comparison to this arrangement is found on the Robartes monument at Truro, dating from around 1614, which presents a grouping of four statues including Death and Time gathered around two effigies reclining on their sides.

When taken together, the key visual components – Unton's reclining effigy, his widow's kneeling effigy, and the use of allegorical statues and cherubs – indicate that the Unton monument as represented on the Unton Portrait must date from no earlier than the mid- to late 1600s. The date of 1606 given in the epitaph on Unton's monument fits perfectly. This thesis holds true regardless of whether the portrait image was that of the finished monument, or of a design for it. There being no indication that the image of the monument was added after the rest of the composition, the portrait as a whole can thus be re-dated to 1606 or thereabouts. It was created at some distance from the immediate circumstances of Unton's death, and is an early Jacobean rather than late Elizabethan cultural production.

Unton's Memorials, Dorothy's Memory

The Unton Portrait is closely linked to the long mourning of the woman who must have been the picture's patron, Unton's widow Dorothy. Dudley Carleton commented on the extent of her mourning when he visited her at her father's house in Wiltshire a few months after Unton's death, observing that the epitaphs she had hung 'do make her chamber look like the house of sorrow'.[19] Dorothy's second marriage in 1598 to George Shirley was a failure, despite (or perhaps because of) an extensive prenuptial agreement: by 1602 she was living in her dower house at Faringdon and still signing herself 'Dorothy, Lady Unton' as if her new husband did not exist.[20] In 1634, when Dorothy herself died, she left instructions to be buried at Faringdon with her first husband, and specifically bequeathed the 'Picture of Sir Henry Unton' to her niece Lady Unton Dering.[21]

The portrait may be read as a widow's tribute to the enduring memory of her husband; Roy Strong observed how the domestic scenes in the bottom right corner must have relied on Dorothy's input, and perhaps made sense to her alone. But the portrait is also testament to the strength of the death ritual in late Elizabethan and early Jacobean England. It was part of an attempt by Dorothy to develop a complex and enduring visual, literary, and musical memorial tradition imitating that of Philip Sidney. In Unton's case, for example, this commemorative programme included a set of memorial verses produced immediately after his death, and John Dowland's pavan 'Sir Henry Umpton's Funerall', published several years later in 1604.[22]

Dorothy Unton's prolonged perpetuation of her first husband's memory resonates with the commemorative activities of contemporary widows. The closest comparison is undoubtedly Elizabeth Cooke Hoby Russell, a prolific patron of monuments who introduced the reclining effigy style into England through the tombs of her two husbands, Thomas Hoby and John Russell.[23] Both Dorothy and Elizabeth were widows of men who died in France and whose mortal remains were transported home across the English Channel. Both women remarried as widows, outliving not one but two husbands, although Elizabeth had surviving children and Dorothy did not. The women certainly knew one another; they were eventually related by marriage when in the early seventeenth century Elizabeth's son Edward Hoby married Dorothy's sister-in-law Cicely Unton.[24]

Dorothy's role in the portrait's creation, and the messages she left for posterity, are suggested by Unton's epitaph on his monument in Faringdon. Indeed, if analysis of the visual culture of monuments permits the Unton Portrait to be dated to the early seventeenth century, interpretation of Unton's epitaph sheds light on the contemporary understandings of memory and mortality. Inscriptions frequently provide the hermeneutical key to understanding the theological narrative of early modern images, in both monuments and portraits.[25] Just as the Unton Portrait leaves little to chance with its lavish use of written labels and heraldic devices to convey its precise messages, so too does the epitaph on Unton's monument unlock meaning. Written in Latin, it records not only the date of the monument's completion but also identifies Dorothy as its patron. Even though the words are almost certainly the work of a third party commissioned by the patron, the epitaph may still be taken as a statement from Dorothy to posterity – that is to say, to us:[26]

> Sacred to Virtue and Honour.
> To Henry Unton, knight, son of Edward Unton, knight, by Anne, Countess of Warwick (daughter of Edward Seymour, Duke of Somerset and Protector of England), who was nourished from an early age by the best of studies at Oxford, and who travelled a great part of the Christian world. Acquiring the dignity of knight from his bellicose virtue at the siege of Zutphen, on account of his singular prudence and faithful observation he was sent many times as Ambassador of the most serene Queen of England to the most Christian King in France, from whence he emigrated to his heavenly fatherland the 23 day of March in the year of salvation 1596.
> Dorothy his most loving wife (daughter of the illustrious Thomas Wroughton, knight) with great grief arranged the transfer of his corpse to this place, and most mournfully erected this monument as a testament of their mutual love and conjugal fidelity, 1606.[27]

The introit to the epitaph points us to the fundamental purpose of memory in a post-Reformation world. No longer was this purpose a request to pray for the dead. Memory was a sacred performance of the attributes of virtue and honour, a performance by and for the deceased, the patron, and the viewer. Like the portrait, the main body of the epitaph focuses on the movement of Unton's body in time and space. It begins with Unton's eminent mother, the Countess of Warwick, traces his studies and travels from Oxford to Zutphen to France. This motion concludes with his 'emigration' to the heavenly home, and is emphasised by Dorothy's care for the unusual 'transfer' of Unton's mortal remains across the English Channel. The epitaph concludes with an affective statement of Dorothy's grief, love, and fidelity, which explains how the tomb came into being. Her emotional state is materialised on Unton's monument in the statue of Faith, the mourning cherubs at the apex, and the vigil kept by the widow kneeling over her late husband.

Fascinatingly, the account given by the epitaph on Unton's monument almost precisely mirrors the imagery of the Unton Portrait. There is a unity of purpose across both memorials suggesting they were erected at the same time as part of one grand, monumental testament. Authored by Dorothy, they indicate her desire to remember her husband, his life and death, and (perhaps above all else) the ritual performance of his death. One testament, the monument, was intended for public viewing in Faringdon Church, a permanent reminder of Unton's lineage, honour, and achievements. The other, the portrait, was relatively private, able to be seen by Dorothy and her household at Wadley. By a twist of fate, the opposite is true today with the portrait on public display at the National Portrait Gallery and only remnants of the monument visible in Faringdon.

It should come as no surprise that Dorothy did not complete her first husband's monument, and perhaps the Unton Portrait itself, for a decade after his death in 1596. The death ritual was a protracted business. Moreover, the delayed creation of monuments to the dead was a phenomenon practised at the highest levels of British culture. In 1606, the new king, James VI and I, completed a monument for his predecessor Elizabeth at Westminster Abbey, while work on the companion tomb for his mother, Mary, Queen of Scots, was not finished until 1612, some twenty-five years after her death.[28] These monuments, like so many others, set forth a particular version of events that suited the needs of a new regime and which shaped historical myth-making for a generation. The death of Unton's contemporary Sir Philip Sidney, soldier and poet, was similarly celebrated over many years through music, poetry, and drama, providing a recipe that Unton's friends and widow followed.[29]

The Unton monument may be understood within this context as a deliberate, delayed commemoration of Sir Henry, ensuring due honour was paid to his name. Both Unton's monument and the portrait point to the significance of the death rituals in early modern England, as rituals themselves worthy of commemoration. The objects capture and perpetuate a turning point in time, when the world stopped to mourn Unton through processions, clothing, and displays of heraldry. They also serve to memorialise Dorothy herself, portrayed to posterity as Unton's grieving, faithful widow – all the while silently erasing her second, unhappy marriage to George Shirley.

Memory and Mortality: The Unton Portrait Reconsidered

What emerges from this analysis is an even more compelling window onto early modern concepts of memory and mortality, and the role commemoration played after the immediate rituals of death were completed. The chapter thereby contributes not only to a reappraisal of the Unton Portrait, but also to developing a theory of memory and commemoration authentic to the English Renaissance. And so, to return to my opening question, what does this case study tell us about how early modern English elite society understood and performed memory?

Key to this analysis is the extraordinary image of Unton's monument, especially its use of a reclining effigy, which became a powerful and influential trope in English sepulchral imagery in the period. It is likely that the portrait and the monument it depicts were produced at the same time in 1606. The intended messages of the reclining effigy are unlocked by, and throw light upon, the world of the Unton Portrait.

The portrait is thus both a memorial and a meta-memorial. It documents the rituals of death and is a substitute for them. It produces an excess of memory: so far as we know, one funeral monument was enough for most mourners, without the need for a second, elaborate pictorial monument. Evidently, the Untons were experts in the new arts of memory emerging in the English Reformation and Renaissance. They remembered to die, and exhorted others to do the same.

The portrait presents the relentless dance of death, from cradle to grave. Unton's journey was more elaborate than most, punctuated by battles and embassies far from home. The portrait also presents a vision of the afterlife. It is nonetheless primarily a vehicle for memory in the here and now, for the commemoration of the past to posterity is finite and mortal, and the eschatological vision of the future is at best blurry.

As a theological and aesthetic performance from England in the early 1600s, the portrait of Sir Henry Unton is as complete as it can be. It satisfies the universal desire of human societies to ensure the ancestors are properly honoured, buried in the right place, and remembered in the right manner.[30] And it records precisely how this was done in the case of one man in Europe at the turn of the seventeenth century. Unton's monumental effigy waits, in contemplation; his mortal remains sit under the tomb, his soul is in some empty Elysian field awaiting the last trumpet, while his memory relies on our remembering at Dorothy's prompting. Unton's central portrait faces towards this dissolution of parts into body, soul, and memory. His pen is poised to begin writing a new letter, a letter we are not able to read from this side of the grave.

The portrait reminds us that our lives are one long funeral procession stretching from our first home to our last, and we must strive to keep our eyes on the hope that lies beyond our knowing. The incomplete elements – the blurry vision of the afterlife – cannot be filled in, at least not by Protestant theology, and both the living and the dead must wait for time to end before the last things are revealed. Like Unton, all that we can do is to wait for the resurrection and the reunion of body, soul, and memory. The best response is to focus on death, on living to die, and on dying well.

Notes

1 Anthony Rooley, 'A Portrait of Sir Henry Unton', in David Fallows and Tess Knighton, eds., *Companion to Medieval and Renaissance Music* (Oxford: Oxford University Press, 1997), pp. 85–92.
2 Roy Strong, 'Sir Henry Unton and His Portrait: An Elizabethan Memorial Picture and Its History', *Archaeologia*, 99 (1965), 53–76.
3 'The Portrait of Sir Henry Unton (c. 1558–1596)', *National Portrait Gallery*, https://npg.org.uk/research/programmes/making-art-in-tudor-britain/case-studies/the-portrait-of-sir-henry-unton-c.-1558-1596.php [accessed 25 June 2021].
4 Nigel Llewellyn, *The Art of Death: Visual Culture in the English Death Ritual c.1500–c.1800* (London: Reaktion Books, 1993), pp. 13–16.
5 Clare Gittings, 'Expressions of Loss in Early Seventeenth Century England', in Peter C. Jupp and Glennys Howarth, eds., *The Changing Face of Death: Historical Accounts of Death and Disposal* (Basingstoke: Macmillan, 1997), pp. 19–33.
6 Judith Pollmann, *Memory in Early Modern Europe, 1500–1700* (Oxford: Oxford University Press, 2017), p. 72.
7 Llewellyn, *Art of Death*, p. 14.
8 Peter Sherlock, *Monuments and Memory in Early Modern England* (Aldershot: Ashgate, 2008), p. 6.

9 Sally Badham, 'A Painted Canvas Funerary Monument of 1615 in the Collections of the Society of Antiquaries of London and its Comparators', *Church Monuments*, 24 (2009), 89–110, 146–53.

10 Livinus de Vogelaare, *The Memorial of Lord Darnley* (1567), oil on canvas, 142.3 cm x 224 cm. RCIN 401230. Royal Collection Trust, London.

11 Elias Ashmole, *The Antiquities of Berkshire*, 3 vols. (London, 1719), vol. I, p. 190.

12 Strong, 'Sir Henry Unton', p. 72.

13 Adam White, 'A Biographical Dictionary of London Tomb Sculptors *c.*1560–*c.*1660', *The Volume of the Walpole Society*, 61 (1999), 1–162.

14 Patricia Phillippy, *Women, Death and Literature in Post-Reformation England* (Cambridge: Cambridge University Press, 2002), pp. 179–210.

15 The Westminster examples include the tombs of Thomas Owen (d. 1598) and Thomas Hesketh (d. 1605). Provincial examples include William Peryam (d. 1605) at Crediton, Devon, and Archbishop Matthew Hutton (d. 1606) at York Minster. Double reclining effigies appear on the tomb of Edward Denny (d. 1600) at Waltham Abbey, Essex, with Edward also presented in his armour. Peter Sherlock, 'Monuments and the Reformation', in Alexandra Walsham, Bronwyn Wallace, Ceri Law, and Brian Cummings, eds., *Memory and the English Reformation* (Cambridge: Cambridge University Press, 2020), pp. 168–84.

16 John Webster, *The Duchess of Malfi*, ed. by Michael Neill (New York and London: W.W. Norton & Company, 2015), p. 83 (4.2.145–50). See Chapter 5, 'Memory, Climate, and Mortality: The Dudley Women among the Fields' by Patricia Phillippy on the cultural cachet of this 'toothache' pose; and also Chapter 12, '"Superfluous Men" and the Graveyard Politics of *The Duchess of Malfi*' by Michael Neill, for a more fulsome discussion of larger socio-political ramifications of the ruins, tombs, and monuments in this play.

17 Katherine Eustace, 'Before or After? A Model of the Monument to Mary Thornhurst (1549–1609) in St Michael's Chapel, Canterbury Cathedral', *Church Monuments*, 25 (2010), 105–20.

18 John Weever, *Ancient Funerall Monuments* (London, 1631), p. 11.

19 Strong, 'Sir Henry Unton', p. 71.

20 See for example Hatfield House, Hertfordshire: The Cecil Papers CP 86/61, Letter of Dorothy, Lady Unton to Sir Robert Cecil, 26 May 1601.

21 Strong, 'Sir Henry Unton', p. 72.

22 Joseph Barnes, ed., *Funebria Nobilissimi Ac Præstantissimi Equitis, D. Henrici Vntoni* (Oxford: 1596); John Dowland, *Lachrimæ, or Seauen Teares* (London, [1604]), F2^v–G1^r.

23 Phillippy, *Women, Death and Literature*, pp. 179–210.

24 Strong, 'Sir Henry Unton', p. 70.

25 Sherlock, *Monuments and Memory*, p. 229.

26 On women's patronage of monuments and their authorship of epitaphs, see Peter Sherlock, 'Monuments and Memory', in Patricia Phillippy, ed., *A History of Early Modern Women's Writing* (Cambridge: Cambridge University Press, 2018), pp. 292–312.

27 My translation. The Latin epitaph is transcribed in Ashmole, *Antiquities of Berkshire*, vol. I, p. 190. The date '1658' was added by Ashmole's time, indicating the year the monument was restored.

28 Peter Sherlock, 'The Monuments of Elizabeth Tudor and Mary Stuart: King James and the Manipulation of Memory', *Journal of British Studies*, 46.2 (2007), 263–89.

29 Despite the frenzy of funerary activity and the efforts of his friend Fulke Greville, Sidney's resting place in St Paul's Cathedral, London, was never crowned by a funeral monument. Jean Wilson, '"Two names of friendship, but one Starre": Memorials to Single-Sex Couples in the Early Modern Period', *Church Monuments*, 10 (1995), 70–83. See also Chapter 11 in this volume, 'The Many Labours of Mourning a Virgin Queen' by Andrew Hiscock, for further insight into the procedural mourning of Sir Philip Sidney.

30 Katherine Verdery, *The Political Lives of Dead Bodies: Reburial and Postsocialist Change* (New York: Columbia University Press, 1999), pp. 41–7.

CHAPTER 10

Andrew Marvell's Taste for Death

Anita Gilman Sherman

In his lyric poetry, Marvell returns again and again to the moment of death, sometimes staging heroic conduct, sometimes staging youthful vulnerability, sometimes staging the precariousness of beauty and thereby ringing changes on the *carpe diem* motif. Arguably his most famous lyric is his *carpe diem* poem, 'To His Coy Mistress' with the lines that T. S. Eliot liked so much that he parodied them. Eliot transformed Marvell's 'But at my back I always hear / Time's winged chariot hurrying near' into 'But at my back in a cold blast I hear / The rattle of the bones, and chuckle spread from ear to ear'.[1] Marvell's morbid, but jocular couplet – 'The grave's a fine and private place / But none I think do there embrace' – qualifies his graveyard speculations, its parenthetical 'I think' introducing a note of comic sceptical doubt about the likes of Romeo and Juliet or John Donne and his lady-loves.[2] The poem's curious revisiting of tried and true mortality motifs (the winged chariot, the marble vault, the worms, ashes and dust) alongside its startling hyperboles like the 'vegetable love' growing 'vaster than empires, and more slow' captures Marvell's alchemical gifts: the way he repurposes conventional images and tropes to achieve poetic gold and an idiosyncratic voice that has been described as 'sounding a note as though blown with subdued breath on the trumpet of the Dweller in the Innermost'.[3] Rather than attributing the poet's gifts to a divine *afflatus*, I suggest that in certain scenes touching on death and the remembrance of mortality, Marvell achieves his special effects by exploring the problem of taste, and, specifically, by worrying the boundary between good and bad taste. He thereby contributes to the secularization of the *ars moriendi*.

Marvell's intellectual circle was not insulated from the emergence of taste as an aesthetic category in the second half of the seventeenth century. In 1674 Nicolas Boileau publishes *L'Art Poétique*, a witty treatise in four cantos ('chants') that holds forth on the criteria of good poetic taste by satirizing and calling out by name those who fall short of his neo-classical standards. Sir William Soame translated it around 1680;

with John Dryden's revisions it was published in 1683, admittedly five years after Marvell's death. Nevertheless, it is probable that Marvell – a voracious and cosmopolitan reader in several languages – would have been aware of Boileau, given that Dryden mentions Boileau in his letters as early as 1673.[4] One of the butts of Boileau's satire is the poet, Marc-Antoine de Gérard, sieur de Saint-Amant, whom he accuses of lapses in taste that he calls burlesque. Saint-Amant was well known to Marvell. His poem on solitude and his encomium on the melon have been discussed as sources for Marvell's poem, 'The Garden'.[5] Furthermore, Sir Thomas Fairfax, Marvell's patron in the years 1650–2, was an admirer and translator of Saint-Amant.[6] Marvell probably read Saint-Amant's long poem, 'La metamorphose de Lyrian et de Sylvie' as 'Englished' by Sir Edward Sherburne. Sherburne published a collection of translated poetry in 1651 that included several metamorphoses in the Ovidian style as well as his own poems.[7] He was part of the Thomas Stanley circle and literary salon, which Marvell likely frequented in his early days.[8] Lyrian's metamorphosis into an ivy vine may have inspired Marvell's ecstatic surrender to nature in 'Upon Appleton House' when he describes ivy winding around him – 'ivy, with familiar trails, / Me licks, and clasps, and curls, and hales' (ll. 589–90) – erotic verses that guardians of taste like Boileau might well have reproved. In *L'Art Poétique*, Boileau criticizes Saint-Amant's account of the parting of the Red Sea in his epic, *Moyse sauvé* (1653):

> N'imitez pas ce fou qui, décrivant les mers,
> Et peignant au milieu de leurs flots entr'ouverts,
> L'Hébreu sauvé du joug des ses injustes maîtres,
> Met, pour le voir passer, les poissons aux fenêtres.   (III.261–4)[9]

Boileau is alluding to Saint-Amant's line: 'Les poisons ébahis le regardent passer.' He faults Saint-Amant for the bathos of sentient fish jostling like spectators for a view, saying that he ruins the 'élégance' (259) of his description with 'basse circonstance' (260), lowly circumstance.[10] My point is that Marvell was aware of literary developments in France.[11] He travelled in France and lived in Saumur for a year (1655–6), 'subjected', says his biographer, 'to French culture at its most tolerant, rich and multifarious; libertine and speculative in its habits'.[12] After his return, he would have been apprised of the French vogue for neo-classicism and its rejection of poetry deemed vulgar, burlesque, gothic or barbarian, adjectives attached to bad taste. He may even have encountered the early works of the Jesuit Dominique Bouhours who not only proselytized among the

English Catholics at Dunkirk, but who published treatises on taste, wit and *je ne sais quoi*, as well as on his doubts about the French language.[13]

In 'The Man of Taste', Giorgio Agamben observes that this novel figure emerges in the middle of the seventeenth century. Agamben describes the man of taste as one 'who is endowed with a particular faculty, almost with a *sixth sense* – as they started to say then – which allows him to grasp the *point de perfection* that is characteristic of every work of art'.[14] Agamben lifts the phrase from Jean de La Bruyère's 1688 *Caractères*, noting that it implies a portrait of the man of bad taste: 'the person who loves what is "short of the right point or beyond it"' (17). Citing a 1671 letter from Madame de Sévigné where she wonders at her own attraction to second-rate novels, Agamben observes that we moderns are no longer surprised at the 'inexplicable inclination of good taste towards its opposite', taking it for granted that 'good taste carrie[s] within itself a tendency to pervert itself' (19, 18). But it is more than a tendency, Agamben argues. Good taste 'is, in some way, the very principle of any perversion, and its appearance in consciousness seems to coincide with the beginning of a process of reversal of all values and all contents' (22). While Agamben may be overstating the importance of taste in the history of European culture, his analysis allows us to see that Marvell wrestles with the burgeoning problematics of the aesthetic sense.

In *The Rehearsal Transpros'd* (1672), his blistering attack on Samuel Parker, Archdeacon of Canterbury, and his programme of religious persecution and intolerance, Marvell repeatedly addresses issues of style, excoriating his opponent for 'Indecencies' in rhetoric and conduct, even as these oblige him – so he claims – to respond in kind and overgo him (*Prose* I. 48).[15] He accuses Parker of 'the highest Indecorum' (55), charging him with affecting an 'Elegancy of Stile' (51) that he describes as 'Trash' (55) and as 'luscious and effeminate', reminiscent of Madeleine de Scudéry's romances (53). He also dubs it 'debauched' (126), 'scurrilous and sacrilegious' (200), petulant (239) and 'Ruffian-like' (244). Marvell proposes to expose and correct Parker's outrages by engaging in vituperative flights of his own. For example, Parker has 'made a constant Pissing-place of his [Calvin's] Grave' (73). Later, he recounts the putative origins of 'a scurvy disease', namely syphilis, noting its 'nasty botches and ugly symptoms', adding: 'What I relate it for is out of no further intention, not is there any more similitude than that the Mind too hath its Nodes sometimes, and the Stile its Buboes' (110). Marvell recognizes ugly 'Nodes' of infection, not just in Parker's mind but in any mind, issuing in 'Buboes' or suppurating sores of style. He defends his method, averring that his *ad hominem* arguments hew to the decorum of animadversions, his chosen genre: 'But I shall, so far as possible, observe *decorum*, and, whatever I talk of, not commit such an Absurdity, as to be grave with a Buffoon' (96). Nevertheless, his defensiveness belies him, betraying a worry that Parker's reprehensible cynicism may get lost, dimmed by the flashes of his own incandescent and 'learnedly impertinent' wit (158).[16] In brief, Marvell represents himself in these prose polemics as patrolling the precincts of style and policing the boundaries between good and bad taste, even as he himself indulges in the occasional breach of decorum. The critical consensus is that he is imitating the style of the Marprelate tracts a century earlier that revelled in exuberant flyting; Alex Garganigo invokes Menippean satire.[17] But several early readers considered them burlesque, including Gilbert Burnet and Anthony à Wood.[18] Anthony Collins in 1729 also thought they evinced an 'Excesse of Burlesque'.[19] As we have seen, burlesque exemplified bad taste for Boileau. Marvell may have been exploring burlesque effects in his tract.

While scenes of death in Marvell's lyric poetry are never burlesque, they nevertheless engage issues of taste and style addressed in *The Rehearsal Transpros'd*, especially as regards gender and religion. In the tract Marvell identifies a Protestant and manly style of writing, contrasting it with excesses of ornament associated with Catholicism. Parker does not recognize his own Papist proclivities, Marvell alleges, such as introducing the Inquisition to England and conferring priestly powers on the king so that he must don 'all the Sacerdotal habiliments, and the Pontifical Wardrobe' (*Prose* I. 98–9). Parker's Italianate tendencies are opposed to 'that Majesty and Beauty which sits upon the Forehead of masculine Truth and generous Honesty' characteristic, for example, of the discourse of John Hales (134). Marvell quotes long passages from Hales's tract on schism published decades earlier, in 1642, and written probably in 1636. A member of the Great Tew Circle, Hales composed his irenic work during the contested debates about ornament, ceremony and liturgical style that rocked Cambridge University (among other locales) in the years when Marvell attended Trinity College (1633–40).[20] In 1639 Hales became one of Archbishop Laud's chaplains. Thus, Marvell's sensitivity to questions of style predates his fight with Parker, going back to the culture wars of his adolescence. His aesthetic coding of rhetoric in terms of both gender and religion, while scarcely unique to him, informs Marvell's revisioning of the *ars moriendi* in his lyric poetry.

For example, in 'An Horatian Ode upon Cromwell's Return from Ireland', Marvell remembers King Charles as exemplifying good taste in the *ars moriendi*. The king is calm as he approaches the scaffold. He tries 'the axe's edge' (60).[21] He does not call 'the Gods with vulgar spite / To vindicate his helpless right' (61–2). Instead, he bows 'his comely head / Down, as upon a bed' (63–4). The king evinces a Stoic dignity of the sort Montaigne admires when he declares just before invoking Seneca, 'All the actions of our life must be tried and tested by this last act. It is the master day, the day that is the judge of all the others' (I.19). Montaigne goes on to add that three of the most execrable people of his time, whose lives were full of abominations, nevertheless 'had deaths that were ordered and in every circumstance composed to perfection' (I.19). Leaving behind the damaging trajectory of his life, King Charles dies well. Yet the bystander who speaks the poem presents him, not as achieving the good death envisioned by Montaigne, but rather as approaching the *point de perfection* of an artwork.[22] He stages the beheading of the king as a play, describing the 'royal actor' as one who 'nothing common did or mean / Upon that memorable Scene' (57–8). The speaker positions himself as an onlooker and member of the execution's audience, offended by 'the armèd bands' who 'Did clap their bloody hands' (55–6).

By contrast, the Ode's Cromwell is forceful and garish. When Marvell likens Cromwell to 'the three-forked lightning' (13) – 'burning through the air he went, / And palaces and temples rent: / And Caesar's head at last / Did through his laurels blast' (21–4) – the simile with its sublime imagery may strike the reader as overblown, perhaps verging on the grotesque.[23] The lightning breaks 'the clouds where it was nursed', dividing its fiery way 'thorough his own side' (14–16). If we understand 'side' as meaning not only the Parliamentarian or Independent party but also Cromwell's rib cage alight with electrified stigmata (15), we glimpse a subliminal flash of Roman Catholic iconography attached to Cromwell's rise.

Is Catholic iconography related to the *ars moriendi* being tapped to overstep the bounds of aesthetic and rhetorical decorum? To pursue this question, consider a parallel scene: the death of Captain Douglas in the 1667 verse satire, 'Last Instructions to a Painter'. Marvell evidently valued the forty-seven lines representing Douglas's death so much that he recycled them with minor variations soon afterward in 'The Loyal Scot' (1667–73). Archibald Douglas was the commander of a company of Scottish troops in the Second Anglo-Dutch War and refused to leave his ship, *The Royal Oak*, after the Dutch attacked it in June 1667. The dying pose of Captain Douglas, described in an inset of eight rhyming couplets, is – I suggest – a foray into the problematics of taste. Marvell revisits the image from the Horatian Ode of bowing the head down 'as upon a bed', but with very different tonal effects, thanks partly to the pun on 'sheets' to denote both fire and bedding. Douglas is portrayed as a heroic, virginal martyr incandescent in his surrender. Stoic dignity is not apparent so much as erotic immolation:

> Like a glad lover, the fierce flames he meets,
> And tries his first embraces in their sheets.
> His shape exact, which the bright flames enfold,
> Like the sun's statue stands of burnished gold.
> Round the transparent fire about him glows,
> As the clear amber on the bee does close,
> And, as on angels' heads their glories shine,
> His burning locks adorn his face divine.
> But when in his immortal mind he felt
> His altering form and soldered limbs to melt,
> Down on the deck he laid himself and died,
> With his dear sword reposing by his side,
> And on the flaming plank, so rests his head
> As one that's warmed himself and gone to bed.
> His ship burns down, and with his relics sinks,
> And the sad stream beneath his ashes drinks.
>
>   ('*Last Instructions*', ll. 677–92; '*Loyal Scot*', ll. 43–58)

Critics have remarked on the Counter-Reformation aesthetic of this passage, supporting their claim with their research that Douglas was probably a Roman Catholic.[24] They detect an allusion to the martyrdom of Saint Lawrence, who was burnt alive on a gridiron, as well as to iconographic motifs popularized in John Foxe's *Book of Martyrs* (1583).[25] The word 'relics' evokes saintly remains.[26] Yet, appropriating images of martyrdom and Counter-Reformation iconography is not in itself a sign of bad taste although some in Marvell's artistic world would have thought so – especially those who hated the way Charles I was portrayed as a martyr. Milton, for example, scorned the king's self-representation in *Eikon Basilike*: 'He who writes himself martyr by his own inscription is like an ill painter who, by writing on the shapeless picture which he hath drawn, is fain to tell passengers what shape it is; which else no man could imagine' (803). Milton's contempt for the king as a pseudo-martyr is here expressed in terms of artistic failure.

More pertinent to the question of discerning the borderlines between good and bad taste is the relation of the Captain Douglas passage in 'Last Instructions' to two other poems: 'The Loyal Scot', as previously mentioned, and 'The Unfortunate Lover'. 'The Loyal Scot' is a Menippean satire responding to John Cleveland's 'The Rebel Scot'. Dryden in his *Essay of Dramatic Poesy* (1666–8) singles out Cleveland as a writer who violates decorum. 'To express a thing hard and unnaturally, is his new way of elocution', Dryden says, accusing Cleveland of catachresis. He adds, 'We cannot read a verse of Cleveland's without making a face at it, as if every word were a pill to swallow: he gives us many times a hard nut to break our teeth, without a kernel for our pains' (445). By deciding to channel Cleveland's voice in 'The Loyal Scot', Marvell aims for several effects, among them testing the parameters of taste.[27] Calling 'the account of Douglas' death ... curiously frigid and even stagy' (278), Elsie Duncan-Jones notes the minor change Marvell made to the recycled passage in 'The Loyal Scot'.[28] 'As one that's warmed himself and gone to bed' (l. 690) now reads: 'As one that hugs himself in a warm bed' (l. 56). Duncan-Jones suggests that with this revision, Marvell wished to avoid a 'homeliness' that 'might be thought dangerously near to burlesque' and to emphasize instead a quality of 'self-enclosedness' (277–8). Her insight that Marvell is choosing to lessen the burlesque tonalities of the simile supports my sense that Marvell is sounding the shoals of taste.

'The Unfortunate Lover', an early poem dated to 1648–9, also draws on a Counter-Reformation aesthetic. Like the Captain Douglas passages that it anticipates by twenty years, it too involves a storm-tossed, eroticized body, wounded, endangered and surrounded by flames. In this instance, however the scene of dying involves a child: a Herculean cherub agonizing on board a fired ship after his bloody birth via Caesarean section. Steven Zwicker and Derek Hirst describe the poem as 'melodramatic, lurid, even garish' (76) and as evincing 'grotesque extravagance ... now safely housed within hyperbole and artificiality' (84).[29] Rosalie Colie observes that the infant 'cuffing the thunder with one hand' (l. 50) derives from the *amorini* popular in emblem books.[30] 'The Lover is distinguished' at the outset, she observes, 'from those happy pairs that play so sweetly with one another through the pages of Otto van Veen's *Amorum Emblemata* or of Herman Hugo's *Pia Desideria*, or of Quarles' *Emblems*' (110). Otto van Veen came from a Belgian Catholic family; he did the engravings for *vitae* of Thomas Aquinas and St Rose of Lima. Hugo was a Jesuit priest. Quarles borrowed the plates of Hugo's emblems for his own Protestant work of meditation. The uncanny counterpoint of the unfortunate lover and the *amorini* featured in Veen's work supports Colie's view that Marvell draws on Catholic devotional works for many of his visual tableaux.[31] To what extent is Marvell deliberately mobilizing Roman Catholic imagery in this poem to explore issues of taste?

Of the poem's eight stanzas, I cite the second, seventh and eighth to give the flavour:

'Twas in a shipwreck, when the seas
Ruled, and the winds did what they please,
That my poor lover floating lay,
And, ere brought forth, was cast away:
Till at the last the master-wave
Upon the rock his mother drave;
And there she split against the stone,
In a Caesarean section.   (ll. 9–16)

See how he nak'd and fierce doth stand,
Cuffing the thunder with one hand;
While with the other he does lock,
And grapple, with the stubborn rock:
From which he with each wave rebounds,
Torn into flames, and ragg'd with wounds;
And all he says, a lover dressed
In his own blood does relish best.   (ll. 49–56)

This is the only banneret
That ever Love created yet:
Who though, by the malignant stars,
Forced to live in storms and wars;
Yet dying leaves a perfume here,
And music within every ear:
And he in story only rules,
In a field sable a lover gules.   (ll. 57–64)

Zwicker and Hirst believe this portrait of 'the orphan of the hurricane' (the concluding line from the fourth stanza) operates as a key that unlocks or decodes much of Marvell's poetry (75). Noting 'gothic moments in the lyric poetry, (90) they see the unfortunate lover's storm-wracked death as an early expression of a preoccupation with heroic drowning which surfaces later in, for example, the hagiographic tribute to Captain Douglas. For them, the through-line is the 'melodrama of the wounded self' (84) and the 'fantasy of ideal and endangered youth' (93). By contrast, Colie distinguishes between the 'frenetic' cherub and the poem itself (111). She interprets 'the anonymous speaker' of 'The Unfortunate Lover' as a 'cool voice' and 'an art critic, enjoying the lover's turning into a heraldic pattern, ending the din, ending the story. Dying, the Lover is far prettier, to say nothing of more manageable than when alive' (50). Rather than seeing the poem as agitated and symptomatic, Colie sees it as detached: an exercise in aesthetic judgement.

All three poems – 'The Unfortunate Lover', 'Last Instructions' and 'The Loyal Scot' – stage extravagant scenes of dying: either fighting the elements (as in the early poem) or surrendering to death with the incandescent suffering of a martyr. These scenes violate the rules of decorum as expressed, for example, in the manuals of the *ars moriendi* with their insistence on contrition, confession and dignified stoicism.[32] The equipoise and serenity that Marvell is famous for in so many of his lyric poems – and that should govern the good death ideally – are absent in these outlandish portraits. Instead, the poetic speaker adopts the pose of a lover, hovering helplessly but adoringly near the expiring subject, memorizing his last gestures in a mirroring paroxysm of similes and painterly metaphors. Douglas is virginal, golden, intact and saintly as he lays himself down on 'the flaming plank', his statuesque and 'soldered limbs' melting in ashy metamorphosis.[33] The unfortunate lover also braves 'the mad tempest' (l. 48), an 'amphibium of Life and Death' (l. 40), even as he is 'torn into flames, and ragg'd with wounds' (l. 54). Philippe Ariès might conclude that Marvell is participating in that 'macabre eroticism' whereby 'death and violence have merged with desire' – a cultural phase that he argues bridges 'the tame death' of the Middle Ages and the Romantic 'age of the beautiful death'.[34] While Ariès's surmises about the unconscious 'sadism' of the seventeenth century merit consideration (370), I see Marvell pushing past what could be a sublime death at its *point de perfection* and going beyond into the realm of hyperbole and grotesque.

The appeal of going almost overboard, as it were – especially coming from a poet who revels in boxing himself into octosyllabic stanzas and rhyming couplets – seems to be the transgressive frisson, not only of violating norms of poetic decorum, but tapping into Catholic iconography. Why would this be so? We can speculate. Marvell was apparently 'seduced' by Jesuits while he was a student at Cambridge – an incident that prompted an intervention by Marvell's Puritan preacher father (Smith 35). A decade later, in the mid-1640s, he was in Rome and attended dinner parties at the English College (Smith 56). His cruel portrait of 'Flecknoe, an English Priest at Rome' dates from that time. Marvell wrote satires with extraordinary gusto, enjoying scatological and misogynist humour. His penchant for mockery also targets, in my view, the sensuality of the Counter-Reformation's aesthetic with its exaltation of the dying body. Gary Kuchar, however, understands Marvell's Protestant poetics as mounting a serious challenge to Catholic precedents. In analysing 'Eyes and Tears', Kuchar argues that 'the poem revises the Catholic literature of tears tradition … in the service of a theological vision, whose irony, epistemological skepticism, and overall philosophy is distinct from previous Catholic and Laudian instances of the genre'.[35] The poem brings the *ars lachrimandi* into a Protestant framework because 'for Marvell, as for

Luther, the order of grace communicates with the order of nature through
differential relations among signs and beings, rather than through analogi-
cal or isomorphic similitude' (100). 'Eyes and Tears', according to Kuchar,
reworks incarnational and sacramental theology. Should we then assume,
mutatis mutandis, that Marvell's revisions of the *ars moriendi* reveal, not
the experimental forays of a man of taste, but enquiries into the incom-
mensurability of the orders of grace and nature?

To consider this question, let us turn to a poem involving tears, youth,
innocence and death. In the pastoral lyric, 'The Nymph Complaining for
the Death of her Fawn', the nymph laments her dying deer in language
redolent of religiosity. She mourns the martyred creature, murdered by
'wanton troopers' (1), with religious devotion as it expires:

> Oh help! Oh help! I see it faint:
> And die as calmly as a saint.
> See how it weeps. The tears do come
> Sad, slowly dropping like a gum.
> So weeps the wounded balsam: so
> The holy frankincense doth flow.   (ll. 93–8)

To whom is the nymph crying for 'help'? Not the gods. Whom is she
beckoning to come 'see'? Is she extending a hand to us, pulling us into the
poem's frame? Several speech-acts overlap: prayer, invitation and ekphra-
sis.[36] In a panic, the nymph prays, inviting anyone (including us) to save
the suffering creature. Yet her adverbs – 'calmly', 'slowly' – lend accents of
resignation to her plea, revealing her awareness that the end has come and
no help is to be had. Meanwhile, her words are ekphrastic, describing the
fawn as it turns into a piece of sacred art before our eyes. Lest the simile of
sainthood be insufficiently clear, the nymph channels the Song of Songs
with its language of balsam and frankincense.

The Song of Songs permeates the poem, freighting the imagery of lilies
and roses with religious significance. In a poignant flashback, the nymph
remembers the fawn loving her garden 'with roses overgrown / And lilies'
(ll. 72–3). She recalls how

> Upon the roses it would feed,
> Until its lips ev'n seemed to bleed:
> And then to me 'twould boldly trip,
> And print those roses on my lip.   (ll. 83–6)

The fawn's blood-coloured lips smudge the nymph's own mouth, its kiss
marking her with the purple colours of the Passion. The fawn gorges
on the garden's roses, but is also pampered with *sucreries dévôts*: 'With

sweetest milk, and sugar, first / I at mine own fingers nursed' (ll. 55–6), the nymph recalls. Even the fawn's breath is 'sweet', mingling with scents of balsam and frankincense in a fragrant haze evoking not only the Song of Songs but also Catholic ceremony.[37] Wistfully the nymph imagines the creature maturing, transmuting its tastes into symbolic sustenance: 'Had it lived long, it would have been / Lilies without, roses within' (ll. 92–3). But that transubstantiation has been cut off, the wanton troopers and the order of nature cancelling it.

Don Cameron Allen has surveyed the literary and religious forbears of the dying fawn, explaining its many metaphorical resonances. 'Deer are blessed creatures', he observes, in both classical and medieval Christian texts.[38] The fawn, at once Christian and pagan, stands for love and sacrifice. Yet Marvell refuses an encounter between the orders of grace and nature in this poem, nor does he dwell on the paradoxes of an incarnational poetics. Instead, he sets in motion an allusive echo chamber in whose wide ambit Catholic arts of dying also play. For example, when the nymph shifts from memory to memorializing, her imagination takes a distinctively Catholic turn. She cherishes the fawn's tears, treating them with holy reverence, and vows to preserve them in a kind of reliquary that will also receive her own tears so that they mingle:

> I in a golden vial will
> Keep these two crystal tears; and fill
> It till it do o'erflow with mine;
> Then place it in Diana's shrine.   (ll. 101–4)

The confluence of the *ars lachrimandi* and the *ars moriendi* floods the pagan, pastoral scene with Catholic tonalities.

In the end, however, Marvell rejects theological transcendence, opting instead for religious ornament as a feature of style. This is not an implicit defence of a Protestant poetics, but rather a turn to aesthetics. In thinking about memory and mortality, Marvell prefers the Ovidian metamorphosis of nature into secular art.[39] The unfortunate lover lives on as a heraldic emblem after his death, described ekphrastically as 'sable' and 'gules' (l. 64). The nymph pictures herself as a kind of Niobe, transformed into stone. As her dying wish, she resolves to memorialize her love and her deer in a set of contiguous statues: one marble, the other alabaster. 'O do not run too fast', she tells the fawn now imagined in Elysium, 'for I / Will but bespeak thy grave and die' (ll. 109–10):

> First my unhappy statue shall
> Be cut in marble; and withal,

> Let it be weeping too: but there
> Th'engraver sure his art may spare;
> For I so truly thee bemoan,
> That I shall weep though I be stone:
> Until my tears, still dropping, wear
> My breast, themselves engraving there.
> There at my feet shalt thou be laid,
> Of purest alabaster made […].   (ll. 111–20)

The funerary ensemble that the nymph imagines is baroque – live tears streaming down her breast and trickling into the clefts and curves of the recumbent creature's effigy. While some might see the sculptural tableau as postmodern, a self-consuming artefact eroding its own engraving, it is also a Mannerist fantasy.[40] The poem stages a scene of dying that is highly aestheticized. Its sugary sweetness with its evocations of sacrifice, innocent blood and prostrate devotion taps into Roman Catholic iconography, testing the limits of decorum. While it may not tip over into bad taste, it hovers on the edge of sentimentality.

Edgar Allen Poe thought 'The Nymph Complaining for the Death of her Fawn' achieved the *point de perfection*, declaring it 'a beautiful poem, abounding in pathos, exquisitely delicate imagination and truthfulness'. Poe praises 'the very hyperbole' of the concluding lines, saying it 'renders them more true to nature when we consider the innocence, the artlessness, the enthusiasm, the passionate grief, and more passionate admiration of the bereaved child'.[41] Poe may also have admired the poem because it presents a 'beautiful death', in Ariès's sense. The nymph is vulnerable, nubile, tender. The statue she envisions might well fit into those cemeteries turned sculpture gardens where nineteenth-century mourners flocked on Sundays, in Ariès's telling (526–32). Poe's aesthetic sensibility notwithstanding, it is hard to isolate the artlessness of the nymph from the artfulness of the poem and its exploratory forays into contested areas of religious taste.

Death shadows beautiful young people in many of Marvell's lyric poems. Yet his fascination with memory and mortality is not confined to variations on the *carpe diem* theme. It leads him beyond into a liminal aesthetic territory where questions of taste and decorum in the *ars moriendi* are investigated. Just as he authorizes himself to be an arbiter of style in his prose polemics, excoriating arguments and rhetoric together, so also in his poetry Marvell is acutely conscious of stylistic extremes, adopting different personae, playing with diction and modulating aesthetic registers. This interest in violations of decorum and breaches of taste corresponds, in my view, with the philosophical emergence of taste as a category on the Continent. The implications of Marvell's stylistic experiments with the death arts are many. They reveal, for example, the sectarian overtones of religious iconography related to death, such that a tasteful Protestant death distinguished by sobriety and stoicism shades into a 'baroque' Catholic death marked by pain and self-display. In the process the conventions for representing martyrdom are revisited. Similarly, Marvell's panoply of dying poses interrogates the preoccupation with dying a good death, evincing scepticism about the project of memorialization.[42] With his focus on scenes of sudden death, Marvell casts doubt on the value of preparing for death, instead preferring to observe how beauty is cut down in its prime. In this way, Marvell's taste for death charts the secularization of the *ars moriendi* and the aestheticization of the art of memory.

Notes

1 See 'The Fire Sermon' from *The Wasteland* in T. S. Eliot, *Selected Poems* (New York: Harcourt, Brace & World, 1934), 58, where the echo repeats: 'But at my back from time to time I hear / The sound of horns and motors'.

2 See Chapter 12, '"Superfluous Men" and the Graveyard Politics of *The Duchess of Malfi*' by Michael Neill, for a contrapuntal treatment of this line by Marvell, where tombs are discussed as 'intensely public constructions'.

3 See H. H. Margoliouth in Elizabeth Story Donno (ed.), *Andrew Marvell: The Critical Heritage* (London: Routledge & Kegan Paul, 1978), 341.

4 See John M. Aden, 'Dryden and Boileau: The Question of Critical Influence', *Studies in Philology* 50.3 (1953), 491–509. See also A. F. B. Clark, *Boileau and the French Classical Critics in England* (Paris: Champion, 1925).

5 Andrew Marvell, *The Poems of Andrew Marvell*, ed. by Nigel Smith (Harlow, UK: Longman Pearson, 2007), 152, 154.

6 Nigel Smith, *Andrew Marvell: The Chameleon* (New Haven, CT: Yale University Press, 2010): 'At Nun Appleton in the early 1650s, Saint-Amant's poetry would be an important resource for both Marvell and his employer Lord Fairfax' (52). See also 97.

7 Sherburne's collection also includes translations of Giambattista Marino and the Polish Jesuit Casimir Sarbiewski.

8 Nicholas McDowell, *Poetry and Allegiance in the English Civil Wars* (Oxford University Press, 2008), 15–16. See also Nicholas McDowell, 'Marvell's French Spirit', in Martin Dzelzainis and Edward Holberton (eds.), *The Oxford Handbook of Andrew Marvell* (Oxford University Press, 2019), 614–36, 619, and Giulio Pertile, 'Marvell as *libertin*: *Upon Appleton House* and the Legacy of Théophile de Viau', *The Seventeenth Century* 28.4 (2013), 395–418

9 Nicolas Boileau, *Oeuvres Poétiques*, ed. F. Brunetière (Paris: Hachette, 1923), 216. Compare Sir William Soames's translation (London, 1683): 'Nor imitate that Fool, who, to describe / The wondrous Marches of the Chosen Tribe, / Plac'd on the sides, to see their Armyes pass, / The Fishes staring through the liquid glass' (44).

10 If Marvell read Boileau's attack on Saint-Amant's taste, one wonders whether he remembered his own lines in 'Upon Appleton House': 'The stupid fishes hang as plain / as flies in crystal overta'en' (Marvell, *The Poems of Andrew Marvell*, ed. by Smith, 677–8). While composing the latter stanzas of that poem, perhaps Donne's whimsical verses featuring fish floated in the back of Marvell's mind – more likely those of 'The Bait' than the self-effacing creatures he offers as exemplars to Sir Henry Wotton: 'but as / Fishes glide, leaving no print where they pass, / Nor making sound, so closely thy course go' (from 'To Sir Henry Wotton', ll. 55–7).

11 Marvell may also have learned about literary developments in Spain when he visited Madrid for several months in 1646–7. He could have come across the works of the Jesuit Baltasar Gracián, one of the earliest theorists of taste. See Anthony J. Cascardi, *Ideologies of History in the Spanish Golden Age* (University Park: Pennsylvania State University Press, 1997), 133–60.

12 Smith, *Andrew Marvell: The Chameleon*, 129. Similarly, McDowell, 'Marvell's French Spirit', describes 'the erudite conversation of the Huguenot *literati* who passed through the academy at Saumur, renowned for its intellectual diversity, in the 1650s' (615).

13 Dominique Bouhours, *Les entretiens d'Ariste et d'Eugène* (1671), which became a best-seller reprinted in various European cities, and *Doutes sur la langue française proposés aux Messieurs de l'Academie française* (1674). Dryden translated some of his later works into English.

14 Giorgio Agamben, *The Man without Content*, trans. by Georgia Albert (Stanford University Press, 1999), 13.

15 Andrew Marvell, *Prose Works*, ed. by Annabel Patterson, with Martin Dzelzainis, Nicholas von Maltzahn, and N. H. Keeble, et al., 2 vols. (New Haven, CT: Yale University Press, 2003).

16 Marvell's recognition that he may have gone too far is most apparent in *The Second Part*, which he published under his own name: 'But how can the Author of an Invective, though never so truly founded, expect approbation (unless from such as love to see mischief at other Mens expence) who, in a World all furnished with subjects of praise, instruction and learned inquiry, shall studiously chuse and set himself apart to comment upon the blemishes and imperfections of some particular person? Such men do seldom miss too of *their own reward*' (*Prose*, I. 237).

17 See Alex Garganigo, '*The Rehearsal Transpros'd* and *The Rehearsal Transpros'd: The Second Part*', in Dzelzainis and Holberton (eds.), *Oxford Handbook*, 517–42.

18 Donno, *Andrew Marvell*, 51, 53.

19 Cited in Jennifer Chibnall, 'Something to the Purpose: Marvell's Rhetorical Strategy in *The Rehearsal Transpros'd* (1672)', *Prose Studies* 9 (1986), 85.

20 Trinity College 'had been slow to move towards a liturgically complex form of service. In the 1636 report on the religious practices of the university that was prepared for Archbishop Laud in advance of his intended visitation, Trinity was criticized for its slovenly services and its mean furnishings. In 1636, perhaps in anticipation of that visit, the college spent about £500 on beautifying

the chapel: the eastern end was raised by several steps, the altar sumptuously adorned, new wainscotting with a gilded frieze put into the chancel, where a black and white marble pavement was laid. The organ was painted. All around the east end were hung large painted cloths showing stories of Christ's life, and near the altar four large pictures, of Christ, the Virgin Mary, Elizabeth and John the Baptist, were placed.' See Graham Parry, *Glory, Laud and Honour: The Arts of the Anglican Counter-Reformation* (Woodbridge: The Boydell Press, 2006), 83.

21 This quatrain in full reads: 'He nothing common did, or mean, / Upon that memorable scene, / But with his keener eye / The axe's edge did try' (57–60).

22 See Anita Gilman Sherman, *Skepticism in Early Modern English Literature* (Cambridge University Press, 2021), 176–224.

23 Donald M. Friedman comments: 'To reify the meaning of a Caesarian birth by picturing the hero as giving birth to himself by bursting "thorough his own Side" (l. 15) is to introduce a mode of metaphorics that we have come to recognize as peculiarly Marvellian.' Friedman, 'Rude Heaps and Decent Order', in Warren Chernaik and Martin Dzelzainis (eds.), *Marvell and Liberty* (New York: St. Martin's Press, 1999), 127.

24 See J. Creaser, '"As one scap't strangely from captivity": Marvell and Existential Liberty', in Chernaik and Dzelzainis (eds.), *Marvell and Liberty*, 145–72; Martin Dzelzainis notes that 'a certain ruthlessness underlies Marvell's otherwise delicate handling of Douglas' in 'Marvell and the Earl of Castlemaine', in Chernaik and Dzelzainis (eds.), *Marvell and Liberty*, 290–312; John R. Knott, *Discourses of Martyrdom in English Literature, 1563–1694* (Cambridge University Press, 1993); Marvell, *The Poems of Andrew Marvell*, ed. by Smith, 387.

25 When visiting Rome in 1645–6, Marvell may have seen (or heard about) Bernini's sculpture of the martyrdom of Saint Lawrence in the Strozzi villa, Via del Viminale. Smith surmises that 'if there is a Bernini statue in the background, it is most likely to be the remarkable ecstasy of St. Teresa, in the Cappella Cornaro, in the church of Santa Maria della Vittoria' (*Andrew Marvell: The Chameleon*, 61). Smith reports that the Sun's statue, to which Douglas is likened, 'was literally a fragment by Marvell's day', exhibited in front of the Lateran Palace as the vestige of a gilded bronze statue from the fourth century that 'was held to have shone in the dark and rotated to face the sun constantly' (60–1).

26 Marvell's use of the term 'relics' in the heroic verse-portrait of Captain Douglas's death ('His ship burns down, and with his relics sinks') bears comparison to Milton's subtle characterization of scattered bones as 'relics' in his Sonnet 18 – a poem perspicaciously discussed by Philip Schwyzer in Chapter 6 of this volume, 'Scattered Bones, Martyrs, Materiality, and Memory in Drayton and Milton'.

27 Smith, *Andrew Marvell: The Chameleon*, 222–6.

28 Elsie Duncan-Jones, 'Marvell: A Great Master of Words', *Proceedings of the British Academy* 61 (1975), 267–90.

29 Derek Hirst and Steven Zwicker, *Andrew Marvell, Orphan of the Hurricane* (Oxford University Press, 2012).

30 Rosalie Colie, *'My echoing song': Andrew Marvell's Poetry of Criticism* (Princeton University Press, 1970).

31 When comparing passages and images from Henry Hawkins's *Partheneia Sacra* (Rouen, 1633) to Marvell's verse involving dew and gardens, Colie acknowledges that it 'is a little book of Catholic devotion' (*'My echoing song'*, 115), but argues that Marvell resists 'that luxuriance of language' in Hawkins that is not necessarily 'a Roman Catholic stylistic device' (116). But see Anthony Raspa on 'The Jesuit Aesthetics of Henry Hawkins' *Partheneia Sacra*', in *The Jesuits and the Emblem Tradition*, ed. by Marc Van Vaeck and John Manning (Turnhout: Brepols, 1999), 25–32.

32 See Nancy Lee Beaty, *The Craft of Dying: A Study in the Literary Tradition of the ars moriendi in England* (New Haven, CT: Yale University Press, 1970).

33 See Diane Treviño Benet, '"The Loyall Scot" and the Hidden Narcissus', in C. J. Summers and T. Pebworth (eds.), *On the Celebrated and Neglected Poems of Andrew Marvell* (Columbia: University of Missouri Press, 1992), 192–206. Benet notes Douglas's Ovidian metamorphosis; as he melts so too the artificial borders between Scotland and England melt. 'At thy flame', Marvell subsequently writes, 'Our nations melting, thy colossus frame, / Shall fix a foot on either neighboring shore, / And join those lands that seemed to part before' (ll. 71–4). See also Earl Miner, 'The "Poetic Picture, Painted Poetry" of "The Last Instructions to a Painter"', *Modern Philology* 63.4 (1966), 288–94. In an effort to explain the odd tonalities of this poem, Miner invokes 'rhetorical amplifications' from 'the neutral norm', ranging from panegyric to libel (292), noting that 'after one has seen [political] cartoons of popes vomiting and worse, one is not surprised at details in *Last Instructions*' (290). Yet Miner concedes that this appeal to rhetoric and decorum is inadequate, pleading 'our lack of familiarity with assumptions about artistic imitation in the seventeenth century' (293) – a plea that defies belief and is moot if one invokes taste.

34 Philippe Ariès, *The Hour of Our Death*, trans. by Helen Weaver (New York: Vintage Books, 1981), 373–5. Ariès's original publication was in 1977.

35 Gary Kuchar, *The Poetry of Religious Sorrow in Early Modern England* (Cambridge University Press, 2008), 99–100.

36 Jonathan Goldberg, *Voice Terminal Echo* (New York and London: Methuen, 1986), elaborates on the nymph's solicitation to the reader: 'The entrance into this text at this point thematizes entrance into a text, the excessive supplementation that takes place upon annihilation. The analogies here dissolve the I/eye and the object in their place of meeting' (34).

37 In *An Account of the Growth of Popery*, Marvell lists 'Whisperings, Sprinklings, Censings' among the 'Phantastical Rites' of Catholicism (*Prose* II. 228). Kendra Packham shows the different ways Catholicism is represented in the text, arguing that it embeds 'the varied uses of Restoration anti-popery' including 'flexible, pragmatic partisan configurations' (578). See 'Marvell, Political Print, and Picturing the Catholic', in Dzelzainis and Holberton (eds.), *Oxford Handbook*, 558–82.

38 Don Cameron Allen, *Image and Meaning: Metaphoric Traditions in Renaissance Poetry* (Baltimore: The Johns Hopkins University Press, 1960), 99.

39 Compare Giulio Pertile, 'Marvell as *libertin*', who sees Marvell turning away from a devotional poetics towards Cesare Vanini's 'libertine philosophy of nature' as relayed through the poetry of Théophile de Viau (409–10). 'Marvell never approaches the frank ribaldry of Théophile's burlesque', Pertile remarks, but is attracted to his 'naturalism' and sensuality (411).

40 See Goldberg, *Voice Terminal Echo*, 35; Warren Chernaik, *The Poet's Time: Politics and Religion in the Work of Andrew Marvell* (Cambridge University Press, 1983), 154; Liam E. Semler, *The English Mannerist Poets and the Visual Arts* (Madison and Teaneck, NJ: Fairleigh Dickinson University Press, 1998), 201–39.

41 Donno, *Andrew Marvell*, 164–5. Thanks to William E. Engel for the Poe reference. See William E. Engel, 'Poe's Cultural Inheritance', in J. G. Kennedy and S. Peeples (eds.), *The Oxford Handbook to Edgar Allen Poe* (Oxford University Press, 2019), 499–519. Engel shows that Poe considered ideas of 'quaintness', 'strangeness' and 'grotesqueness' as criteria of poetic merit, using these words to convey his appreciation for seventeenth-century metaphysical poetry (508–9).

42 But see D. Vance Smith in *Arts of Dying* (University of Chicago Press, 2020) who argues that 'the literature of dying places so much stress on questions of style and lexicon' because 'the answer to endless dying lies somewhere in the terms of language itself' (4) including 'as the dispersal into an archive' (6).

CHAPTER II

The Many Labours of Mourning a Virgin Queen

Andrew Hiscock

Age cannot wither her, nor custom stale
Her infinite variety. Other women cloy
The appetites they feed, but she makes hungry
Where most she satisfies.

Antony and Cleopatra, II.ii.240–3

Enobarbus' speech to Maecenas in *Antony and Cleopatra* represents one of the most familiar eulogies in the Shakespearean canon and its opening has frequently been incorporated into contemporary usage, with ironic emphasis or otherwise. However, the present discussion, exploring some of the many and various ways in which the last Tudor monarch was mourned, does not seek to propose the celebrated tragedy as a specific act of royal commemoration. Rather, Enobarbus' speech is highlighted at the opening of this discussion because it draws attention to an increasingly consuming source of anxiety in the second half of the sixteenth century for the Tudor state – the highly scrutinised relationship of the female sovereign to the remorseless passage of time.

Shakespeare's tragedy devotes much space and energy to the depiction of ageing rulers (and lovers) richly sensitive to, but ultimately failing to defy, the combined forces of Fortuna and Chronos. However, it seems that such a situation not only was uppermost in the minds of mourners in 1603, but characterised responses to Elizabeth I throughout her forty-five-year reign. At the turn of the Tudor century, panegyrists located the declining queen with increasing urgency in a realm which apparently exceeded the grasp of Time itself. Francis Davison's *A Poeticall Rhapsody* (1602) contains a lyric performed during a royal entertainment some two years before, in 1600. Here, auditors were reminded of the very particular situation of their political (lunar) mistress Cynthia: 'Only Time which all doth mowe, / Her alone doth cherish. / Times yong howres attend her still'.[1] Elsewhere, the loyal Catholic Edmund Bolton, like Shakespeare's Enobarbus, refused to acknowledge the onset of age for the peerless female monarch. In his 'Canzon Pastorall in Honour of her Maiestie', also penned three years before the queen's death, her subjects might seek solace in the knowledge that in their land, 'No Ice dooth christallize the running Brooke, / No blast deflowers the flower – adorned field /... Winter though euery where / Hath no abiding heere.'[2] When the virgin queen was well past her child-bearing years and, indeed, approaching death, there might be every reason for those seeking royal favour to offer the possibility of *stopping the clocks*, casting the realm as held fast in some newly minted Golden Age under the sway of Astraea.[3] In the final year of her life, the Lord Keeper, Sir Thomas Egerton, welcomed Elizabeth and the court to his Middlesex residence, Harefield Place. Among the verse dialogues, allegorical stagings, courtly petitions and pastoral diversions of the *Harefield Entertainment* (1602) was included 'The Dialogue of Place and Time'. Here, even Place itself queries why its partner should remain in an environment which resists its powers: 'Farwell, Time, are you not gone, doe you stay heare? I wonder that Time should stay any wheare, what is the cause?' Without demur, her auditor is only too willing to concede that 'I stay to entertaine the wonder of this time' – a wonder who had seemingly overcome mortal life itself.[4]

In the event, the vigorous concern with the restraining of, or testifying to, the relentless march of Time towards a queen, who was bringing to a close (rather than spawning) a new dynasty, remained a constant feature of responses to her political career from its very outset. Indeed, the ageing queen was not averse to finding herself in the midst of a constantly rejuvenating society, as Rowland Whyte acknowledged in his correspondence to Robert Sidney describing the court's summer progress in August 1600:

> Her Maiestie removed vpon tuesday to Tooting, and vpon wednesday came to Nonsuch, where she stayes till Tuesday and then very constantly resolues to goe one her long progress to Tottenham the earl of Hartfords. The lords are sorry for y[t], butt her Maiestie byds the old stay behind and the young and able to goe along with her.

Ultimately, however, the strategy backfired. Whyte added, 'Her Maiestie misliked and had iust cawse to be offended that at her remoue to this place she was soe poorely attended. for I never saw such a dearth of nobility.'[5]

Attending to Loss and Memory

> [W]hen letters were written to her Ambassadors in France, to deliver some private message to the Queen-Mother [Catherine de'Medici] then of Valois; wherein her Secretary, as it were, to curry favour, had inserted this clause,

that the Ambassador should say, They two were two such Queens, so versed
in Soveraign Arts, and seen in politick affairs, as no Kings nor men in the
world went beyond them; She misliked the assotiation, and commanded it
to be blotted out, saying, The Arts she had learned were of a better stamp,
and the principles of a far higher nature, whereby she ruled her people.[6]

This extract, from Francis Bacon's posthumously published *In felicem memoriam Elizabethae* (Latin version published 1626; English translation first published 1651) had been composed in 1608 to challenge the late queen's Catholic
detractors. It serves as just one instance, among a host of examples surviving
from the period, in which the queen is seen to demonstrate her keen appreciation of the narratives which were being formulated about her for posterity
and of how these might be subsequently unpicked by future generations.

As one decade succeeded the next, the deployment of heroising seemingly transcendent but thoroughly gender-marked identities for the last
Tudor monarch remained evident in all forms of artistic creativity. The so-
called Sieve Portrait (*c.* 1583) by Quentin Mestys the Younger rehearsed yet
another narrative of an immaculate heroine impervious to the common laws
restraining lesser beings: the vestal virgin Tuccia refuted charges of unchas-
tity by transporting water in a sieve without spilling a drop.[7] Two years later,
this apotropaic anxiety of keeping death and decline at bay was reinterpreted
in Nicholas Hilliard's Ermine Portrait (1585), aligning the royal person on
this occasion with a creature of legend: the latter, it was recounted, perished
if its coat of purest white came into contact with any source of contamina-
tion.[8] In a pattern that recurs across the span of Elizabeth's life, we find
such iconographic associations were frequently taken up at the moment of
mourning her death: in this case, decades later, on the occasion of the publication of the University of Oxford's official elegiac verse collection in Latin
commemorating the queen's passing – *Oxoniensis academæ funebre officium
in memoriam honoratissimam serenissimæ et beatissiamæ elisabethæ* (1603). In
one contribution, as part of a succession of extravagant similes celebrating
that the 'fresh fame, [of] Eliza, is sent across the whole world', the reader was
reminded (here in English translation) that

> just as the ermine fears to touch the heaps of mud,
> Is surrounded and captured in the freezing north,
> So that the garments of royalty, its snow-white pelt, is not stained,
>   Just so did you breathe with the power of the Christ you adored,
>   Such, Eliza, was the radiance of your life.[9]

Here, the ermine is deployed not only as an emblematic focus for recalling
the late queen's pure and virginal status, but also for configuring her in a
Christological discourse of superlative exemplarity.

As a whole sequence of distinguished scholars, such as Frances A. Yates, Marie Axton, Roy Strong, Susan Doran, John N. King and Helen Hackett, have argued, the forms of reverence proffered to the last Tudor monarch transformed over the course of her reign as the young, marriageable princess of the Reformed faith matured into the virgin queen.[10] In a post-Reformation nation which had witnessed acts of iconoclasm in the decades following Henry VIII's break with Rome, images of the monarch that were promoted by the state would inevitably attract marked and widespread attention. Apart from the queen's image on the coins circulating throughout the kingdom, engravings and portraits became a highly significant cultural locus for the appreciation of the Supreme Governor of Church and State.[11] Furthermore, while miniatures of the queen might be offered by Elizabeth herself as tokens of royal favour, the periodic commissioning of the often-costly portraits remained notably for the attention of a wider public. The key power of cultural intervention that these representations might wield was swiftly realised by government ministers. William Cecil, for example, drew up the following proclamation which was issued from Windsor on 6 December 1563:

> [H]ir Maiesty … shall shortly make a pourtraict of hir person or visage … [and] commandeth all manner of persons in the meane tyme to forbeare from payntyng graving pryntyng or making of any pourtraicture of hir Maiesty, vntill some special person that shall be by hir allowed shall have first finished a purtraictvure therof, after which finished … all other payntors or grauors … shall and maye at ther pleasvres follow the sayd patron or first portraictvr.[12]

This decree would prove to be but the first in a number of government endeavours to circumscribe the ways in which the queen would be represented to her subjects and audiences abroad, leading ultimately to, what Roy Strong termed, the issuing of the 'mask of youth' for prescribed usage in artists' workshops.[13] If Elizabeth might sometimes appear in tributes during her lifetime as a *Venus armata*, for those mourning her death she could equally often be located in mythological scenes. The University of Cambridge produced its own elegiac verse collection in Latin commemorating the death of the monarch: *Threno-thriambeuticon, cantabrigiæ* (1603). At its opening, William Smith, the university Vice-Chancellor, began by lamenting in one of his poetic contributions the fateful 'day of Jove' (Thursday) which had struck down all the rulers of the Tudor dynasty since Henry VIII. Nonetheless, in this instance, 'By her death, she is reborn, and flourishes, / Just as the moon is reborn and renews its light.'[14]

The very multifariousness of the iconographic and panegyric productions of Elizabeth circulating throughout the realm was appreciated by her
subjects even during her reign. By way of recalling this, in *The discouerie
of a gaping gulf whereinto England is like to be swallowed by another French
marriage* (1579) John Stubbes had hailed 'our Queene, the chiefe officer
in England, our most precious rych treasure, our Elizabeth IONAH and
ship of good speede, the royall ship of our ayde, the hyghest tower, the
strongest hold, and castle in the land' – and he lost his right hand for his
pains.[15] (At such moments, we may be reminded of the mock encomium
devoted to Ben Jonson's very own 'Faerie Queene' in *The Alchemist* (1612):
'our Dol, our Castle, our Cinque-Port, / Our Douer Pire, our what thou
wilt'.[16]) Elsewhere, at the close of Elizabeth's reign, the opening to Thomas
Dekker's *Old Fortunatus*, a Christmas entertainment performed by the
Admiral's Men in 1600, reviewed some of the many and various ways
in which the ageing queen had been revered and celebrated during her
long reign: 'Some cal her Pandora: some Gloriana, some Cynthia: some
Delphaebe, some Astraea.'[17] In fact, Elizabeth was frequently called upon
to keep company with the classical pantheon of goddesses. In the Latin
verses addressed to her by scholars of Eton school in 1563, for example, the
royal auditor was duly informed that 'Juno has filled you, Queen, with
most abundant riches, Pallas Athena has given you a full share of serious
wisdom … but Venus (as she is the goddess of beauty) … has added an
attractive appearance.'[18] Elizabeth was similarly matched in Hans Eworth's
painting *Elizabeth and the Three Goddesses* (1569). Interestingly, this scene
was renewed some twenty years later in the recently discovered, and rather
more accomplished, miniature (*c.* 1590) attributed to Isaac Oliver.[19] This
sustained association with Olympian deities would be revisited on the
occasion of her death.[20] The presence of Venus, Juno and Athena could
not fail to lend magnitude to any tribute addressed to the last Tudor
monarch, alive or dead. Keen to exploit such poetic strategies for his own
extended elegy in English, 'T. W. gentleman' penned *The lamentation
of Melpomene, for the death of Belphaebe our late Queene* (1603), paying
due homage to 'The chast Belphaebe [who] is of life depriu'de, / Merrour
of Chastetie, when shee suruiu'de.'[21] Moreover, the constant paralleling
of Elizabeth with pagan goddesses often formed a discursive continuum
with other accounts of her miraculous, transcendent presence, notably in
the celebrations of her as a *donna angelicata* composed by those mining
the enormously rich and popular seam of the *Petrarchismo*. Strikingly,
Elizabeth was as guilty of this lively fascination with the Italian poet as
any of her subjects: like Mary Sidney, she rendered sections of Petrarch's

Trionfi into English verse.[22] Amongst the wider society of her subjects, she was also situated pictorially on at least two occasions as leading the illustrious cortège of the *Trionfo della Fama*.[23] In addition, blazoning Elizabeth forth as a Petrarchan mistress, the critic and poet George Puttenham is attributed with the verse collection *Partheniads* offered to the sovereign as a New Year's gift in 1579: the seventh 'Partheniad' (or virgin-song) was dedicated to the muse of music (Euterpê) and recounted, 'I saw march in a meadow green / A fairer wight than Fairy Queen, ... Of silver was her forehead high, / Her brows two bows of ebony. / Her tresses trussed were to behold, / Frizzled and fine as fringe of gold.'[24]

Developing even further this panegyric mode hailing a queen who surpassed the bounds of mortal life, the 'Hymnus in Cynthiam' in George Chapman's *The Shadow of the Night* (1594) constituted but one in a whole sequence of verse offerings in the latter period of her reign that unveiled the sovereign as the moon goddess: 'Peacefull, and warlike, and the power of fate, / In perfect circle of whose sacred state, / The circles of our hopes are compassed.'[25] This lunar identity for the queen was also exploited in the visual arts. Headdresses incrusted with images of the moon might be found in a number of representations of her, including Isaac Oliver's 'Rainbow' portrait (*c.* 1600, inscribed motto: *'Non sole sine iris'*–no rainbow without the sun) at the Cecils' residence in Hatfield House: here, the heavenly goddess held the celestial promise of peace in her hand.[26] In *Colin Clouts Come Home Againe* (1595), Edmund Spenser had drawn attention to the 'Shepherd of the Ocean', Sir Walter Ralegh, whose

> song was all a lamentable lay,
> Of great vnkindnesse, and of vsage hard,
> Of *Cynthia* the Ladie of the sea ...[27]

If, in the surviving 'books' of the 'Ocean's love to Scinthia', discovered in Ralegh's own hand in the mid-nineteenth century in the Cecil family archive, the court favourite as forsaken suitor paid extended tribute to his cruel fair ('Shee gave, shee tooke, she wounded, she appeased. /... what stormes so great but Cinthias beames apeasd?'[28]), he was not alone in configuring Elizabeth, Cynthia and the passage of time in the same poetic discourse.[29] Given the currency of this vein of panegyric until the very end of her reign, such emphases would again be taken up in the poetic mourning for the dead queen. John Lane's *An elegie vpon the death of the high and renowned princesse, our late Soueraigne Elizabeth* (1603) urged the wider company of the pastoral scene to mourn the passing of 'the Lady of the

Faiery-land / … weepe, and wayle, and melt away to teares, / … For siluer
Cynthia has eclipst her light / And with her absence makes eternall night'.[30]

New Heaven, New Earth: Elizabeth and the New Jerusalem

In 1559, the beleaguered queen was keenly aware of the hostility to her sovereignty at home and abroad. It was thus imperative that Elizabeth assert
the legitimacy of her political authority from the outset by affirming her
Christian piety. The need for such demonstrations could only be rendered
more pressing when Pope Pius V declared her excommunicate in 1570.[31]
Such an emphasis would be taken up both during her life (e.g. woodcut
from John Day's *Christian Prayers and Meditations* (1569)[32]) as well as in
the commemorative publications of 1603. In Henry Chettle's *England's
Mourning Garment* (1603), for example, with its Spenserian dialogue
between the shepherds Collin and Thenot, we learn that, 'Her Highnes
therefore taught all her people the vndoubted truth: faith in Christ alone,
the waye, the doore, and the life.' In addition, Chettle's publication also
included 'The order and proceeding at the Funerall of the Right High and
Mightie Princesse Elizabeth.'[33] By the Jacobean period, this strategic point
was still being made by William Camden's *Annales* (1625) where the reader
was informed, 'Queen ELIZABETH was truely godly, pious, and zeal-
ously deuoted: for her Maiestie was not so soone out of her bed, but fell
vpon her knees in her priuate Closet, praying to God deuoutly.'[34]

If early modern monarchs, such as Henry VIII, might regularly be compared to David, Moses or Solomon, panegyrists in the opening decades
of her reign also aligned Elizabeth with Old Testament heroines, such as
Deborah, Judith and Esther. Within a few years of her accession in 1558,
the queen was being transposed to landscapes where England jostled with
Judaea and Palestine for the audience's attention. In the Latin addresses
recited to the queen at Windsor in 1563 by scholars at Eton school,
Elizabeth was placed among the '*Iehovæ populum*' as Deborah protect-
ing 'Judah from the rage of Jabin' and as Judith '*fœmina fortis*' defeating
Holofernes: 'thus you (o Queen) will put warlike enemies to flight – thus
you will defeat your enemies, Elizabeth'.[35] Equally significantly, Elizabeth
herself acknowledged the justness of the comparison. In her only surviving
works composed in Spanish and dating from the opening decades of her
reign, one of the texts of her prayers includes a petition ('O my God, O my
Father') that she might be given strength 'so that I, like another Deborah,
like another Judith, like another Esther, may free Thy people of Israel from
the hands of Thy enemies'.[36]

Elsewhere, in a Latin address during entertainments at Woodstock in 1575, Elizabeth was hailed as '*Constantinæ nostræ*'. The speaker, Laurence Humphrey, Dean of Gloucester and Regius Professor of Divinity and Vice-Chancellor at Oxford University, declared 'I see Solomon's kingdom renewed and recalled by the kindness of a divine power.'[37] Although the comparison of Elizabeth with Old Testament heroines has often been principally consigned by critics to the initial decades of her reign, examples of this form of panegyric persisted on into the latter part of the sixteenth century. For the title page of 'The Second Lamp of Virginitie' in Thomas Bentley's *Monument of Matrons* (1582), for instance, the kneeling Elizabeth is counterpointed in the opposing column of the page with a similarly devout Esther.[38] Elsewhere, at the end of the decade, in Leonard Wright's *The hunting of Antichrist* (1589), Jehovah's 'faythfull annoynted handmayde' is duly compared with earlier English monarchs and Old Testament heroes and heroines.[39] Indeed, such eulogies continued to have currency into the final years of the reign as Richard Vennar's manuscript collection *The Right Way to Heaven* (1601) bears witness. Here in a 'Prayer for the Prosperous Successe of Hir Maiesties Forces in Ireland', the desire is explicitly articulated that 'our Soueraigne may sing with Debora after the victorie, hauing with Hester preserued hir people, and with chast Iudith cut of the head of harme pretending Holofernes'.[40]

As we have seen, the extravagant nature of the encomia addressed to Elizabeth led again and again to an emphasis upon political and spiritual transcendence. In Vennar's *The Right Way to Heaven* (1601), mentioned above, we discover the image of Elizabeth attended upon and crowned by angels; and this was just the note that a more lyrically minded Gabriel Harvey struck on one occasion for his own evocation of the sovereign: 'words, hand, eyes, face, everything was filled with an angelic grace'.[41] Here, we broach perhaps the liveliest and most strenuously discussed area of Elizabethan iconography. Key contributions to the field in studies by Helen Hackett, John N. King and Susan Doran, for example, have rightly advised against giving credence to any formalised or government-sponsored cult of Elizabeth designed to replace that attributed to the Virgin Mary in pre-Reformation Britain.[42] However, there are some individual instances of remarkable forms of veneration expressed during her lifetime. Michael Drayton, for example, drew attention in his poetic collection *Idea* (1593) to a celestial 'Betha' whose symbolism partook of the Greco-Roman and Christian worlds as well as that of the *Petrarchismo*:

> Beta long may thine Altars smoke, with yeerely sacrifice,
> And long thy sacred Temples may their Saboths solemnize,
> Thy shepheards watch by day and night,
> Thy Mayds attend the holy light,
> And thy large empyre stretch her armes from east vnto the west,
> And thou vnder thy feet mayst tread, that soule seuen-headed beast.[43]

Late sixteenth-century copies of images of the young Elizabeth in her coronation robes with her auburn hair spread out on her shoulders *may* also recall pictorial evocations of the Marian coronation widely circulating in pre-Reformation and Counter-Reformation Europe.[44] The Ditchley and Rainbow portraits certainly portray a queen who towers above and holds sway over the mortal world; and Doran draws attention to the visit of Baron Waldstein to Hampton Court where he remarked upon a ceiling representation of Elizabeth being received into heaven, now lost.[45] Camden pursued this theme in his own commemoration of the late queen for his *Annales* (Latin edition 1615; English translation 1625): 'Shortly after, vpon the 24. of March, being the Eue of the Annunciation of the blessed Virgin Mary, (being the very same day whereon she was borne) being called out of the prison of her flesh, into her heauenly Country, she quietly departed this life.'[46]

Whatever the interpretation or status placed upon such examples, these forms of tribute occur only intermittently in the queen's lifetime and, as has been underlined in studies by Hackett, King and Doran, many of the major contributors to Elizabethan panegyric consciously avoided Marian discourse.[47] Not least among the reasons for this are that the Reformists had sought to establish incontrovertible principles of difference between the practices of the Catholic and Protestant cultures of worship, notably a rejection of what was perceived as the old faith's investment in idolatry. In addition, any notion of a widespread neo-Marian cult of Elizabeth must be placed severely in question when such allusions are mostly restricted, chronologically, to the later phases of her reign and, socially, to the confines of the court and its (aspiring) clientage. Nonetheless, certain examples of Mariological allusion are apparent in elegies upon the late queen. For the *Threno-thriambeuticon, cantabrigiæ*, Samuel Walsall from Corpus Christi College stressed that, 'As on the eve, behold, of the Annunciation / Of Mary, the maiden Bearer of God, / Then was the sad death first announced of Eliza, the maiden who worshipped God. / How fittingly! As this maiden was next to that one / In virginity, so she was in the day.'[48] However, if John Webbe, of Christ Church College, Oxford, insisted in his own Latin tribute for the *Oxoniensis academæ* that 'when Elizabeth descended from the height of Heaven, / She allowed her kingdom to possess eternal light', his fellow scholar, Francis Alexander, Fellow of New College, pursued the analogy even more extravagantly, construing both virgins as almost twin-like ('*cùm cætera pœne gemellæ*'):

> Do you wish to know the reason why holy Eliza ascended
>   To the realms above, on the day before the virgin's day? …
> Mary and she were virgins. Mary was blessed,
>   And so was Beth, among the ranks of women.
> To one, a king was heir; the other was the king's heir.
>   This one carried God in her womb; that one, in her heart.[49]

Thus, if there is no evidence of a state-sponsored initiative to render the virgin queen as a latter-day *regina caeli*, it was possible for single individuals to evoke and, on occasions, to give explicit expression to such sentiments both before and after her death.[50]

Semper Eadem

Inherited from her mother, Anne Boleyn, one of the most celebrated mottoes adopted by Elizabeth during her reign was that of *semper eadem* – always the same.[51] Conversely, the thrust of the present discussion has been to explore just some of the endlessly proliferating meanings associated with the last Tudor monarch that crossed over from her life into her death.

George Browne of Magdalen College took up the celebrated motto for his own Latin verse 'Semper eadem' in the *Oxoniensis Academæ Funebre Officium*, deploying the voice of a scoffing critic to dramatic effect: 'Arrogant woman, do you think you are immortal?' In the event, the tirade at the opening of Browne's offering swiftly transforms into eulogy, hailing one who was 'always the same … / On Earth, she was a goddess, and shines out among the stars, just the same'.[52] If, as we have seen, prominent figures, such as Ralegh, figured forth poetic personae who engaged primarily with the sovereign during her lifetime in Petrarchan terms of languishing, grieving and lamentation, one of the earliest and most significant mourners of the last Tudor monarch might be identified as Elizabeth herself. Challenging her Catholic detractors after her death, Bacon's *In felicem memoriam Elizabethae* insisted that, 'It is most untrue, for many years before her end she was not nice, often, and with much grace to call herself old woman, and used to discourse of her Tomb' – indicating thus that rumours had long been circulating of the queen's tendency towards morbidity. Bacon did, however, acknowledge that 'not long before her death, sitting pensive, and, as it were, musing of mortality, as one came and told her, that divers places stood too long vacant in the State; she rose up somewhat offended, and said, *She knew well enough that her place would not stand an instant empty*.⁵³

Even as a relatively young woman, shortly after her accession at twenty-five years of age, she was discovered on public, state occasions urging her audiences to contemplate her own demise. Instances of what Scott L. Newstok characterises as the 'preliminary auto-epitaph'⁵⁴ are interestingly being given voice by Elizabeth in these opening phases of her reign when hopes of marriage and motherhood might still be reasonably held. In her many and various interactions with Parliament, Elizabeth was compelled to reflect not only upon her role as sovereign, but also as an agent of political transmission. Some five years after her accession in April 1563, Francis Bacon's father, Nicholas, the Lord Keeper, delivered Elizabeth's response to the House of Lords in the royal presence on the question of the succession, ending 'I hope I shall die in quiet with *Nunc dimittis*, which cannot be without I see some glimpse of your following surely after my graved bones.'⁵⁵ In 1576, in a speech closing the parliamentary session, Elizabeth insisted with notable animation that 'I know I am but mortal, which good lesson Mr. Speaker in his third division of a virtuous prince's properties required me with reason to remember ... [I] prepare myself to welcome death whensoever it shall please almighty God to send it.'⁵⁶

Clearly, this sentiment had become thematic to many of her public pronouncements, strategically enhancing her authority as the pious philosopher-queen. It was, however, in 1564 in a Latin address to the University of Cambridge that Elizabeth seems to have seized the opportunity to explore publicly her relationship to death under more extended terms:

> [S]o may I, before I pay my debt to nature (if Atropos does not sever the thread of life more quickly than I hope), do some famous and noteworthy work ... And if it should come to pass (which clearly I do not know how soon it might) that I have to die before I am able to complete that which I promise, yet will I leave an exceptional work after my death, by which not only may my memory be renowned in the future, but others may be inspired by my example, and I may make you all more eager for your studies.⁵⁷

In the event, the ailing Elizabeth appears to have been somewhat less steadfast, more humanly vulnerable, if the accounts of her final hours are to be believed – accounts which seem to summon up the vivid rendering of the ageing queen in the 'Allegorical Portrait' of Elizabeth (English School, *c.* 1600).⁵⁸ Elizabeth's goddaughter and maid of honour, Elizabeth Southwell, recorded that nearing death in the melancholy of her sicknes [the queen] desired to see a true looking glasse, which in twenty yeares she had not sene, but only such a one as was made of purpose to deceue her sight, which glase being brought her she fell presently into exclaymyng against them which had so commended her and toke it so offensiuely that some which before had flattered her dourst not come in to her sight.[59]

The limits of time and space have rendered it impossible to do full justice to the many and various commemorations of the last Tudor monarch. However, by way of conclusion, it should be added that eulogists might also strategically exploit a redemptive logic of compensation, so frequently in evidence in discourses of mourning. This emphasis is struck in Shakespeare and Fletcher's *Henry VIII* or *All is True* (1613) by Thomas Cranmer at the infant Elizabeth's baptism: 'The bird of wonder dies, the maiden phoenix, / Her ashes new create another heir/ As great in admiration as herself' (V.iv.40–2).[60] The textual anxiety in evidence in the Archbishop's prophecy to reconfigure demise-as-parturition is widely reiterated in a most politic fashion in the commemorative outpourings of 1603. If a poetic 'Lamentation' included in the *Oxoniensis academæ* duly recorded that 'The splendour of the English nation, the glory of Europe, / The phoenix of the world has fallen into ash'[61], the induction to Henry Petowe's *Elizabetha Quasi Vivens, Eliza's Funerall* (1603) asserted, 'She was, she is, and euermore shall bee, / the blessed Queene of sweet eternitie.' For the present, however, Petowe's poetic persona was compelled to 'sorowe with my pen, / Till dead *Eliza* doth reuiue agen'.[62] In such ways, Petowe's text, amongst a host of others, may draw attention to what R. Clifton Spargo has identified as the way in which 'mourning frequently deploys a psychological trick of time, treating its retrospective concern for the other as if it were anticipatory or potentially preventive of loss'.[63]

Nonetheless, like many of his compatriots, choosing not to remain in this minor key, Phineas Fletcher submitted for the *Threno-thriambeuticon, cantabrigiæ*: '[Let whoever] Sing of you, Eliza, of you and of your death / ... At the same time, let him celebrate you, James.'[64] In this way, like the shepherds in *The Winter's Tale*, readers were invited to contemplate both 'things dying ... [and] things new-born' (III.iii.104–5), marking a point of loss and the subsequent restoration of integrity for the nation as a whole. Such a therapeutic emphasis upon the labours of mourning and renewal is also in evidence in Anthony Nixon's *Elizaes memoriall. King Iames his arriuall. And Romes downefall* (1603) where, after poetic eulogies to the queen's political achievements, he passes on in the second phase of the publication 'to Englands present state, / [where] sudden ioy ore-come the former feare'.[65] Alternatively, the full title of T. W.'s 1603 verse publication cited earlier in this chapter was *The lamentation of Melpomene, for the death of Belphaebe our late Queene With a ioy to England for our blessed King* – in the event, the 'joy' of the title was consigned to the final lines of the extended elegy in English.

In the closing moments of this discussion, lest such laudatory publications should be seen to monopolise all forms of response across the nation as a new dynasty acceded to the English throne, it might be added that attitudes to Elizabeth in life and in death remained as many and various as we have seen the iconographical representations to be. Panegyric might not universally hold sway over opinion as the Tudor century drew to a close, nor might biting political critique be the preserve solely of Catholic antagonists. Loss inevitably prompts the living to seize an opportunity for reflection and re-evaluation; and Dennis Kay notes with regard to the vernacular elegy that although a 'significant number of poets did write on the Queen's death ... [there were] many fewer than had mourned Sidney or would mourn Prince Henry'.[66] Already, in the final decade of the queen's reign, Lady Penelope Rich, sister to Robert Devereux, Earl of Essex, could be discovered penning messages to James VI, acknowledging that her brother was 'excedinge wery[,] accomptyng it a thrale he lyves nowe in and wysshes the change'.[67] Elsewhere, at some distance from the Elizabethan *fin-de-siècle*, in the Caroline period Godfrey Goodman, Bishop of Gloucester, observed that, 'The people were very generally weary of an old woman's government. And this no doubt might be some cause of the Queen's melancholy.'[68] More broadly, whatever the subject's line of political vision as one century yielded to the next, *mutatis mutandis* the island nation would negotiate a quite different court culture and, indeed, a quite different political trajectory in the new, Stuart, century.

Notes

1 Francis Davison, *A Poeticall Rhapsody* (London: V. Sims, 1602), L7ᵛ.
2 See *Englands Helicon* (London: I. Roberts for John Flasket, 1600), C4ᵛ.
3 This aspect of Elizabethan iconography was explored at length in Frances A. Yates' seminal study, *Astraea: The Imperial Theme in the Sixteenth Century* (London: Routledge & Kegan Paul, 1975).
4 See Elizabeth Goldring et al., eds., *John Nichols's The Progresses and Public Processions of Queen Elizabeth I: A New Edition of the Early Modern Sources*, 5 vols. (Oxford: Oxford University Press, 2014), IV.182.
5 Ibid., IV.128.

6 Sir Francis Bacon, *The felicity of Queen Elizabeth …* (London: Thomas Newcombe for George Latham, 1651), pp. 40–1. William Camden also completed his *Annales* (1615) at the request of James I. The English translation of books I–III was published in 1625.

7 The portrait forms part of the collection in the Pinacoteca Nazionale in Siena. There is also another earlier, less accomplished version of this scene in the 'Plimpton' portrait (*c.* 1579) by the English painter George Gower. See https://luna.folger.edu/luna/servlet/detail/FOLGERCM1-6-6-29241-102094:The-Plimpton--Sieve--portrait-of-Qu (accessed 15 December 2021).

8 This portrait is located in the King James Drawing Room of Hatfield House, Hertfordshire.

9 Goldring et al., eds., *Nichols's The Progresses*, IV.483, 661. Roy Strong also draws a link between the Ermine Portrait and Petrarch's *Trionfo della Castità*. See Strong, *The Tudor and Stuart Monarchy. Pageantry, Painting, Iconography*, vol. II: *Elizabethan* (Woodbridge: Boydell Press, 1995), p. 12.

10 See Yates, *Astraea*; Marie Axton, *The Queen's Two Bodies: Drama and the Elizabethan Succession* (London: Royal Historical Society, 1977); Roy Strong, *Gloriana: The Portraits of Queen Elizabeth I* (London: Thames & Hudson, 1987); Helen Hackett, *Virgin Mother, Maiden Queen: Elizabeth I and the Cult of the Virgin Mary* (London: Palgrave, 1995); Susan Doran, 'Virginity, Divinity and Power: The Portraits of Elizabeth I', in Susan Doran and Thomas S. Freeman (eds.), *The Myth of Elizabeth* (Basingstoke: Palgrave, 2003), pp. 171–99; John N. King, *Tudor Royal Iconography: Literature and Art in an Age of Religious Crisis* (Princeton, NJ: Princeton University Press, 1989).

11 For examples of engravings of Elizabeth I by William Rogers, see www.npg.org.uk/collections/search/person/mp57930/william-rogers (accessed 15 December 2021).

12 Proclamation 6 December 1563. See Goldring et al., eds., *Nichols's The Progresses*, I.371–2. In this context, see also Strong, *The Tudor and Stuart Monarchy*, II.11.

13 Strong, *Gloriana*, p. 16.

14 Goldring et al., eds., *Nichols's The Progresses*, IV.254, 315–16.

15 John Stubbes, *The discouerie of a gaping gulf* (London: Henry Singleton, 1579), C2ʳ.

16 Ben Jonson, *The Alchemist* (London: Thomas Snodham for Walter Burre, 1612), G2ᵛ.

17 Thomas Dekker, *The pleasant comedie of old Fortunatus* (London: S. S. for William Aspley, 1600), A1ᵛ.

18 Edward Franckline, epigram 17 from 'Verses Addressed to the Queen at Windsor by Eton Scholars, 9 September 1563'. See Goldring et al., eds., *Nichols's The Progresses*, I.328–9.

19 See, respectively, www.rct.uk/collection/403446/elizabeth-i-and-the-three-goddesses and www.npg.org.uk/collections/search/portrait/mw224945/Queen-Elizabeth-I-Elizabeth-I-and-the-Three-Goddesses (accessed 15 December 2021). For a fascinating discussion of the latter, see Helen Hackett, 'A New Image of Elizabeth I: The Three Goddesses Theme in Art and Literature', *Huntington Library Quarterly*, 77.3 (September 2014), 225–56.

20 In this context, see Latin verse elegies in the *Oxoniensis Academæ* by Thomas Antrobus and Henry Shelley in vol. IV of Goldring et al., eds., *Nichols's The Progresses*, 503, 685; 510, 694.

21 'T. W. gentleman', *The lamentation of Melpomene, for the death of Belphaebe our late Queene With a ioy to England for our blessed King* (London: W. White, 1603), A3ᵛ.

22 See Elizabeth I, *Translations 1544–1589*, ed. by Janel Mueller and Joshua Scodel (Chicago: University of Chicago Press, 2009).

23 See, respectively, British Library manuscript Sloane 1832 fols. 7ᵛ–8ʳ (dated 1570), www.bl.uk/learning/timeline/item104117.html (accessed 15 December 2021) and Anthony Munday, *Zelauto* (London: John Charlewood, 1580), p. 34. Moreover, by way of tribute to the Elizabethan *Petrarchismo*, one of the mottoes in the background of the Sieve Portrait is from the *Trionfo d'Amore*: 'stancho riposo e riposato affano' (weary I rest and having rested I am still weary).

24 Anthologised in Susan M. Felch and Donald V. Stump, eds., *Elizabeth I and Her Age* (New York: W. W. Norton & Norton, 2008), p. 569. For further discussion, see Hackett, *Virgin Mother, Maiden Queen*, p. 98. In this context, see also a lyric composed for a 1591 court entertainment anthologised in Felch and Stump, *Elizabeth I and Her Age*, p. 576; and Sir John Davies, 'Hymne I: Of Astraea', in John Davies, *Hymnes of Astraea in acrosticke verse* (London: I.S., 1599), A2ʳ.

25 George Chapman, *Skia nyktos – The shadow of night containing two poeticall hymnes* (London: Richard Field for William Ponsonby, 1594), C2ᵛ.

26 See www.hatfield-house.co.uk/house/the-house/the-rainbow-portrait/ (accessed 15 December 2021).

27 Edmund Spenser, *Colin Clouts Come Home Againe* (London: Thomas Creede, 1595), A4ʳ, B1ᵛ.

28 'The 21th and last booke of the Ocean to Scinthia', ll. 56, 118. See Sir Walter Ralegh, *The Poems of Sir Walter Ralegh: A Historical Edition*, ed. by Michael Rudick (Tempe: Arizona Center for Medieval and Renaissance Studies/ Renaissance English Text Society, 1999), pp. 50, 52.

29 See also the 1588 portrait of Ralegh in London's National Portrait Gallery where this follower of Cynthia is represented with a fugitive image of the crescent moon in the background: www.npg.org.uk/collections/search/portrait/mw05204/Sir-Walter-Ralegh-Raleigh (accessed 15 December 2021).

30 John Lane, *An elegie vpon the death of the high and renowned princesse, our late Soueraigne Elizabeth* (London: W. White, 1603), A3ʳ. For other examples of Cynthia-inspired lyrics, see Goldring et al., eds., *Nichols's The Progresses*, IV.256, 317; 448, 615; 512, 696–7. On the poetic trope turning upon the dialectic of presence and absences, see Chapter 3 'Recollection and Pre-emptive Resurrection in Shakespeare' by John S. Garrison.

31 In this context, see also Alexandra Walsham, '"A Very Deborah?" The Myth of Elizabeth I as a Providential Monarch', in Doran and Freeman (eds.), *Myth of Elizabeth*, pp. 143–68 (p. 144).

32 See John Day, *Christian prayers and meditations in English French, Italian, Spanish, Greeke, and Latine* (London: John Day, 1569), A1ᵛ.

33 Henry Chettle, *Englands mourning garment* (London: 1603), D4ʳ, E4ᵛ–F2ʳ.

34 William Camden, *Annales*... (London: George Purslowe, Humphrey Lownes, and Miles Flesher for Benjamin Fisher, 1625), p. 13.
35 Goldring et al., eds., *Nichols's The Progresses*, I.294, 348.
36 Elizabeth I, *Elizabeth I: Collected Works*, ed. by Leah S. Marcus, Janel Mueller and Mary Beth Rose (Chicago: University of Chicago Press, 2002), p. 157.
37 Goldring et al., eds., *Nichols's The Progresses*, II.441, 460.
38 Thomas Bentley, *The monument of matrons* (London: Henry Denham, 1582), F2ʳ. See also Doran, 'Virginity, Divinity and Power', p. 182.
39 Leonard Wright, *The hunting of Antichrist* (London: John Wolfe, 1589), pp. 14–15.
40 Goldring et al., eds., *Nichols's The Progresses*, IV.146–7. In this context, see also contributions to *Oxoniensis academæ* by Thomas Holland and Richard Etkins, anthologised in vol. IV of *Nichols's The Progresses*, 393, 547; 449, 618.
41 Goldring et al., eds., *Nichols's The Progresses*, II.657.
42 Helen Hackett, 'Rediscovering Shock: Elizabeth I and the Cult of the Virgin Mary', *Critical Quarterly*, 35.3 (September 1993), 30–42. See also David Scott Wilson-Okamura, 'Belphoebe and Gloriana', *ELR*, 39.1 (2009), 47–73; Peter McClure and Robin Headlam Wells, 'Elizabeth I as a Second Virgin Mary', *Renaissance Studies*, 4.1 (March 1990), 38–70; Yates, *Astraea*, p. 79; Julia M. Walker, *The Elizabeth Icon: 1603–2003* (London: Palgrave, 2004), p. 35.
43 Michael Drayton, *Idea* (London: Thomas Orwin for Thomas Woodcocke, 1593), p. 18.
44 For further discussion here, see Andrew Hiscock, 'Élisabeth Iᵉʳᵉ: Iconographie, Matérialité et *Côté Obscur*', in *Actes du colloque tenu au château de Bournazel* (Montpellier: Édition du Buisson/Presses Universitaires de la Méditerranée, forthcoming). However, it should be noted that a maturer Elizabeth does not have her hair arranged in this manner, for example, when she is crowned by Mercy and Justice on the title page of the Bishops' Bible (London: Richard Jugge, 1569); in a decorative initial for the dedication of John Foxe's *Acts and Monuments* (London: John Day, 1563), B1ʳ; or in the frontispiece to Christopher Saxton's *Atlas of England and Wales* (London: n.p., 1579).
45 See Doran, 'Virginity, Divinity and Power', p. 185.
46 William Camden, *The historie of the life and reigne of that famous princesse Elizabeth* (London: for William Webbe, 1634), pp. 383–4.
47 See respectively: Hackett, *Virgin Mother, Maiden Queen*, pp. 7–10; Hackett, 'Rediscovering Shock', pp. 30–42; Helen Hackett, 'Dreams or Designs, Cults or Constructions? The Study of Images of Monarchs', *The Historical Journal*, 44.3 (2001), 811–23; Doran, 'Virginity, Divinity and Power', pp. 172, 177–8; King, *Tudor Royal Iconography*, pp. 183, 199; John N. King, 'Queen Elizabeth I: Representations of the Virgin Queen', *Renaissance Quarterly*, 43.1 (1990), 30–74.
48 Goldring et al., eds., *Nichols's The Progresses*, IV.260, 322.
49 Ibid., IV.488, 668.
50 For a discussion of the medieval inheritance of medieval queens being associated with the iconography of the Virgin Mary, see King, *Tudor Royal Iconography*, pp. 197ff.

51 John N. King draws attention draws comparison between this motto and that of Mary I – *Veritas Temporis Filia* – Truth is the Daughter of Time. See *Tudor Royal Iconography*, p. 103.

52 Goldring et al., eds., *Nichols's The Progresses*, IV.493–4, 674–5.

53 Bacon, *Felicity*, pp. 24–5.

54 Scott L. Newstok, '"Turn thy Tombe into a Throne": Elizabeth I's Death Rehearsal', in Annaliese Connolly and Lisa Hopkins (eds.), *Goddesses and Queens: The Iconography of Elizabeth I* (Manchester: Manchester University Press, 2007), pp. 169–90 (p. 177).

55 *Elizabeth I: Collected Works*, p. 80. See also Elizabeth's response to a parliamentary delegation and a Latin oration to the University of Oxford: ibid., respectively pp. 95, 91.

56 Ibid., p. 170.

57 Ibid., pp. 88–9.

58 See www.corsham-court.co.uk/Pictures/Commentary.html (accessed 15 December 2021).

59 Goldring et al., eds., *Nichols's The Progresses*, IV.225.

60 *The Arden Shakespeare Complete Works*, ed. by Richard Proudfoot, Ann Thompson and David Scott Kastan (London: Thomson Learning/Arden, 1998).

61 Goldring et al., eds., *Nichols's The Progresses*, IV.430, 593. In this context, see also the Phoenix medal struck in 1574 and reproduced in Strong, *Gloriana*, p. 82.

62 Henry Petowe, *Elizabetha quasi viuens Eliza's funerall* (London: E. Allde for M. Lawe, 1603), A3ʳ–A3ᵛ.

63 R. Clifton Spargo, *The Ethics of Mourning* (Baltimore, MD: Johns Hopkins University Press, 2004), p. 4.

64 Goldring et al., eds., *Nichols's The Progresses*, IV.258, 321.

65 Anthony Nixon, *Elizaes memoriall. King Iames his arriuall. And Romes downefall* (London: Thomas Creede, 1603), B2ʳ.

66 Dennis Kay, *Melodious Tears: The English Funeral Elegy from Spenser to Milton* (Oxford: Clarendon Press, 1990), pp. 78–9. See also Chapter 9, 'The Unton Portrait Reconsidered' by Peter Sherlock, with reference to how Sir Philip Sidney was mourned and remembered.

67 See Penelope Rich to James VI. Hatfield House, Cecil Papers, 18/50. Quoted in Chris Laoutaris, '"Toucht with bolt of Treason": The Earl of Essex and Lady Penelope Rich', in Annaliese Connolly and Lisa Hopkins (eds.), *Essex: The Cultural Impact of an Elizabethan Courtier* (Manchester: Manchester University Press, 2013), pp. 201–36 (p. 206).

68 Godfrey Goodman, *At the Court of King James the First ... Now first published from the original manuscripts*, ed. by John S. Brewer, 2 vols. (London: Richard Bentley, 1839), I.97.

CHAPTER 12

'Superfluous Men' and the Graveyard Politics of The Duchess of Malfi

Michael Neill

Sinking into nothing, I cease to be superfluous ...
                                            Ivan Turgenev, *Diary of a Superfluous Man*

In 1598 Philip Henslowe drew up the now celebrated list of properties belonging to his company, the Admiral's Men:[1] it consists mainly of small, portable pieces of equipment, ranging from weapons, tools, and musical instruments, to animal skins, crowns, and a papal mitre; larger, more spectacular properties, though they include items as various as 'I Hell mought [mouth]', 'the sittie of Rome', a 'wooden canepie', 'Faeton charete [Phaeton's chariot]', and 'i dragon in Fostes [*Faustus*]', are relatively few – which makes it all the more surprising that, at the head of his catalogue, Henslowe includes no fewer than three tombs: 'i tombe .... i tome of Guido, i tome of Dido'. Given the lavish ornamentation characteristic of sixteenth-century funeral monuments, these must have been expensive items, and the entrepreneur's need to acquire more than one suggests something about the importance of memorial display on the early modern stage – a suggestion borne out by the surprisingly large number of plays from the surviving repertoire in which a tomb becomes a focus of the action.[2] As I have argued elsewhere,[3] the theatrical prominence given to such properties reflects significant developments in the post-Reformation culture of death, when the spate of iconoclastic vandalism that followed the break with Rome was succeeded by an extraordinary upsurge in the demand for expensive church tombs – monuments whose emphasis on posthumous fame helped to mend a relationship with the living that had been so painfully fractured by the abolition of purgatory and of the entire practice of intercession for the dead.[4]

No play of the period is more preoccupied with such memorial artifice than John Webster's *The Duchess of Malfi*: especially striking are three episodes involving the Duchess herself. In the opening scene her wooing of Antonio is coloured by oddly disturbing references to 'a winding sheet' and to 'the figure cut in alabaster / Kneels at my husband's tomb' (I.1.380, 442–3); while in Act IV, her murder is prefaced by a piece of macabre theatre when Bosola enters in the guise of an old man, announcing himself a 'tomb-maker' whose 'trade is to flatter the dead' (ll. 135–6).[5] Advising the Duchess that 'I am come to make thy tomb' (l. 110), he proceeds to discourse on the iconographic niceties of 'fashion in the grave' (ll. 144–50), before bringing her 'By degrees to mortification' (l. 164). But the tomb he promises never appears, becoming instead a conspicuous absence at the centre of the action – one closely bound up with contemporary events and thus with the dissident politics on which Webster's great tragedy is grounded.

* * * * *

On 6 November 1612 there occurred an event that shook England to its core: the death from typhoid of King James's eldest son, Henry, Prince of Wales. The eighteen-year-old prince had emerged as the hero of the country's more militant Protestants: inclined towards Calvinism, he was imagined as the engineer of a future second Reformation: 'Henry the 8. Pull'd down abbeys and cells,' went the jingle, 'But Henry the 9. shall pull down Bishops and bells.'[6] Heralded as a champion against the threat from Catholic Spain, he had presided over a household that, in the last two years of his life, became an ideological rival to the court of his father, the self-proclaimed *rex pacificus*. As a result, Henry's passing was the occasion for an unprecedented exhibition of public grief. A flood of mourning publications included accounts of his life, descriptions of his funeral, and more than fifty elegiac volumes from leading poets of the day – among them Webster himself, who must have put aside work on *The Duchess of Malfi* to compose the first of his tributes to the dead prince, *A Monumental Column* (1613).[7]

For four weeks Henry's body lay in state at his palace of St James. Then, on 7 December, it was transferred to a superbly ornamented hearse – the tomb-like structure, devised by his Surveyor of Works, the architect and stage-designer, Inigo Jones, which formed the centrepiece of his magnificent funeral procession. An enormous cortège – larger even than that accorded to Queen Elizabeth – consisting of over 2000 mourners then accompanied the body to Westminster. Crowds in the street, as they caught sight of Henry's waxwork effigy, made 'a fearefull outcrie … as if they felt … their own ruine in that losse …. [and their] streaming eyes made knowen howe much inwardly their harts did bleed'.[8] The funeral climaxed in a magnificent service at the Abbey, where the prince was duly buried.[9] There, in Henry VII's Lady Chapel, King James had recently installed a grand monument for his predecessor, Elizabeth I (1606), as well as elegant marble tombs for his infant daughters, Mary and Sophia (1607), before, in the very year of Henry's death, completing an especially impressive edifice in which to re-inter his mother, Mary, Queen of Scots.

Mary had been executed by Elizabeth for involvement in Anthony Babington's treasonous papist conspiracy (1587); and the erection of her monument (significantly larger than Elizabeth's) was an act of symbolic recuperation. For all the splendour of his obsequies, however, the Protestant hero was to receive no such dignity, his body being simply consigned to lie beside his Catholic grandmother in the vault beneath her tomb. Rumours circulated regarding plans to build him an equally lavish memorial, but nothing eventuated. James would no doubt have pleaded penury; but, given their fractious relationship, the neglect must have seemed conspicuous; and it was no doubt partly in reaction to it that for three decades Henry's greatness continued to be proclaimed by adherents of the Protestant and parliamentary cause. Webster himself wrote a 'monument of gratitude' to the prince as the climax to his 1624 mayoral pageant, *Monuments of Honour*; and there, in a telling metaphor, he imagined 'fame's best president' as having been 'Called to a higher Court of Parliament'. As late as 1641, in the months leading up to parliament's rebellion against King Charles, two biographies appeared in print:[10] each optimistically dedicated to the current Prince of Wales as 'the true inheritour of your noble Uncle's vertues'. Both works were attributed to Henry's former treasurer, the late Sir Charles Cornwallis (d. 1629), who in 1614 had been sent to the Tower for organising parliamentary opposition to James.

Cornwallis's *Discourse* pointed to the absence of any tomb for his master by concluding with the regretful 'wish [that] it were in my power to raise such a monument unto his fame, as might eternise it unto all posterities'. In this he echoed a number of the 1613 elegists who had already seemed to anticipate the king's neglect, by suggesting that only their words would preserve Henry's fame: William Drummond, for example, in the pyramid-shaped verse that he contributed to the collection fittingly named *Mausoleum* (1613), predicted that 'no great Marble Atlas trembl[ing] with gold' would be erected 'To please a vulgar eye'; instead the tears of Apollo and the Muses would form 'A Chrystal tombe' to show the dead prince's worth. In his own elegy, *A Monumental Columne* (1613), Webster makes use of a similar conceit: 'The greatest of the kingly race is gone,' he begins, with a defiant superlative; but, although humbly 'laid in the earth', Henry now resembles 'a perfect diamond set in lead [whose] glories do break forth' adorned by 'those colors, which Truth calls her own'. No matter that the prince lacks the material grandeur of a 'Darius' tomb', his fame will be preserved by poets, who alone have power to immortalise great men.

The idea of literature-as-monument, offering immortality to its creator as well as to its subject, was of course a venerable trope, deriving from Horace and other Latin poets, 'I have built a monument more lasting than bronze, and loftier than the pyramids of kings' Horace had declared of his own poetry (*Odes*, III.30). Famously elaborated in Shakespeare's Time sonnets,[11] it is a theme of John Weever's study of *Ancient Funeral Monuments* (1631) whose opening chapter reminds its readers that 'the Muses works are of all monuments the most permanent, for of all things else there is vicissitude, a change both of cities and nations' (B2[r]). The memorialising power of poetry was again in Webster's mind when *The Duchess of Malfi* went to press, providing the theme of his dedicatory epistle with its insistence that 'such poems as this ... when the poets themselves [are] bound up in their winding-sheets' will make their patrons 'live in [their] grave and laurel spring out of it' (ll. 15–20); and the resonance of this conceit for the play as a whole is confirmed by the self-consciously chosen compliments of the encomiastic verses which Webster's fellow-playwrights contributed to the printed text. This 'masterpiece', wrote John Ford, would endow the poet himself with 'A lasting fame to raise his monument' (l. 6), while Thomas Middleton, echoing the playwright's own graveyard politics, announced that

> Thy monument is raised in thy lifetime;
> And 'tis most just; for every worthy man
> Is his own marble, and his merit can
> Cut him to any figure and express
> More art than Death's cathedral palaces,
> Where royal ashes keep their court.   (ll. 6–11)

Middleton's sardonic vision of royal ashes holding court recalls the language of Webster's villain-satirist, Bosola; but it also encodes a reference to the immediate circumstances of the play's creation, echoing the way in which *A Monumental Columne* remembered 'when churches in the land were thought rich jewel boxes': 'this age', the elegy declared 'hath brought / That time again' – not, however, through a revival of papist ornamentation, but through a more metaphysical transformation. Middleton's insistence on the fragility of worldly 'greatness' – of 'all our scepters and our chairs of state' – together with his dismissive reference to 'Death's cathedral palaces', recalls the way in which Webster's elegy urged its readers to visit 'Henry the Seventh's chapel', where 'the dust of a rich diamond [lies] enshrined', setting its display of monumental grandeur against a spectacle of decay like that which confronts Antonio and Delio in the ruined cloister of Act V:

> What a dark night piece of tempestuous weather,
> Have the enragèd clouds summoned together,
> As if our loftiest palaces should grow
> To ruin, since such highness fell so low.[12]

The Muses, however, enable 'great men' to transcend the ruins of time: – 'For they shall live by them, when all the cost / Of gilded monuments shall fall to dust'; and Henry's patronage of the 'noble arts' will make his 'beams … break forth from [his] hollow tomb / Stain the time past and light the time to come' (pp. 181, 180).

The playwright would return to that figure of illuminated fame in *Malfi*, where Antonio's first paean to the Duchess ('She stains the time past, lights the time to come', I.i.202) anticipates his visionary moment in the ruined abbey, where a 'clear light' (V.iii.45) illuminates the mysterious sorrowing face that may be his wife's. Nor is this the scene's only imagistic connection with the poetry of Prince Henry's death; for its suggestive Echo turns out to be modelled on another of the 1613 elegies – George Wither's fiercely anti-Catholic *Prince Henry's Obsequies*. In Wither's poem, the allegorical figure of Britain summons the prince to rise from his grave and defend his people against the swarming menace of 'Rome's locusts'. He is answered by a voice that consoles his countrymen with the apocalyptic promise that 'Babel's [i.e., Rome's] fall and Jacob's [i.e. James's] rising [are] near.'[13] Although the title-page promises 'A supposed Inter-locution betweene the Ghost of Prince Henrie and Great Brittaine', Wither's text identifies this prophetic voice only as a 'Spirit'; and (since Protestant doctrine did not allow for the return of the dead) it is carefully distinguished as being neither 'my prince's ghost, or fiend' – its divinations coming only as uncanny echoes of Britain's own words. Webster's version is even more careful to discount any suggestion of papist superstition, since Delio explains that, though 'many have supposed it is a spirit', the voice results simply from the acoustics of 'a piece of cloister which … gives the best echo you ever heard' (V.iii.5–9); and the stage name dubs it only 'Echo'. For Antonio, however, Echo's words are given supernatural significance by its sounding 'like my wife's voice' (l. 26); although, in contrast to Wither's Spirit, it has no uplifting prophecy to offer, speaking only of its interlocutor's mortality – 'Thou art a dead thing' – and of his wife's fearful absence, warning that he will 'Never see her more' (ll. 40, 45). What are we to make of this bleak transformation of Wither's optimistic vision? It is, I think, a product of Webster's disillusioned response to the sudden death of the Prince of Wales and its politically contentious aftermath.

The Duchess of Malfi is not usually thought of as an especially political play: to its first audiences, however, it may have appeared a more controversial work than it does to us. Most obviously, given James I's determination to maintain peace with Spain and to cultivate the loyalty of his own Catholic subjects, it is likely to have seemed implicitly oppositional in its treatment of the Duchess's brothers: not only does it emphasise their arrogant pride in 'The royal blood of Aragon and Castile' (II.v.22), but it is openly anti-papist in its portrait of the war-mongering, lecherous Cardinal, whose cold-blooded murder of his own mistress with a poisoned Bible is among Webster's more lurid additions to his sources.[14] The intention behind this vicious caricature was perfectly evident to Horatio Busino, chaplain to the Venetian ambassador, who, when the King's Men re-staged the play in 1618, took offence at the ways in which it sought to 'deride our religion as detestable and superstitious'.[15]

Occurring just as the country moved towards a crisis over the proposed marriage between Prince Charles and the Catholic Infanta of Spain, this revival looks like a loaded gesture; and it is probably no coincidence that *Malfi* was finally published in 1623, just as the conflict between James and parliament over the Spanish match reached its peak, and a matter of months before Webster's own sympathies were once again made plain in *Monuments of Honour*, published after Charles, by turning his back on the Infanta, appeared to have thrown in his lot with parliament. Of course hostility to Spain as Europe's principal instrument of Catholic reaction had been a recurrent feature of English theatre since at least the 1580s. But what makes *Malfi*'s political and religious attitudes distinctive is the way in which they are bound up with an equally oppositional social vision.

A key to this aspect of the tragedy is to be found in the Echo scene: at first sight it might seem to have very little to do with politics, just as it can seem imperfectly integrated into the design of the play itself. That design is itself an odd one, since it allows the action to continue for an entire act after the death of the nominal protagonist; but, in addition to making that act – most of which is of the playwright's own invention[16] – the longest in the play, Webster placed at its centre an episode that is not only without equivalent in other versions of the story, but that contributes almost

nothing to an already overstretched plot. As a result, the scene is routinely
cut from modern productions of the play. Why then did Webster choose
to include it? The answer has everything to do with what might be called
the politics of the graveyard.

'The grave's a fine and private place,' wrote Andrew Marvell to his coy
mistress; tombs, by contrast, are intensely public constructions.[17] In early
modern England issues of interment became, for reasons I have begun to
suggest, especially fraught. Webster's tragedy is full of graves, figurative as
well as literal – a sign, according to T. S. Eliot, that 'Webster was much
possessed by death': but there are reasons for thinking that this preoccupation had less to do with 'the skull beneath the skin', than with the
contested ideology of monumental display.

In Bosola's imagination the living body itself is no more than an animated cadaver: inhabiting 'a shadow or deep pit of darkness'; human
beings are merely 'dead walls or vaulted graves' (V.v.99, 95) whose condition anticipates the oblivion and corruption of the boneyard:

> Though we are eaten up of lice and worms,
> And though continually we bear about us
> A rotten and dead body. All our fear –
> Nay, all our terror – is lest our physician
> Should put us in the ground to be made sweet.   II.i.55–60

In the Duchess's brothers he sees 'a pair of hearts are hollow graves, /
Rotten and rotting others' (IV.ii.303–4); while Ferdinand himself, tormented by jealousy, complains that his sister has 'ta'en that massy sheet of
lead, / That hid thy husband's bones, and folded it / About my heart' (III.
ii.112–14). Following her murder he imagines that 'The wolf shall find her
grave and scrape it up – / Not to devour the corpse, but to discover / The
horrid murder' (IV.ii.293–4); and the figure uncannily anticipates his own
lycanthropic madness, when, convinced he has himself become a wolf, he
'Steal[s] forth to churchyards in the dead of night / [To] dig dead bodies
up' (V.i.10–12).

Set against the grave's harsh reminders of mutability are the lavish edifices by which great men seek to ensure their own immortality. But this is
mere vanity: the 'huge pyramid' to which Bosola compares the Cardinal,
'Begun upon a large and ample base', ends 'in a little point, a kind of nothing' (V.v.75–7); while to Cariola, the imprisoned Duchess herself resembles
'some reverend monument / Whose ruins are even to be pitied' (IV.ii.32–3);
and it is to just such ruinous nullity that the play leads its audience in the
derelict necropolis of the Echo scene.

On a first reading, the scene can easily seem like a piece of gratuitous melodrama, intended simply to match the hauntings of plays like *Hamlet* and George Chapman's *Bussy D'Ambois*, or the graveyard scene of Cyril Tourneur's *Atheist's Tragedy*. At the beginning of the act, Antonio, still unaware of his wife's murder, has informed his friend Delio that he intends to seek 'reconcilement' with her brothers, the Cardinal and Duke Ferdinand (V.i.1, 72). Now, as the two friends approach the Cardinal's castle they find themselves amid the remains of an 'ancient abbey', where their conversation is punctuated by the ominous responses of a voice that, even as it insists that Antonio will never see his Duchess again (l. 43), exposes him to a fearful hallucination: 'on the sudden, a clear light / Presented me a face folded in sorrow' (ll. 45–6). Whose face it is, he does not say; and critics readily assume that, like the apparition that tormented Bosola at the end of the previous scene, it is the Duchess's. Supposing that the mysterious Echo must issue from her own grave, they conjecture that Webster, taking advantage of a spectacular property which the King's Men had built a little earlier for *The Lady's Tragedy* (1611), actually intended the Duchess's spectral form to appear on stage.[18] In Middleton's play, when the hero Govianus visits the grave of his murdered love, her monument suddenly flies open and 'a great light appears in the midst of the tomb' revealing her figure, 'standing just before him all in white, stuck with jewels and a great crucifix on her breast' (IV.iv.42). Webster's 'clear light', it is suggested, signalled his intention to reuse this expensive device; but, given the way that dialogue and stage directions describe the spectacular effects that are required elsewhere – in the Cardinal's military investiture, for example (III.iv.), or Ferdinand's display of waxwork bodies (IV.i)[19] – this seems unlikely. Antonio speaks of the ruined graves that 'questionless' must lie beneath their feet (V.iii.9–17), but there is nothing to indicate the presence of anything like the 'richly set forth' monument that dominates two whole scenes of *The Lady's Tragedy* (IV. iii–iv).[20] In place of Middleton's eloquent ghost, whose dialogue with Govianus extends for nearly fifty lines, Webster's scene offers only the insubstantial Echo which (however it may sound to Antonio) is simply the distorted reverberation of the characters' own voices; and, given that the 'face folded in sorrow' seems invisible to Delio, it is likely that the audience were no more supposed to see it than they were allowed to witness the previous haunting that Bosola dismissed as the illusory product of his own 'melancholy' (V.ii.346).

Insofar, then, as the scene remembered Middleton's staging, it was surely just to emphasise Webster's refusal to indulge in such fantasy: what matters here, as Brian Chalk has recently suggested,[21] is the scene's very lack of monumental display. In its place there is only the desolate ruin conjured into the audience's minds by Antonio's rumination on the 'reverend history' represented by the remains of an 'ancient abbey':

> ... questionless, here is this open court,
> Which now lies naked to the injuries
> Of stormy weather, some men lie interred
> Loved the church so well, and gave so largely to't,
> They thought it should have canopied their bones
> Till doomsday; but all things have their end:
> Churches and cities, which have diseases like to men,
> Must have like death that we have.   (ll. 11–19)

It is worth asking, however, why, in a work that is generally parsimonious with scenic detail, this decaying cloister should be so vividly imagined.[22]

The prospect envisioned in Antonio's extended *vanitas* or *memento mori* will have seemed uncomfortably familiar to Webster's audience, of course: for it belongs not to the play's nominal setting in Renaissance Italy, but to early modern England, whose landscape had been left scarred with such remains by the iconoclastic violence of the Reformation.[23] The 'bare ruined choirs' that Shakespeare lamented were painful reminders of the contentious politics of monumental display, to which recent historical events had given an especially sharp edge.[24] The most explicit contemporary reflection on their significance is to be found Weever's treatise, *Ancient Funeral Monuments*. To this antiquarian, the sight of the vandalised tombs that had once adorned the aisles and chantries of abbeys, churches, and cathedrals was so disturbing that, in an effort to preserve their derelict record, he set about compiling a detailed catalogue of all that he could find. In it he contemplated the sad effects of 'the small continuance ... [of such] magnificent strong buildings', while quoting an anonymous sonneteer's lament for 'the sudden fall of our religious houses' in language that strikingly resembles Antonio's own meditation:

> What sacred structures did our Elders build,
> Wherein Religion gorgeously sat deckt?
> Now all throwne downe, Religion exiled ...
> Or ruind so that to the viewers eye,
> In their owne ruines they intombed lie;
> The marble urnes of their so zealous Founders
> Are digged up, and turn'd to sordid uses;
> Their bodies are quite cast out of their bounders,
> Lie un-interr'd....[25]

For Weever, such monuments, whatever their pious inscriptions, had less to do with religion than with the advertisement and preservation of the social order: 'Sepulchres', he declared, 'should bee made according to the qualitie and degree of the person deceased, that by the Tombe everyone might be discerned of what ranke hee was living.'[26] Even as he lamented the destruction of tombs that had embodied this ideal, Weever railed against the way in which the church monuments of his own day appeared to flout it, so that 'more honour is attributed to a rich quondam Tradesman, or griping usurer than is given to the greatest Potentate entombed in Westminster'.[27] Moralising on such futile ostentation, he is forced to concede that 'It is vanitie for a man to thinke to perpetuate his name and memory by strange and costly great Edifices', for they serve only to demonstrate 'the vanity of our mindes, vailed under our fantasticke habits and attires'.[28] *The Duchess of Malfi* expresses a similar scorn for 'fantasticke' ostentation in the grave, but pushes it towards a levelling conclusion that would have been anathema to the conservative Weever.

The Echo scene may not show us the Duchess's monument, but immediately before her murder a disguised Bosola offers to build her one: presenting himself as a tomb-maker, whose 'trade is to flatter the dead' (IV. ii.136), he enquires 'of what fashion' she desires to have hers built; 'Why', she responds with defensive irony, 'do we grow fantastical in our death-beds? Do we affect fashion in the grave?' (ll. 143–4). 'Most ambitiously', he replies, offering a lesson on contemporary style:

> Princes' images on their tombs do not lie as they were wont, seeming to pray up to heaven, but with their hands under their cheeks as if they died of the toothache. They are not carved with their eyes fixed upon the stars, but as their minds were wholly bent upon the world, the same way they seem to turn their faces. (ll.145–50)

Just such an image appears in a well-known Jacobean portrait; and thinking about that painting can, I believe, help to illuminate the politics of Webster's monuments.[29] The painting traces the life-story of Sir Henry Unton, Queen Elizabeth's ambassador to France: beginning with his birth at Wadley House, the family seat in Berkshire, it moves through his marriage and subsequent career to his death and to the imposing heraldic funeral that preceded his interment in the parish church of Faringdon in 1596 (Chapter 9; see Figures 9.1 and 9.2). The climax of the narrative is supplied by a splendid tomb, whose armour-clad effigy lies in precisely the 'toothache' posture that Bosola describes; behind it kneels the figure of Unton's wife, Dorothy, gesturing at a pedestal on which a pious book lies open.[30] Frozen for eternity, Lady Unton seems to belong, like her husband, to the grave; but in fact her presence on the monument merely signalled the mourning death-in-life to which a dutiful widow was consigned. Lady Unton would live on – not just to see the completion of Sir Henry's monument in 1606, but to commission the portrait itself – whose programme she no doubt supplied. She would, moreover, get married a second time, resembling in this Webster's defiant Duchess who, as she woos her new husband, is made to repudiate just such an image of widowly piety:

> This is flesh and blood, sir;
> 'Tis not the figure cut in alabaster
> Kneels at my husband's tomb. (I.i.441–3)

We do not know how Lady Unton's family reacted to her remarriage; but Webster's protagonist undertakes hers in outright defiance of her brothers' opinions: 'You are a widow', she is reminded. 'They are most luxurious [lustful] will wed twice …. The marriage night is the entry into some prison … Wisdom begins at the end. Remember it' (ll. 285–317).[31] Compounding her offence by choosing to marry one of her own servants, in what was known as a 'marriage of disparagement', the Duchess presents her wooing of Antonio as nothing less than an heroical quest: 'as men in some great battles … have achieved / Almost impossible actions … So I, through frights and threat'nings, will assay / This dangerous venture …. Wish me good speed, / For I am going into a wilderness / Where I shall find nor path nor friendly clew to be my guide' (1.1.334–51). Then, as she places her ring upon his finger, the Duchess raises her steward from his own kneeling position, symbolically reversing the deferential hierarchy embodied by her figure on the tomb ('This goodly roof of yours is too low built', I.i.404). For all her rebellious rhetoric, however, she is compelled to marry in secret, and will remain dogged by reminders of that mortal 'end' where wisdom begins too late, and of the tomb to which her first husband's death was meant to relegate her. When at last she is forced to accept her brothers' 'gift' of death (IV.ii. 11), she does so in a posture that painfully recalls the alabaster figure she sought to repudiate:

> Yet stay – heaven gates are not so highly arched
> As princes' palaces: they that enter there
> Must go upon their knees. (ll. 18–20)

Here it might seem as if the Duchess has come full circle, finally submitting to the role of pious widow; and if this were all, the play could appear to endorse, with only minor qualifications, those earlier versions of the

story that had presented her life as a warning against princely irresponsibil-
ity and the consequences of undutiful widowhood. The monument that
Bosola's tomb-maker promises is never realised: instead, the nearest thing
we see is a mocking parody of tomb sculpture: the 'sad spectacle' of 'the
artificial figures of ANTONIO and his Children, appearing as if they were
dead', the 'excellent property' that Bosola presents to the Duchess in the
first scene of her imprisonment (IV.i.54 SD, 56, 64).

But there is more to the play's graveyard politics than this; and again,
we can find pointers in the Unton Portrait. Among this painting's oddities
is the way in which it asks to be read in more than one way. Insofar as its
biographical design is shaped by the funeral procession that dominates its
foreground, its action seems to lead directly from cradle to grave, with only
a wedding to intervene. Unton's career as a diplomat, figured above, is
reduced to a kind of digression from this insistent narrative; and, although
in each of its episodes his figure is lit by the sun in the top right-hand
corner, it is his tomb at the bottom left which its beams illuminate with
special magnificence, making it appear the proper culmination of a life
well lived. Beneath the tomb, however, the painter shows us Sir Henry's
shrouded cadaver, a reminder of the sordid reality beneath that monumental display; and it is not, after all, to the monument that the viewer's eye is
most insistently drawn. Instead, the image that dominates the entire composition – even as it remains conspicuously unintegrated into its narrative
design – is a formal portrait of the diplomat at work, his head framed by
two figures who compete to possess him: on his left, Death presents Unton
with an ominous hourglass, but on his right the winged figure of Fame – as
if set free from her other representation beneath the canopy of the monument – swoops down to claim him, blowing her trumpet. The portrait
figure, then, appears to stand for a renown that, as it displaces the progress
of mortality, transcends the merely material ostentation of the tomb.

A similar effect is created, I think, in the last scene of the *Duchess of
Malfi*, where Bosola's despairing epitaph – 'We are only like dead walls or
vaulted graves / That, ruined, yields no echo' (V.v.95–6) – sends us back
to the Echo that resounded among those other ruined graves – one whose
significance is finally spelt out in Delio's response to the 'great ruin' by
which he is surrounded:

> These wretched eminent things
> Leave no more fame behind 'em than should one
> Fall in a frost and leave his print in snow –
> As soon as the sun shines, it ever melts
> Both form and matter. I have ever thought

> Nature doth nothing so great for great men
> As when she's pleased to make them lords of truth:
> *Integrity of life is Fame's best friend,*
> *Which nobly, beyond death, shall crown the end.* (V.v.111–19)

It is the Duchess's integrity whose fame Delio proclaims; but it is no accident that he should speak of 'great men', for his is the generalised elegiac language of *A Monumental Columne*: 'Oh greatness! What shall we compare thee to? To giants, beasts, of towers framed out of snow … *The evening shows the day and death crowns life.*'[32] It would resound once more in *Monuments of Honour*, where, as if remembering Bosola's 'huge pyramid', the closing 'Monument of Gratitude' begins with a display of 'foure curious Paramids charged with the Princes Armes … which are Monuments for the Dead, that hee is deceased', before claiming for Henry a greatness whose fame transcends such empty display:

> Such was this prince, such are the noble hearts
> Who, when they die, yet die not in all parts,
> But from the *integrity of a brave mind*,
> Leave a most *clear* and eminent fame behind,
> Thus hath this *jewel* not quite lost his ray,
> Only cased up 'gainst a more glorious day....[33] (I.i.334–51)

The echo of *Malfi*'s 'Integrity of life' is unmistakeable; and it is important that the concluding lines of the pageant claim that same princely virtue for the bourgeois Lord Mayor himself '*Integrity*, that keeps / The safest watch and breeds the soundest sleeps'[34] – since Henry is implicitly presented here as a patron of Sir John Gore's Merchant-Tailors and their citizen world.

In *Malfi*, as the Duchess prepares to face the imprisonment that will separate her forever from Antonio, she is urged by Bosola to 'forget this base, low fellow …. One of no birth' (III.v.112–14); she responds with a parable that exposes conventional ideas of rank to question, 'Men oft are valued high when they're most wretch'd,' it concludes, 'There's no deep valley, but near some great hill' (ll. 135–9). In the virtual epilogue that announces the play's tragic conclusion, Delio provides a gloss for these somewhat enigmatic *sententiae*: 'Let us make noble use of this *great* ruin …. Nature doth nothing so *great* for *great* men, /As when she's pleased to make them lords of truth' (V.v.108–17). His insistent repetition of 'great' comes as a final reminder of the semantic pressure that the play has put on that bland-seeming adjective: together the words 'great' and 'greatness' appear no fewer than fifty-six times in Webster's tragedy – a frequency matched only in two plays that subject the idea of 'greatness' to similar interrogation – Shakespeare's *Troilus and Cressida* (fifty-seven) and *Antony and Cleopatra* (fifty-three). The court world, though haunted by fears of 'a great man's ruin' (III.i.93–4), is full of so-called '*great* men': Ferdinand 'the *great* Calabrian Duke' (I.i.83) claims the privileges that belong to '*great* men' (l. 233), the Cardinal is called 'this *great* fellow' (l. 44), 'the *great* Cardinal' (5.2.185), and a '*great* man' (l. 290), their sister is 'the *great* Duchess' (l. 268), a '*great* woman' (IV.ii.125) whose downfall is ironically assured when she becomes '*great* with child' (II.i.108). Among the other characters, the foolish Malateste is called 'the *great* Count' (III.i.41), while Julia, the Cardinal's mistress, boastingly numbers herself among '*great* women of pleasure' (V.ii.192). Even Bosola, Antonio sneeringly suggests, is 'studying to become a *great* wise fellow' (II.i.77). Ferdinand, who scorns Antonio as 'A slave that only smelt of ink and counters, / [Who] never in his life looked like a gentleman' (III.iii.72–3), sarcastically dubs this social-climber 'the *great* master of [the Duchess's] household' (I.i.86); but it is Antonio himself who (in a figure uncannily brought to life by the madmen who are sent to torment the imprisoned Duchess) dismisses all ambition as 'a *great* man's madness … girt with the wild noise of prattling visitants / Which makes it lunatic beyond all cure' (I.i.408–12); and it is Antonio who, at the point of death, dismisses life itself as a deluded 'quest of *greatness*' in which 'We follow after bubbles blown in th'air' (V.v.62). 'The great are like the base,' he reflects, pondering the Duchess's efforts to conceal her pregnancy, 'nay, they are the same, / When they seek shameful ways to avoid shame' (II.iii.51–2).

The 'integrity of life', which for Delio sets the Duchess apart from such folly, self-consciously translates the famous opening of Horace's *Odes* I.22: 'Integer vitae, scelerisque purus.' With its implicit rejection of martial greatness, the phrase becomes a reminder of the way in which the Duchess's course of life has rewritten the heroic aspiration expressed in her wooing of Antonio ('As men in some *great* battles …', I.i.334–51); and it reaches back to the question with which Cariola opens the play's debate about the nature of greatness: 'Whether the spirit of *greatness* or of woman / Reign most in her, I know not' (l. 487) (emphasis added). In recent criticism the play's apparent endorsement of the Duchess's secret marriage is often read as a response to 'women's issues';[35] and it is admittedly crucial to the playwright's purpose that Delio's final speech should promise to establish Antonio's surviving son 'In's *mother's* right' (l. 111, emphasis added). In Webster's sources, by contrast, this son was 'forced to fly out of Milan, to change his name, and to retire himself far off, where he died unknown', while the Duchess, along with her murdered husband and her other strangled children, was reduced to a 'ruin' that set an 'example to all posterity'.[36] But in the play's characteristic oxymoron it is the corpses of those 'wretched eminent things', Ferdinand and the Cardinal, that are consigned to the oblivion of 'ruined graves', while the play itself, with its wholesale reimagining of the Duchess's story, becomes a monument to the unbroken 'integrity' that defines her greatness. Webster's proto-feminism is easily exaggerated, however; and the much less generous treatment of figures like Julia, or Vittoria Corombona in his earlier tragedy, *The White Devil*, suggests that his sympathy for the Duchess was inspired by something other than straightforward indignation at the plight of women.

It was less the inequities of gender than the tyrannies of rank that seem to have stirred the playwright's resentment, as we can see from the dedicatory epistle, addressed to 'To the Right Honorable George Harding, Baron Berkeley of Berkeley Castle, and Knight of the Order of the Bath to the Illustrious Prince Charles', that framed *Malfi*'s published text. Beginning in the deferential manner expected of such appeals for patronage, Webster breaks into a sudden truculence that is unlikely to have pleased his aristocratic addressee: 'I do not altogether look up at your title, the ancientest nobility being but a relic of time past. And the truest honor indeed being for a man to confer honor on himself.' But this, significantly, is the same attitude expressed in one of the satiric diatribes given to the villain-hero, Bosola, when he confronts Antonio early in the second act:

> A duke was your cousin-german removed[?] Say you were lineally descended from King Pippin – or he himself; what of this? Search the heads of the *greatest* rivers in the world, you shall find them but bubbles of water. Some would think the souls of princes were brought forth by some more weighty cause than those of meaner persons. They are deceived: there's the same hand to them; the like passions sway them. The same reason that makes a vicar go to law for a tithe pig and undo his neighbours makes them spoil a whole province and batter down a goodly city with the cannon. (II.i.94–103 [emphasis added])

If titles, like ruined monuments, are no more than 'relics of time past', for Bosola the order of degree, on which others set so much store, amounts to nothing more than a hierarchy of humiliation: 'for places in court are but like beds in a hospital, where this man's head lies at that man's foot, and so lower and lower' (I.i.64–6).

Webster's choice of a story to illustrate this contentious attitude to rank was hardly an obvious one: a century after her death, the history of Giovanna d'Aragona, the widowed Duchess of Malfi – of her marriage of disparagement to her steward, Antonio da Bologna, of her honour-killing at the behest of her jealous brothers, with the butchery of her children, and the hunting down of her husband – had become widely known. But, told and retold by a succession of moralising writers in Italian, French, and English, it was typically offered as an admonition to the great – and to great women in particular – against the danger of subordinating public duty to private emotion and to the 'shameless lusts', 'libidinous appetite', and 'ticklish instigations of … wanton flesh' denounced in William Painter's *Palace of Pleasure*.[37] In the hands of Webster, as he adapted Painter's version for the London stage, the meaning of the story was effectively turned on its head. It is true that the play's opening dialogue seems at first to recall the source writers' warnings: 'a prince's court', the audience is reminded, 'Is like a common fountain … if't chance / Some cursed example poison't near the head / Death and diseases through the whole land spread' (I.i.11–15). But it is the Duchess's brothers who, shortly afterwards, are made to voice the familiar denunciations of her behaviour: it is the hypocritical Cardinal who insists that she must be governed by the obligations of rank, demanding that his sister allow nothing 'without the addition, honour, / [to] Sway [her] high blood' (I.i.286–7); it is the psychopathic Ferdinand, tormented by his own incestuous fantasies, who rails against the weakness of her female flesh, declaring that 'They are most luxurious / [who] Will wed twice' (ll. 289–90). The play, by contrast, with its insistence upon the Duchess's 'integrity of life', becomes a subversive celebration of all that Painter and others had deplored, even as it invites scorn for the vanities of rank that so possess the Aragonian brothers.

The corollary to Bosola's levelling invective against the imaginary greatness attributed to 'the souls of princes' is to be found in Act III, Scene iii, where Bosola's indignation at Antonio's betrayal by the Duchess's officers prompts a diatribe against the obsequious hypocrisy of the court world –

> these are rogues, that in's prosperity,
> But to have waited on his fortune, could have wished
> His dirty stirrup through their noses ….
> Would have prostituted their daughters to his lust,
> Made their firstborn intelligencers, thought none happy
> But such as … wore his livery.   (ll. 224–31)

And when the Duchess defends her apparent banishment of Antonio with a reminder that 'he was basely descended' (l. 250), Bosola responds with an expression of disdain for the 'painted honors' (l. 267) by which social status is proclaimed: 'Will you make yourself a mercenary herald, rather to examine men's pedigrees than virtues' (ll. 251–2).

The reason for Bosola's uncharacteristically sincere riposte is that Antonio's apparent disgrace allows him to recognise in the steward's base descent – and consequent vulnerability to the whims of the great – a mirror for his own condition. But the cruel irony of the scene lies in the fact that it is precisely this spontaneous outburst of feeling, breaking through Bosola's politic mask, that tempts the Duchess into revealing the secret that all his intelligencer's wiles could not uncover: 'This good one that you speak of is my husband' (l. 263). However, Bosola's wonder that 'this ambitious age' can 'prefer a man merely for worth' (ll. 264–5) will not allow him any escape from the treadmill of 'courtly reward, / And punishment' (*White Devil*, I.i.3–4): if Antonio looks like his own virtuous *alter ego*, then Bosola's accidental killing of 'The man I would have saved 'bove my own life' (V.iv.50) simply epitomises his own self-destructive career. It is easy to recognise a Calvinistic determinism in his tormented recognition 'we cannot be suffered / To do good when we have a mind to it!' (IV.ii.344–5); but this 'perspective that shows us hell' is as much social as it is theological.

In his recent study, *Age of Anger*, Pankaj Mishra explores the present-day predicament of the educated precariat, 'superfluous young people condemned to the anteroom of the modern world' and possessed by the *ressentiment* that arises from 'the contradiction between extravagant promise and meagre means'[38] – outcasts who remind him of that archetypal figure from nineteenth-century literature, Turgenev's Rudin, an 'alienated young man of promise [who] … educated into a sense of hope and entitlement, [but] rendered adrift by his limited circumstances, [finds himself] exposed to feelings of weakness, inferiority and envy … [and becomes] the wandering outlaw of his own dark mind'.[39] Alienation of the kind Mishra describes is hardly peculiar to the social crises of the nineteenth and twenty-first centuries, however; and much of what he has to say about the bitter discontents of life in the societal antechamber could readily be applied to the group whom M. H. Curtis once described as 'The Alienated Intellectuals of Early Stuart England'[40] – well-educated and talented young men to whom the cash-strapped Jacobean state offered no secure employment. Bosola is just the kind of 'superfluous man' that both Curtis and Mishra describe. A character almost entirely of Webster's invention, he becomes the vehicle for social resentments that often seem to voice those of his creator – an Inns of Court man who, apparently finding no proper career in the law, became the jobbing writer famously sneered at by a more privileged contemporary as 'Crabbed Websterio, / The playwright-cartwright.'[41] Bosola's too is an anger that results from frustrated social ambition: a university graduate whose determination to seek the favour of

the great has made a murderer of him, and won him nothing better than
a seven-year sentence to the galleys (I.i.30–5, 67–9), he first appears railing
bitterly at the master who suborned his crime:

> I have done you
> Better service than to be slighted thus.
> Miserable age, where the only reward
> Of doing well is the doing of it.   (I.i.29–32)

In Act III, Scene iii, Delio supplies Pescara and Silvio with a revelatory
back-story for this malcontent:

> I knew him once in Padua – a fantastical scholar, like some who study to
> know how many knots was in Hercules' club, of what color Achilles's beard
> was, or whether Hector was troubled with the toothache. He hath studied
> himself half-blear eyed to know the true symmetry of Caesar's nose by a shoe-
> ing-horn; and this he did to gain the name of a speculative man. (ll. 41–7)

Webster's tragedy is named for a royal Duchess; but this low-born, frustrated scholar becomes her rival as tragic protagonist, for not only are the
two given an equally large number of lines, but the catastrophe of the last
act effectively belongs to him. Looked at from this perspective the play
becomes what (adapting a term from the lexicon of comedy) we might call
a 'citizen tragedy'. It was not that the playwright chose to flout the propri-
eties of what Sir Philip Sidney had called 'the high and excellent tragedy':
there was to be no question of relocating tragic action to the bourgeois
world of generic outliers like *Arden of Faversham* or *A Woman Killed with
Kindness*. Indeed Webster would surely have concurred with Sidney's claim
that the principal function of tragedy was precisely to make 'kings fear to be
tyrants', exposing their vulnerability by showing 'upon how weak founda-
tions gilden roofs are builded';[42] it is the 'great Cardinal', after all, with his
'large and ample base' who is reduced to 'a little point, a kind of nothing',
exposed as a superfluous man who now longs only to be 'laid by and never
thought of' (V.v.88); it is the 'great Duke' who dismisses himself as a diamond 'cut with our own dust'; while it is the Duchess who recognises in her
own fate an exemplum of 'the misery of us that are born great' (I.i.429), just
as in the murder scene Bosola points to her grey hairs as evidence that 'thou
art some great woman, sure' (IV.ii.125). But it is also the Duchess whose
parable of the salmon and the dogfish invites reinterpretation of her apparent downfall: 'There's no deep valley but near some great hill.'

With her fable the Duchess makes explicit the question on which the
action of the tragedy proves to turn: 'I prithee, who is greatest, can you
tell?' (III.v.118); and Webster addresses this question from the resolutely

sceptical perspective of one whose allegiance was to the values of the (over-whelmingly Protestant) urban middle class – a man who, on the title-page of the civic pageant he wrote for the Lord Mayor was proud to call himself 'John Webster Merchant-Taylor'. Announcing his citizen credentials as a member of the very company to which the Lord Mayor himself belonged, he was at pains to remind his audience that, like Edward III and others in its 'Royall conventicle of Kings', Prince Henry himself was a member of the livery company, having been inducted as a freeman in 1607.[43] The 'Monument of Gratitude', spoken by the chivalric hero Amade le Grand (Amadis the Great), presents Henry as 'of all your brotherhood the joy': boasting that 'our company / Hath not forgot him who ought ne'er to die', it offers him, like the Duchess, as an exemplar of 'integrity, that keeps / The safest watch, and breeds the soundest sleeps'.[44] *The Duchess of Malfi* itself is not – at least in any straightforward way – a contribution to the extended chorus of lament for the dead prince; but, as I have tried to show, it is a work profoundly inflected by the grief into which his death plunged the nation; and it remains Webster's greatest monument to the values for which Prince Henry had, in the minds of his admirers, come to stand.

Notes

1 For a full transcript of the list and some discussion of its contents, see Andrew Gurr, *The Shakespearean Stage, 1574–1642* (Cambridge: Cambridge University Press, 1970), pp. 123–4.

2 Conspicuous examples include Shakespeare's (and George Peele's?) *Titus Andronicus* (1589?), *Much Ado About Nothing* (1598), (with Thomas Middleton?) *Timon of Athens* (1606), (with George Wilkins?) *Pericles, Prince of Tyre* (1608), John Marston's *Antonio's Revenge* (1600), George Chapman's *The Widow's Tears* (1605), Middleton's *The Revenger's Tragedy* (1606) and *The Lady's Tragedy* [*Second Maiden's Tragedy*] (1611), Thomas John Fletcher's *Knight of Malta* (1618) and *A Wife for a Month* (1624), and John Ford's *Love's Sacrifice* (1632). To these we should probably add 'Ninus' tomb' in *A Midsummer Night's Dream* (1596), and Paulina's monumental statue in *The Winter's Tale* (1609). In *Romeo and Juliet* (1595) *John* and *Antony and Cleopatra* (1607), the stage itself becomes a tomb interior; while the grave-yard scenes of *Hamlet* (1601) and Cyril Tourneur's *The Atheist's Tragedy* (1610) may well have used tomb properties for their *mise-en-scènes*.

3 See my *Issues of Death: Mortality and Identity in English Renaissance Tragedy* (Oxford: Clarendon Press, 1997), pp. 39–42, 280–1.

4 On the shifting place of purgatory in early modern English thought and ritual practices, see the Introduction to this volume; Chapter 2, 'Spiritual Accountancy in the Age of Shakespeare' by Jonathan Baldo; and Chapter 3, 'Recollections and Pre-emptive Resurrection in Shakespeare' by John S. Garrison

5 John Webster, *The Duchess of Malfi*, ed. by Michael Neill, Norton Critical Editions (New York: W.W. Norton & Co., 2015). All citations from *Malfi* are to this edition.

6 Roy Strong, *Henry, Prince of Wales and England's Lost Renaissance* (London, Thames & Hudson, 1986), p. 225. Strong also cites a letter written by a Mr Beaulieu to William Trumbull six days after Henry's death: 'God had reserved and destined him as chosen Instrument to the Standard-bearer of his Quarrell in these miserable Times, to work the Restoration of his Church and the Destruction of Romish idolatry.'

7 For another poem in the same collection of elegies, see entry IV.12 'Cyril Tourneur, Selected Works', in William E. Engel, Rory Loughnane, and Grant Williams, eds., *The Death Arts in Renaissance England* (Cambridge: Cambridge University Press, 2022).

8 Contemporary account from the National Archives, cited in Catherine MacLeod, ed., *The Lost Prince: The Life and Death of Henry Stuart* (London: National Portrait Gallery, 2012), p. 161.

9 The waxwork effigy was put on show thereafter. As Jennifer Woodward notes: '[Henry Stuart's] body and effigy lay in state during the two-hour funeral oration, delivered by the Archbishop of Canterbury, and for a further three days of services for the dead. Both remained in the catafalque "to be seene of all" for nine more days until 19 December when the coffin was interred.' See *Theatre of Death: The Ritual Management of Royal Funerals in Renaissance England, 1570–1624* (Woodbridge: Boydell Press, 1997), p. 151.

10 *A Discourse of The Most Illustrious Prince, Henry, Late Prince of Wales, Written Anno 1626 by Sir Charles Cornwallis* (London, 1641), and *The Life and Death of Our Late and most Incomparable and Heroique Prince, Henry Prince of Wales … Written by Sir Charles Cornwallis* (London, 1641).

11 On the immortality *topos* in Horace and its relationship to Shakespeare's Time sonnets, see Andrew Hui, *The Poetics of Ruins in Renaissance Literature* (New York: Fordham University Press, 2017), pp. 35–51.

12 Cited from *A Monumental Columne* in Webster, *The Duchess of Malfi*, ed. by Neill, p. 180. All citations from the elegy are to this text.

13 See Webster, *The Duchess of Malfi*, ed. by Neill, pp. 171–2. For a reading of Webster's Echo scene that stresses its connection with Ovid's story of Echo and Narcissus, see Agnès Lafont, '"I am truly more fond and foolish than ever Narcissus was": Webster's *Duchess of Malfi* and Ovidian Resonances', in Pascale Drouet and William C. Carroll, eds., *'The Duchess of Malfi': Webster's Tragedy of Blood* (Paris: Belin, 2018), pp. 60–77. See also the treatment of ruined structures cast within culturally circumscribed literary contexts in Stewart Mottram, *Ruin and Reformation in Spenser, Shakespeare, and Marvell* (Oxford: Oxford University Press, 2019).

14 For an account of contemporary rumours suggesting that Prince Henry himself had been the victim of 'a nefarious popish poison-plot', see James Bellamy and Thomas Cogswell, *The Murder of James I* (New Haven, CT: Yale University Press, 2015), pp. 181–3 (p. 182).

15 See Leah S. Marcus's introduction to her Arden Early Modern Drama edition of John Webster, *The Duchess of Malfi* (London: A & C Black, 2009), pp. 24–5.

16 Of the main events in the act, only Antonio's murder at the hands of Bosola is recorded in the sources, which say nothing about the fate of the Duchess's brothers or of Bosola himself. It is true that the details of Ferdinand's lycanthropia in V.ii are closely modelled on the account of that disease in Edward Grimeston's translation of Simon Goulart's *Admirable and Memorable Histories* (1607); but these come from a portion of Goulart's text quite unconnected with the Malfi story.

17 See Chapter 10, 'Andrew Marvell's Taste for Death' by Anita Gilman Sherman, for a more nuanced and rhetorically informed interpretation this 'morbid, but jocular couplet'.

18 See e.g., John Russell Brown's landmark Revels edition of this play by Webster: *The Duchess of Malfi*, ed. by John Russell Brown, 2nd ed., Revels Plays (Manchester: Manchester University Press), p. xxxv. I was formerly attracted to this conjecture myself – see 'Monuments and Ruins as symbols in *The Duchess of Malfi*', in James Redmond, ed., *Drama and Symbolism*, Themes in Drama 4 (Cambridge: Cambridge University Press, 1982), pp. 71–87, and 'Fame's Best Friend: The Endings of *The Duchess of Malfi*', in Neill, *Issues of Death*, pp. 328–53.

19 Although the stage direction's 'artificial figures' suggest that Webster envisaged the use of waxworks, like those displayed in royal funerals, it remains possible, of course, that the company would have used actors for the purpose.

20 *The Lady's Tragedy* is cited from Julia Briggs's edition in *Thomas Middleton: The Collected Works*, gen. ed. by Gary Taylor and John Lavagnino (Oxford: Clarendon Press, 2007).

21 Brian Chalk, 'Webster's "Worthyest Monument": The Problem of Posterity in *The Duchess of Malfi*', *Studies in Philology*, 108 (2011), 379–402, reprinted in Webster, *The Duchess of Malfi*, ed. by Neill, pp. 335–53.

22 Mottram, *Ruin and Reformation*, pp. 4–5, explores the significance of the ruins in this scene as a complex, temporally dilated *memento mori*: 'Antonio approaches these abbey ruins as might an antiquarian', seeing them 'as windows on the past, but Webster's ruins demand we see them as prospective mirrors on the future, reminding Antonio, and Webster's audience, that he, and we, will also fall to ruin'.

23 See e.g. Elizabeth I's *Proclamation against Breakinge of Defacing of Monumentes of Antiquitie beyng set up in Churches or other publique places for memory, and not for superstition* (1560).

24 Shakespeare, Sonnet 73, l. 4.9, in *Shakespeare's Sonnets*, ed. by Francis X. Connor, in *The New Oxford Shakespeare: Modern Critical Edition*, gen. ed. by Gary Taylor, John Jowett, Terri Bourus, and Gabriel Egan (Oxford: Oxford University Press, 2016), pp. 2819–82 (p. 2848–9).

25 John Weever, *Ancient Funeral Monuments* (London, 1631), B3^v, in Webster, *The Duchess of Malfi*, ed. by Neill, p. 184.

26 Ibid., p. 185.

27 Ibid., p. 186.

28 Weever, *Ancient Funeral Monuments*, B2, B6.

29 In addition to the reproduction provided in this volume, Chapter 9, 'The Unton Portrait Reconsidered' by Peter Sherlock, a coloured detail of the painting can be found on the cover of my Norton edition.

30 In this regard, one might well imagine Unton's wife as providing precisely the 'lifeless tomb' posture on the funeral monument for her husband that the Duchess fears she has become in the monument for her first husband.

31 For a detailed analysis of significance of the Cardinal's monitory aphorism, see Rory Loughnane, 'Studied Speech and *The Duchess of Malfi*: The Lost Arts of Rhetoric, Memory, and Death', *Sillages Critiques*, 26 (2019), 'Nouvelles perspectives sur *The Duchess of Malfi*' (https://journals.openedition.org/sillage scritiques/6847?lang=en).

32 Webster, *The Duchess of Malfi*, ed. by Neill, pp. 176, 181.

33 Ibid., p. 182.

34 In his 1625 *Funeral Elegie* for King James, the playwright Thomas Heywood, who had been one of Henry's elegists, would nostalgically repeat the phrase, celebrating 'what doth grace even Princes honesty, / Integrity of life', B4. See *Funeral Elegie* [for King James I] (London, 1625; STC 13324).

35 See Webster, *The Duchess of Malfi*, ed. by Marcus, pp. 1, 11–13.

36 Painter and Goulart in Webster, *The Duchess of Malfi*, ed. by Neill, pp. 160, 163.

37 Painter, ibid., pp. 136, 146, 132. See also entry IV.5 on William Painter in Engel, Loughnane, and Williams, eds., *The Death Arts in Renaissance England*.

38 Pankaj Mishra, *The Age of Anger: A History of the Present* (London: Penguin Books, 2017), pp. 330–1.

39 Ibid., p. 23.; and cf. p. 296.

40 M. H. Curtis, 'The Alienated Intellectuals of Early Stuart England', *Past & Present*, 23 (1962), 25–43.

41 Henry Fitzgeffrey, *Satyres and Satyricall Epigrams* (London, 1617). For further discussion of this aspect of Webster's writing, see Michael Neill, '"Crabbed Websterio": *The Duchess of Malfi* and the Character of a Dramatic Poet', in Drouet and Carroll, eds., *'The Duchess of Malfi': Webster's Tragedy of Blood*, pp. 31–4.

42 Sir Philip Sidney, 'An Apology for Poetry', in Edmund D. Jones, ed., *English Critical Essays (Sixteenth, Seventeenth and Eighteenth Centuries)* (London and New York: Oxford University Press, 1947), p. 26.

43 See Gregory McNamara, '"Grief was as clothes to their backs": Prince Henry's Funeral viewed from the Wardrobe', in Timothy Wilks, ed., *Prince Henry Revived: Image and Exemplarity in Early Modern England* (Southampton: Southampton Solent University and Paul Holberton Publishing, 2007), pp. 259–79 (p. 260); and N.V. Sleigh-Johnson, 'The Merchant-Taylors Company of London, 1580–1645' (PhD thesis, University College, London, 1985).

44 Webster, *The Duchess of Malfi*, ed. by Neill, pp. 181, 182.

Parting Epigraph

O prepare me for the time of my great account that so when my dust shall return to the earth as it was, my spirit may return unto thee who didst give it. Let his spectacle of mortality live in my memory, that so when I consider that the time will come that as naked as I came out of my mother's womb, so naked shall I thither return again; I may wholly endeavour, and seek to be clothed with the righteousness of thy Son. With him thou hast been graciously pleased that by baptism I should be buried into death: grant also, good God, that like as he was raised up from the dead by the glory of thee the eternal Father, even so I also may walk in newness of life. Make me ever think upon death which will seize on me, judgment which will examine me, and hell which would devour mee, that heaven may receive me.

John Featley, *A fountaine of teares* (Amsterdam: 1646; Wing F598), Y12ᵛ

Bibliography

Manuscripts

BL MS Sloane 1911–13. Thomas Browne (selected correspondence).

BL MS Sloane 1847. Thomas Browne (selected correspondence).

BL MS Sloane 4062. Thomas Browne (selected correspondence).

BL Add. MS 46378 (B). Thomas Browne (selected correspondence).

BL Add MS 12514, fol. 277. 'Order of the proceeding to the funerall of the Lady Alice, Dutchesse Dudley, 16 Martii, 1668, in the handwriting of Sir Will. Dugdale'.

Camden Local Studies and Archives. P/GF, St Giles in the Fields 'Minutes of the Vestry, 1618–1900'.

Shakespeare Birthplace Trust. Cat. DR18/2/82. 'Acquittance of William Wright of London, March 27, 1655'.

Staffordshire and Stoke on Trent Record Office. Cat. D868/2/4. Katherine Dudley to Richard Leveson, n.d.

TNA PROB 11/138/369, 'Will of Alicia Dudley of St. Giles in the Fields, Middlesex', 7 November 1621.

TNA PROB 11/149/258, 'Will of Sir Thomas Leigh', 24 May 1626.

TNA PROB 11/182/163, 'Will of Dame Katherine Leigh', 8 February 1640.

TNA PROB 11/312/122, 'Will of Anne Holburne', 27 August 1663.

TNA PROB 11/329/325, 'Will of Lady Alicia Duches Duddeley', 9 March 1669.

Warwickshire Record Office. 'Warwickshire, England, Church of England Baptisms, Marriages, and Burials, 1535–1812: Stoneleigh, 1616–1699'.

Primary and Secondary Sources

Acker, Faith D., 'John Benson's *Poems* and Its Literary Precedents', in *Canonising Shakespeare: Stationers and the Book Trade, 1640–1740*, ed. by Emma Depledge and Peter Kirwan (Cambridge: Cambridge University Press, 2017), pp. 89–106.

Adams, Simon, 'Sir Robert Dudley (1574–1649)', *Oxford Dictionary of National Biography Online Edition*, https://doi.org/10.1093/ref:odnb/8161.

Aden, John M., 'Dryden and Boileau: The Question of Critical Influence', *Studies in Philology*, 50.3 (1953), 491–509.

Adlard, George, *Amye Robsart and the Earl of Leycester* (London: John Russell Smith, 1870).

Agamben, Giorgio, *The Man without Content*, trans. by Georgia Albert (Stanford, CA: Stanford University Press, 1999).

Aho, James, 'Rhetoric and the Invention of Double Entry Bookkeeping', *Rhetorica: A Journal of the History of Rhetoric*, 3.1 (1985), 21–43.

Allen, Don Cameron, *Image and Meaning: Metaphoric Traditions in Renaissance Poetry* (Baltimore, MD: Johns Hopkins University Press, 1960).

Anon., *Englands Helicon* (London: I. Roberts for John Flasket, 1600).

Anon., *Mausoleum or, The Choicest Flowers of the Epitaphs, Written on the Death of the Never-Too-Much Lamented Prince Henry* (London, 1613; STC 13160).

Appleford, Amy, *Learning to Die in London, 1380–1540* (Philadelphia: University of Pennsylvania Press, 2015).

Ariès, Philippe, *The Hour of Our Death*, trans. by Helen Weaver (New York: Vintage, 1981).

Ariès, Philippe, *The Hour of Our Death: The Classic History of Western Attitudes toward Death over the Last One Thousand Years*, trans. by Helen Weaver, 2nd ed. (New York: Vintage Books, 2008).

Ashmole, Elias, *The Antiquities of Berkshire*, 3 vols. (London, 1719).

Assmann, Jan, *Cultural Memory and Early Civilization: Writing, Remembrance, and Political Imagination* (Cambridge: Cambridge University Press, 2011).

Aston, Margaret, *Broken Idols of the English Reformation* (Cambridge: Cambridge University Press, 2015).

Atkinson, David W., 'The English Ars Moriendi: Its Protestant Transformation', *Renaissance and Reformation*, 6.1 (1982), 1–10.

Atkinson, David W., ed., *The English Ars Moriendi* (Bern and New York: Peter Lang, 1992).

Augustine, *The Confessions of Saint Augustine*, trans. by R. S. Pine-Coffin (New York: Penguin, 1961).

Augustine, *Answer to Faustus, A Manichean*, trans. by Roland Teske (Hyde Park, NY: New City Press, 2007).

Axton, Marie, *The Queen's Two Bodies: Drama and the Elizabethan Succession* (London: Royal Historical Society, 1977).

Bacon, Sir Francis, *The Felicity of Queen Elizabeth* (London: Thomas Newcombe for George Latham, 1651).

Bacon, Sir Francis, *The Advancement of Learning and New Atlantis*, ed. by Arthur Johnston (Oxford: Clarendon Press, 1974).

Badham, Sally, 'A Painted Canvas Funerary Monument of 1615 in the Collections of the Society of Antiquaries of London and Its Comparators', *Church Monuments*, 24 (2009), 89–110, 146–53.

Baker, Nicholson, *The Size of Thoughts: Essays and Other Lumber* (New York: Penguin Random House, 1996).

Baldo, Jonathan, *Memory in Shakespeare's Histories: Stages of Forgetting in Early Modern England* (New York: Routledge, 2012).

Barkan, Leonard, 'What Did Shakespeare Read?' in *The Cambridge Companion to Shakespeare*, ed. by Margreta de Grazia and Stanley Wells (Cambridge: Cambridge University Press, 2001), pp. 31–47.

Barnes, Joseph, ed., *Funebria Nobilissimi Ac Præstantissimi Equitis, D. Henrici Vntoni* (Oxford, 1596).

Barthes, Roland, *A Lover's Discourse: Fragments*, trans. by Richard Howard (New York: Hill and Wang, 2010).

Battista della Porta, Giovanni, *L'Arte del ricordare* (Naples: Marco Antonio Passaro, 1566).

Beaty, Nancy Lee, *The Craft of Dying: A Study in the Literary Tradition of the Ars Moriendi in England* (New Haven, CT: Yale University Press, 1970).

Beecher, Donald and Grant Williams, eds., *Ars Reminiscendi: Mind and Memory in Renaissance Culture* (Toronto: Centre for Reformation and Renaissance Studies, 2009).

Bellamy, James and Thomas Cogswell, *The Murder of James I* (New Haven, CT: Yale University Press, 2015).

Benet, Diane Treviño, '"The Loyall Scot" and the Hidden Narcissus', in *On the Celebrated and Neglected Poems of Andrew Marvell*, ed. by C. J. Summers and T. Pebworth (Columbia: University of Missouri Press, 1992), pp. 192–206.

Bentley, Thomas, *The Monument of Matrons* (London: Henry Denham, 1582).

Berger, Harry, Jr., '*Ars Moriendi* in Progress, or John of Gaunt and the Practice of Strategic Dying', *Yale Journal of Criticism*, 1.1 (1987), 39–65.

Berlant, Lauren, *Desire/Love* (Brooklyn, NY: Punctum Books, 2012).

Berry, Wendell, 'Manifesto: The Mad Farmer Liberation Front', in *Collected Poems*, ed. by Wendell Berry (San Francisco, CA: North Point Press, 1985), p. 151.

Bishop, Jeffrey P., '*Scientia Mortis* and the *Ars Moriendi*: To the Memory of Norman', in *Health Humanities in Health Humanities Reader*, ed. by Therese Jones, Delese Wear, and Lester D. Friedman (New Brunswick, NJ: Rutgers University Press 2014), pp. 387–402.

[Bishops'] Bible (London: Richard Jugge, 1569).

Blair, Ann, *Too Much to Know: Managing Scholarly Information before the Modern Age* (New Haven, CT: Yale University Press, 2010).

Boileau, Nicolas, *The Art of Poetry*, trans. by William Soame and John Dryden (London, 1683).

Boileau, Nicolas, *Oeuvres Poétiques*, ed. by F. Brunetière (Paris: Hachette, 1923).

Bolzoni, Lina, *La stanza della memoria* (Turin: Einaudi, 1995).

Bolzoni, Lina, *The Gallery of Memory: Literary and Iconographic Models in the Age of the Printing Press*, trans. by Jeremy Parzen (Toronto: University of Toronto Press, 2001).

Boreman, Robert, *A Mirror of Christianity and a Miracle of Charity* (London: E. C. for Robert Royston, 1669).

Borlik, Todd, '"The Way to Study Death": New Light on a Variant in F2 *Macbeth*', *The Explicator*, 70.2 (2012), 144–8.

Boughen, Edward, *The Principles of Religion* (London, 1646).

Bouhours, Dominique, *Les entretiens d'Ariste et d'Eugène* (Paris, 1671).

Bouhours, Dominique, *Doutes sur la langue française proposés aux Messieurs de l'Academie française* (Paris, 1674).

Boyle, Robert, 'Accidents of an Ague', in *Occasional Reflections* (London, 1665).

Bradbrook, M. C., *Shakespeare the Craftsman* (London: Chatto & Windus, 1969).

Braithwaite, Richard, *A Spiritual Spicerie containing sundrie sweet tractates of devotion and piety* (London, 1638; STC 3586).

Bray, Gerald, 'Evangelicals, Salvation, and Church History', in *Catholics and Evangelicals: Do They Share a Common Future?*, ed. by Thomas P. Rausch (New York: Paulist Press, 2000), pp. 77–100.

Brock, Kathryn Gail, 'Milton's "Sonnet XVIII" and the Language of Controversy', *Milton Quarterly*, 16.1 (1982), 3–6.

Browne, Thomas, *Religio Medici* (London, 1643).

Browne, Thomas, *Hydriotaphia, Urne-Buriall …. Together with The Garden of Cyrus* (London, 1658).

Browne, Thomas, *A Letter to a Friend, Upon occasion of the Death of his Intimate Friend* (London, 1690).

Browne, Thomas, *Christian Morals* (London, 1716).

Browne, Thomas, *Religio Medici and Other Works*, ed. by L. C. Martin (Oxford: Clarendon Press, 1964).

Browne, Thomas, *Pseudodoxia Epidemica*, ed. by Robin Robbins, 2 vols. (Oxford: Clarendon Press, 1981).

Budra, Paul, 'The Emotions of Tragedy: Middleton or Shakespeare?' in Gary Taylor and Trish Thomas Henley, eds., *The Oxford Handbook of Thomas Middleton* (Oxford: Oxford University Press, 2012), pp. 487–501.

Burbery, Timothy J., 'From Orthodoxy to Heresy: A Theological Analysis of Sonnets XIV and XVIII', *Milton Studies*, 45.1 (2006), 1–20.

Burnet, Thomas, *The Theory of the Earth* (London, 1684).

Burrow, Colin, *Shakespeare and Classical Antiquity* (Oxford: Oxford University Press, 2013).

Burton, Robert, *The Anatomy of Melancholy*, ed. by T. C. Faulkner, N. K. Kiessling, and R. L. Blair, with intro. and comm. by J. B. Bamborough and M. Dodsworth, 6 vols. (Oxford: Clarendon Press, 1989–2000).

Butler, F. G., 'Erasmus and the Deaths of Cordelia and Lear', *English Studies*, 73.1 (1992), 10–21.

Butler, Judith, *Precarious Life: The Powers of Mourning and Violence* (London and New York: Verso, 2004).

Butler, Katy, *The Art of Dying Well: A Practical Guide to a Good End of Life* (New York: Scribner, 2019).

Callaghan, Dympna, *Shakespeare's Sonnets* (Malden and Oxford: Wiley-Blackwell, 2007).

Camden, William, *Annales …* (London: George Purslowe, Humphrey Lownes, and Miles Flesher for Benjamin Fisher, 1625).

Camden, William, *The historie of the life and reigne of that famous princesse Elizabeth* (London: William Webbe, 1634).

Carey, Kevin, *The End of College: Creating the Future of Learning and the University of Everywhere* (New York: Riverhead Books, 2015).

Carlson, Christina Marie, 'The Rhetoric of Providence: Thomas Middleton's *A Game at Chess* (1624) and Seventeenth-Century Political Engraving', *Renaissance Quarterly*, 67.4 (2014), 1224–64.

Carlson, Peter, 'The Art and Craft of Dying', in *The Oxford Handbook of Early Modern Literature and Religion*, ed. by Andrew Hiscock and Helen Wilcox (Oxford: Oxford University Press, 2017), pp. 634–49.

Carruthers, Mary J., *The Book of Memory: A Study of Memory in Medieval Culture* (Cambridge: Cambridge University Press, 1990).

Carruthers, Mary J., *The Book of Memory: A Study of Memory in Medieval Culture*, 2nd ed. (Cambridge: Cambridge University Press, 2008).

Carruthers, Mary J. 'Moving Back in Memory Studies', *History Workshop Journal*, 77.1 (2014), 275–82.

Carter, John, *The Nail and the Wheel* (London, 1646).

Cascardi, Anthony J., *Ideologies of History in the Spanish Golden Age* (University Park: Pennsylvania State University Press, 1997).

Chernaik, Warren L., *The Poet's Time: Politics and Religion in the Work of Andrew Marvell* (Cambridge: Cambridge University Press, 1983).

Chernaik, Warren L. and Martin Dzelzainis, eds., *Marvell and Liberty* (New York: St. Martin's Press, 1999).

Chibnall, Jennifer, 'Something to the Purpose: Marvell's Rhetorical Strategy in *The Rehearsal Transpros'd* (1672)', *Prose Studies*, 9.2 (1986), 80–104.

Chakrabarty, Dipesh, 'The Climate of History: Four Theses', *Critical Inquiry*, 35.2 (2009), 197–222.

Chalk, Brian, 'Webster's "Worthyest Monument": The Problem of Posterity in *The Duchess of Malfi*', *Studies in Philology*, 108.3 (2011), 379–402.

Chalk, Brian, *Monuments and Literary Posterity in Early Modern Drama* (Cambridge: Cambridge University Press, 2015).

Chapman, George, *Skia nyktos – The shadow of night containing two poeticall hymnes* (London: Richard Field for William Ponsonby, 1594).

Charney, Maurice, *Wrinkled Deep in Time: Aging in Shakespeare* (New York: Columbia University Press, 2009).

Chettle, Henry, *Englands mourning garment* (London, 1603).

Christian prayers and meditations in English French, Italian, Spanish, Greeke, and Latine (London: John Day, 1569).

Cicero, *De oratore in Cicero on Oratory and Orators*, trans. by J. S. Watson (Evanston: Southern Illinois University Press, 1970).

Cicero, *Laelius, On Friendship (Laelius de Amicitia) & The Dream of Scipio*, trans. by J. G. F. Powell (Warminster: Aris and Phillips Ltd., 1990).

Cicero, *De oratore: Books I and II*, trans. by E. W. Sutton and H. Rackham, 2 vols. (Cambridge, MA, and London: Harvard University Press, 1996).

Clark, A. F. B., *Boileau and the French Classical Critics in England* (Paris: Champion, 1925).

Clayton, Peter A. and Martin J. Price, 'Introduction', in *Seven Wonders of the Ancient World*, ed. by Peter A. Clayton and Martin J. Price (London: Routledge, 1988), pp. 1–12.

Clegg, Roger and Lucie Skeaping, *Singing Simpkin and Other Bawdy Jigs: Musical Comedy on the Shakespearean Stage* (Exeter: University of Exeter Press, 2014).

Cogan, Thomas, *Haven of Health* (London, 1588).

Colie, Rosalie, *'My echoing song': Andrew Marvell's Poetry of Criticism* (Princeton, NJ: Princeton University Press, 1970).

Cormack, Bradin, 'Shakespeare's Narcissus, Sonnet's Echo', in *The Forms of Renaissance Thought: New Essays on Literature and Culture*, ed. by Leonard Barkan, Bradin Cormack, and Sean Keilen (New York: Palgrave Macmillan, 2009), pp. 127–49.

Cornwallis, Charles, *A Discourse of The Most Illustrious Prince, Henry, Late Prince of Wales, Written Anno 1626* (London, 1641; Wing C6329).

Cornwallis, Charles, *The Life and Death of Our Late and most Incomparable and Heroique Prince, Henry Prince of Wales* (London, 1641; Wing C6330).

Cotgrave, Randle, *A Dictionarie of the French and English Tongues* (London, 1611).

Crane, Mary Thomas, *Framing Authority: Sayings, Self, and Society in Sixteenth-Century England* (Princeton, NJ: Princeton University Press, 2016).

Cranmer, Thomas, *The Book of Common Prayer* (London, 1549).

Crashaw, Richard, 'On a Treatise of Charity', in *The Poems of Richard Crashaw*, ed. by L. C. Martin, 2nd ed. (Oxford: Oxford University Press, 1957).

Creaser, John, '"As one scap't strangely from captivity": Marvell and Existential Liberty', in *Marvell and Liberty*, ed. by Warren Chernaik and Martin Dzelzainis (New York: St. Martin's Press, 1999), pp. 145–72.

Cressy, David, *Bonfires and Bells: National Memory and the Protestant Calendar in Elizabethan and Stuart England* (Berkeley and Los Angeles: University of California Press, 1989).

Cressy, David, *Birth, Marriage, and Death: Ritual, Religion, and the Life-Cycle in Tudor and Stuart England* (Oxford: Oxford University Press, 1997).

Critchley, Simon, 'To Philosophize Is to Learn How to Die: Facing Death Can Be a Key to Our Liberation and Survival', *New York Times* (11 April 2020).

Crosby, Alfred W., *Ecological Imperialism* (Cambridge: Cambridge University Press, 1986).

Cummings, Brian, '"Dead March": Liturgy and Mimesis in Shakespeare's Funerals', *Shakespeare*, 8.4 (2012), 368–85.

Cummins, Neil, Morgan Kelly, and Cormac Ó Gráda, 'Living Standards and Plague in London, 1550–1665', *Economic History Review*, 69.1 (2016), 3–34.

Curtis, M. H., 'The Alienated Intellectuals of Early Stuart England', *Past & Present*, 23 (1962), 25–43.

D'Urfey, Thomas, *Collins Walk through London and Westminster* (London, 1690).

da Ravenna, Pietro, *Memoriae ars quae Phoenix inscribitur* (Vienna: Mathias Bonhome, 1541).

Daniell, Christopher, *Death and Burial in Medieval England 1066–1550* (London: Routledge, 2005).

Davidson, Clifford and Sophie Oosterwijk, *John Lydgate, 'The Dance of Death', and its Model, the French 'Danse Macabre'*, ed. by Clifford Davidson and Sophie Oosterwijk (Leiden: Brill, 2021).

Davies, Sir John, *Hymnes of Astraea in acrostike verse* (London: I. S., 1599).

Davis, Lydia, 'Grammar Questions', in *110 Stories*, ed. by Ulrich Baer (New York: New York University Press, 2002), p. 72.

Davison, Francis, *A Poeticall Rhapsody* (London: V. Sims, 1602).

Degroot, Dagomar, 'Climate Change and Society in the 15th to 18th Centuries', *Wiley Interdisciplinary Reviews: Climate Change*, 9.3 (May/June 2018), pp. 1–20, https://doi.org/10.1002/wcc.518.

Dekker, Thomas, *The pleasant comedie of old Fortunatus* (London: S. S. for William Aspley, 1600).

Dekker, Thomas (attrib.), *The Great Frost. Cold Doings in London* (London: Henry Gosson, 1608).

Dekker, Thomas, *The Cold Year 1614* (London: W. W. for Thomas Langley, 1615).

della Porta, Giovanni, *L'Arte del ricordare* (Naples: Marco Antonio Passaro, 1566).

DeLoughrey, Elizabeth M., *Allegories of the Anthropocene* (Durham, NC: Duke University Press, 2019).

Dent, R. W., *Shakespeare's Proverbial Language: An Index* (Berkeley: University of California Press, 1981).

Derrida, Jacques, 'The Ends of Man', in Jacques Derrida, *Margins of Philosophy*, trans. by Alan Bass (Chicago: University of Chicago Press, 1972), pp. 111–36.

Derrida, Jacques, *Of Grammatology*, trans. by Gayatri Chakravorty Spivak (Baltimore, MD: Johns Hopkins University Press, 1976).

Derrida, Jacques, *Specters of Marx*, trans. by Peggy Kamuf (London and New York: Routledge, 1994).

Dewey, John, *Democracy and Education* (New York: The Macmillan Company, 1916).

Dobie, Rowland, *History of the United Parishes of St. Giles in the Fields and St. George Bloomsbury* (London: printed for the author, 1829).

Dobson, Mary J., *Contours of Death and Disease in Early Modern England* (Cambridge: Cambridge University Press, 2002).

Doebler, Bettie Anne, 'Othello's Angels: The Ars Moriendi', *ELH*, 34.2 (June 1967), 156–72.

Donne, John, 'A Feaver', in *Poems by J.D. With elegies on the authors death* (London, 1633).

Donne, John, *LXXX Sermons Preached by that Learned and Reverend Divine, John Donne* (London, 1640).

Donne, John, *The Sermons of John Donne*, ed. by George R. Potter and Evelyn M. Simpson (Berkeley and Los Angeles: University of California Press, 1962).

Donne, John, *John Donne: Selected Prose*, ed. by Evelyn Simpson, Helen Gardner, and T. S. Healy (Oxford: Oxford University Press, 1967).

Donne, John, *The Complete English Poems*, ed. by A. J. Smith (London: Penguin, 1971).

Donne, John, *The Complete English Poems*, ed. by A. J. Smith (London: Penguin, 1986).

Donne, John, *The Variorum Edition of the Poetry of John Donne, Vol. 6: The Anniversaries and the Epicedes and Obsequies*, ed. by Gary A. Stringer (Bloomington: Indiana University Press, 1995).

Donne, John, *The Complete English Poems*, ed. by A. J. Smith (New York: Penguin, 1996).

Donne, John, *The Sermons of John Donne, Vol. 12: Sermons Preached at St Paul's Cathedral, 1626*, ed. by Mary Ann Lund (Oxford: Oxford University Press, 2017).

Donno, Elizabeth Story, ed., *Andrew Marvell: The Critical Heritage* (London: Routledge & Kegan Paul, 1978).

Doran, Susan, 'Virginity, Divinity and Power: The Portraits of Elizabeth I', in *The Myth of Elizabeth*, ed. by Susan Doran and Thomas S. Freeman (Basingstoke: Palgrave, 2003), pp. 171–99.

Doran, Susan and Thomas S. Freeman, eds., *The Myth of Elizabeth* (Basingstoke: Palgrave, 2003).

Dowland, John, *Lachrimæ, or Seauen Teares* (London, [1604]).

Drayton, Michael, *Idea* (London: Thomas Orwin, 1593).

Drayton, Michael, *Englands Heroicall Epistles* (London, 1597).

Drayton, Michael, *Englands Heroicall Epistles*, in *The Works of Michael Drayton, Volume 2*, ed. by J. W. Hebel (Oxford: Shakespeare Head, 1933).

Drayton, Michael, *Poly-Olbion*, in *The Works of Michael Drayton, Volume 4*, ed. by J. W. Hebel (Oxford: Shakespeare Head, 1933), 11.359–60, 16.79–80.

Drouet, Pascale and William Carroll, eds., '*The Duchess of Malfi': Webster's Tragedy of Blood* (Paris: Belin, 2018).

Dryden, John, *Selected Works*, ed. by William Frost (New York: Holt, Rinehart and Winston, 1971).

Dubrow, Heather, *Deixis in the Early Modern English Lyric: Unsettling Spatial Anchors Like 'Here', 'This', 'Come'* (Basingstoke and New York: Palgrave, 2015).

Duffy, Eamon, *The Stripping of the Altars: Traditional Religion in England, 1400–1580* (New Haven, CT: Yale University Press, 1992).

Dugan, Holly, *The Ephemeral History of Perfume: Scent and Sense in Early Modern England* (Baltimore, MD: Johns Hopkins University Press, 2011).

Dugdale, Lydia S., *The Lost Art of Dying: Reviving Forgotten Wisdom* (New York: HarperOne, 2020).

Dugdale, William, 'Dugdale's Account of Duchess Dudley', *The Gentleman's Magazine* (April 1820), 309–11.

Dugdale, William, *Diary*, in *The Life, Diary and Correspondence of Sir William Dugdale, Knight*, ed. by William Hamper (London: Harding and Lepard, 1827).

Duncan-Jones, Elsie, 'Marvell: A Great Master of Words', *Proceedings of the British Academy*, 61 (1975), 267–90.

Dutton, Richard, 'Thomas Middleton's *A Game at Chess*: A Case Study', in *The Cambridge History of British Theatre*, vol. 1, ed. by J. Milling and P. Thomson (Cambridge: Cambridge University Press, 2004), pp. 424–38.

Dwelly, Edward, ed., *Dwelly's Parish Records* (London: E. Dwelly, 1864).

Dzelzainis, Martin, 'Marvell and the Earl of Castlemaine', in *Marvell and Liberty*, ed. by Warren L. Chernaik and Martin Dzelzainis (New York: St. Martin's Press, 1999), pp. 290–312.

Dzelzainis, Martin and Edward Holberton, eds., *The Oxford Handbook of Andrew Marvell* (Oxford: Oxford University Press, 2019).

Edmondson, Paul and Stanley Wells, *Shakespeare's Sonnets* (Oxford: Oxford University Press, 2004).

Eire, Carlos M. N., *A Very Brief History of Eternity* (Princeton, NJ: Princeton University Press, 2010).

Eire, Carlos M. N., *Reformations: The Early Modern World, 1450–1650* (New Haven, CT: Yale University Press, 2016).

Eliot, T. S., *Selected Poems* (New York: Harcourt, Brace & World, 1934).

Eliot, T. S., *Selected Essays*, 3rd ed. (London: Faber and Faber, 1951).

Elizabeth I, *Elizabeth I: Collected Works*, ed. by Leah S. Marcus, Janel Mueller, and Mary Beth Rose (Chicago: University of Chicago Press, 2002).

Elizabeth I, *Translations 1544–1589*, ed. by Janel Mueller and Joshua Scodel (Chicago: University of Chicago Press, 2009).

Elyot, Thomas, *The Dictionary of Sir Thomas Eliot Knight* (London, 1538; STC 7659).

Endfield, Georgina H., 'Exploring Particularity: Vulnerability, Resilience, and Memory in Climate Change Discourses', *Environmental History*, 19.2 (April 2014), 303–10.

Engel, William E., *Mapping Mortality: The Persistence of Memory and Melancholy in Early Modern England* (Amherst: University of Massachusetts Press, 1995).

Engel, William E., 'What's New in Mnemology?', *Connotations*, 11.2–3 (2001–2002), 241–61.

Engel, William E., *Death and Drama in Renaissance England: Shades of Memory* (Oxford: Oxford University Press, 2002).

Engel, William E., 'Poe's Cultural Inheritance', in *The Oxford Handbook of Edgar Allen Poe*, ed. by J. G. Kennedy and S. Peeples (Oxford: Oxford University Press, 2019), pp. 499–519.

Engel, William E., Rory Loughnane, and Grant Williams, eds., *The Memory Arts in Renaissance England* (Cambridge: Cambridge University Press, 2016).

Engel, William E., Rory Loughnane, and Grant Williams, eds., *The Death Arts in Renaissance England* (Cambridge: Cambridge University Press, 2022).

Enterline, Lynn, *Shakespeare's Schoolroom* (Philadelphia: University of Pennsylvania Press, 2012).

Epictetus, *The Manuell of Epictetus*, trans. by James Sanford (London: Imprinted by H. Bynneman for Leonard Maylard, 1567).

Epictetus, *The Enchiridion*, trans. by Thomas Wentworth Higginson, in *The Works of Epictetus* (Boston: Little, Brown, and Company, 1865).

Erasmus, Desiderius, *De praeparatione ad mortem* (Basel: Froben and Episcopius, 1534).

Erasmus, Desiderius, *Preparation to deathe*, trans. by Anon. (London, 1538; STC 10505).

Erasmus, Desiderius, *Opus epistolarum Des. Erasmi Roterdami*, vol. 11, ed. by Percy Stafford Allen (Oxford: Clarendon Press, 1906).

Erasmus, Desiderius, *Preparing for Death* in *Spiritualia and Pastoralia*, trans. by John N. Grant, in *Collected Works of Erasmus*, vol. 70, ed. by John W. O'Malley (Toronto: University of Toronto Press, 1998).

Erasmus, Desiderius, *Correspondence of Erasmus: Letters 2803 to 2939*, trans. by Clarence H. Miller, in *Collected Works of Erasmus*, vol. 20, ed. by James M. Estes (Toronto: University of Toronto Press, 2020).

Erne, Lukas, '"Our Other Shakespeare": Thomas Middleton and the Canon', *Modern Philology*, 107.3 (February 2010), 493–505.

Eustace, Katherine, 'Before or After? A Model of the Monument to Mary Thornhurst (1549–1609) in St Michael's Chapel, Canterbury Cathedral', *Church Monuments*, 25 (2010), 105–20.

Evelyn, John, *A Philosophical Discourse of Earth* (London, 1676).

Farrow, Thomas J., 'The Dissolution of St. Paul's Charnel: Remembering and Forgetting the Collective Dead in Late Medieval and Early Modern England', *Mortality* (2021), https://doi.org/10.1080/13576275.2021.1911976.

Felch, Susan M. and Donald V. Stump, eds., *Elizabeth I and Her Age* (New York: W.W. Norton & Company, 2008).

Fenner, Dudley, *The Song of Songs, That Is, the Most Excellent Song Which Was Solomon's* (Middelburg, 1587; STC 2769).

Finn, Margot C., *The Character of Credit: Personal Debt in English Culture, 1740–1914*, Cambridge Social and Cultural Histories (Cambridge: Cambridge University Press, 2003).

Fitzgeffrey, Henry, *Satyres and Satyricall Epigrams* (London, 1617; STC 10945).

Floyd-Wilson, Mary, *English Ethnicity and Race in Early Modern Drama* (Cambridge: Cambridge University Press, 2003).

Fortin, Simon, 'Dying to Learn, Learning to Die, The Craft of Dying in Early Modern English Drama and the Cultivation of Dying-Voice Literacy' (unpublished doctoral dissertation, CUNY, 2016).

Foster, Joseph, ed., *The Pedigrees of the County Families of Yorkshire*, 3 vols. (London: W. Wilfred Head, 1874).

Foxe, John, *Acts and Monuments* (London: John Day, 1563).

Frarinus, Petrus, *An Oration against the Unlawfull Insurrections of the Protestantes of our Time* (Antwerp: Joannes Foulerus, 1566).

Freud, Sigmund, 'Thoughts of the Times on War and Death', in *The Standard Edition of the Complete Psychological Works of Sigmund Freud*, gen. ed. by James Strachey, vol. 14 (London: Hogarth Press, 1957), pp. 275–300.

Friedman, Donald M., 'Rude Heaps and Decent Order', in *Marvell and Liberty*, ed. by Warren L. Chernaik and Martin Dzelzainis (New York: St. Martin's Press, 1999), pp. 123–44.

Galen, *Methodus Medendi [Method of Medicine]*, ed. and trans. by Ian Johnston and G. H. Horsely (Cambridge, MA: Harvard University Press/Loeb Classical Library, 2011).

Garganigo, Alex, '*The Rehearsal Transpros'd* and *The Rehearsal Transpros'd: The Second Part*', in *The Oxford Handbook of Andrew Marvell*, ed. by Martin Dzelzainis and Edward Holberton (Oxford: Oxford University Press, 2019), pp. 517–42.

Garrison, John S., *Shakespeare and the Afterlife* (Oxford: Oxford University Press, 2018).

George, Kathleen, *Winter's Tales: Reflections on the Novelistic Stage* (Newark: University of Delaware Press, 2005).

Ginsberg, Allen, 'An Interview by Gary Pacernick' (1997), in *First Thought: Conversations with Allen Ginsberg*, ed. by Michael Schumacher (Minneapolis: University of Minnesota Press, 2017).

Gittings, Clare, 'Expressions of Loss in Early Seventeenth Century England', in *The Changing Face of Death: Historical Accounts of Death and Disposal*, ed. by Peter C. Jupp and Glennys Howarth (Basingstoke: Macmillan, 1997), pp. 19–33.

Gleeson-White, Jane, *Double Entry: How the Merchants of Venice Created Modern Finance* (New York and London: W.W. Norton & Company, 2011).

Goethe, Johann Wolfgang von, *Wilhelm Meister's Apprenticeship*, in *The Collected Works*, vol. 9, ed. and trans. by Eric A Blackall in cooperation with Victor Lange (Princeton, NJ: Princeton University Press, 1989; repr. 1995).

Goldberg, Jonathan, *Voice Terminal Echo: Postmodernism and English Renaissance Texts* (New York and London: Methuen, 1986).

Goldring, Elizabeth et al., eds., *John Nichols's The Progresses and Public Processions of Queen Elizabeth I: A New Edition of the Early Modern Sources*, 5 vols. (Oxford: Oxford University Press, 2014).

Goodman, Godfrey, *At the Court of King James the First ... Now First Published from the Original Manuscripts*, ed. by John S. Brewer, 2 vols. (London: Richard Bentley, 1839).

Gordon, Bruce and Peter Marshall, eds., *The Place of the Dead: Death and Remembrance in Late Medieval and Early Modern Europe* (Cambridge: Cambridge University Press, 2000).

Goulart, Simon, *Admirable and Memorable Histories*, trans. by Ed[ward] Grimeston (London, 1607; STC 12135).

Graunt, John, Observations on the Bills of Mortality, in *The Economic Writings of Sir William Petty*, vol. 2, ed. by Charles Henry Hull (Cambridge: Cambridge University Press, 1899).

Greenblatt, Stephen, *Hamlet in Purgatory* (Princeton, NJ: Princeton University Press, 2001).

Gregory of Nyssa, 'On the Soul and the Resurrection', in *Nicene and Post-Nicene Fathers, Series 2, Volume 5*, ed. by Philip Schaff (London, 1893).

Greville, Fulke, *The life of the renowned S[i]r Philip Sidney* (London: for Henry Seile, 1652).

Greville, Fulke, *Poems and Dramas of Fulke Greville: First Lord Brooke, Volume 1*, ed. by Geoffrey Bullough (Oxford: Oxford University Press, 1945).

Grimald, Nicholas, 'Of Friendship', in *Tottel's Miscellany*, ed. by Richard Tottel (London: s.n., 1867).

Guibbory, Achsah, 'John Donne and Memory as "The Art of Salvation"', *Huntington Library Quarterly*, 43.4 (1980), 261–74.

Gurr, Andrew, *The Shakespearean Stage, 1574–1642* (Cambridge: Cambridge University Press, 1970).

Guth, DeLloyd J. 'The Age of Debt, the Reformation and English Law', in *Tudor Rule and Revolution: Essays for G. R. Elton from His American Friend*, ed. by Delloyd J. Guth and John W. McKenna (Cambridge: Cambridge University Press, 1982), pp. 69–86.

Guy-Bray, Stephen, 'Remembering to Forget: Shakespeare's Sonnet 35 and Sigo's "XXXV"', in *Sexuality and Memory in Early Modern England: Literature and the Erotics of Recollection*, ed. by John S. Garrison and Kyle Pivetti (London and New York: Routledge, 2015), pp. 43–50.

Habl, Jan, '"Only that man who governs himself may govern others": Jan Amos Comenius and His Anthropological Assumptions of Moral Politics', *Pro Rege*, 43.4 (2015), 8–14.

Hackenbracht, Ryan, *National Reckonings: The Last Judgment and Literature in Milton's England* (Ithaca, NY: Cornell University Press, 2019).

Hackett, Helen, 'Rediscovering Shock: Elizabeth I and the Cult of the Virgin Mary', *Critical Quarterly* 35.3 (September 1993), 30–42.

Hackett, Helen, *Virgin Mother, Maiden Queen: Elizabeth I and the Cult of the Virgin Mary* (London: Palgrave, 1995).

Hackett, Helen, 'Dreams or Designs, Cults or Constructions? The Study of Images of Monarchs', *The Historical Journal*, 44.3 (2001), 811–23.

Hackett, Helen, 'A New Image of Elizabeth I: The Three Goddesses Theme in Art and Literature', *Huntington Library Quarterly*, 77.3 (September 2014), 225–56.

Halbwachs, Maurice, *On Collective Memory*, ed. and trans. by Lewis A. Coser (Chicago: University of Chicago Press, 1992).

Haraway, Donna, *The Companion Species Manifesto: Dogs, People, and Significant Otherness* (Chicago: Prickly Paradigm Press, 2003).

Harding, Vanessa, *The Dead and the Living in Paris and London, 1500–1670* (Cambridge: Cambridge University Press, 2002).

Harington, John, *A Preface, or rather a Briefe Apologie of Poetrie, prefixed to the translation of Orlando Furioso* (London, 1591).

Harward, Simon, *Two Godly and Learned Sermons* (London, 1582).

Hatton, Edward, *A New View of London*, 2 vols. (London: R. Chiswell and A. and J. Churchill, 1708).

Heffernan, Virginia, 'The Beautiful Benefits of Contemplating Doom', *Wired* (April 2019), www.wired.com/story/the-beautiful-benefits-of-contemplating-doom/.

Helfer, Rebeca, *Spenser's Ruins and the Art of Recollection* (Toronto: University of Toronto Press, 2012).

Helfer, Rebeca, 'The State of the Art of Memory and Shakespeare Studies', in *The Routledge Handbook of Shakespeare and Memory*, ed. by Andrew Hiscock and Lina Perkins Wilder (London: Routledge, 2018), pp. 315–28.

Helms, Lorraine, '"The High Roman Fashion": Sacrifice, Suicide, and the Shakespearean Stage', *PMLA*, 107.3 (1992), 554–65.

Herrick, Robert, '225. The Plaudite, or End of Life', in *The Complete Poetry of Robert Herrick: Volume I*, ed. by Tom T. Cain and Ruth Connolly (Oxford: Oxford University Press, 2013).

Heskyns, Thomas, *The Parliament of Chryste* (Antwerp, 1566).

Heywood, Thomas, *Funeral Elegie* [for King James I] (London, 1625; STC 13324).

Hildreth, R. W., 'What Good Is Growth? Reconsidering Dewey on the Ends of Education', *Education & Culture*, 27.2 (2011), 28–47.

Hippocrates, *Prognostic*, trans. by W. H. S. Jones (Cambridge, MA: Harvard University Press/Loeb Classical Library, 1923).

Hirst, Derek and Steven Zwicker, *Andrew Marvell, Orphan of the Hurricane* (Oxford: Oxford University Press, 2012).

Hiscock, Andrew, *Reading Memory in Early Modern English Literature* (Cambridge: Cambridge University Press, 2011).

Hiscock, Andrew, 'Élisabeth Ière: Iconographie, Matérialité et *Côté Obscur*', in *Actes du colloque tenu au château de Bournazel* (Montpellier: Édition du Buisson/Presses Universitaires de la Méditerranée, forthcoming).

Holland, Peter, *Shakespeare and Forgetting* (London: Bloomsbury, 2021).

The Holy Bible (London, 1611; STC 2216).

Holst, Jonas, 'The Fall of the *Tektōn* and the Rise of the Architect: On the Greek Origins of Architectural Craftsmanship', *Architectural Histories*, 5.1 (2017), https://doi.org/10.5334/ah.239.

Horace, *Horace: The Odes and Epodes*, trans. by Charles E. Bennett (Cambridge, MA; London: Harvard University Press; Heinemann, 1964).

Houlbrooke, Ralph, *Death, Religion and the Family in England, 1480–1750* (Oxford: Oxford University Press, 1998).

Howard, Henry, Earl of Surrey, 'Complaint of the Absence of Her Lover, Being on the Sea', in *The Broadview Anthology of Sixteenth-Century Poetry and Prose*, ed. by Marie Loughlin, Sandra Bell, and Patricia Brace (Peterborough, ON: Broadview Press, 2011), p. 192.

Howard, Jackson Joseph, *Miscellanea Genealogica et Heralidica*, 3rd series, vol. 4 (London: Hamilton, Adams, and Co., 1902).

Huffman, Carl, 'Pythagoreanism', in *The Stanford Encyclopedia of Philosophy* (Fall 2019), ed. by Edward N. Zalta, https://plato.stanford.edu/archives/fall2019/entries/pythagoreanism/.

Hui, Andrew, *The Poetics of Ruins in Renaissance Literature* (New York: Fordham University Press, 2017).

Hulme, Mike, 'Climate', in *The Cambridge Guide to the Worlds of Shakespeare. Shakespeare's World, 1500–1660*, ed. by Bruce R. Smith, 2 vols. (Cambridge: Cambridge University Press, 2016), 1:29–34.

Hunter, William B., Jr., 'Milton and the Waldensians', *Studies in English Literature, 1500–1900*, 11.1 (Winter 1971), 153–64.

Huntley, Frank Livingstone, *Sir Thomas Browne: A Biographical and Critical Study* (Ann Arbor: University of Michigan Press, 1962; pbk 1968).

Hurtig, Judith, 'Seventeenth-Century Shroud Tombs: Classical Revival and Anglican Context', *The Art Bulletin*, 64.2 (June 1982), 217–28.

Hutton, Patrick H., *Philippe Ariès and the Politics of French Cultural History* (Amherst: University of Massachusetts Press, 2004).

Ivic, Christopher and Grant Williams, eds., *Forgetting in Early Modern English Literature and Culture: Lethe's Legacies* (London: Routledge, 2004).

Jerome, 'To Pammachius against John of Jerusalem', trans. by W. H. Fremantle, in *Nicene and Post-Nicene Fathers, Series 2, Volume 6*, ed. by Philip Schaff (Christian Classics Ethereal Library), www.ccel.org/ccel/schaff/npnf206.vi.viii.html.

Johnson, Samuel, *The Idler*, no. 103 (Saturday, 5 April 1760), *Yale Digital Edition of the Works of Samuel Johnson*, www.yalejohnson.com/frontend/sda_viewer?n=107591.

Jonas, Hans, 'Tool, Image, and Grave: On What Is Beyond the Animal in Man', in *Mortality and Morality: A Search for Good after Auschwitz*, ed. by Lawrence Vogel (Evanston, IL: Northwestern University Press, 1996), pp. 75–86.

Jones, Emrys, *The Origins of Shakespeare* (Oxford: Oxford University Press, 1977).

Jonson, Ben, *The Alchemist* (London: Thomas Snodham, 1612).

Jonson, Ben, 'To the Memory of My Beloved the Author, Mr. William Shakespeare, and what he hath left us', in *Mr. William Shakespeares Comedies, Histories, & Tragedies*, ed. by John Heminges and Henry Condell (London, 1623).

Jonson, Ben, *Timber, or Discoveries*, in *Ben Jonson, Vol. 8: The Poems; The Prose Works*, ed. by C. H. Herford, Percy Simpson, and Evelyn Simpson (Oxford: Oxford University Press, 1947), pp. 555–649.

Kalanithi, Paul, *When Breath Becomes Air* (New York: Random House, 2016).

Karremann, Isabel, *The Drama of Memory in Shakespeare's History Plays* (Cambridge: Cambridge University Press, 2015).

Kathman, David, 'Players, Livery Companies, and Apprentices', in *The Oxford Handbook of Early Modern Theatre*, ed. by Richard Dutton (Oxford: Oxford University Press 2009), pp. 413–28.

Kay, Dennis, *Melodious Tears: The English Funeral Elegy from Spenser to Milton* (Oxford: Clarendon Press, 1990).

Keers, Robert Young, *Pulmonary Tuberculosis* (London: Baillière Tindal, 1978).

Kerrigan, John, *Shakespeare's Binding Language* (Oxford: Oxford University Press, 2016).

Kezar, Dennis, *Guilty Creatures: Renaissance Poetry and the Ethics of Authorship* (Oxford: Oxford University Press, 2001).

Kiernan, Stephen P., *Last Rights: Rescuing the End of Life from the Medical System* (New York: St. Martin's Press, 2006).

King, John N., *Tudor Royal Iconography: Literature and Art in an Age of Religious Crisis* (Princeton, NJ: Princeton University Press, 1989).

King, John N., 'Queen Elizabeth I: Representations of the Virgin Queen', *Renaissance Quarterly*, 43.1 (1990), 30–74.

Kircher, Athanasius, *The vulcano's: or, Burning and fire-vomiting mountains, famous in the world: with their remarkables* (London, 1669).

Kishlansky, Mark, *A Monarchy Transformed: Britain, 1603–1714* (London: Penguin Books, 1997).

Knapp, Jeffrey, *Pleasing Everyone: Mass Entertainment in Renaissance England and Golden-Age Hollywood* (Oxford: Oxford University Press, 2016).

Knott, John R., *Discourses of Martyrdom in English Literature, 1563–1694* (Cambridge: Cambridge University Press, 1993).

Koller, Kathrine, 'Falstaff and the Art of Dying', *Modern Language Notes*, 60.6 (June 1945), 383–6.

Krier, Theresa M., 'Psychic Deadness in Allegory: Spenser's House of Mammon and Attacks on Linking', in *Imagining Death in Spenser and Milton*, ed. by E. J. Bellamy, P. Cheney, M. Schoenfeldt (London: Palgrave, 2003), pp. 46–64.

Kuchar, Gary, *The Poetry of Religious Sorrow in Early Modern England* (Cambridge: Cambridge University Press, 2008).

La Marche, Olivier de, *The Travelled Pilgrim*, trans. by Stephen Batman (London, 1569; STC 1585).

Lafont, Agnès, '"I am truly more fond and foolish than ever Narcissus was": Webster's *Duchess of Malfi* and Ovidian Resonances', in *The Duchess of Malfi: Webster's Tragedy of Blood*, ed. by Pascale Drouet and William C. Carroll (Paris: Belin, 2018), pp. 60–77.

Lane, John, *An elegie vpon the death of the high and renowned princesse, our late Soueraigne Elizabeth* (London: W. White, 1603).

Langlands, Alexander, *Cræft: An Inquiry into the Origins and True Meaning of Traditional Crafts* (New York: W.W. Norton & Company, 2018).

Laoutaris, Chris, '"Toucht with bolt of Treason": The Earl of Essex and Lady Penelope Rich', in *Essex: The Cultural Impact of an Elizabethan Courtier*, ed. by Annaliese Connolly and Lisa Hopkins (Manchester: Manchester University Press, 2013), pp. 201–36.

Latour, Bruno, *Politics of Nature: How to Bring the Sciences into Democracy*, trans. by Catherine Porter (Cambridge, MA: Harvard University Press, 2004).

Le Goff, Jacques, 'The Usurer and Purgatory', in *The Dawn of Modern Banking* (New Haven, CT, and London: Yale University Press, 1979), pp. 25–52.

Le Goff, Jacques, *The Birth of Purgatory*, trans. by Arthur Goldhammer (Chicago: University of Chicago Press, 1984).

Lehmberg, Stanford E., *Cathedrals under Siege: Cathedrals in English Society, 1600–1700* (University Park: Pennsylvania University Press, 1996).

Leppin, Volker, 'Preparing for Death: From the Late Medieval *Ars Moriendi* to the Lutheran Funeral Sermon', in *Preparing for Death, Remembering the Dead*, ed. by Jon Øygarden Flæten and Tarald Rasmussen (Göttingen: Vandenhoeck & Ruprecht, 2015), pp. 9–24.

Letters and Papers, Foreign and Domestic, Henry VIII, Volume 13 Part 2, August–December 1538, ed. by James Gairdner (London, 1893), *British History Online*, www.british-history.ac.uk/letters-papers-hen8/vol13/no2.

Lewalski, Barbara Kiefer, *Protestant Poetics and the Seventeenth-Century Religious Lyric* (Princeton, NJ: Princeton University Press, 1979).

Lewis, Simon L. and Mark A. Maslin, 'Defining the Anthropocene', *Nature*, 159 (March 2015), 171–80.

Lim, Vanessa, '"To be or not to be": Hamlet's Humanistic *Quaestio*', *The Review of English Studies*, 70.296 (2019), 640–58.

Llewellyn, Nigel, *Art of Death: Visual Culture in the English Death Ritual, c. 1500– c. 1800* (London: Reaktion, 1991).

Llewellyn, Nigel, *Funeral Monuments in Post-Reformation England* (Cambridge: Cambridge University Press, 2000).

Loughnane, Rory, 'The Medieval Inheritance', in *The Oxford Handbook of Shakespearean Tragedy*, ed. by Michael Neill and David Schalkwyk (Oxford: Oxford University Press, 2016), pp. 35–53.

Loughnane, Rory, 'Studied Speech and *The Duchess of Malfi*: The Lost Arts of Rhetoric, Memory, and Death' *Sillages Critiques*, 26 (2019), 'Nouvelles perspectives sur *The Duchess of Malfi*', https://journals.openedition.org/sillagescritiqu es/6847?lang=en.

Lowenthal, David, *The Past is a Foreign Country – Revisited* (Cambridge: Cambridge University Press, 2015).

Lyne, Raphael, *Memory and Intertextuality in Renaissance Literature* (Cambridge: Cambridge University Press, 2016).

MacLeod, Catherine, ed., *The Lost Prince: The Life and Death of Henry Stuart* (London: National Portrait Gallery, 2012).

Malo, Robyn, 'Intimate Devotion: Recusant Martyrs and the Making of Relics in Post-Reformation England', *Journal of Medieval and Early Modern Studies*, 44.3 (2014), 531–48.

Marlowe, Christopher, *Doctor Faustus: A- and B-Texts*, ed. by David Bevington and Eric Rasmussen (Manchester: Manchester University Press, 1993).

Marlowe, Christopher, *Doctor Faustus* (A-text), in *Doctor Faustus and Other Plays*, ed. by David Bevington and Eric Rasmussen (Oxford: Oxford University Press, 1998).

Marotti, Arthur F., 'Southwell's Remains: Catholicism and Anti-Catholicism in Early Modern England', in *Texts and Cultural Change in Early Modern England*, ed. by C. C. Brown and A. F. Marotti (London: Palgrave, 1997), pp. 37–65.

Marshall, Peter, *Beliefs and the Dead in Reformation England* (Oxford: Oxford University Press, 2002).

Marvell, Andrew, *Prose Works,* ed. by Annabel Patterson, with Martin Dzelzainis, Nicholas von Maltzahn, and N. H. Keeble, 2 vols. (New Haven, CT: Yale University Press, 2003).

Marvell, Andrew, *The Poems of Andrew Marvell,* ed. by Nigel Smith (Harlow, UK: Longman Pearson, 2007).

Maughan, Philip, '"I think the dead are with us": John Berger at 88', *New Statesman* (11 June 2015).

McClure, Peter and Robin Headlam Wells, 'Elizabeth I as a Second Virgin Mary', *Renaissance Studies*, 4.1 (March 1990), 38–70.

McDonald, Russ, 'Planned Obsolescence or Working at the Words', in *Teaching Shakespeare: Passing it On*, ed. by G. B. Shand (Chichester and Malden, MA: Wiley 2009), pp. 25–42.

McDowell, Nicholas, *Poetry and Allegiance in the English Civil Wars: Marvell and the Cause of Wit* (Oxford: Oxford University Press, 2008).

McDowell, Nicholas, 'Marvell's French Spirit', in *The Oxford Handbook of Andrew Marvell*, ed. by Martin Dzelzainis and Edward Holberton (Oxford: Oxford University Press, 2019), pp. 614–36.

McKenzie, Andrea, *Tyburn's Martyrs: Execution in England, 1675–1775* (London: Bloomsbury, 2007).

McNamara, Gregory, '"Grief was as clothes to their backs": Prince Henry's Funeral Viewed from the Wardrobe', in *Prince Henry Revived: Image and Exemplarity in Early Modern England*, ed. by Timothy Wilks (Southampton: Southampton Solent University and Paul Holberton Publishing, 2007), pp. 259–79.

Meres, Francis, *Palladis Tamia, Wit's Treasury* (London, 1598).

Middleton, Thomas, *A Game at Chess*, ed. by J. W. Harper (London: Ernest Benn Limited, 1966).

Middleton, Thomas, *The Collected Works*, gen. ed. by Gary Taylor and John Lavignino (Oxford: Clarendon Press, 2007).

Milton, John, *Complete Poems and Major Prose*, ed. by Merritt Y. Hughes (Indianapolis: Odyssey Press, 1957).

Milton, John, 'On the Late Massacher in Piemont', in *The Complete Works of John Milton, Vol. 3: The Shorter Poems,* ed. by Barbara Kiefer Lewalski and Estelle Haan (Oxford: Oxford University Press, 2012), p. 245.

Miner, Earl, 'The "Poetic Picture, Painted Poetry" of "The Last Instructions to a Painter"', *Modern Philology*, 63.4 (1966), 288–94.

Mishra, Pankaj, *The Age of Anger: A History of the Present* (London: Penguin Books, 2017).

Monta, Susannah Brietz, 'Representing Martyrdom in Tudor England', in *Oxford Handbooks Online* (2016), https://doi.org/10.1093/oxfordhb/9780199935338.013.71.

Montaigne, Michel de, *The Essayes of Michael Lord of Montaigne, Translated by John Fiorio, The First Booke* (London, 1603).

Montaigne, Michel de, *The Complete Essays of Montaigne*, trans. by Donald M. Frame (Stanford, CA: Stanford University Press, 1958).

Mottram, Stewart, *Ruin and Reformation in Spenser, Shakespeare, and Marvell* (Oxford: Oxford University Press, 2019).

Moul, Victoria, 'English Elegies of the Sixteenth and Seventeenth Century', in *The Cambridge Companion to Latin Love Elegy*, ed. by T. S. Thorsen (Cambridge: Cambridge University Press, 2013), pp. 306–19.

Munday, Anthony, *Zelauto* (London: John Charlewood, 1580).

Nashe, Thomas, *The Terrors of the Night* (London, 1594).

Neill, Michael, 'Monuments and Ruins as Symbols in *The Duchess of Malfi*', in *Drama and Symbolism,* ed. by James Redmond, Themes in Drama 4 (Cambridge: Cambridge University Press, 1982), pp. 71–87.

Neill, Michael, *Issues of Death: Mortality and Identity in English Renaissance Tragedy* (Oxford: Clarendon Press, 1997).

Neill, Michael, '"Crabbed *Websterio*": *The Duchess of Malfi* and the Character of a Dramatic Poet', in *'The Duchess of Malfi': Webster's Tragedy of Blood*, ed. by Pascale Drouet and William Carroll (Paris: Belin, 2018), pp. 31–46.

New Oxford Annotated Bible, ed. by Bruce Metzger and Roland Murphy (Oxford: Oxford University Press, 1994).

Newstok, Scott L., '"Turn thy Tombe into a Throne": Elizabeth I's Death Rehearsal', in *Goddesses and Queens: The Iconography of Elizabeth I*, ed. by Annaliese Connolly and Lisa Hopkins (Manchester: Manchester University Press, 2007), pp. 169–90.

Newstok, Scott L., *Quoting Death in Early Modern England: The Poetics of Epitaphs Beyond the Tomb* (New York: Palgrave Macmillan, 2009).

Newstok, Scott L., *How to Think Like Shakespeare: Lessons from a Renaissance Education* (Princeton, NJ: Princeton University Press, 2020).

Nichols, Shaun, 'Imagination and Immortality: Thinking of Me', *Synthese* 159 (2007), 215–33.

Nixon, Anthony, *Elizaes memoriall. King Iames his arriuall. And Romes downefall* (London: Thomas Creede, 1603).

Nora, Pierre, 'Between Memory and History: Les Lieux de Mémoire', *Representations*, 26 (1989), 7–24.

Norbrook, David, '"A Liberal Tongue": Language and Rebellion in *Richard II*', in *Shakespeare's Universe: Renaissance Ideas and Conventions: Essays in Honour of W. R. Elton*, ed. by John M. Mucciolo with Steven J. Doloff and Edward A. Rauchut (Aldershot: Scolar Press, 1996), pp. 37–51.

Norfolk Historic Environment Service, Norfolk Heritage Explorer, www.heritage.norfolk.gov.uk.

Nuland, Sherwin B., *How We Die: Reflections on Life's Final Chapter* (New York: Random House, 1995).

Nunberg, Geoffrey, 'The Organization of Knowledge', *History of Information i218* (18 February 2010), www.sambuz.com/doc/the-organization-of-knowledge-ppt-presentation-934520.

O'Connor, Sister Mary Catharine, *The Art of Dying Well: The Development of the Ars Moriendi* (New York: Columbia University Press, 1942).

Ong, Walter J., *Ramus, Method, and the Decay of Dialogue: From the Art of Discourse to the Art of Reason* (Cambridge, MA, and London: Harvard University Press, 1958).

Ong, Walter J., 'Maranatha: Death and Life in the Text of the Book' (1977), in Walter J. Ong, *Interfaces of the Word: Studies in the Evolution of Consciousness and Culture* (Ithaca, NY: Cornell University Press, 2012), pp. 230–71.

Otes, Samuel, *An Explanation of the General Epistle of Saint Jude* (London, 1633; STC 18896).

Packham, Kendra, 'Marvell, Political Print, and Picturing the Catholic: An Account of the Growth of Popery and Arbitrary Government', in *The Oxford Handbook of Andrew Marvell*, ed. by Martin Dzelzainis and Edward Holberton (Oxford: Oxford University Press, 2019), pp. 558–82.

Palfrey, Simon and Emma Smith, *Shakespeare's Dead* (Oxford: Bodleian Library, 2016).

'Parishes: Stoneleigh', in *A History of the County of Warwick: Vol. 6, Knightlow Hundred*, ed. by L. F. Salzman (London: Victoria County History, 1951), pp. 229–40, *British History Online*, www.british-history.ac.uk/vch/warks/vol6/pp229-240.

Parker, Geoffrey, *Global Crisis: War, Climate Change and Catastrophe in the Seventeenth Century*, abridged and revised (New Haven, CT, and London: Yale University Press, 2017).

Parker, Patricia, 'Cassio, Cash, and the "Infidel O": Arithmetic, Double-Entry Bookkeeping, and *Othello's* Unfaithful Accounts', in *A Companion to the Global Renaissance*, ed. by Jyotsna G. Singh (Oxford: Wiley-Blackwell, 2009), pp. 223–41.

Parker, Patricia, '*Cymbeline:* Arithmetic, Double-Entry Bookkeeping, Counts, and Accounts', *Sederi*, 23 (2013), 95–119.

Parry, Graham, *Glory, Laud and Honour: The Arts of the Anglican Counter-Reformation* (Woodbridge, UK: Boydell Press, 2006).

Parton, John, *Some Account of the Hospital and Parish Church of St. Giles in the Fields* (London: Luke Hansard, 1822).

Pascal, Blaise, Letter 16, in *Les Provinciales, or, The Mystery of Jesuitisme*, 2nd ed. (London, 1658).

Peacham, Henry, *The Garden of Eloquence* (London, 1593).

Pelikan, Jaroslav et al., eds., *Luther's Works*, 55 vols. (St. Louis, MO: Concordia Publishing House, 1955–1986).

Pertile, Giulio, 'Marvell as *Libertin*: *Upon Appleton House* and the Legacy of Théophile de Viau', *The Seventeenth Century*, 28.4 (2013), 395–418.

Petowe, Henry, *Elizabetha quasi viuens Eliza's funerall* (London: E. Allde for M. Lawe, 1603).

Pfau, Thomas, 'The Lost Art of Dying', *Hedgehog Review* (Fall 2018), https://hedgehogreview.com/issues/the-evening-of-life/articles/the-lost-art-of-dying.

Phillippy, Patricia, *Women, Death and Literature in Post-Reformation England* (Cambridge: Cambridge University Press, 2002).

Phillippy, Patricia, *Shaping Remembrance from Shakespeare to Milton* (Cambridge: Cambridge University Press, 2018).

Pinsky, Robert, 'How a 16th-Century Poem Inspired the Clarity of the Prose in *When Breath Becomes Air*', *Slate* (9 September 2016), https://slate.com/culture/2016/09/paul-kalanithis-when-breath-becomes-air-became-a-best-seller-for-a-nearly-unheard-of-reason-the-quality-of-its-prose.html.

Plat, Hugh, *The Jewell House of Art and Nature* (London, 1594).

Plato, *Collected Dialogues of Plato Including the Letters*, ed. by Edith Hamilton and Huntington Cairns (New York: Pantheon, 1961).

Plato, *Phaedrus* in *The Critical Dialogues of Plato*, ed. by Edith Hamilton and Huntington Cairns (Princeton, NJ: Princeton University Press, 1961).

Playfere, Thomas, *The Pathway to Perfection* (1593), in *The Memory Arts in Renaissance England: A Critical Anthology*, ed. by William E. Engel, Rory Loughnane, and Grant Williams (Cambridge: Cambridge University Press, 2016).

Pollmann, Judith, *Memory in Early Modern Europe, 1500–1700* (Oxford: Oxford University Press, 2017).

Poole, Kristin, *Supernatural Environments in Shakespeare's England: Spaces of Demonism, Divinity, and Drama* (Cambridge: Cambridge University Press, 2011).

Poovey, Mary, *A History of the Modern Fact: Problems of Knowledge in the Sciences of Wealth and Society* (Chicago: University of Chicago Press, 1998).

Pratt, Aaron T., 'A Conversation on "Dying Well in Early Modern England"', *Ransom Center Magazine* (30 October 2018).

Preston, Claire, 'The Laureate of the Grave: Urne-Buriall and the Failure of Memory', in Claire Preston, *Thomas Browne and the Writing of Early Modern Science* (Cambridge: University Press Cambridge, 2005), pp. 123–54.

Puttenham, George, *The Art of English Poesy: A Critical Edition*, ed. by Frank Whigham and Wayne A. Rebhorn (Ithaca, NY: Cornell University Press, 2007).

Pye, David, *The Nature and Art of Workmanship* (Cambridge: Cambridge University Press, 1968).

Queen Elizabeth I, *Proclamation against Breakinge of Defacing of Monumentes of Antiquitie beyng set up in Churches or other publique places for memory, and not for superstition* (London, 1560; STC 7913).

Ralegh, Sir Walter, *The Poems of Sir Walter Ralegh. A Historical Edition*, ed. by Michael Rudick (Tempe: Arizona Center for Medieval and Renaissance Studies/Renaissance English Text Society, 1999).

Raspa, Anthony, 'The Jesuit Aesthetics of Henry Hawkins' *Partheneia Sacra*', in *The Jesuits and the Emblem Tradition*, ed. by John Manning and M. Van Vaeck (Turnhout: Brepols, 1999), pp. 25–32.

Reading, John, *Christmass Revived* (London, 1660).

Rhodes, Neil and Jonathan Sawday, eds., *The Renaissance Computer: Knowledge Technology in the First Age of Print* (London: Routledge, 2000).

Romm, James, 'How to Die: What Author James Romm Learned from Seneca's Writings on Death', *Daily Stoic*, https://dailystoic.com/james-romm/.

Rooley, Anthony, 'A Portrait of Sir Henry Unton', in *Companion to Medieval and Renaissance Music*, ed. by David Fallows and Tess Knighton (Oxford: Oxford University Press, 1997), pp. 85–92.

Rossi, Paolo, *Clavis Universalis* (Milan: Ricciardi, 1960).

Rossi, Paolo, *Logic and the Art of Memory: The Quest for a Universal Language*, trans. by Stephen Clucas (Chicago: University of Chicago Press, 2000).

Ryrie, Alec, *Being Protestant in Reformation Britain* (Oxford: Oxford University Press, 2013).

Ryves, Bruno, *Angliæ ruina: or, Englands ruine* (London, 1648).

Sadler, John Edward, *J. A. Comenius and the Concept of Universal Education* (London: Routledge, 1966; repr. 2013).

Sauer, Elizabeth, *Milton, Toleration, and Nationhood* (Cambridge: Cambridge University Press, 2013).

Saunders, Claire, "'Dead in His Bed": Shakespeare's Staging of the Death of the Duke of Gloucester in *2 Henry VI*, *The Review of English Studies*, New Series, 36.141 (February 1985), 19–34.

Saxton, Christopher, *Atlas of England and Wales* (London, 1579).

Schopenhauer, Arthur, *Studies in Pessimism*, trans. by T. B. Bailey Saunders (Whitefish, MT: Kessinger Publishing, 2010).

Schwyzer, Philip, *Literature, Nationalism, and Memory in Early Modern England and Wales* (Cambridge: University Press Cambridge, 2005).

Schwyzer, Philip, *Archaeologies of English Renaissance Literature* (Oxford: Oxford University Press, 2007).

Schwyzer, Philip, *Shakespeare and the Remains of Richard III* (Oxford: Oxford University Press, 2013).

Scranton, Roy, *Learning to Die in the Anthropocene* (San Francisco, CA: City Lights Publishers, 2015).

Semler, L. E., *The English Mannerist Poets and the Visual Arts* (Madison and Teaneck, NJ: Fairleigh Dickinson University Press, 1998).

Sennett, Richard, *The Craftsman* (New Haven, CT: Yale University Press, 2008).

Shakespeare, William, *Poems: Written by Wil. Shake-speare. Gent.* (London, 1640).

Shakespeare, William, *Measure for Measure*, Arden Second Series, ed. by J. W. Lever (London: Methuen and Co., 1965).

Shakespeare, William, *Romeo and Juliet*, Arden Second Series, ed. by Brian Gibbons (London: Methuen and Co., 1980).

Shakespeare, William, *Romeo and Juliet*, The New Cambridge Shakespeare, ed. by G. Blakemore Evans (Cambridge: Cambridge University Press, 1984).

Shakespeare, William, *Antony and Cleopatra*, Arden Third Series, ed. by John Wilders (London: Routledge, 1995).

Shakespeare, William, *King Henry V*, Arden Third Series, ed. by T. W. Craik (London: Routledge, 1995).

Shakespeare, William, *The Two Noble Kinsmen*, Arden Third Series, ed. by Lois Potter (Walton-on-Thames: Thomas Nelson and Sons, 1997).

Shakespeare, William, *The Arden Shakespeare Complete Works*, ed. by Richard Proudfoot, Ann Thompson, and David Scott Kastan (London: Thomson Learning/Arden, 1998).

Shakespeare, William, *Hamlet*, ed. by A. R. Braunmuller (New York: Penguin Books, 2001).

Shakespeare, William, *King Henry IV, Part 1*, Arden Third Series, ed. by David Scott Kastan (London: The Arden Shakespeare, 2002).

Shakespeare, William, *The Complete Sonnets and Poems*, ed. by Colin Burrow (Oxford: Oxford University Press, 2002).

Shakespeare, William, *King Richard III*, ed. by James R. Siemon (London: Methuen, 2009).

Shakespeare, William, *The Norton Shakespeare*, ed. by Stephen Greenblatt et al. (New York: W.W. Norton & Company, 2016).

Shakespeare, William, *Shakespeare's Sonnets*, ed. by Francis X. Connor, in *The New Oxford Shakespeare: Modern Critical Edition*, gen. ed. Gary Taylor, John Jowett, Terri Bourus, and Gabriel Egan (Oxford: Oxford University Press, 2016), pp. 2819–82.

Shakespeare, William, *Hamlet*, Arden Third Series, rev. ed., ed. by Ann Thompson and Neil Taylor (London: The Arden Shakespeare, 2016).

Shakespeare, William, *King Henry IV, Part 2*, Arden Third Series, ed. by James C. Bulman (London: Bloomsbury Arden Shakespeare, 2016).

Shannon, Laurie, *Sovereign Amity: Figures of Friendship in Shakespearean Contexts* (Chicago: University of Chicago Press, 2002).

Shelford, Robert, *Five Pious and Learned Discourses* (Cambridge, 1635).

Sherburne, Edward, *Salmacis, Lyrian & Sylvia, Forsaken Lydia, The Rape of Helen, A Comment thereon, with severall other Poems and Translations* (London, 1651).

Sherlock, Peter, 'The Monuments of Elizabeth Tudor and Mary Stuart: King James and the Manipulation of Memory', *Journal of British Studies*, 46.2 (2007), 263–89.

Sherlock, Peter, *Monuments and Memory in Early Modern England* (Aldershot: Ashgate, 2008).

Sherlock, Peter, *Monuments and Memory in Early Modern England* (London: Routledge, 2016).

Sherlock, Peter, 'Monuments and Memory', in *A History of Early Modern Women's Writing*, ed. by Patricia Phillippy (Cambridge: Cambridge University Press, 2018), pp. 292–312.

Sherlock, Peter, 'Monuments and the Reformation', in *Memory and the English Reformation*, ed. by Alexandra Walsham, Bronwyn Wallace, Ceri Law, and Brian Cummings (Cambridge: Cambridge University Press, 2020), pp. 168–84.

Sherman, Anita Gilman, *Skepticism and Memory in Shakespeare and Donne* (New York: Palgrave Macmillan, 2007).

Sherman, Anita Gilman, *Skepticism in Early Modern English Literature: The Problems and Pleasures of Doubt* (Cambridge: Cambridge University Press, 2021).

Shirley, James, 'Upon Mr Charles Beaumont who died of a Consumption', in James Shirley, *Poems* (London, 1646).

Shrank, Cathy, 'Reading Shakespeare's *Sonnets*: John Benson and the 1640 *Poems*', *Shakespeare*, 5.3 (September 2009), 271–91.

Sidney, Philip, 'An Apology for Poetry', in *English Critical Essays (Sixteenth, Seventeenth and Eighteenth Centuries)*, ed. by Edmund D. Jones (London and New York: Oxford University Press, 1947).

Sidney, Philip, *The Poems of Sir Philip Sidney*, ed. by William A. Ringler, Jr. (London: Clarendon, 1977).

Sidney, Philip, *Sidney's 'The Defence of Poesy' and Selected Renaissance Literary Criticism* (London: Penguin, 2004).

Sillars, Stuart, *Shakespeare and the Visual Imagination* (Cambridge: Cambridge University Press, 2015).

Sinfield, Alan, *Faultlines: Cultural Materialism and the Politics of Dissident Reading* (Berkeley and Los Angeles: University of California Press, 1992).

Slayback, Zachary, *The End of School: Reclaiming Education from the Classroom* (Coldwater, MI: Remnant Publishing, 2016).

Sleigh-Johnson, N. V., 'The Merchant-Taylors Company of London, 1580–1645' (unpublished doctoral thesis, University College London, 1985).

Smith, D. Vance, *Arts of Dying: Literature and Finitude in Medieval England* (Chicago: University of Chicago Press, 2020).

Smith, Nigel, *Andrew Marvell: The Chameleon* (New Haven, CT: Yale University Press, 2010).

Smith, Pamela H., 'Making as Knowing: Craft as Natural Philosophy', in *Ways of Making and Knowing: The Material Culture of Empirical Knowledge*, ed. by Pamela H. Smith, Amy R. W. Meyers, and Harold J. Cook (Ann Arbor: University of Michigan Press, 2014).

Smith, Samuel, *Moses his Prayer* (London, 1656).

Sokol, B. J., *Art and Illusion in The Winter's Tale* (Manchester: Manchester University Press, 1994).

Southwell, Robert, *An Epistle of Comfort to the Reverend Priestes* (London, 1587).

Southwell, R. Clifton, *The Ethics of Mourning* (Baltimore, MD: Johns Hopkins University Press, 2004).

Spenser, Edmund, *Colin Clouts Come Home Againe* (London: Thomas Creede, 1595).

Spenser, Edmund, *The Faerie Queene*, ed. by A. C. Hamilton et al., 2nd ed. (Harlow, UK: Pearson Education, 2007).

Spenser, Edmund, *The Faerie Queene,* ed. by A. C. Hamilton et al., rev. 2nd ed. (London: Longman, 2007).

Spinrad, Phoebe S., '*Measure for Measure* and the Art of Not Dying', *Texas Studies in Literature and Language*, 26.1 (1984), 74–93.

Stein, Arnold, *House of Death: Messages from the English Renaissance* (Baltimore, MD: Johns Hopkins University Press, 1986).

Stewart, Susan, *The Ruins Lesson: Meaning and Material in Western Culture* (Chicago and London: University of Chicago Press, 2020).

Strode, George, *The Anatomy of Mortality* (London, 1618; STC 23364).

Strong, Roy, 'Sir Henry Unton and His Portrait: An Elizabethan Memorial Picture and Its History', *Archaeologia*, 99 (1965), 53–76.

Strong, Roy, *Henry, Prince of Wales and England's Lost Renaissance* (London: Thames & Hudson, 1986).

Strong, Roy, *Gloriana: The Portraits of Queen Elizabeth I* (London: Thames & Hudson, 1987).

Strong, Roy, *The Tudor and Stuart Monarchy: Pageantry, Painting, Iconography, Vol. 2: Elizabethan* (Woodbridge, UK: Boydell Press, 1995).

Strong, Roy, *The Elizabethan Image: An Introduction to English Portraiture, 1558–1603* (New Haven, CT: Yale University Press, 2019).

Stuart, James, *King James VI and I: Political Writings*, ed. by Johann P. Somerville (Cambridge: Cambridge University Press, 1994).

Stubbes, John, *The discouerie of a gaping gulf* (London: Henry Singleton, 1579).

Sullivan, Garrett A., Jr., *Memory and Forgetting in English Renaissance Drama* (Cambridge: Cambridge University Press, 2005).

Sutcliffe, Mathew, *A True Relation of Englands Happinesse* (London, 1629).

Sutton, Christopher, *Disce mori. = Learne to die. A religious discourse, moouing euery Christian man to enter into a serious remembrance of his ende. Wherein also is contained the meane and manner of disposing himselfe to God, before, and at the time of his departure* (London, 1600; STC 23474).

Sutton, John, 'Spongy Brains and Material Memories', in *Environment and Embodiment in Early Modern England*, ed. by Mary Floyd-Wilson and Garrett Sullivan (Basingstoke: Palgrave, 2007), pp. 14–34.

Swann, Marjorie, 'Vegetable Love: Botany and Sexuality in Seventeenth-Century England', in *The Indistinct Human in Renaissance Literature*, ed. by Jean E. Feerick and Vin Nardizzi (New York: Palgrave Macmillan, 2012), pp. 139–58.

Swiss, Margo and David A. Kent, *Speaking Grief in English Literary Culture: Shakespeare to Milton* (Pittsburgh, PA: Duquesne University Press, 2002).

Tamm, Marek and Alessandro Arcangeli, eds., *The Early Modern Age*, vol. 3, in *A Cultural History of Memory*, gen. ed. by Stefan Berge and Jeffrey K. Olick (London: Bloomsbury, 2020).

Targoff, Ramie, *John Donne, Body and Soul* (Chicago: University of Chicago Press, 2008).

Targoff, Ramie, *Posthumous Love: Eros and the Afterlife in Renaissance England* (Chicago: University of Chicago Press, 2014).

Taylor, Gary, 'The Fortunes of Oldcastle', *Shakespeare Survey*, 38 (1985), 85–100.

Taylor, Gary, 'A Game at Chesse: An Early Form', in *Thomas Middleton: The Collected Works*, gen. ed. Gary Taylor and John Lavagnino (Oxford: Oxford University Press, 2007), pp. 1773–88.

Taylor, Gary, 'A Game at Chesse: An Early Form', in *Thomas Middleton: The Collected Works*, gen. ed. Gary Taylor and John Lavagnino (Oxford: Oxford University Press, 2007), pp. 1825–9.

Taylor, Gary, 'Thomas Middleton: Lives and Afterlives', in *Thomas Middleton: The Collected Works*, gen. ed. by Gary Taylor and John Lavagnino (Oxford: Oxford University Press, 2007), pp. 25–58.

Taylor, Gary, and John Lavagnino, eds., *Thomas Middleton and Early Modern Textual Culture* (Oxford: Oxford University Press, 2007).

Taylor, Jeremy, *The Rule and Exercises of Holy Dying* (London, 1651; Wing T361A).

Tennyson, Alfred, Lord, 'The Skipping Rope', 1842, in *The Complete Poetical Works of Tennyson*, ed. by William James Rolfe (Boston: Houghton Mifflin Company, 1898), p. 791.

Teskey, Gordon, *The Poetry of John Milton* (Cambridge, MA: Harvard University Press, 2015).

Thomas, Keith, *Religion and the Decline of Magic: Studies in Popular Beliefs in Sixteenth and Seventeenth Century England* (New York: Oxford University Press, 1971).

Thompson, Grahame, 'Early Double-Entry Bookkeeping and the Rhetoric of Accounting Calculations', in *Accounting as a Social and Institutional Practice*, ed. by Anthony G. Hopwood and Peter Miller (Cambridge: Cambridge University Press, 1994), pp. 40–66.

Throness, Laurie, *A Protestant Purgatory: Theological Origins of the Penitentiary Act, 1779* (Farnham: Ashgate Publishing, 2008).

Tillich, Paul, *Theology of Peace*, ed. by Ronald H. Stone (Louisville, KY: Westminster John Knox Press, 1990).

Tingle, Elizabeth, 'Changing Western European Visions of Christian Afterlives, 1350–1700: Heaven, Hell, and Purgatory', in *A Companion to Death, Burial, and Remembrance in Late Medieval and Early Modern Europe, c. 1300–1700*, ed. by Philip Booth and Elizabeth Tingle (Leiden: Brill, 2021).

Tingle, Elizabeth, 'The Counter Reformation and Preparations for Death in the European Roman Catholic Church, 1550–1700', in *A Companion to Death, Burial, and Remembrance in Late Medieval and Early Modern Europe, c. 1300–1700*, ed. by Philip Booth and Elizabeth Tingle (Leiden: Brill, 2021).

Tisdale, Sallie, *Advice for Future Corpses (and Those Who Love Them): A Practical Perspective on Death and Dying* (New York: Simon & Schuster, 2018).

Traub, Valerie, *Thinking Sex with the Early Moderns* (Philadelphia: University of Pennsylvania Press, 2016).

Tribble, Evelyn B. and Nicholas Keane, *Cognitive Ecologies and the History of Remembering Early Modern England* (London: Palgrave, 2011).

Tuke, Thomas, *A Discourse of Death, Bodily, Ghostly, and Eternal* (London, 1613; STC 24307).

'T. W. gentleman', *The lamentation of Melpomene, for the death of Belphaebe our late Queene With a ioy to England for our blessed King* (London: W. White, 1603).

Uricchio, William, 'A Palimpsest of Place and Past: Location-Based Digital Technologies and the Performance of Urban Space and Memory', *Performance Research*, 17.3 (2012), 45–9.

Vendler, Helen, 'Formal Pleasure in the Sonnets', in *A Companion to Shakespeare's Sonnets*, ed. by Michael Schoenfeldt (Oxford: Blackwell, 2007), pp. 27–44.

Verdery, Katherine, *The Political Lives of Dead Bodies: Reburial and Postsocialist Change* (New York: Columbia University Press, 1999).

Villani, Stefano, 'The British Invention of the Waldenses', in *Remembering the Reformation*, ed. by Alexandra Walsham, Brian Cummings, Ceri Law, and Karis Riley (London: Routledge, 2020), pp. 192–206.

Vinter, Maggie, *Last Acts: The Art of Dying on the Early Modern Stage* (New York: Fordham University Press, 2019).

Vogelaare, Livinus de, *The Memorial of Lord Darnley* (1567), oil on canvas, 142.3cm x 224cm. RCIN 401230. Royal Collection Trust, London.

Volkmann, Ludwig, *Ars memorative* (Vienna: Schroll, 1929).

Volkmann, Ludwig, *Hieroglyph, Emblem, and Renaissance Pictography*, trans. by Robin Raybould (Leiden: Brill, 2018).

Vovelle, Michel, *La Mort et l'Occident de 1300 à nos jours* (Paris: Gallimard, 1983).

Walker, Julia M., *The Elizabeth Icon: 1603–2003* (London: Palgrave, 2004).

Wallace, Andrew, *The Presence of Rome in Medieval and Early Modern Britain: Texts, Artefacts and Beliefs* (Cambridge: Cambridge University Press, 2020).

Walsham, Alexandra, '"A Very Deborah?" The Myth of Elizabeth I as a Providential Monarch', in *The Myth of Elizabeth*, ed. by Susan Doran and Thomas S. Freeman (Basingstoke: Palgrave, 2003), pp. 143–68.

Walsham, Alexandra, 'Skeletons in the Cupboard: Relics after the English Reformation', *Past & Present*, 206, supplement 5 (2010), 121–43.

Walsham, Alexandra, Bronwyn Wallace, Ceri Law, and Brian Cummings, eds., *Memory and the English Reformation* (Cambridge: Cambridge University Press, 2020).

Walton, Izaak, *Walton's Lives: John Donne, Sir Henry Wotton, Richard Hooker, George Herbert and Robert Sanderson* (London: Falcon Educational Books, 1951).

Watson, Robert, *The Rest Is Silence: Death as Annihilation in the English Renaissance* (Berkeley: University of California Press 1994).

Weatherweb, *Weather in History, 1650–1669 AD*, https://premium.weatherweb.net/weather-in-history-1650-to-1699-ad/.

Webster, John, *The Duchess of Malfi*, ed. by John Russell Brown, 2nd ed., Revels Plays (Manchester: Manchester University Press, 2009).

Webster, John, *The Duchess of Malfi*, ed. by Leah S. Marcus, Arden Shakespeare (London: A. & C. Black, 2009).

Webster, John, *The Duchess of Malfi*, ed. by Michael Neill (New York and London: W.W. Norton & Company, 2015).

Weever, John, *Ancient Funeral Monuments* (London, 1631; STC 25223).

West, William, 'The *Idea of a Theater*: Humanist Ideology and the Imaginary Stage in Early Modern Europe', *Renaissance Drama*, 28 (1999), 245–87.

White, Adam, 'A Biographical Dictionary of London Tomb Sculptors c.1560–c.1660', *The Volume of the Walpole Society*, 61 (1999), 1–162.

White, John, *The troubles of Jerusalems restauration* (London, 1646).

White, R. S., *Let Wonder Seem Familiar: Shakespeare and the Romance Ending* (London: Bloomsbury, 2000).

Wilder, Lina Perkins, *Shakespeare's Memory Theatre: Recollection, Properties, and Character* (Cambridge: Cambridge University Press, 2010).

Wilder, Lina Perkins, 'Veiled Memory Traces in *Much Ado About Nothing, Pericles* and *The Winter's Tale*', in *Routledge Handbook of Shakespeare and Memory*, ed. by Andrew Hiscock and Lina Perkins Wilder (London: Routledge, 2018), pp. 239–52.

Wilks, Timothy, ed., *Prince Henry Revived: Image and Exemplarity in Early Modern England* (Southampton: Southampton Solent University and Paul Holberton Publishing, 2007).

Willet, Andrew, *An Harmony upon the First Book of Samuel* (London, 1607; STC 25678).

Williams, Grant, 'Monumental Memory and Little Reminders: The Fantasy of Being Remembered by Posterity', in *The Routledge Handbook of Shakespeare and Memory*, ed. by Andrew Hiscock and Lina Perkins Wilder (New York: Routledge, 2017), pp. 297–311.

Williams, Linda, 'The Anthropocene and the Long Seventeenth Century, 1550–1750', in *A Cultural History of Climate Change*, ed. by Tom Bristow and Thomas H. Ford (London: Routledge, 2016), pp. 87–107.

Wilson-Okamura, David Scott, 'Belphoebe and Gloriana', *ELR*, 39.1 (2009), 47–73.

Wilson, Jean, '"Two names of friendship, but one Starre": Memorials to Single-Sex Couples in the Early Modern Period', *Church Monuments*, 10 (1995), 70–83.

Wilson, Thomas, *The Arte of Rhetorique* (London: John Kingston, 1560).

Woodward, Jennifer, *Theatre of Death: The Ritual Management of Royal Funerals in Renaissance England, 1570–1624* (Woodbridge, UK: Boydell Press, 1997).

Woolf, Virginia, 'Craftsmanship' (broadcast 20 April 1937), in *Selected Essays*, ed. by David Bradshaw (Oxford: Oxford University Press, 2009), pp. 85–94.

Wright, Leonard, *The Hunting of Antichrist* (London: John Wolfe, 1589).

Yates, Frances A., *The Art of Memory* (New York: Routledge and Keegan Paul, 1966).

Yates, Frances A., *Astraea: The Imperial Theme in the Sixteenth Century* (London: Routledge & Kegan Paul, 1975).

Zwicky, Jan, 'A Ship from Delos', in *Learning to Die: Wisdom in the Age of Climate Crisis*, ed. by Robert Bringhurst and Jan Zwicky (Regina, Saskatchewan: University of Regina Press, 2018).

Electronic References of Portraits

Anon., 'The Portrait of Sir Henry Unton (*c.* 1558–1596)', *National Portrait Gallery*, https://npg.org.uk/research/programmes/making-art-in-tudor-britain/case-studies/the-portrait-of-sir-henry-unton-c.-1558-1596.php.

Anon., Portrait of Walter Ralegh (1588), www.npg.org.uk/collections/search/portrait/mw05204/Sir-Walter-Ralegh-Raleigh.

English School, 'Allegorical Portrait' of Elizabeth I (*c.* 1600), www.corsham-court.co.uk/Pictures/Commentary.html.

George Gower, The Plimpton or Sieve Portrait (1579), https://luna.folger.edu/luna/servlet/detail/FOLGERCM1-6-6-29241-102094:The-Plimpton--Sieve--portrait-of-Qu.

Hans Eworth, 'Elizabeth and the Three Goddesses' (1569), www.rct.uk/collection/403446/elizabeth-i-and-the-three-goddesses.

Isaac Oliver, 'The Rainbow Portrait' (*c.* 1600), www.hatfield-house.co.uk/house/the-house/the-rainbow-portrait/.

Isaac Oliver (attr.), 'Elizabeth and the Three Goddesses' (*c.* 1590), www.npg.org.uk/collections/search/portrait/mw224945/Queen-Elizabeth-I-Elizabeth-I-and-the-Three-Goddesses.

Petrarch, Elizabeth I figured in Petrarch's *Trionfo Della Fama* (British Library: Sloane 1832, fols. 7ᵛ–8), www.bl.uk/learning/timeline/item104117.html.

William Rogers, Examples of engravings of Elizabeth I, www.npg.org.uk/collections/search/person/mp57930/william-rogers.

Index

Acker, Faith, 66
aesthetics
    boundary between good and bad taste, 201,
        203–9, 212–13
    Counter-Reformation aesthetics, 206–13
    emergence of, 201–3
    of John Cleveland, 206–7
    in Marvell's poetry, 201
Agamben, Giorgio, 203
Aho, James, 54–5
Allen, Don Cameron, 211
anamnesis, 31–3
Ariès, Philippe, 4, 209, 212
Aristotle, 80
ars moriendi see also craft of dying
    in *A Letter to a Friend* (Browne), 161–2
    of Charles I in Marvell, 204–6
    De praeparatione ad mortem (Erasmus), 1–2,
        10, 83
    handbooks, 78
    instructional wisdom, 1
    literary echoes of, 82
    memory and mortality in, 2
    performative elements, 82–3
    secularization of, 201, 212–13
art of memory
    architectural mnemotechnics, 71, 72
    as the art of salvation in Donne, 27–30,
        35–42
    classical *ars memorativa*, 23, 32–3
    concept of, 28–9
    as a cumulative process, 186
    in early modern culture, 23–4
    intersection with the art of dying, 10–14,
        178–9
    memory and sexual fantasy, 72, 73
    mnemonic poetics, 29, 33
    preparedness for death, 24
    Simonides and the invention of, 11, 32, 84, 97
    visual and aural prompts, 7, 23–4
Augustine, 9, 19, 23–4, 30-34, 36–7, 39–41, 43

Bacon, Francis, 159, 219–20, 227–8
Barthes, Roland, 65
Batman, Stephen, 2
Benson, John, 66–8
Bentley, Thomas, 225
Boileau, Nicolas, 201–2, 204
Bible, 9–10, 19, 233, 240
    Genesis, 31, 34, 168, 175
    Job, 168
    Matthew, 140
    Psalm 32, 31, 39, 43
    Psalm 119, 19
    Psalm 132, 197
    Samuel, 102
    Song of Solomon, 267
    Revelation, 166
Boleyn, Anne, 1, 227
Boleyn, Thomas, 1
Bolton, Edmund, 218–19
Bolzoni, Lina, 73
bones
    Catholic martyrs in Robert Southwell, 129–30
    Jane Grey's call for the gathering of martyrs
        bones in Drayton, 126–30
    in Milton's Sonnet 18, 123–7, 135–6
    old bones and political regime change, 129, 136
    as a practical problem post-Reformation, 133
    re-gathering of scattered bones, 132–3
    re-gathering of scattered bones and ashes in
        Browne, 167
    scattered bones imagery in Donne, 130–1
    scattered bones trope and moral imperative,
        134–6
    scattered bones trope in Shakespeare, 133, 134
    scattered bones trope in Spenser, 133–4
    scattered dry bones of Ezekiel 37, 131–2
    from scattered to sown in Milton, 136–7
    scattering of saints' bones
        in the Reformation, 124–5
Book of Christian Prayer, A, 13
Boyle, Thomas, 166